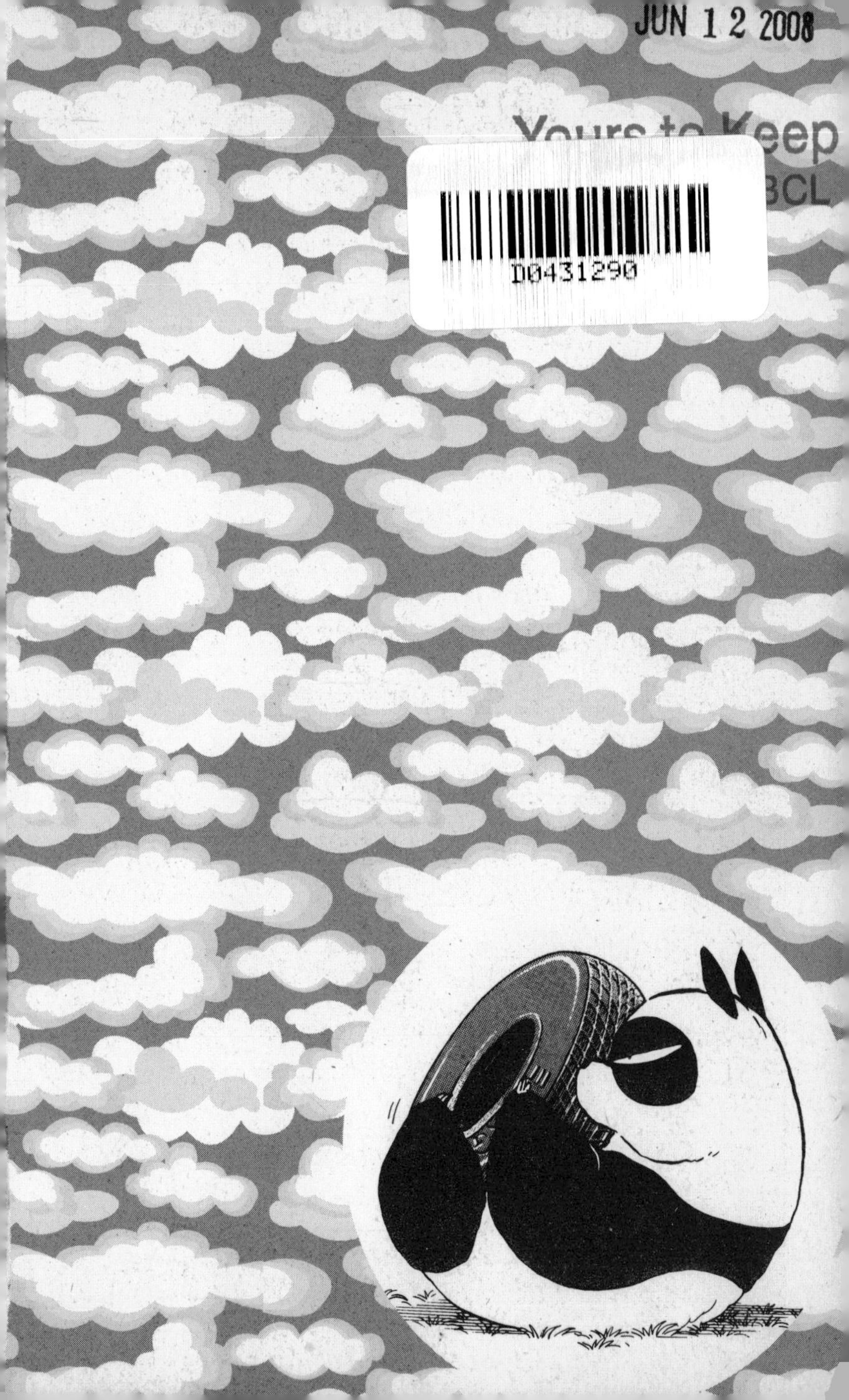

Ranma ½

VOL. 24
VIZ Media Edition

Story and Art by
RUMIKO TAKAHASHI

English Adaptation by Gerard Jones
Translation by Kaori Inoue
Touch-Up Art & Lettering/Wayne Truman
Cover Design/Yuki Ameda
Graphics & Design/Sean Lee
Supervising Editor/Julie Davis
Editor/Avery Gotoh

Editor in Chief, Books/Alvin Lu
Editor in Chief, Magazines/Marc Weidenbaum
VP of Publishing Licensing/Rika Inouye
VP of Sales/Gonzalo Ferreyra
Sr. VP of Marketing/Liza Coppola
Publisher/Hyoe Narita

Printed in Canada

Published by VIZ Media, LLC
P.O. Box 77010
San Francisco, CA 94107

VIZ Media Edition
10 9 8 7 6 5 4 3 2
First printing, October 2003
Second printing, February 2008

www.viz.com

PARENTAL ADVISORY
RANMA 1/2 is rated T+ for Older Teen and is
recommended for ages 16 and up. This volume may
contain violence, language, alcohol or tobacco use,
or suggestive situations.
ratings.viz.com

store.viz.com

Ranma 1/2

VOL. 24   VIZ Media Edition

STORY & ART BY
RUMIKO TAKAHASHI

STORY THUS FAR

The Tendos are an average, run-of-the-mill Japanese family—at least on the surface, that is. Soun Tendo is the owner and proprietor of the Tendo Dojo, where "Anything-Goes Martial Arts" is practiced. Like the name says, anything goes, and usually does.

When Soun's old friend Genma Saotome comes to visit, Soun's three lovely young daughters—Akane, Nabiki, and Kasumi—are told that it's time for one of them to become the fiancée of Genma's teenage son, as per an agreement made between the two fathers years ago. Youngest daughter Akane—who says she hates boys—is quickly nominated for bridal duty by her sisters.

Unfortunately, Ranma and his father have suffered a strange accident. While training in China, both plunged into one of many "accursed" springs at the legendary martial arts training ground of Jusenkyo. These springs transform the unlucky dunkee into whoever—or whatever—drowned there hundreds of years ago.

From now on, a splash of cold water turns Ranma's father into a giant panda, and Ranma becomes a beautiful, busty young woman. Hot water reverses the effect...but only until next time.

Ranma and Genma weren't the only ones to take the Jusenkyo plunge—it isn't long before they meet several other members of the "cursed." And although their parents are still determined to see Ranma and Akane marry and carry on the training hall, Ranma seems to have a strange talent for accumulating extra fiancées, and Akane has a few suitors of her own. Will the two ever work out their differences, get rid of all these extra people, or just call the whole thing off? And will Ranma ever get rid of his curse?

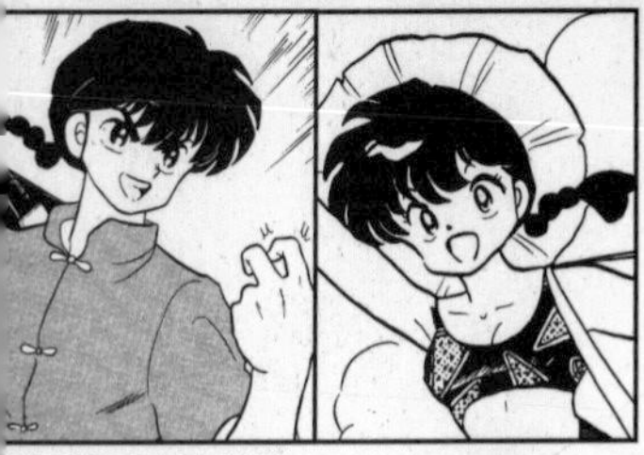

RANMA SAOTOME
Martial artist with far too many finacées, and an ego that won't let him take defeat easily. He changes into a girl when splashed with cold water.

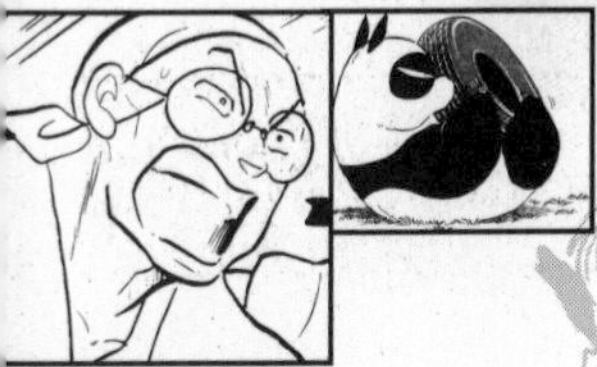

GENMA SAOTOME
Ranma's lazy father, who left his home and wife years ago with his young son to train in the martial arts. He changes into a panda.

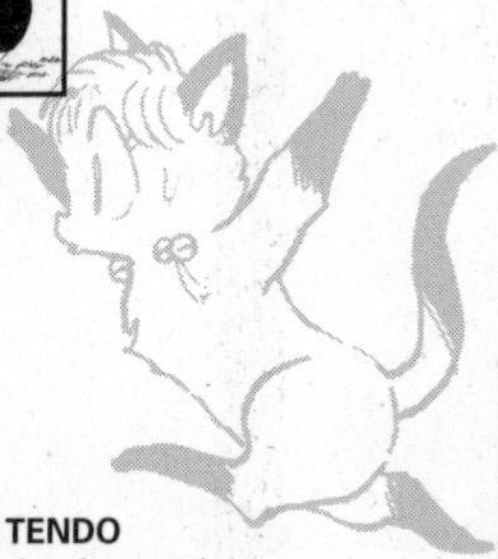

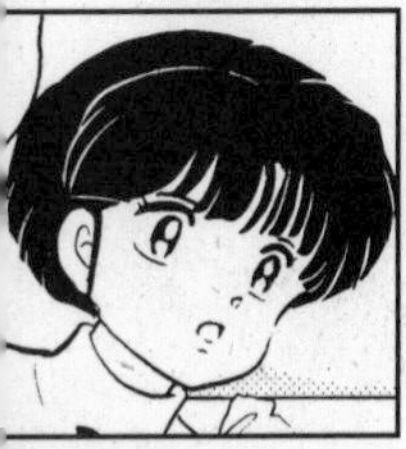

AKANE TENDO
A martial artist, tomboy, and Ranma's fiancée by parental arrangement. She has no clue how much Ryoga likes her, or what relation he has to her pet black pig, P-chan.

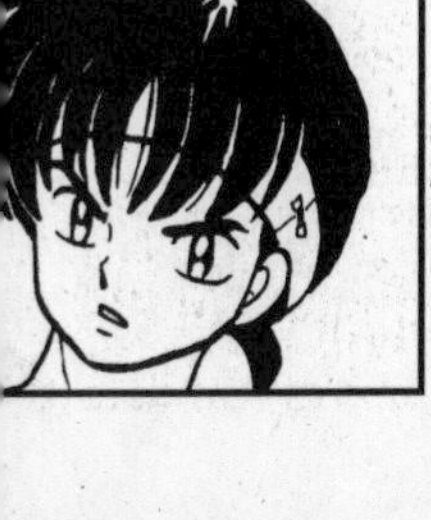

SHINNOSUKE
A forgetful young man who Akane first met in childhood.

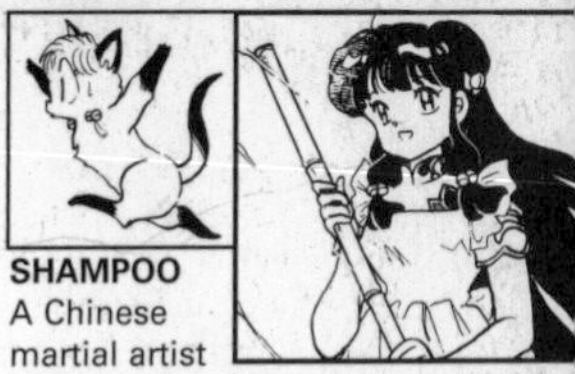

SHAMPOO
A Chinese martial artist from a village of amazons who is in love with Ranma and claims that he must marry her due to village law. She changes into a cat.

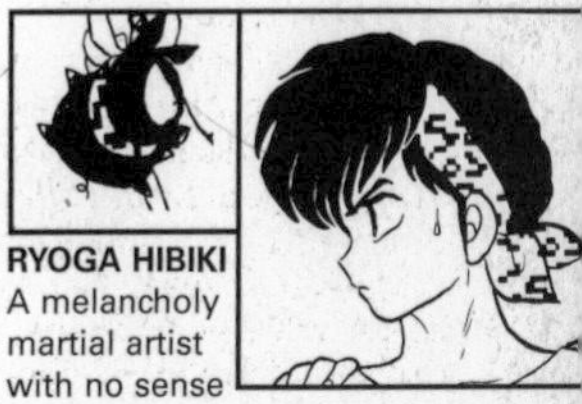

RYOGA HIBIKI
A melancholy martial artist with no sense of direction, a crush on Akane, and a grudge against Ranma. He changes into a small, black pig Akane calls "P-chan."

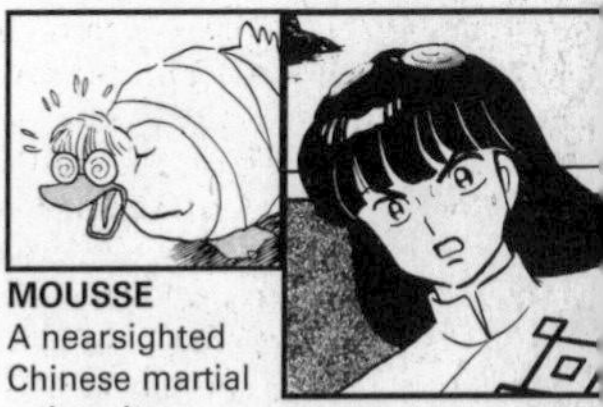

MOUSSE
A nearsighted Chinese martial artist whose specialty is hidden weapons, Mousse has been Shampoo's suitor since childhood. He changes into a duck.

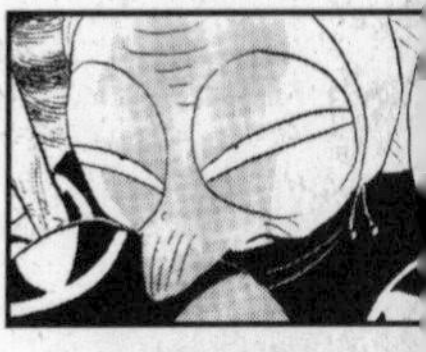

COLOGNE
Great-grandmother to Shampoo who's looking forward to getting a new grandson-in-law in Ranma.

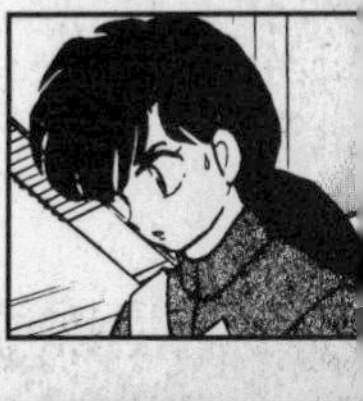

UKYO KUONJI
Another of Ranma's fianceés, Ukyo is both a martial artist and *okonomiyaki* chef.

CONTENTS

Part 1

THE SECRET OF THE FOREST

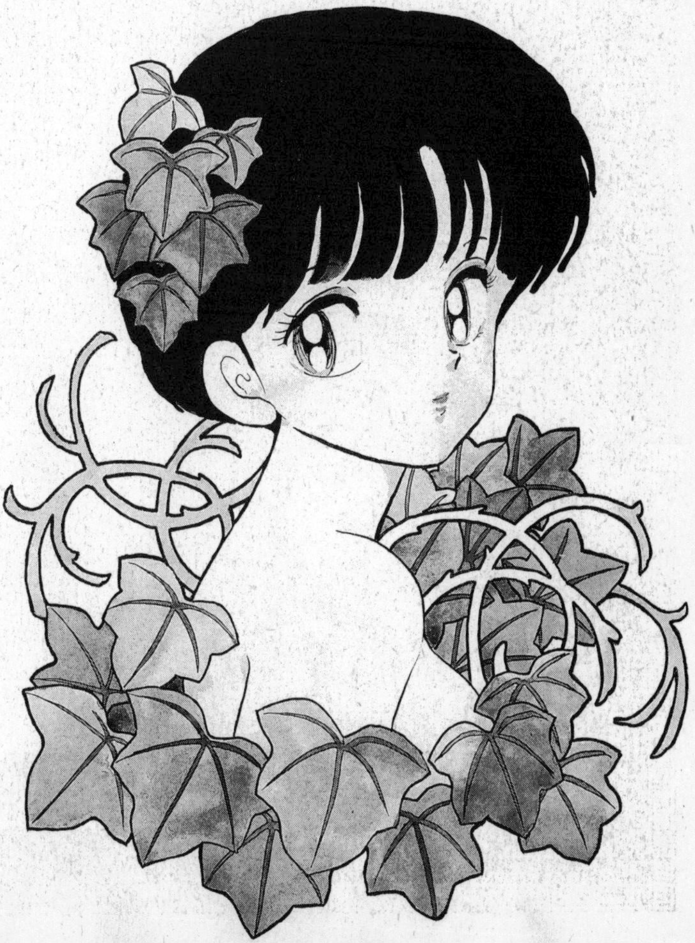

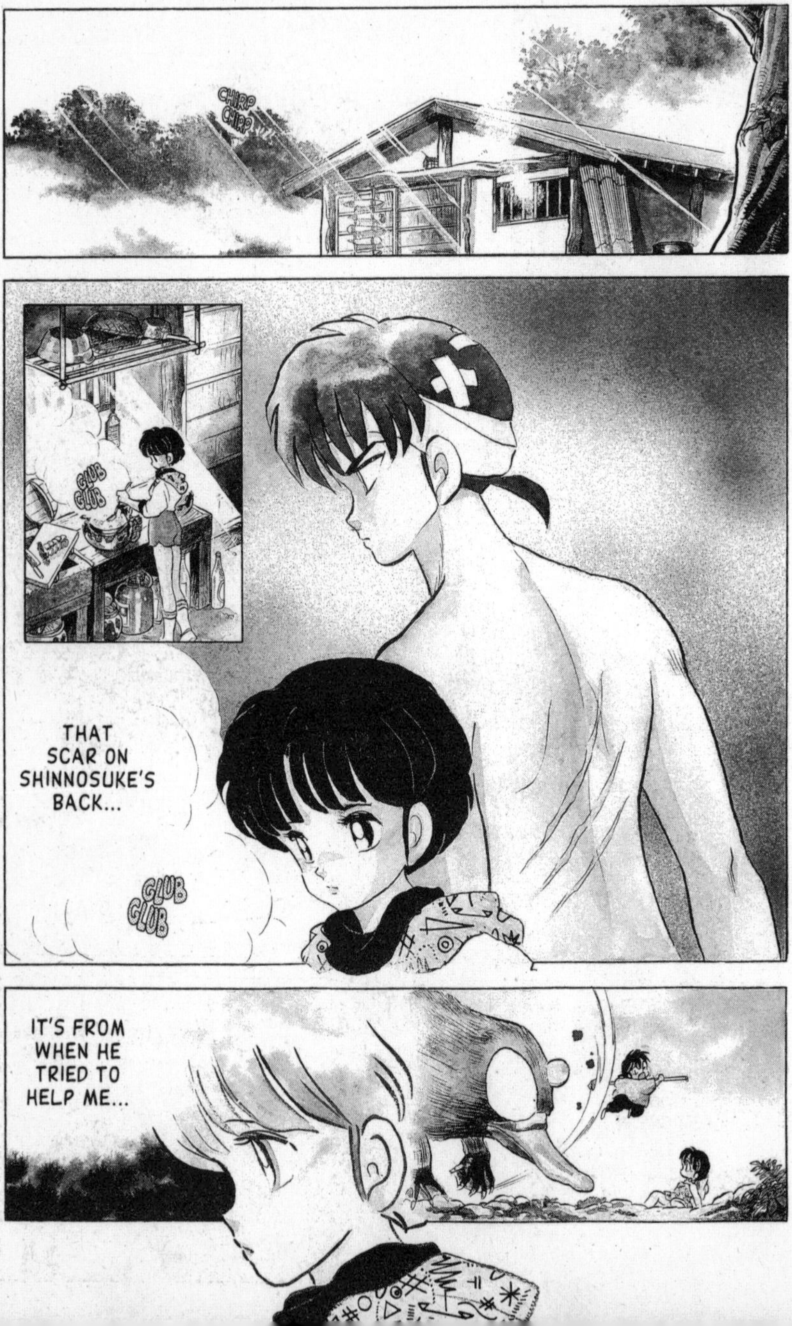
CHIRP
CHIRP
GLUB
GLUB
THAT SCAR ON SHINNOSUKE'S BACK...
GLUB
GLUB
IT'S FROM WHEN HE TRIED TO HELP ME...

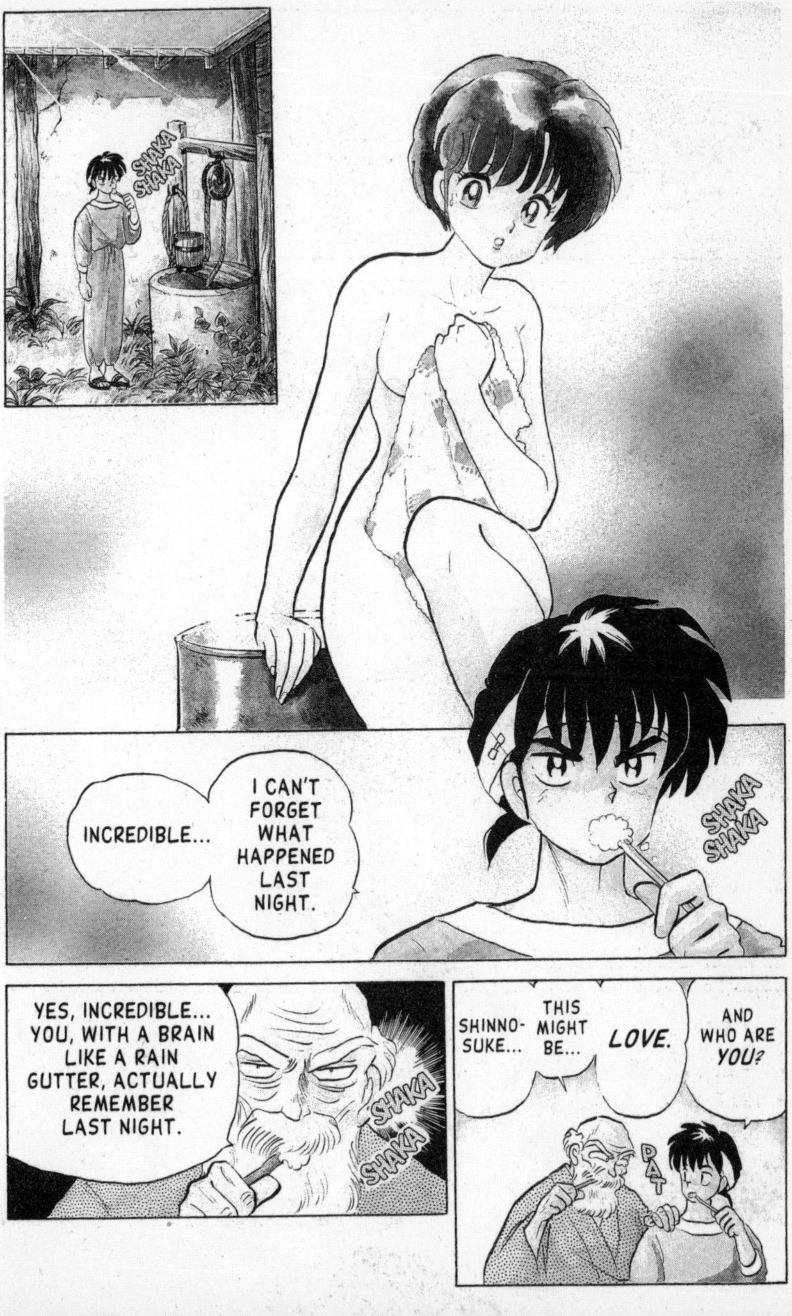
SHAKA SHAKA
INCREDIBLE...
I CAN'T FORGET WHAT HAPPENED LAST NIGHT.
SHAKA SHAKA
YES, INCREDIBLE... YOU, WITH A BRAIN LIKE A RAIN GUTTER, ACTUALLY REMEMBER LAST NIGHT.
SHAKA SHAKA
SHINNO-SUKE...
THIS MIGHT BE...
LOVE.
AND WHO ARE *YOU?*
PAT

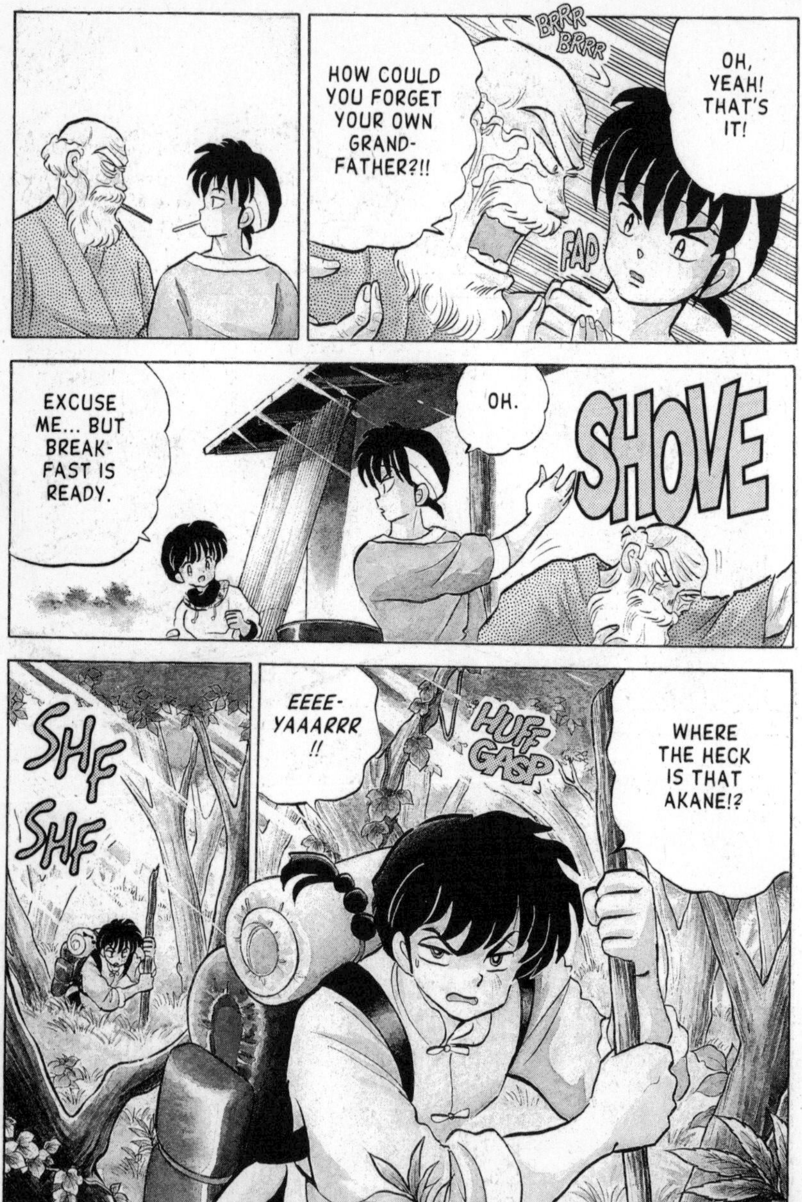
HOW COULD YOU FORGET YOUR OWN GRAND-FATHER?!!
BRRR BRRR
OH, YEAH! THAT'S IT!
FAP
EXCUSE ME... BUT BREAK-FAST IS READY.
OH.
SHOVE
SHF
SHF
EEEE-YAAARRR!!
HUFF GASP
WHERE THE HECK IS THAT AKANE!?

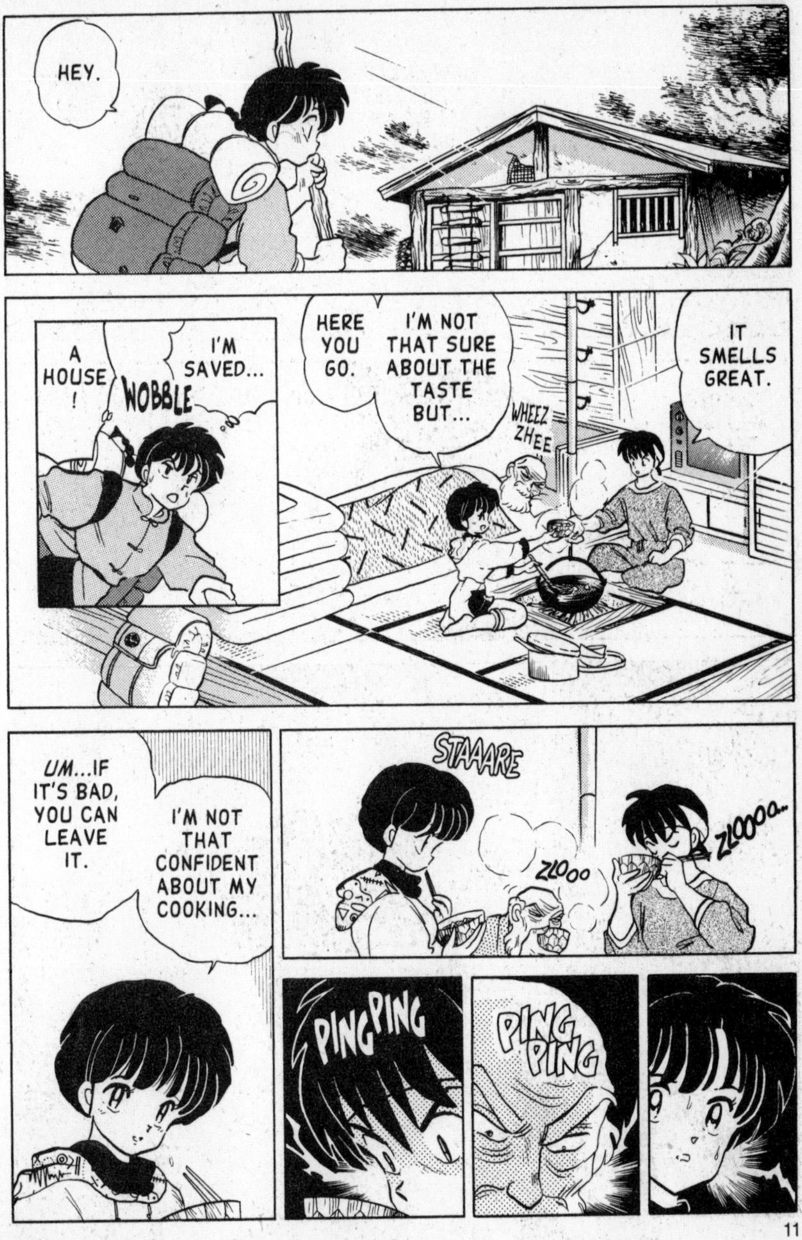
HEY.
A HOUSE!
I'M SAVED...
WOBBLE
HERE YOU GO.
I'M NOT THAT SURE ABOUT THE TASTE BUT...
WHEEZ ZHEE
IT SMELLS GREAT.
UM...IF IT'S BAD, YOU CAN LEAVE IT.
I'M NOT THAT CONFIDENT ABOUT MY COOKING...
STAAARE
ZLOOO
ZLOOOO...
PING PING
PING PING

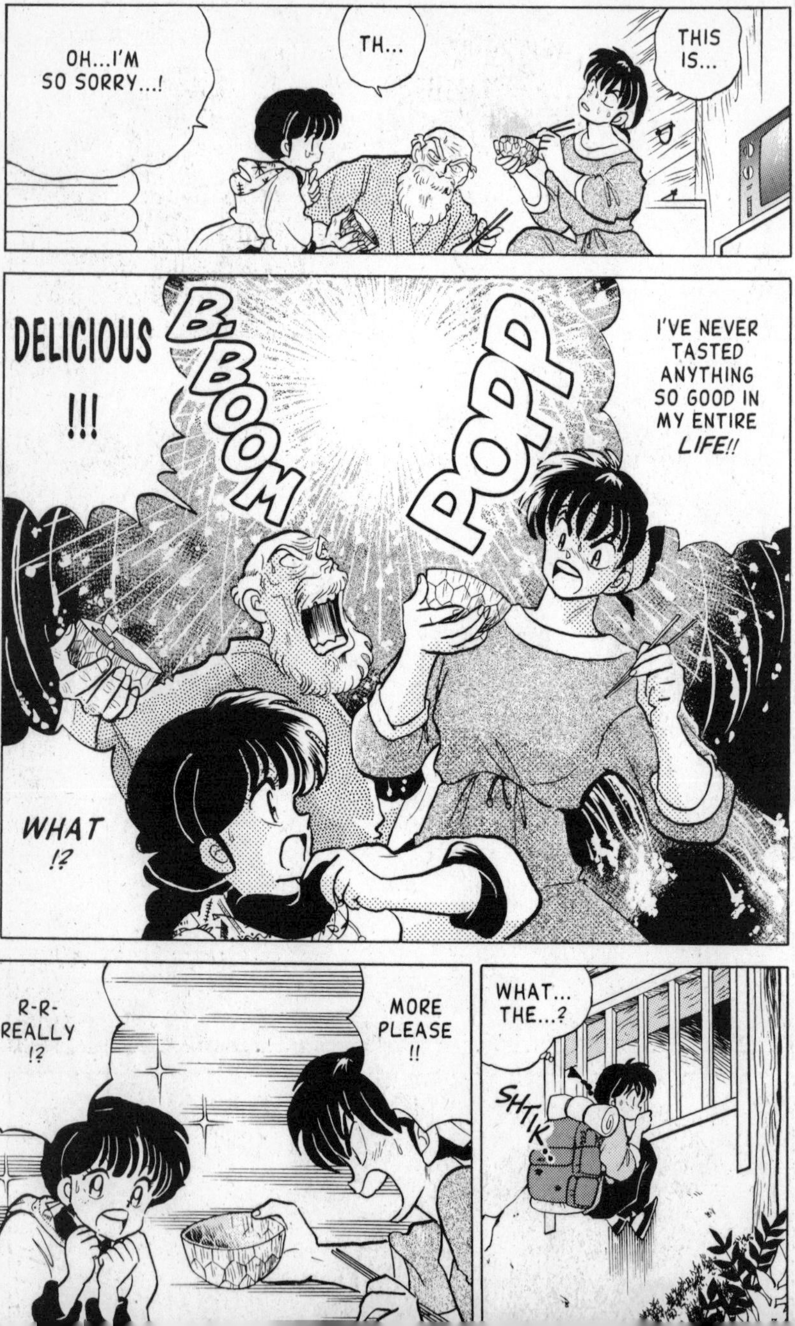

OH...I'M SO SORRY...!
TH...
THIS IS...
DELICIOUS !!!
B-BOOM
POPP
I'VE NEVER TASTED ANYTHING SO GOOD IN MY ENTIRE *LIFE*!!
WHAT !?
R-R-REALLY !?
MORE PLEASE !!
WHAT... THE...?
SHTIK

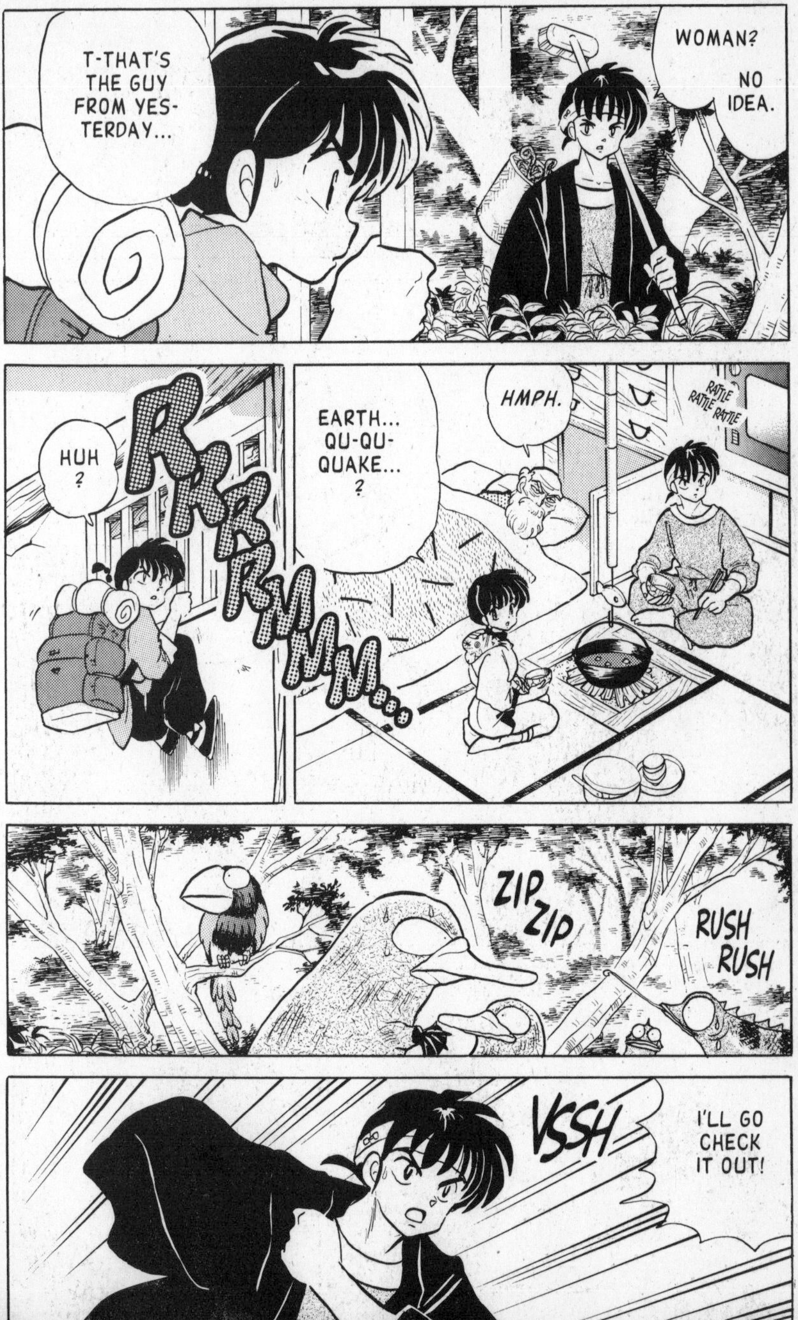
T-THAT'S THE GUY FROM YES-TERDAY...
WOMAN?
NO IDEA.
HUH?
RRRRMMMM...
EARTH... QU-QU-QUAKE...?
HMPH.
RATTLE RATTLE RATTLE
ZIP ZIP
RUSH RUSH
VSSH
I'LL GO CHECK IT OUT!

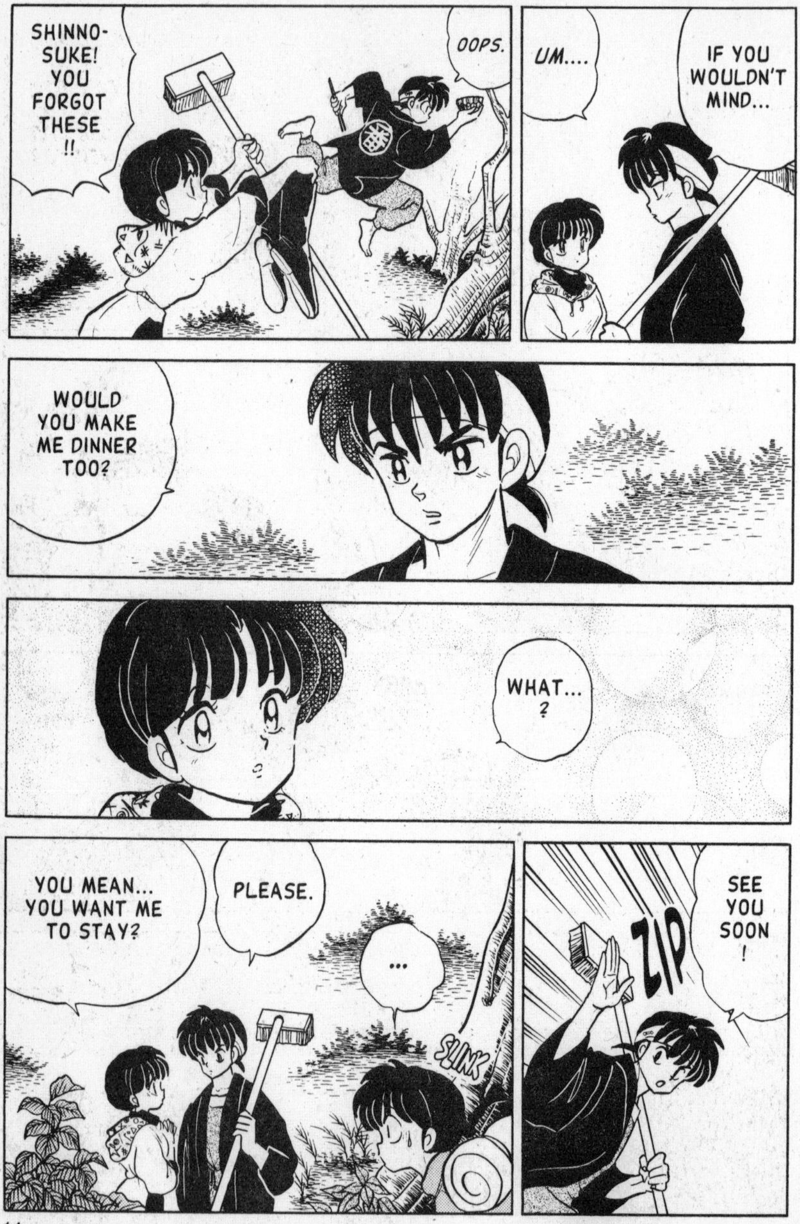
SHINNO-SUKE! YOU FORGOT THESE !!
OOPS.
UM....
IF YOU WOULDN'T MIND...
WOULD YOU MAKE ME DINNER TOO?
WHAT...?
YOU MEAN... YOU WANT ME TO STAY?
PLEASE.
...
SLINK
ZIP
SEE YOU SOON!

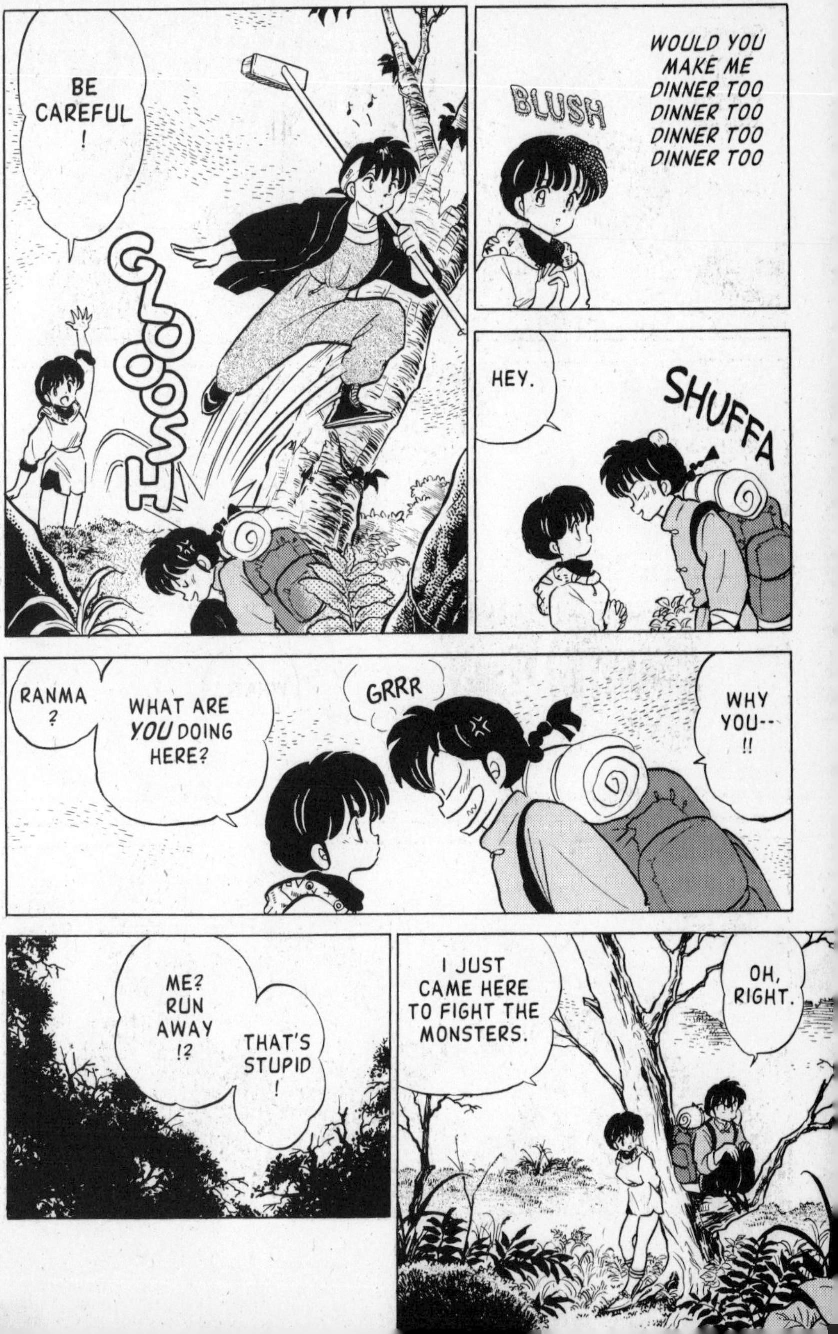
BE CAREFUL !
GLOOOSH
WOULD YOU MAKE ME DINNER TOO DINNER TOO DINNER TOO DINNER TOO
BLUSH
HEY.
SHUFFA
RANMA ?
WHAT ARE *YOU* DOING HERE?
GRRR
WHY YOU-- !!
ME? RUN AWAY !?
THAT'S STUPID !
I JUST CAME HERE TO FIGHT THE MONSTERS.
OH, RIGHT.

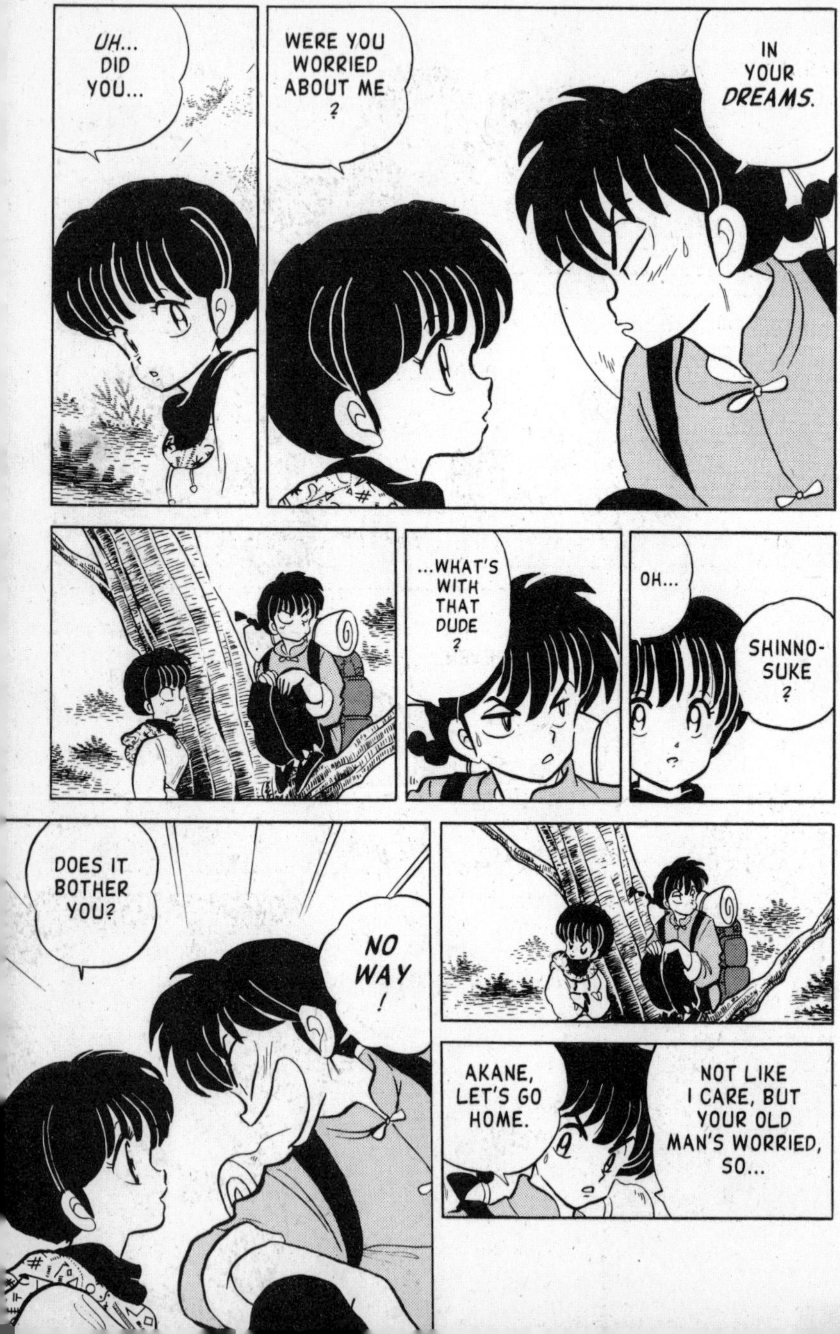
UH... DID YOU...
WERE YOU WORRIED ABOUT ME ?
IN YOUR DREAMS.
...WHAT'S WITH THAT DUDE ?
OH...
SHINNO-SUKE ?
DOES IT BOTHER YOU?
NO WAY !
NOT LIKE I CARE, BUT YOUR OLD MAN'S WORRIED, SO...
AKANE, LET'S GO HOME.

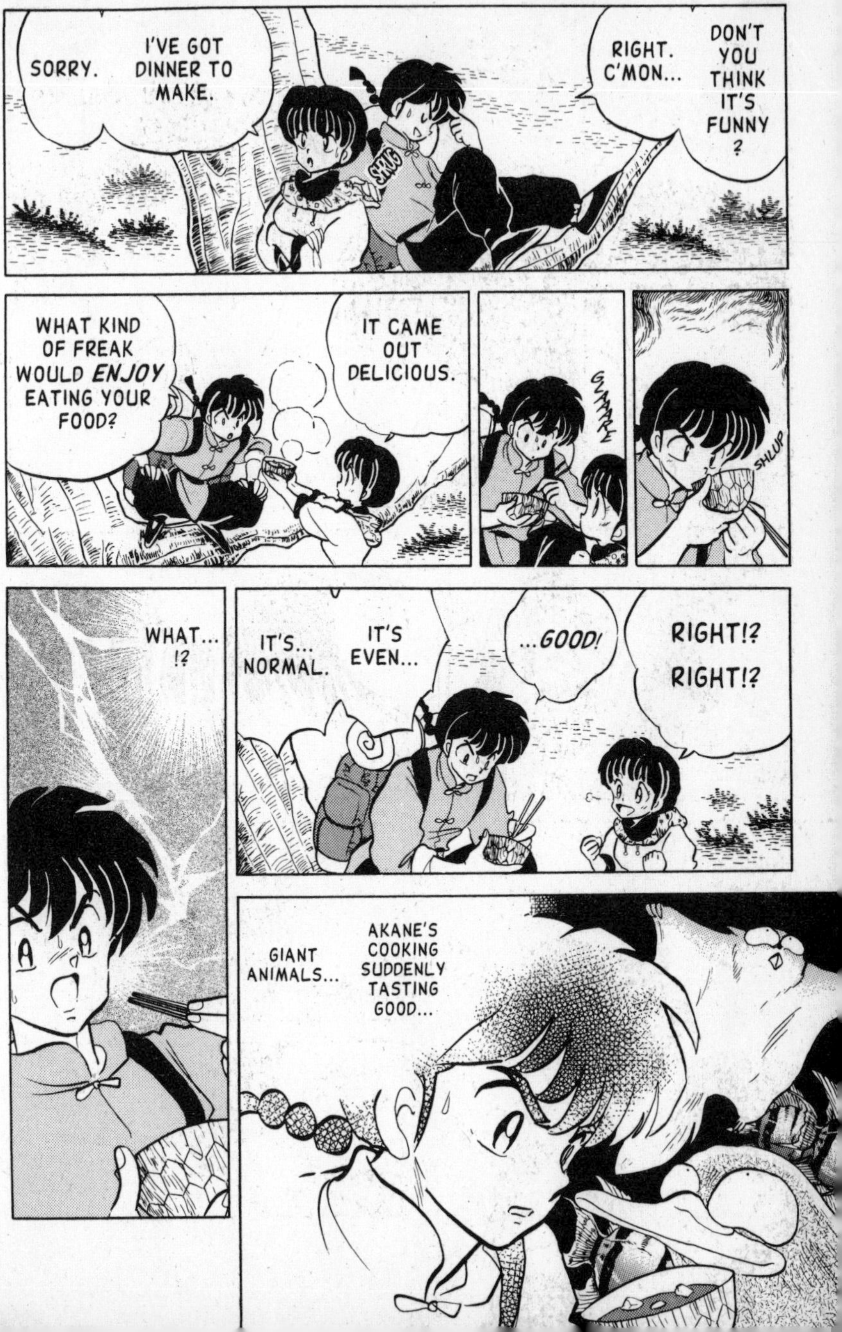
SORRY.
I'VE GOT DINNER TO MAKE.
RIGHT. C'MON...
DON'T YOU THINK IT'S FUNNY?
SHRUG
WHAT KIND OF FREAK WOULD ENJOY EATING YOUR FOOD?
IT CAME OUT DELICIOUS.
SHLUP
WHAT... !?
IT'S... NORMAL.
IT'S EVEN...
...GOOD!
RIGHT!? RIGHT!?
GIANT ANIMALS...
AKANE'S COOKING SUDDENLY TASTING GOOD...

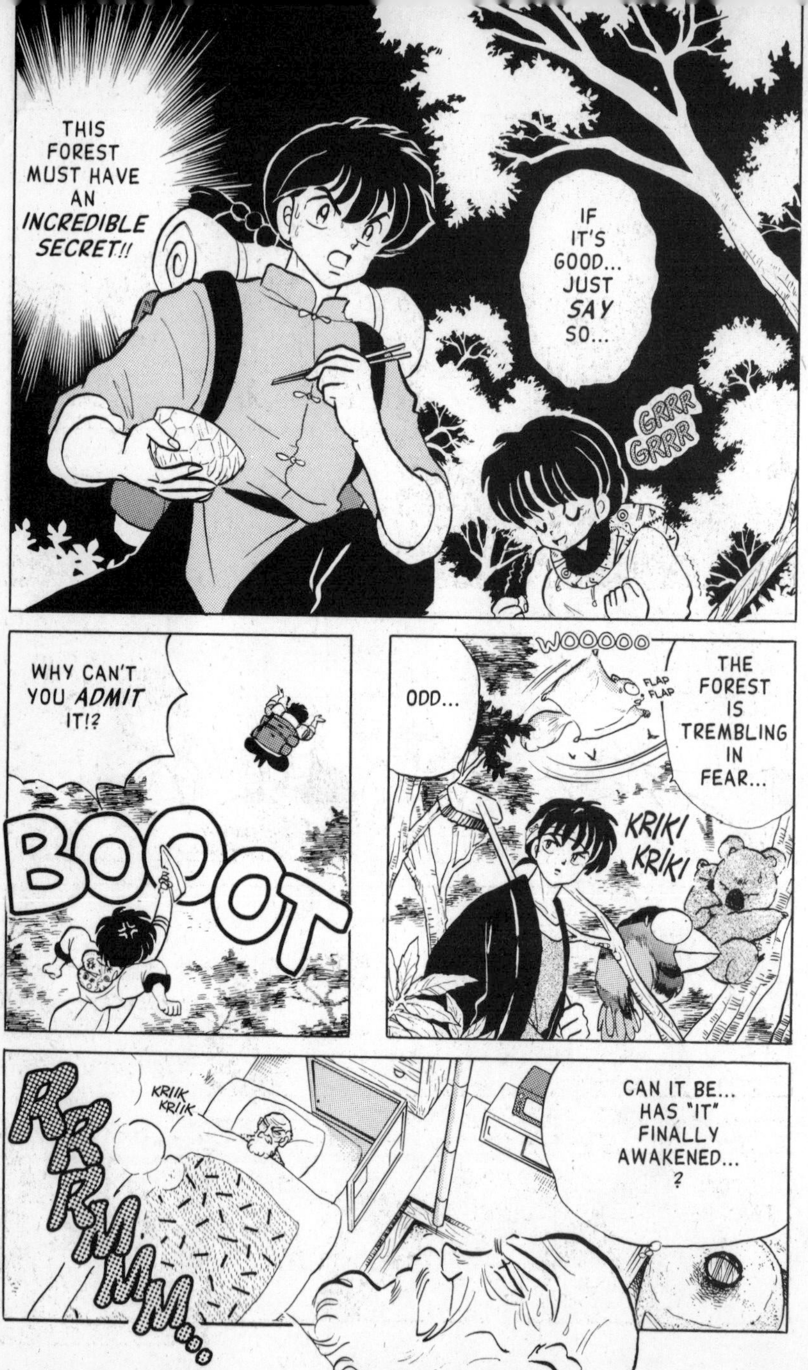
THIS FOREST MUST HAVE AN INCREDIBLE SECRET!!
IF IT'S GOOD... JUST SAY SO...
GRRR GRRR
WHY CAN'T YOU ADMIT IT!?
BOOOT
ODD...
WOOOOO
FLAP FLAP
THE FOREST IS TREMBLING IN FEAR...
KRIKI KRIKI
RRRMMM...
KRIIK KRIIK
CAN IT BE... HAS "IT" FINALLY AWAKENED...?

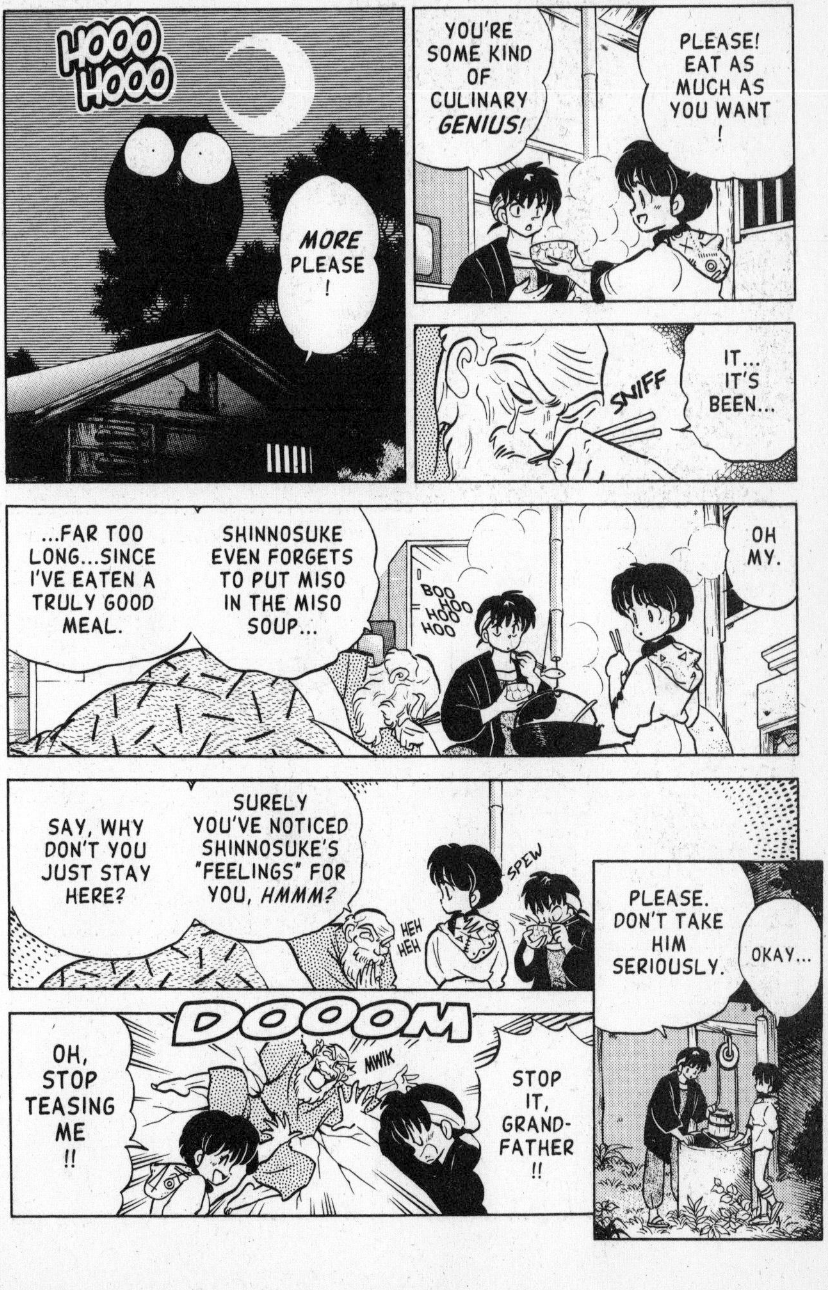
HOOO HOOO
MORE PLEASE!
YOU'RE SOME KIND OF CULINARY GENIUS!
PLEASE! EAT AS MUCH AS YOU WANT!
SNIFF
IT... IT'S BEEN...
...FAR TOO LONG...SINCE I'VE EATEN A TRULY GOOD MEAL.
SHINNOSUKE EVEN FORGETS TO PUT MISO IN THE MISO SOUP...
BOO HOO HOO HOO
OH MY.
SAY, WHY DON'T YOU JUST STAY HERE?
SURELY YOU'VE NOTICED SHINNOSUKE'S "FEELINGS" FOR YOU, HMMM?
SPEW
HEH HEH
DOOOM
OH, STOP TEASING ME!!
MWIK
STOP IT, GRAND-FATHER!!
PLEASE. DON'T TAKE HIM SERIOUSLY.
OKAY...

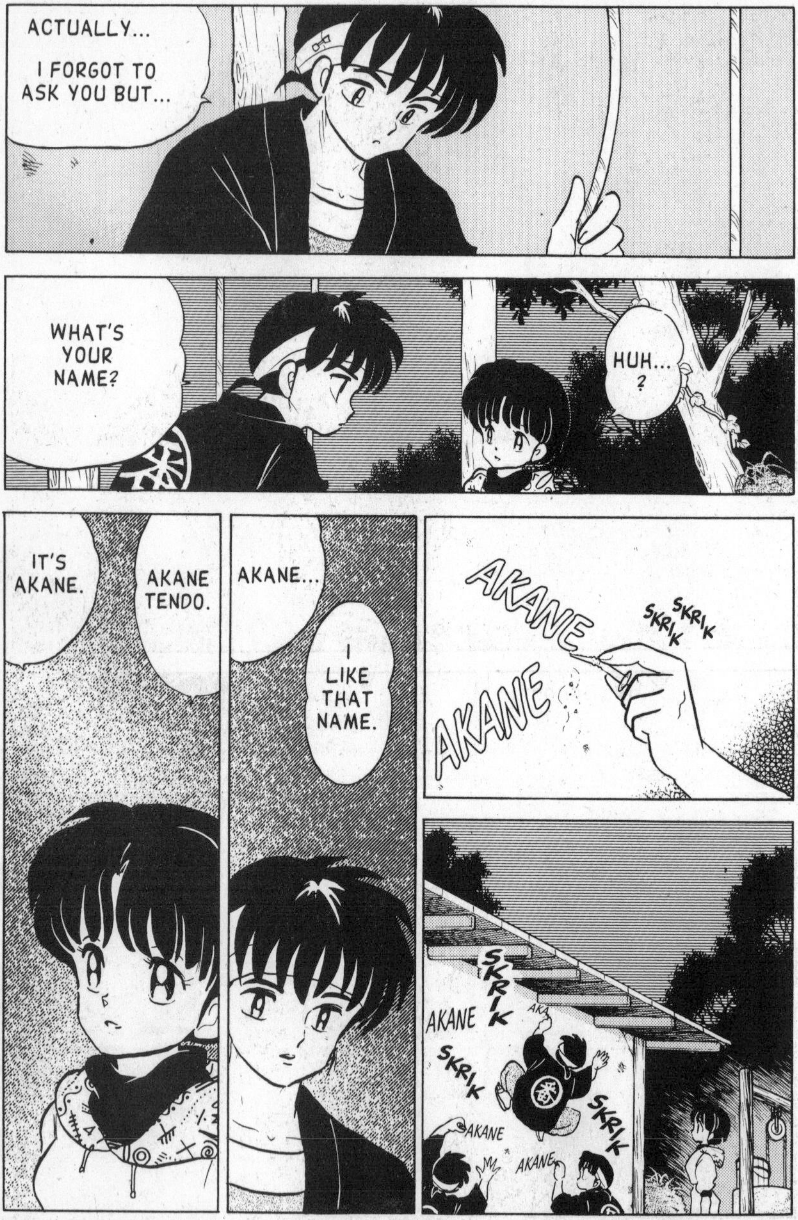
ACTUALLY...
I FORGOT TO ASK YOU BUT...
WHAT'S YOUR NAME?
HUH...?
IT'S AKANE.
AKANE TENDO.
AKANE...
I LIKE THAT NAME.
AKANE
SKRIK SKRIK
AKANE
SKRIK
AKANE
AKA
SKRIK
AKANE
AKANE
SKRIK

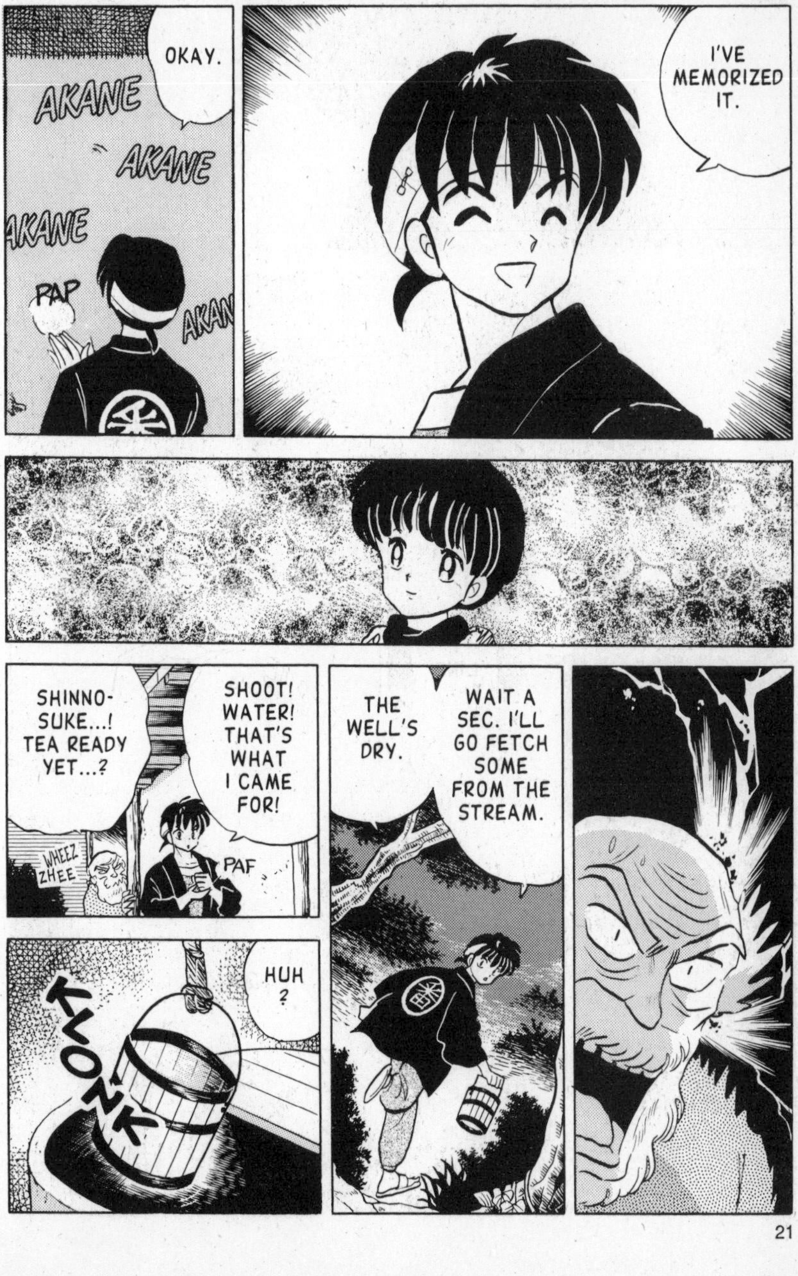
OKAY.
AKANE
AKANE
AKANE
PAP
AKAN
I'VE MEMORIZED IT.
SHINNO-SUKE...! TEA READY YET...?
SHOOT! WATER! THAT'S WHAT I CAME FOR!
WHEEZ ZHEE
PAF
KLONK
HUH ?
THE WELL'S DRY.
WAIT A SEC. I'LL GO FETCH SOME FROM THE STREAM.

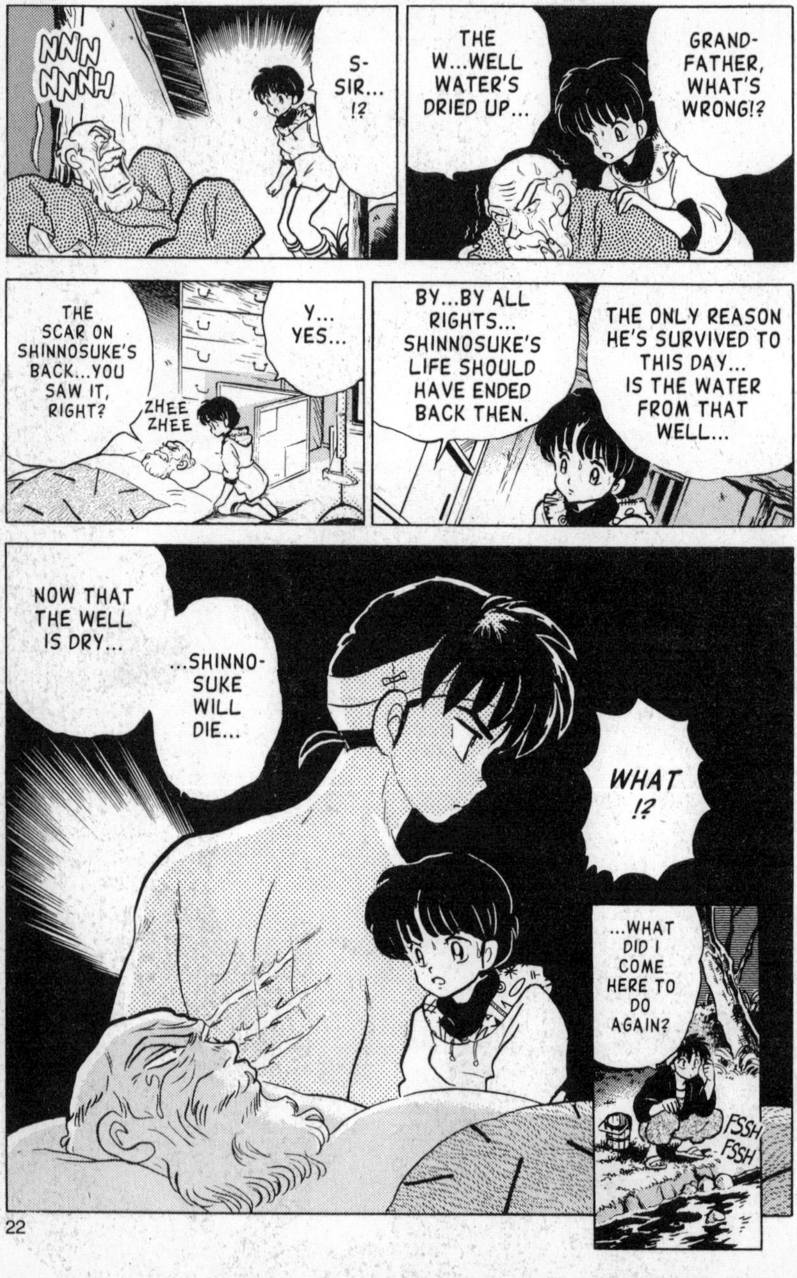
NNNNNNH
S-SIR...!?
THE W...WELL WATER'S DRIED UP...
GRAND-FATHER, WHAT'S WRONG!?
THE SCAR ON SHINNOSUKE'S BACK...YOU SAW IT, RIGHT?
Y...YES...
ZHEE ZHEE
BY...BY ALL RIGHTS... SHINNOSUKE'S LIFE SHOULD HAVE ENDED BACK THEN.
THE ONLY REASON HE'S SURVIVED TO THIS DAY... IS THE WATER FROM THAT WELL...
NOW THAT THE WELL IS DRY...
...SHINNOSUKE WILL DIE...
WHAT!?
...WHAT DID I COME HERE TO DO AGAIN?
FSSH FSSH

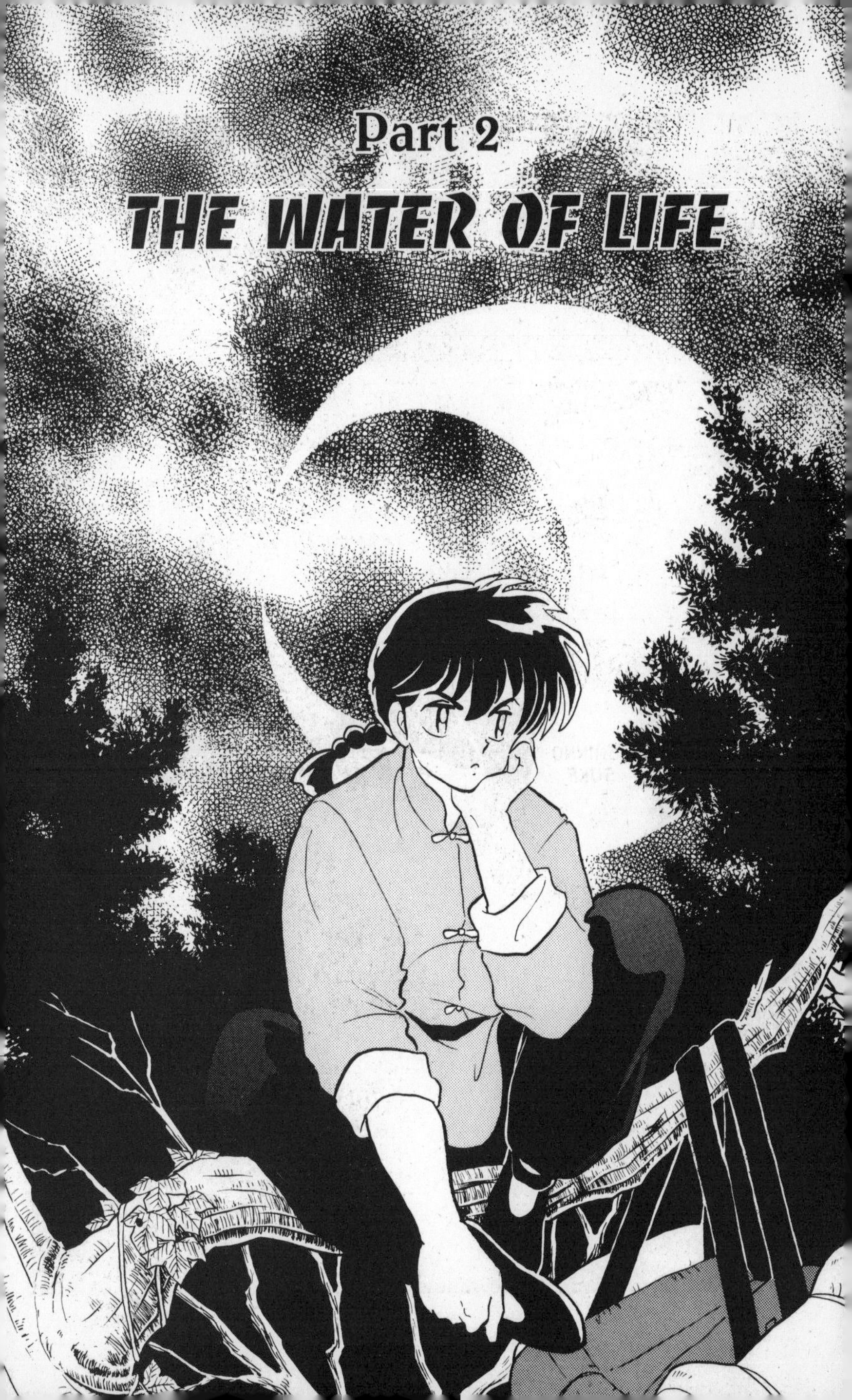
Part 2
THE WATER OF LIFE

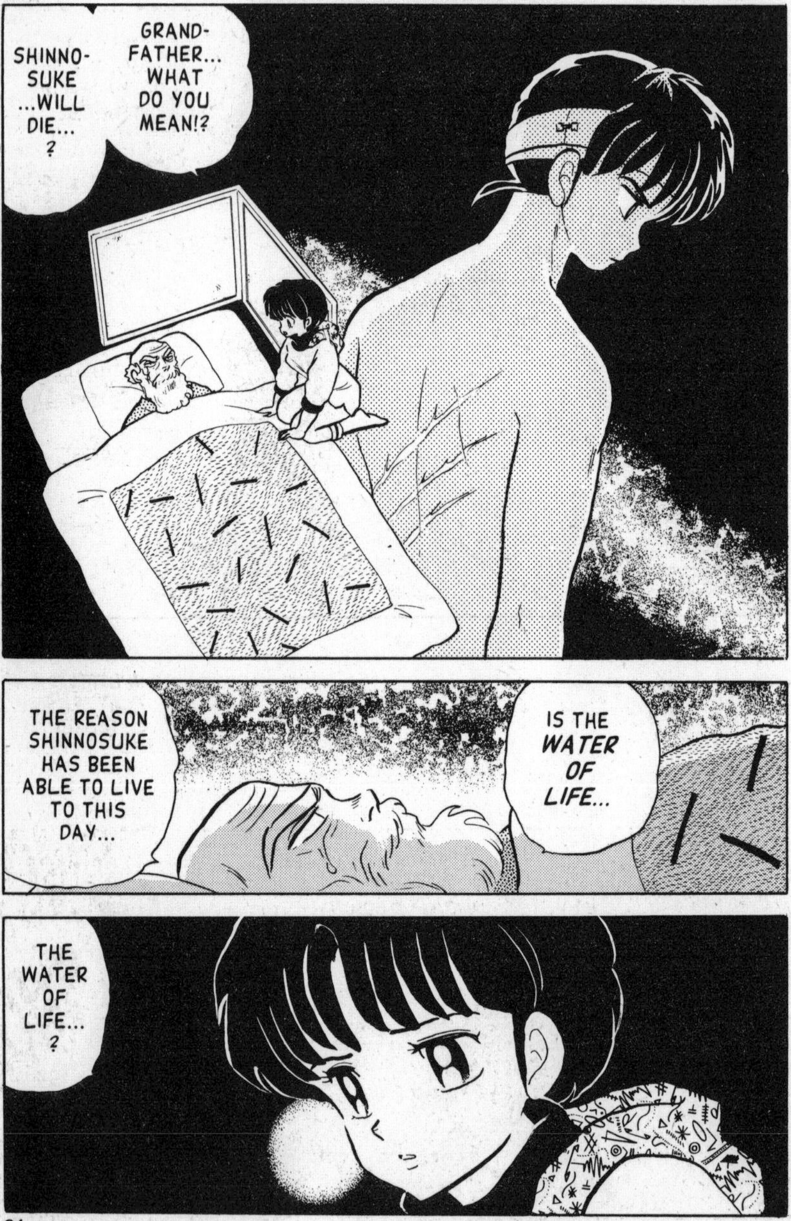

SHINNOSUKE ...WILL DIE...?
GRAND-FATHER... WHAT DO YOU MEAN!?
THE REASON SHINNOSUKE HAS BEEN ABLE TO LIVE TO THIS DAY...
IS THE WATER OF LIFE...
THE WATER OF LIFE...?

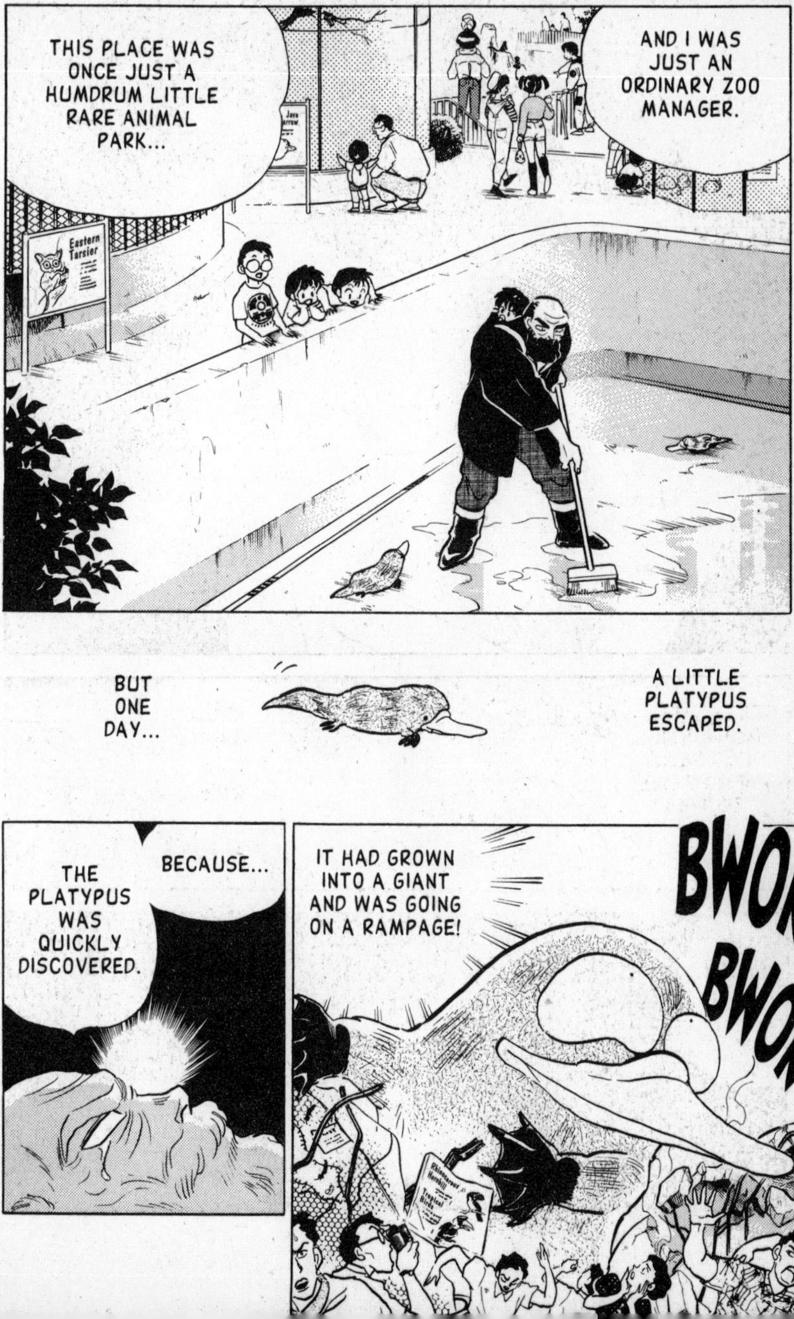
THIS PLACE WAS ONCE JUST A HUMDRUM LITTLE RARE ANIMAL PARK...
AND I WAS JUST AN ORDINARY ZOO MANAGER.
Eastern Tarsier
BUT ONE DAY...
A LITTLE PLATYPUS ESCAPED.
THE PLATYPUS WAS QUICKLY DISCOVERED.
BECAUSE...
IT HAD GROWN INTO A GIANT AND WAS GOING ON A RAMPAGE!
BWOK
BWOK

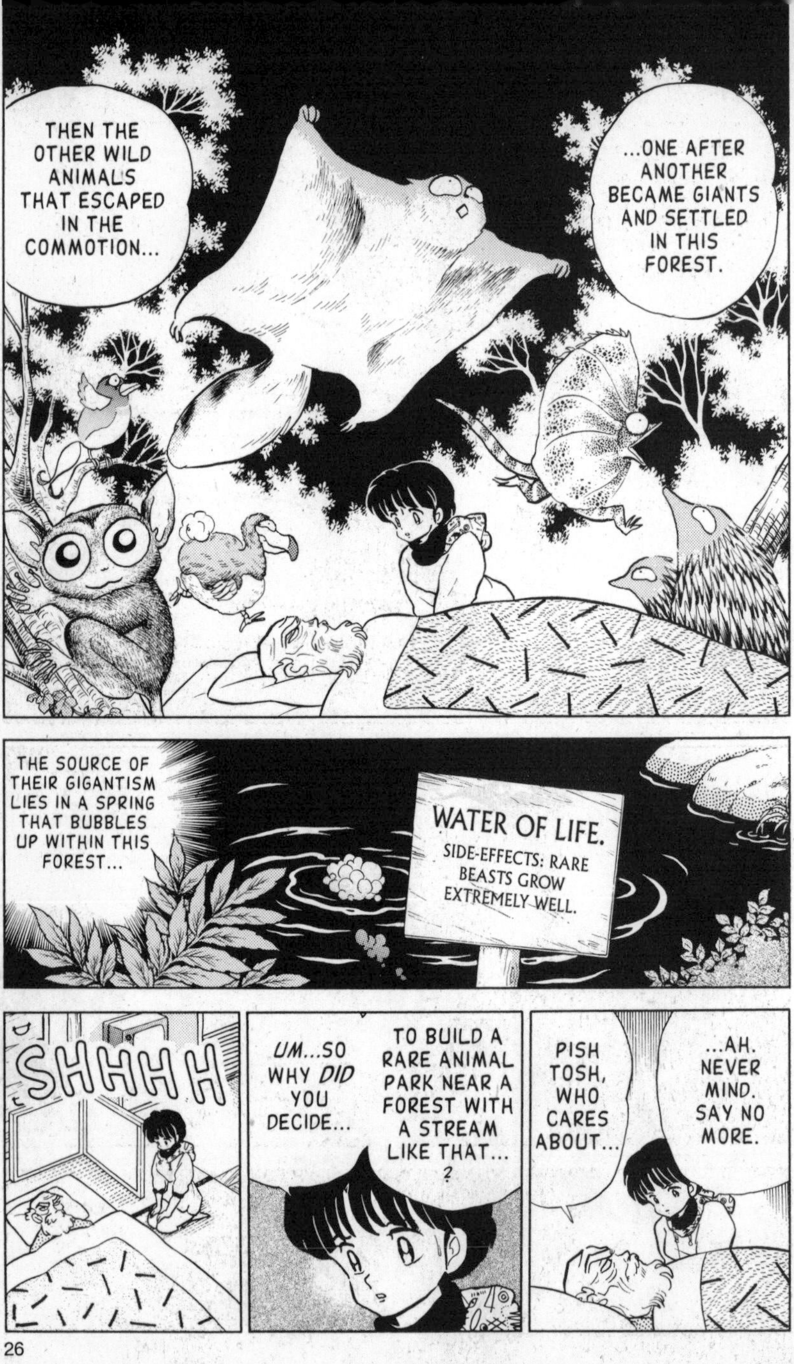
THEN THE OTHER WILD ANIMALS THAT ESCAPED IN THE COMMOTION...
...ONE AFTER ANOTHER BECAME GIANTS AND SETTLED IN THIS FOREST.
THE SOURCE OF THEIR GIGANTISM LIES IN A SPRING THAT BUBBLES UP WITHIN THIS FOREST...
WATER OF LIFE.
SIDE-EFFECTS: RARE BEASTS GROW EXTREMELY WELL.
SHHHH
UM...SO WHY *DID* YOU DECIDE...
TO BUILD A RARE ANIMAL PARK NEAR A FOREST WITH A STREAM LIKE THAT...?
PISH TOSH, WHO CARES ABOUT...
...AH. NEVER MIND. SAY NO MORE.

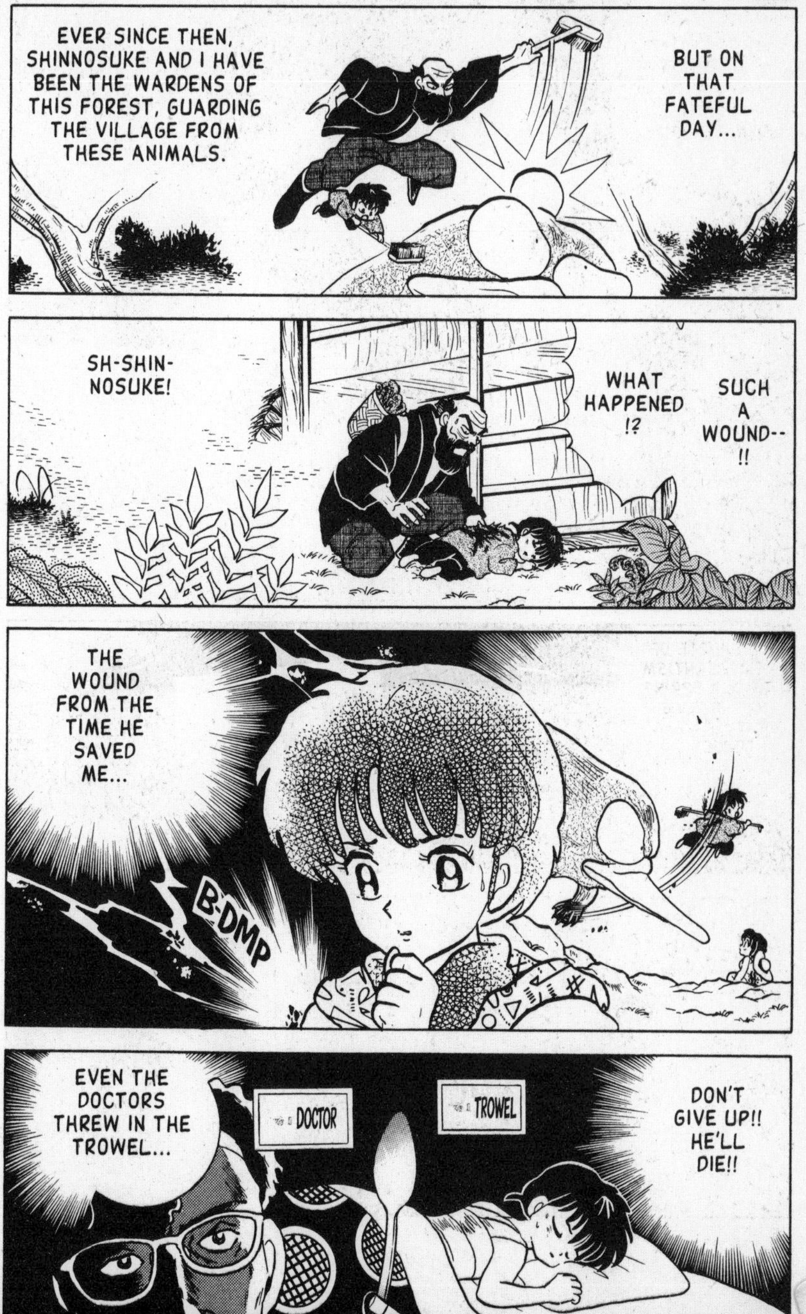
EVER SINCE THEN, SHINNOSUKE AND I HAVE BEEN THE WARDENS OF THIS FOREST, GUARDING THE VILLAGE FROM THESE ANIMALS.
BUT ON THAT FATEFUL DAY...
SH-SHIN-NOSUKE!
WHAT HAPPENED !?
SUCH A WOUND-- !!
THE WOUND FROM THE TIME HE SAVED ME...
B-DMP
EVEN THE DOCTORS THREW IN THE TROWEL...
DOCTOR
TROWEL
DON'T GIVE UP!! HE'LL DIE!!

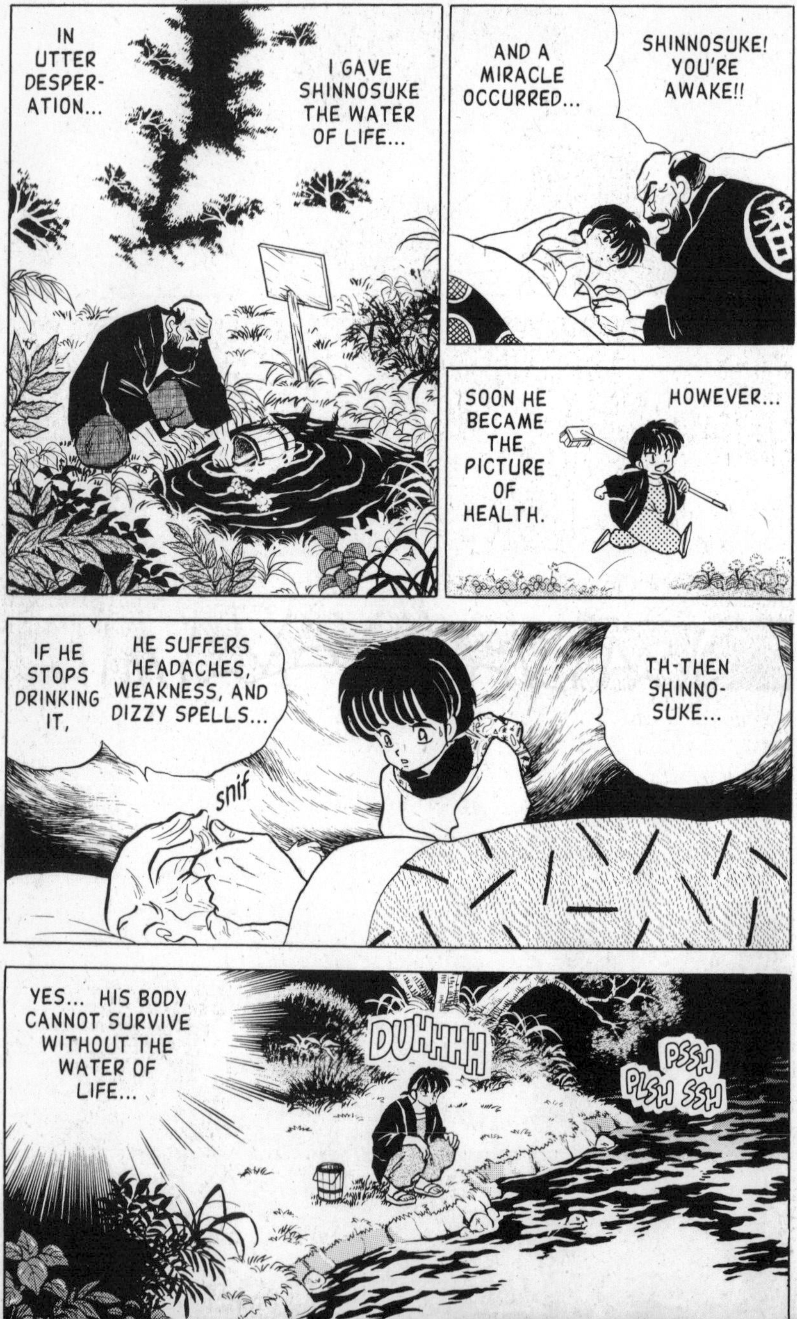
IN UTTER DESPERATION...
I GAVE SHINNOSUKE THE WATER OF LIFE...
AND A MIRACLE OCCURRED...
SHINNOSUKE! YOU'RE AWAKE!!
SOON HE BECAME THE PICTURE OF HEALTH.
HOWEVER...
IF HE STOPS DRINKING IT,
HE SUFFERS HEADACHES, WEAKNESS, AND DIZZY SPELLS...
snif
TH-THEN SHINNOSUKE...
YES... HIS BODY CANNOT SURVIVE WITHOUT THE WATER OF LIFE...
DUHHHH
PSSH
PLSH SSH

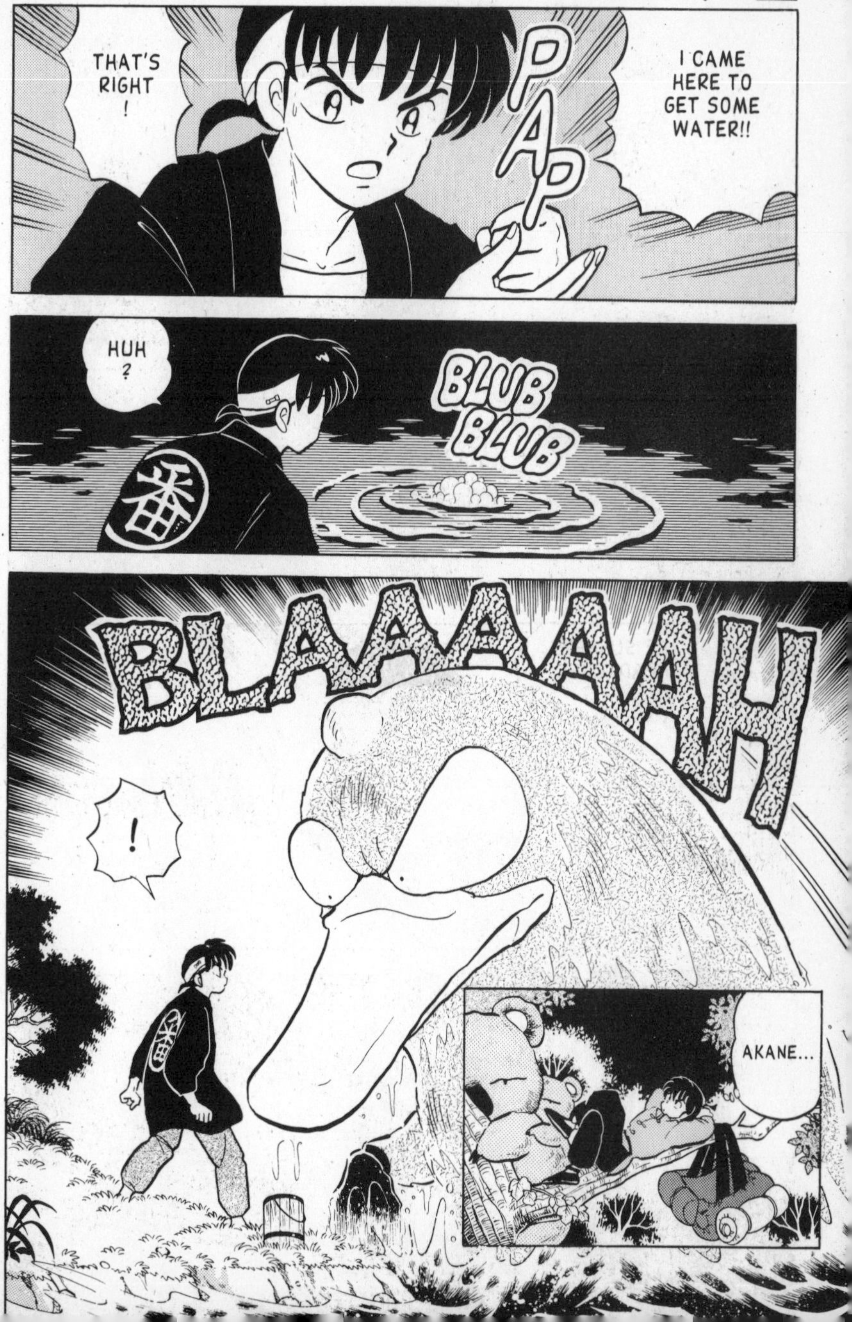
THAT'S RIGHT !
PAP
I CAME HERE TO GET SOME WATER!!
HUH ?
BLUB BLUB
BLAAAAH
!
AKANE...

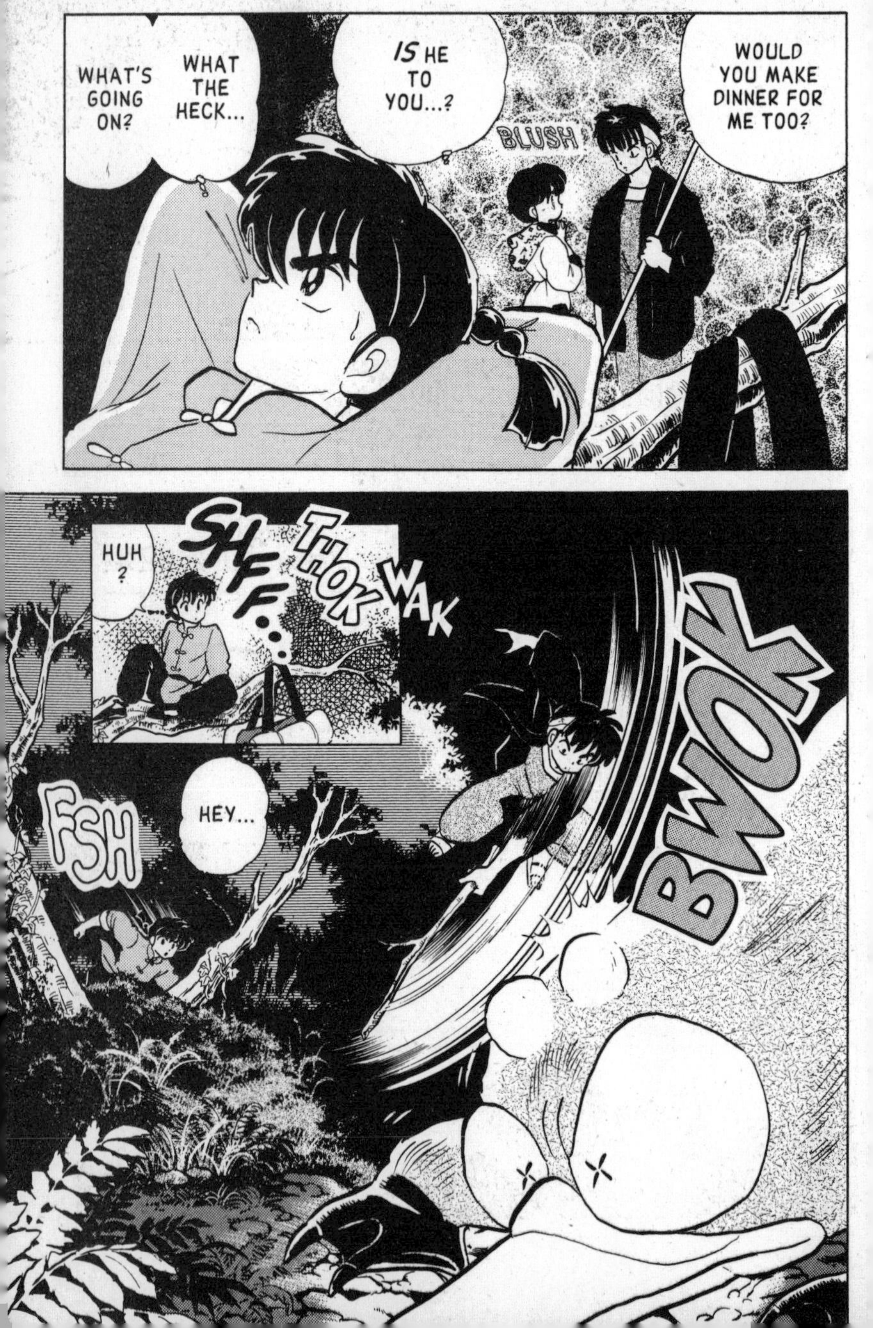
WHAT THE HECK...
WHAT'S GOING ON?
IS HE TO YOU...?
BLUSH
WOULD YOU MAKE DINNER FOR ME TOO?
HUH ?
SHFF...
THOK
WAK
BWOK
FSH
HEY...

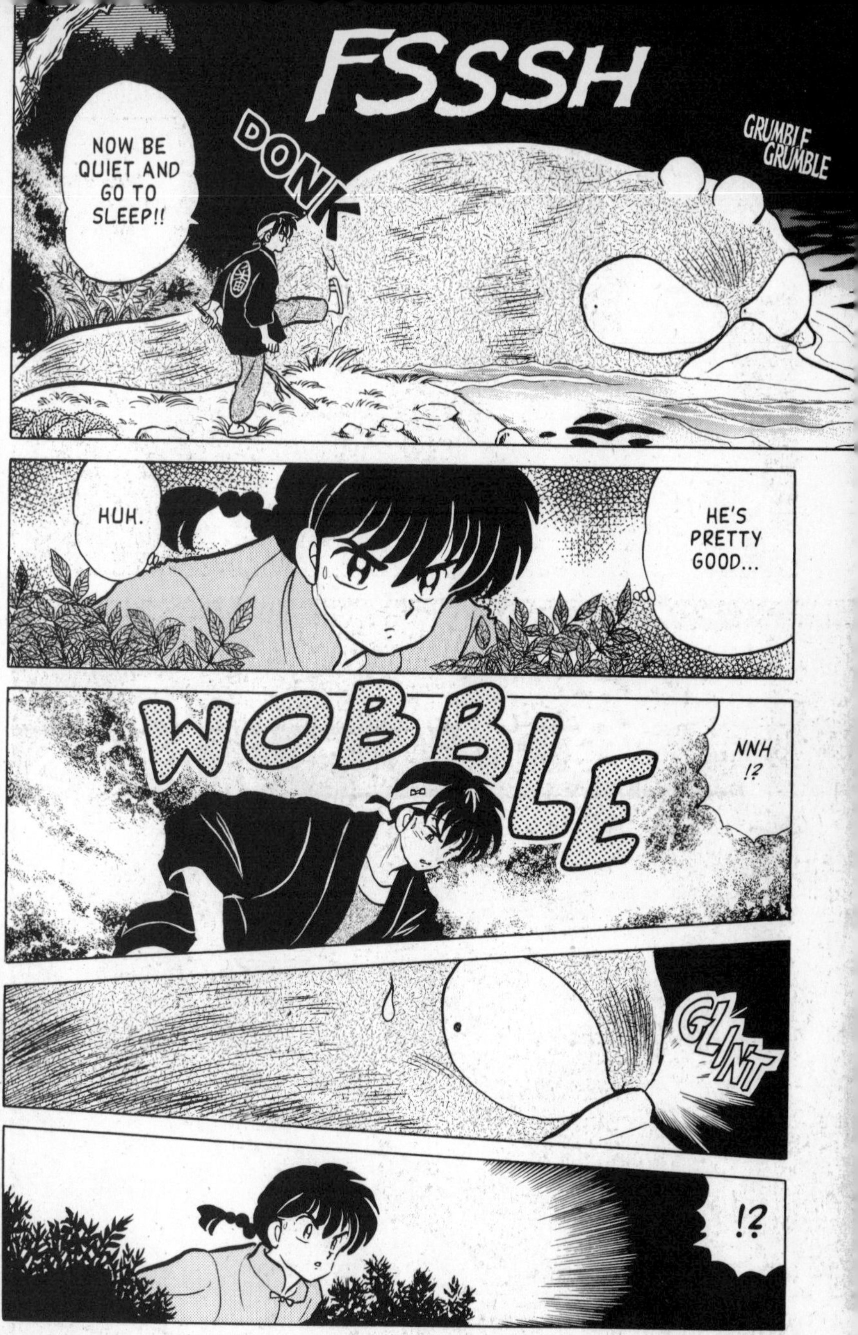
FSSSH
NOW BE QUIET AND GO TO SLEEP!!
DONK
GRUMBLE GRUMBLE
HUH.
HE'S PRETTY GOOD...
WOBBLE
NNH !?
GLINT
!?

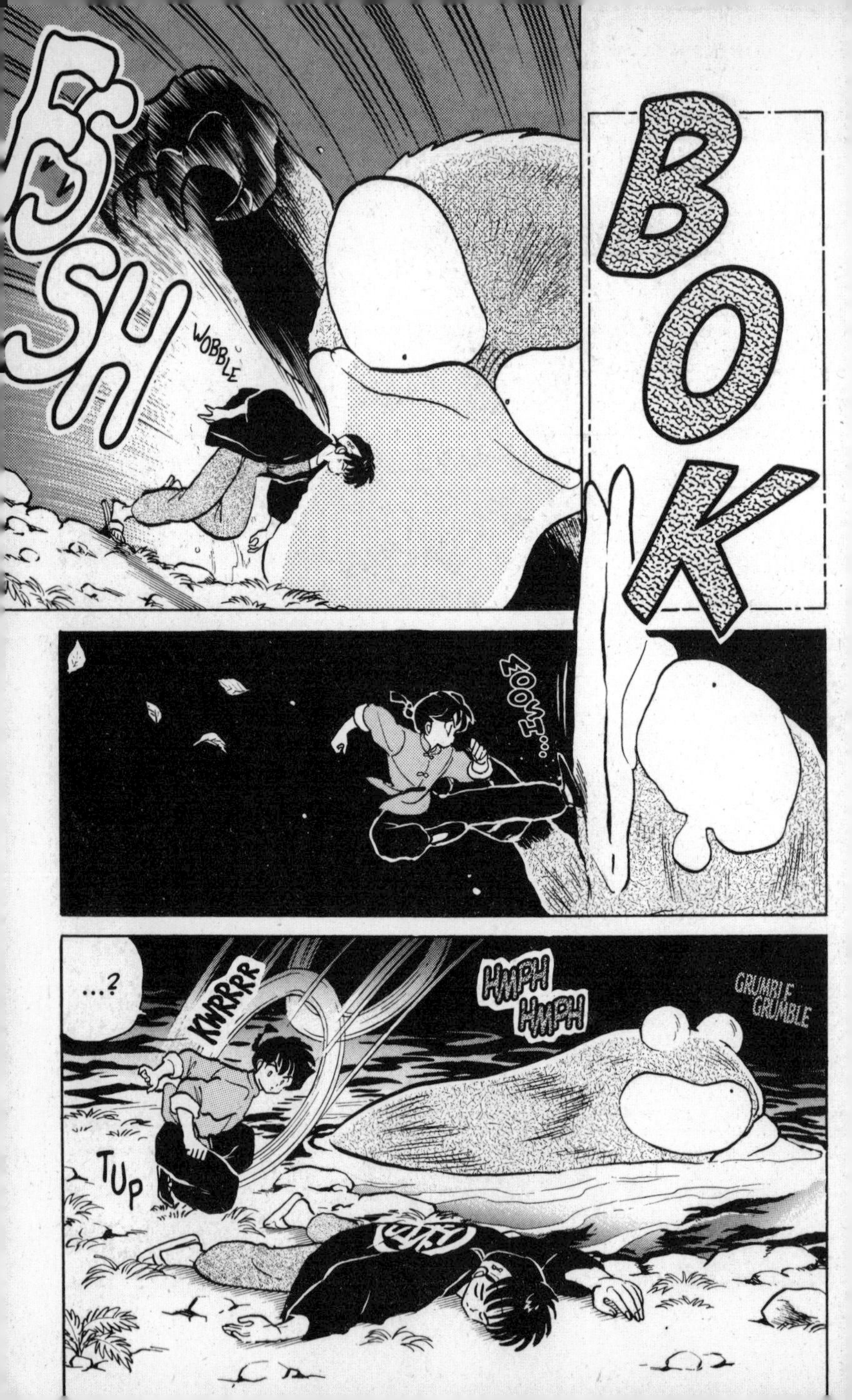
FSSH
WOBBLE
BOK
WOOSH...
...?
KWRRRR
HMPH HMPH
GRUMBLE GRUMBLE
TUP

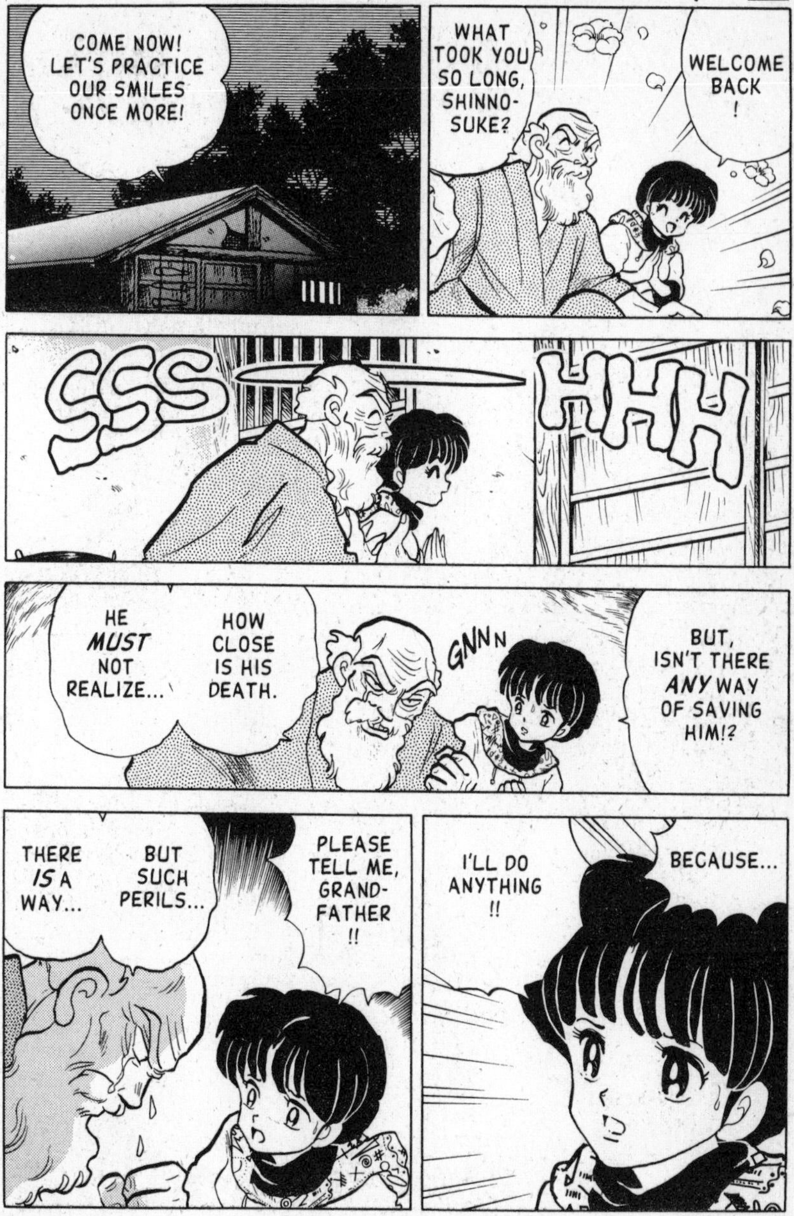
COME NOW! LET'S PRACTICE OUR SMILES ONCE MORE!
WHAT TOOK YOU SO LONG, SHINNO-SUKE?
WELCOME BACK!
SSS
HHH
HE MUST NOT REALIZE...
HOW CLOSE IS HIS DEATH.
GNNN
BUT, ISN'T THERE ANY WAY OF SAVING HIM!?
THERE IS A WAY...
BUT SUCH PERILS...
PLEASE TELL ME, GRAND-FATHER!!
I'LL DO ANYTHING!!
BECAUSE...

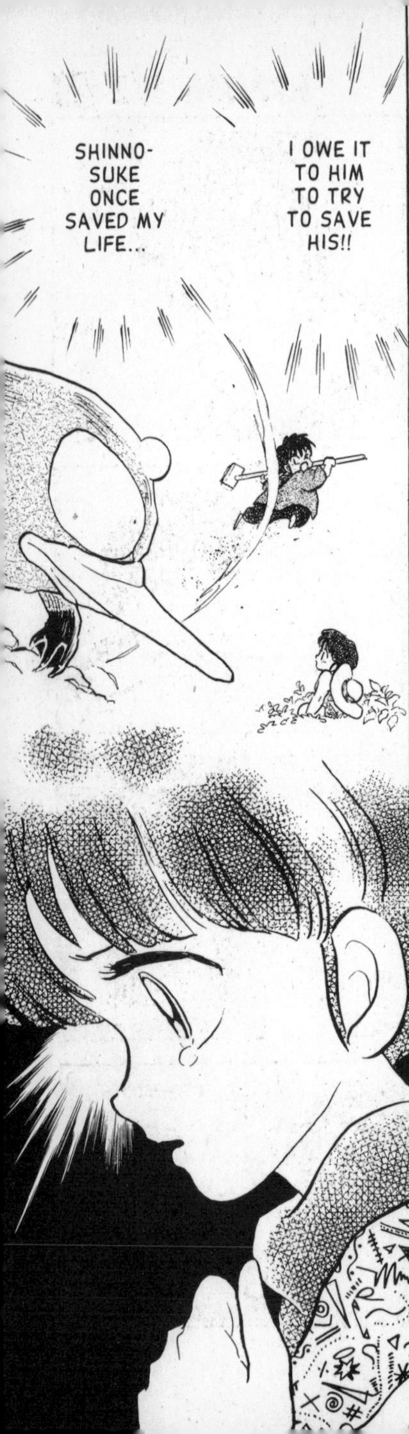
SHINNO-SUKE ONCE SAVED MY LIFE...
I OWE IT TO HIM TO TRY TO SAVE HIS!!
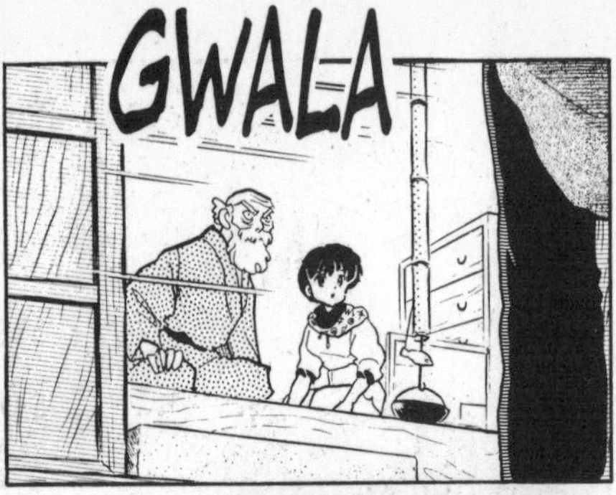
GWALA
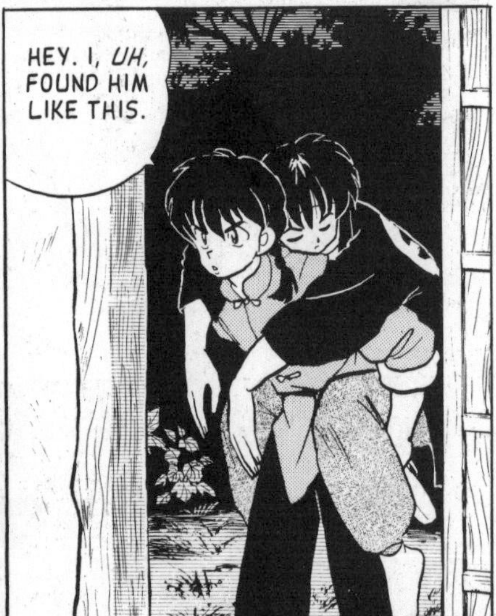
HEY. I, *UH,* FOUND HIM LIKE THIS.
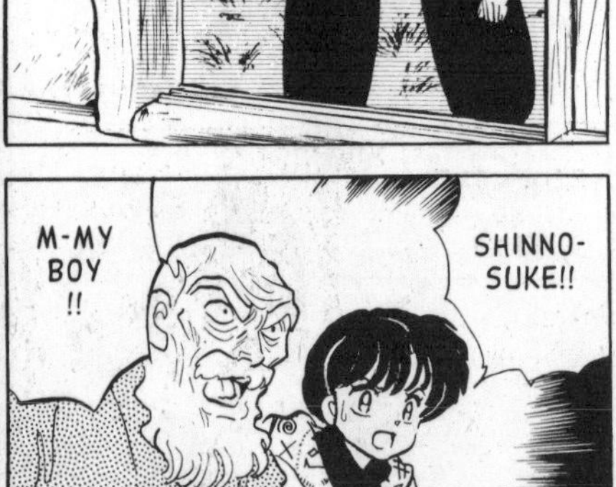
M-MY BOY !!
SHINNO-SUKE!!

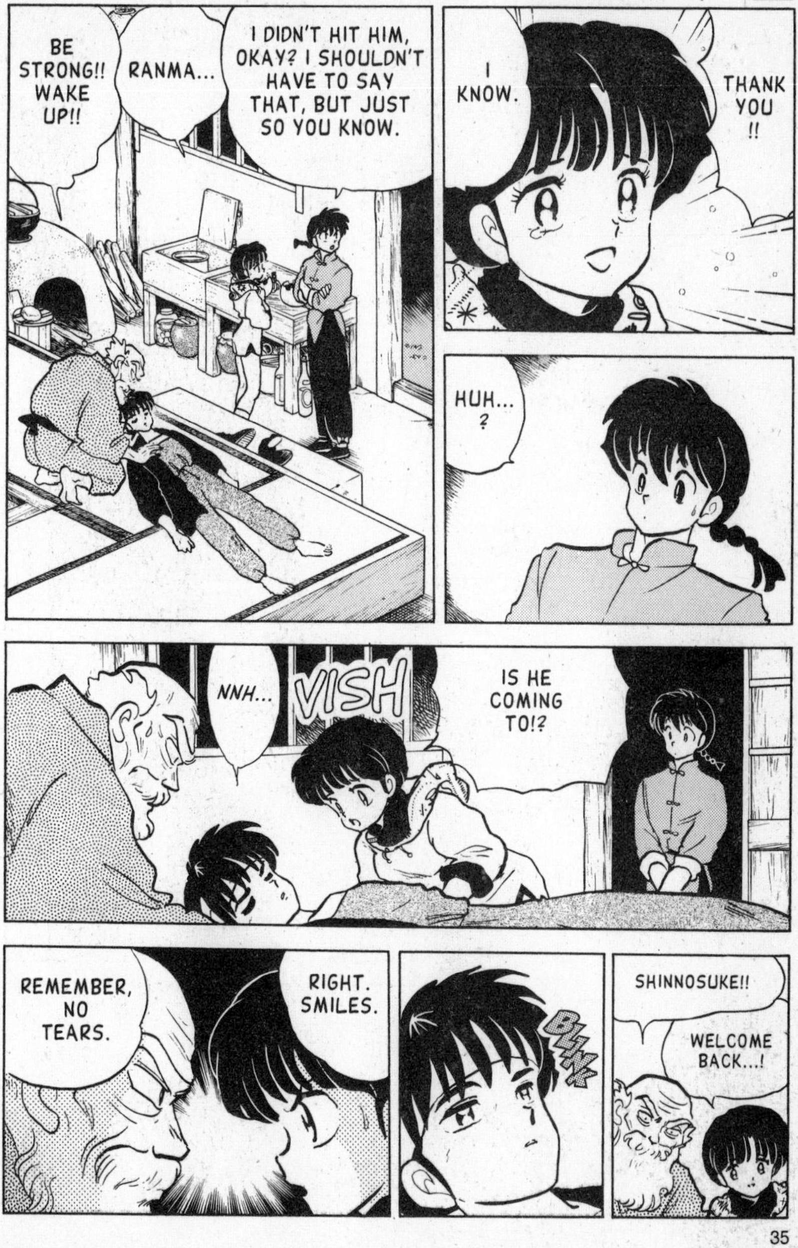
BE STRONG!! WAKE UP!!
RANMA...
I DIDN'T HIT HIM, OKAY? I SHOULDN'T HAVE TO SAY THAT, BUT JUST SO YOU KNOW.
I KNOW.
THANK YOU !!
HUH... ?
NNH...
VISH
IS HE COMING TO!?
REMEMBER, NO TEARS.
RIGHT. SMILES.
BLINK
SHINNOSUKE!!
WELCOME BACK...!

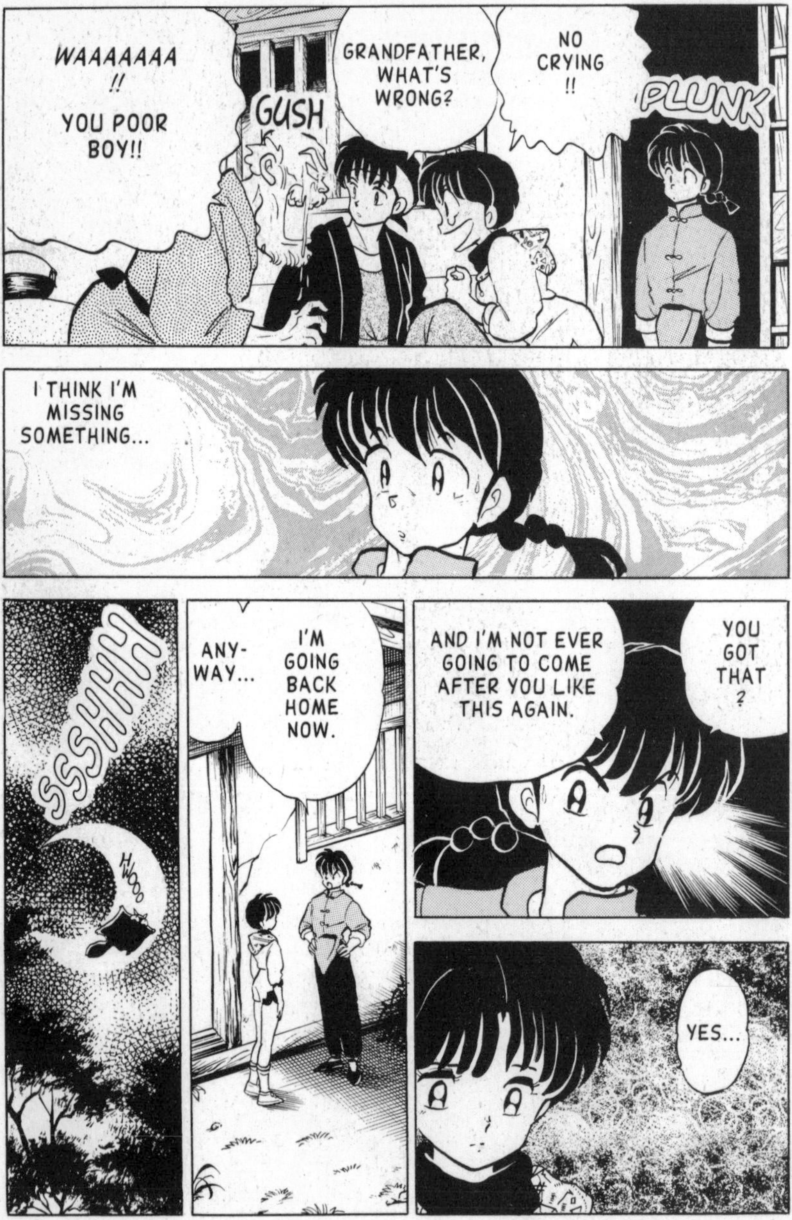
WAAAAAAA !!
YOU POOR BOY!!
GUSH
GRANDFATHER, WHAT'S WRONG?
NO CRYING !!
PLUNK
I THINK I'M MISSING SOMETHING...
SSSHHH
HWOOO
ANY-WAY...
I'M GOING BACK HOME NOW.
AND I'M NOT EVER GOING TO COME AFTER YOU LIKE THIS AGAIN.
YOU GOT THAT ?
YES...

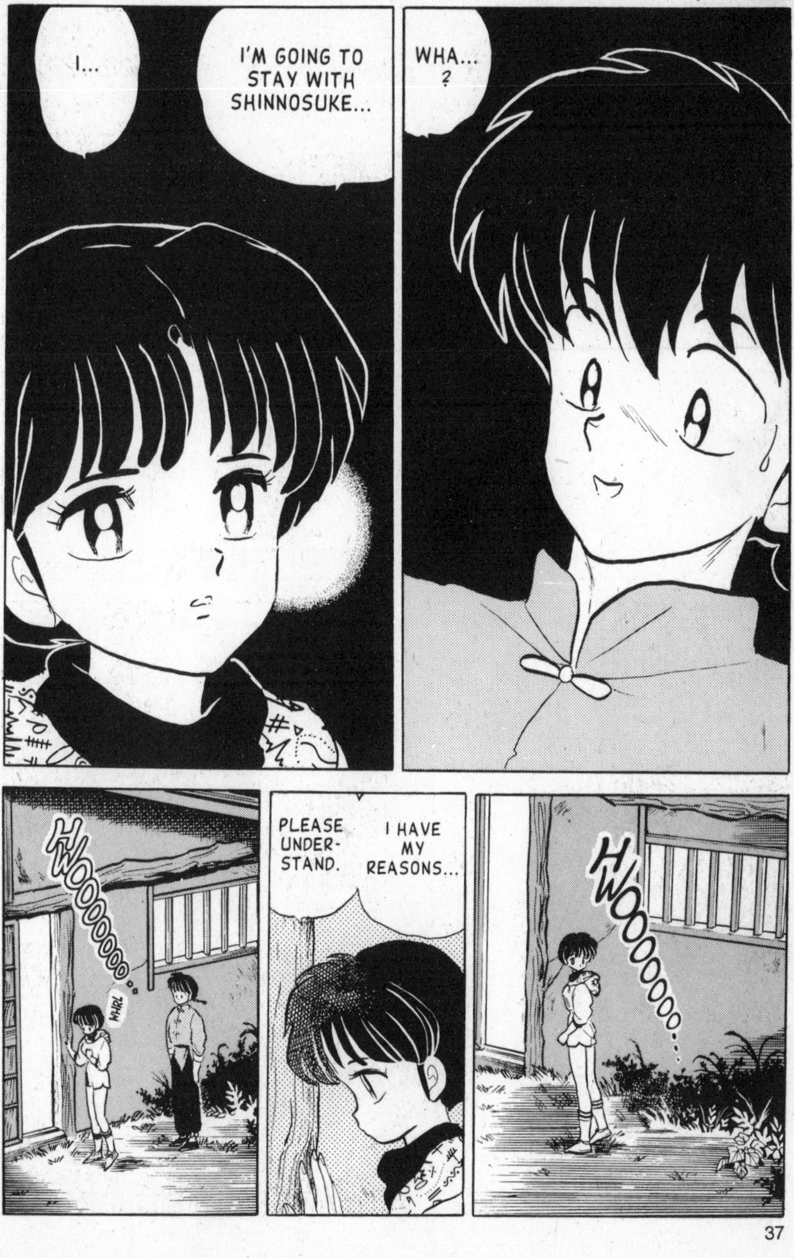
I...
I'M GOING TO STAY WITH SHINNOSUKE...
WHA...?
HWOOOOOOO...
WHRL
PLEASE UNDER-STAND.
I HAVE MY REASONS...
HWOOOOOOO...

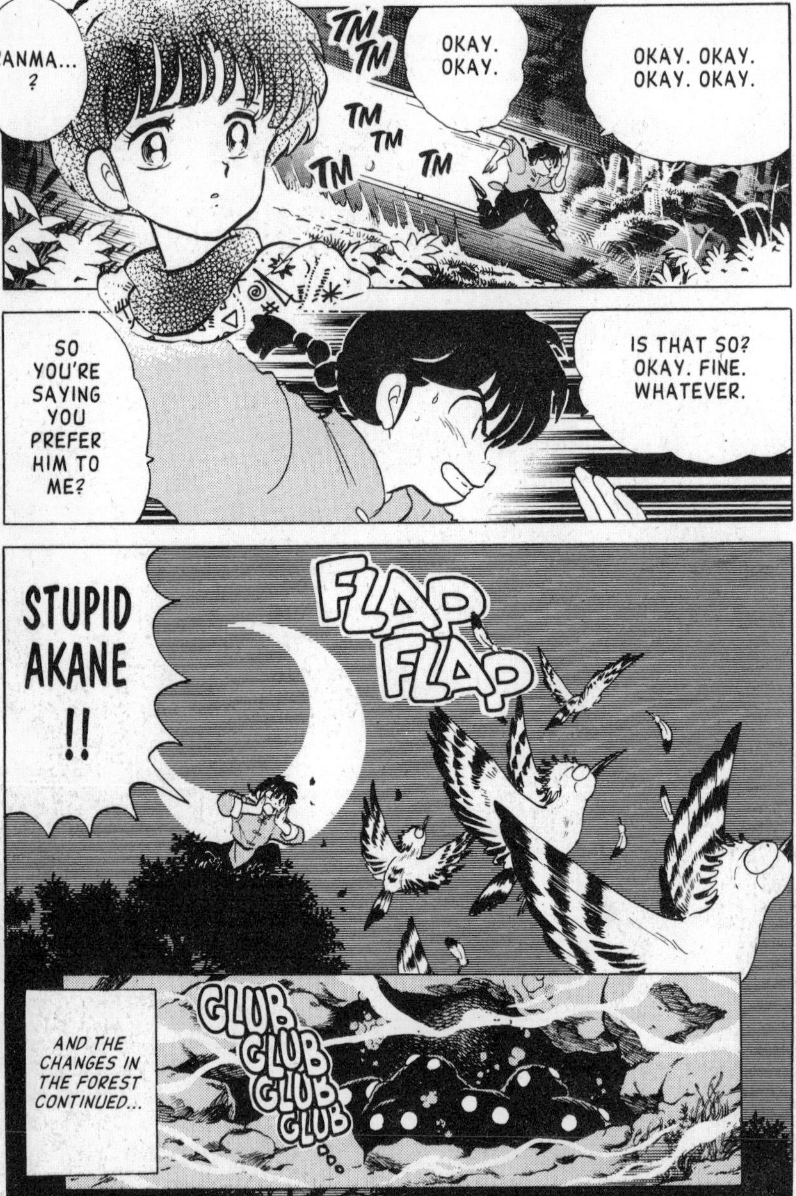
RANMA... ?
TM TM
OKAY. OKAY.
TM TM TM TM
OKAY. OKAY. OKAY. OKAY.
SO YOU'RE SAYING YOU PREFER HIM TO ME?
IS THAT SO? OKAY. FINE. WHATEVER.
STUPID AKANE !!
FLAP FLAP
AND THE CHANGES IN THE FOREST CONTINUED...
GLUB GLUB GLUB GLUB

Part 3

IN THE SHADE OF THE FOREST

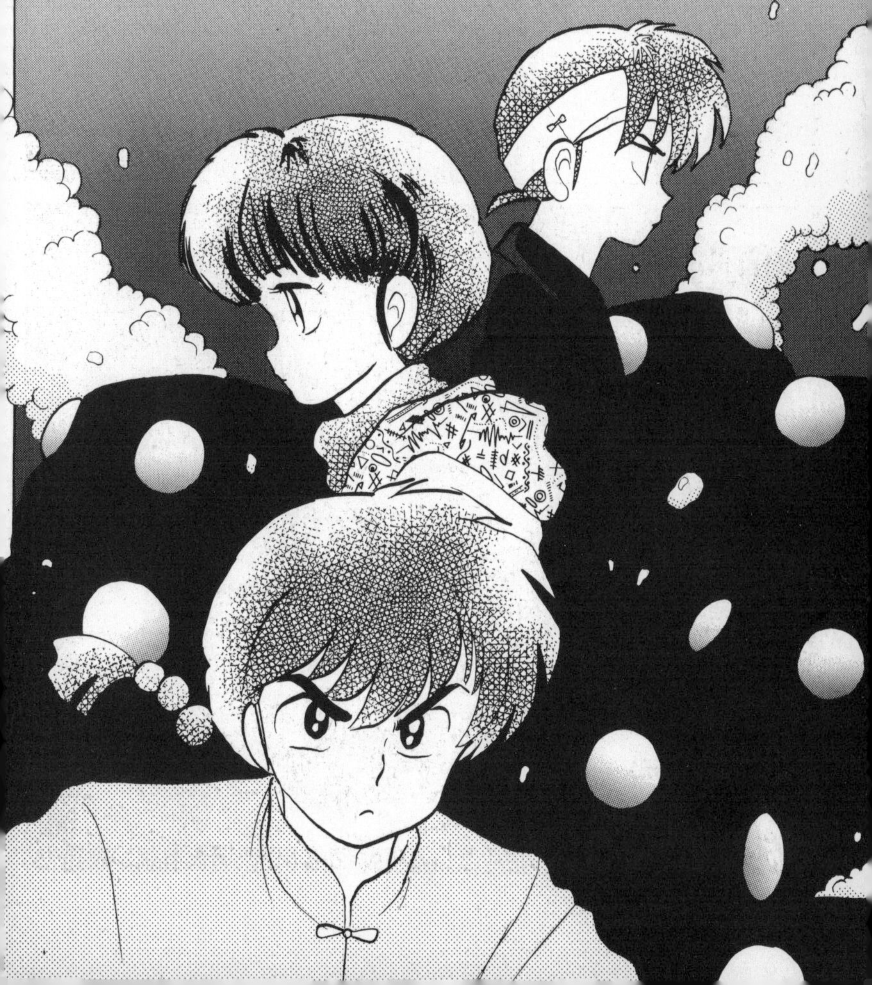

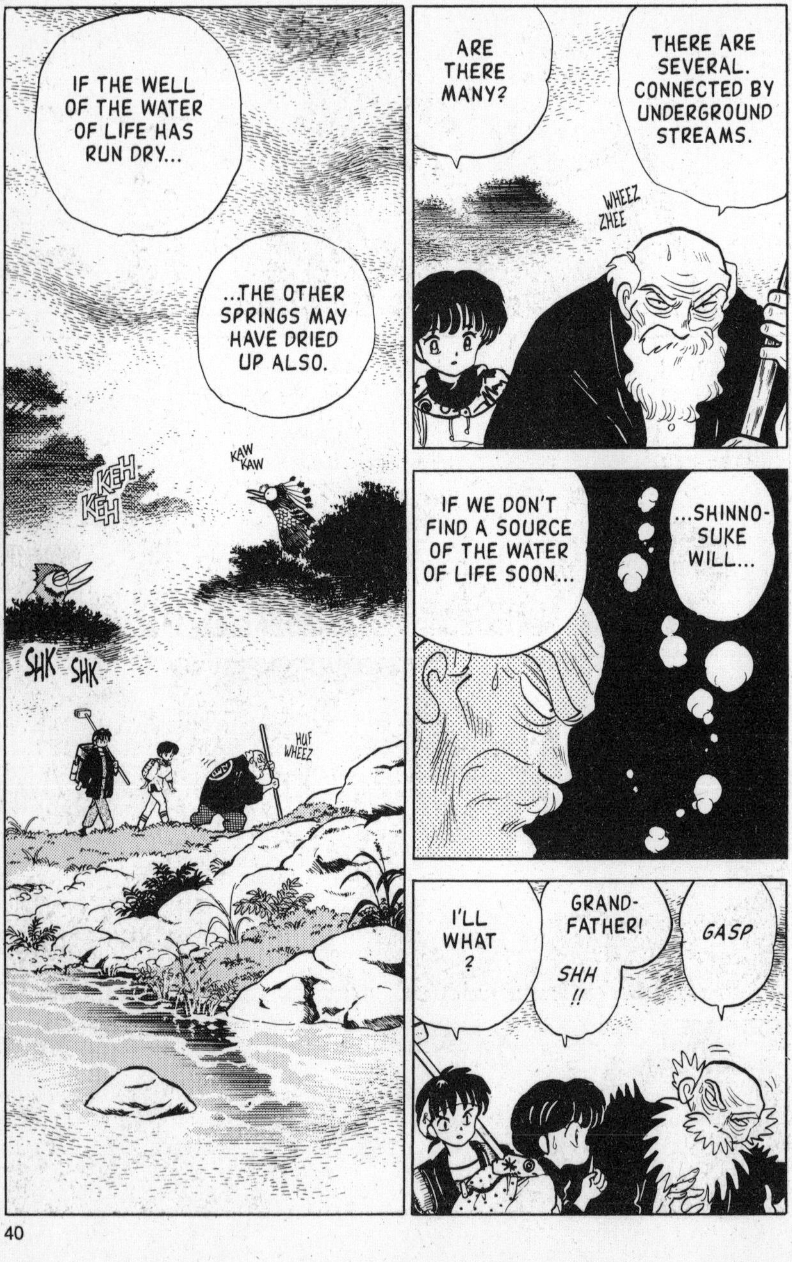
IF THE WELL OF THE WATER OF LIFE HAS RUN DRY...
...THE OTHER SPRINGS MAY HAVE DRIED UP ALSO.
KAW KAW
KEH KEH
SHK SHK
HUF WHEEZ
ARE THERE MANY?
THERE ARE SEVERAL. CONNECTED BY UNDERGROUND STREAMS.
WHEEZ ZHEE
IF WE DON'T FIND A SOURCE OF THE WATER OF LIFE SOON...
...SHINNO-SUKE WILL...
I'LL WHAT ?
GRAND-FATHER!
SHH !!
GASP

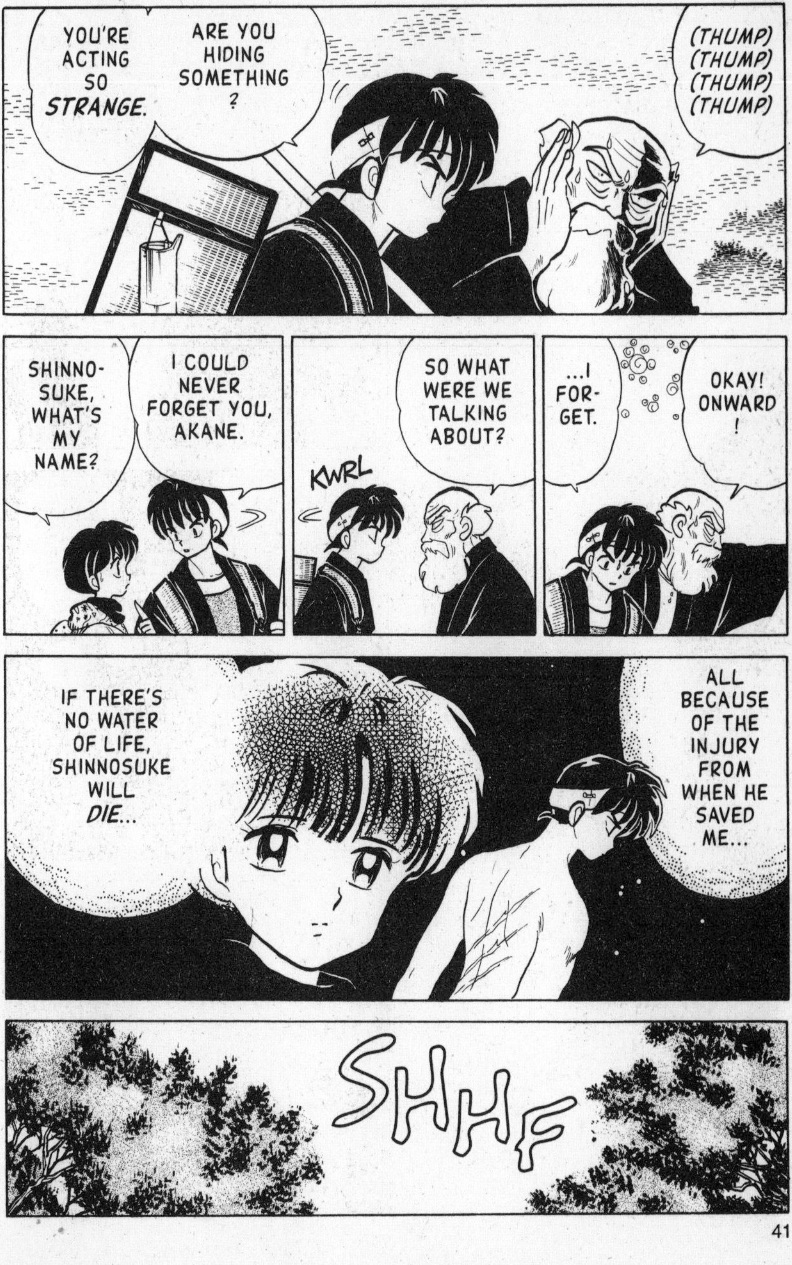
YOU'RE ACTING SO *STRANGE*.
ARE YOU HIDING SOMETHING?
(THUMP) (THUMP) (THUMP) (THUMP)
SHINNOSUKE, WHAT'S MY NAME?
I COULD NEVER FORGET YOU, AKANE.
KWRL
SO WHAT WERE WE TALKING ABOUT?
...I FORGET.
OKAY! ONWARD!
IF THERE'S NO WATER OF LIFE, SHINNOSUKE WILL *DIE*...
ALL BECAUSE OF THE INJURY FROM WHEN HE SAVED ME...
SHHF

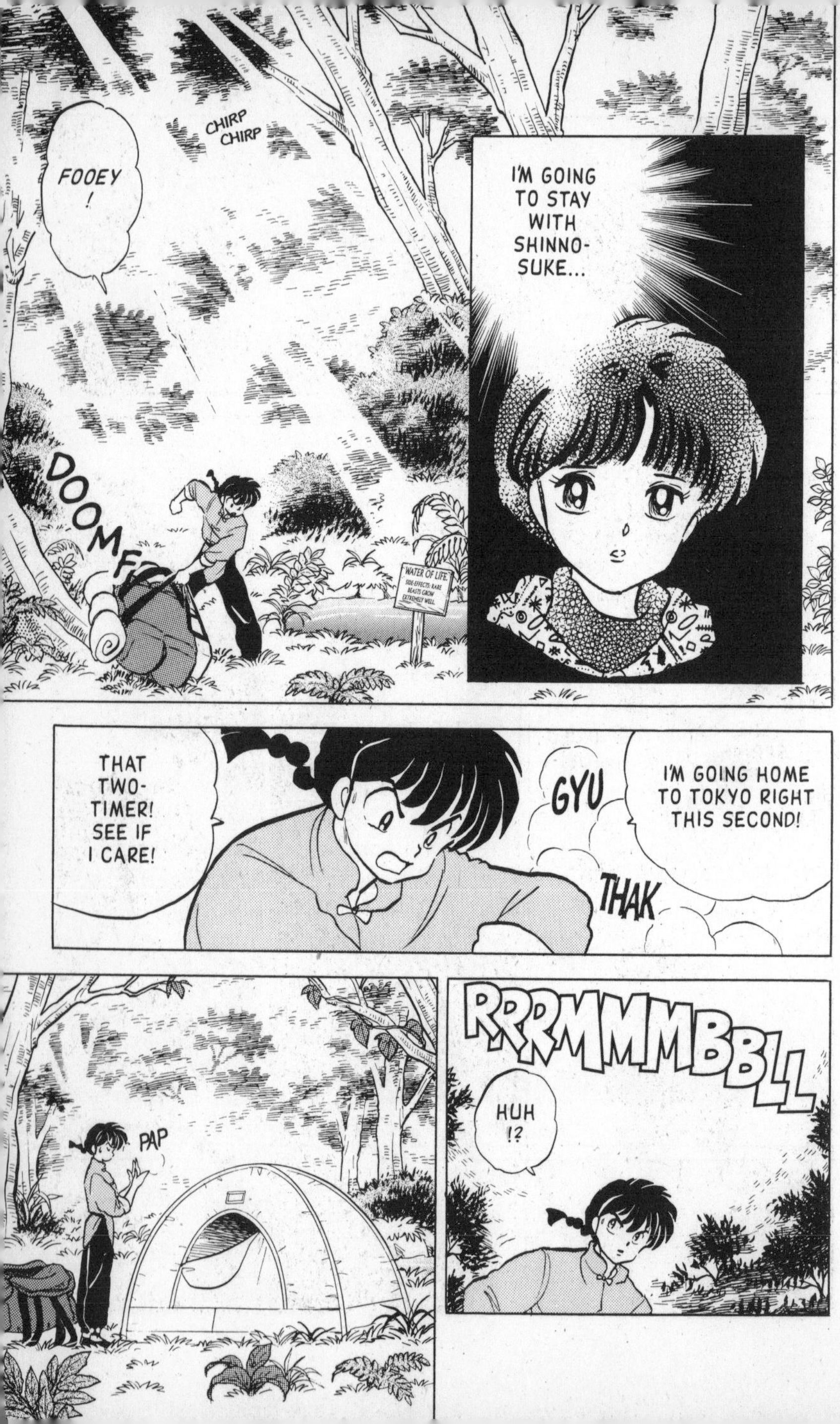
I'M GOING TO STAY WITH SHINNO-SUKE...
FOOEY !
CHIRP CHIRP
DOOMF
WATER OF LIFE.
SIDE-EFFECTS: RARE BEASTS GROW EXTREMELY WELL.
I'M GOING HOME TO TOKYO RIGHT THIS SECOND!
GYU
THAK
THAT TWO-TIMER! SEE IF I CARE!
RRRMMMMBBLL
HUH !?
PAP

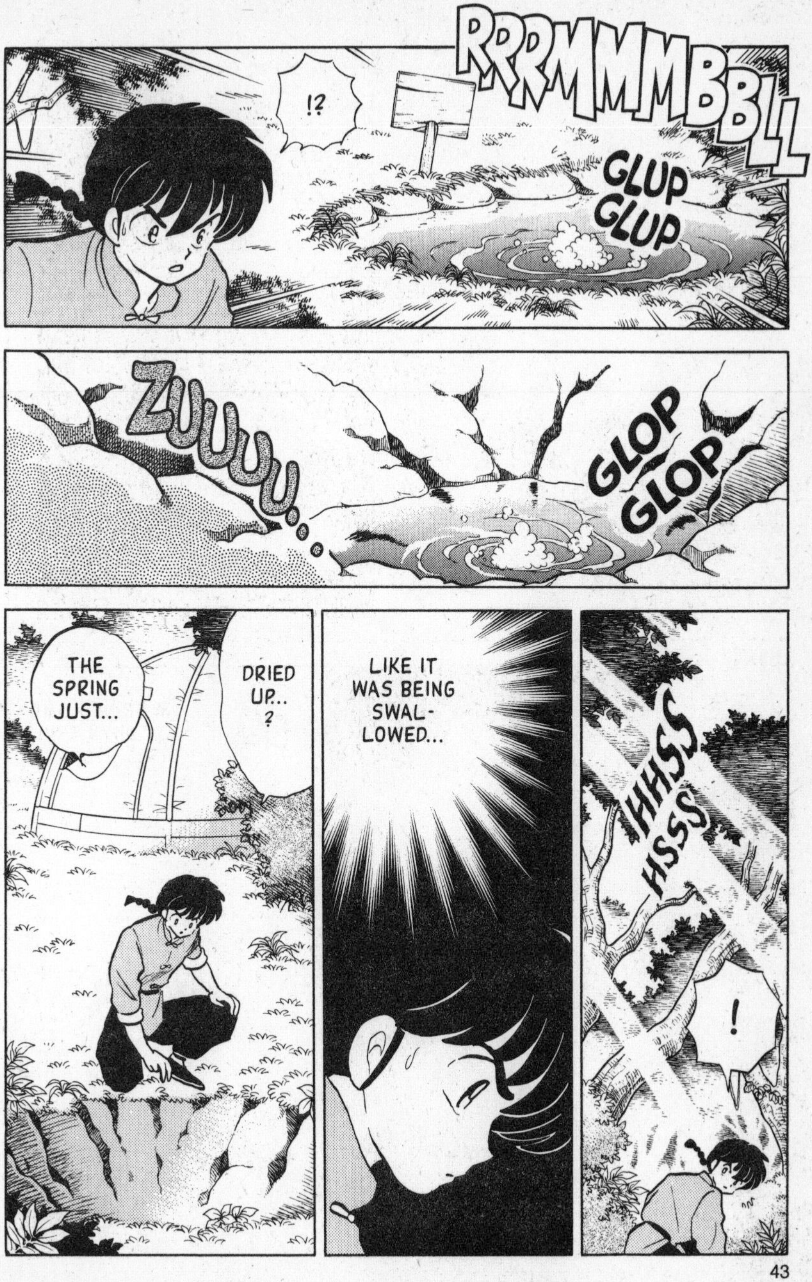
!?
RRRMMMBBLL
GLUP GLUP
ZUUUU...
GLOP GLOP
THE SPRING JUST...
DRIED UP... ?
LIKE IT WAS BEING SWAL-LOWED...
HHSS HSSS
!

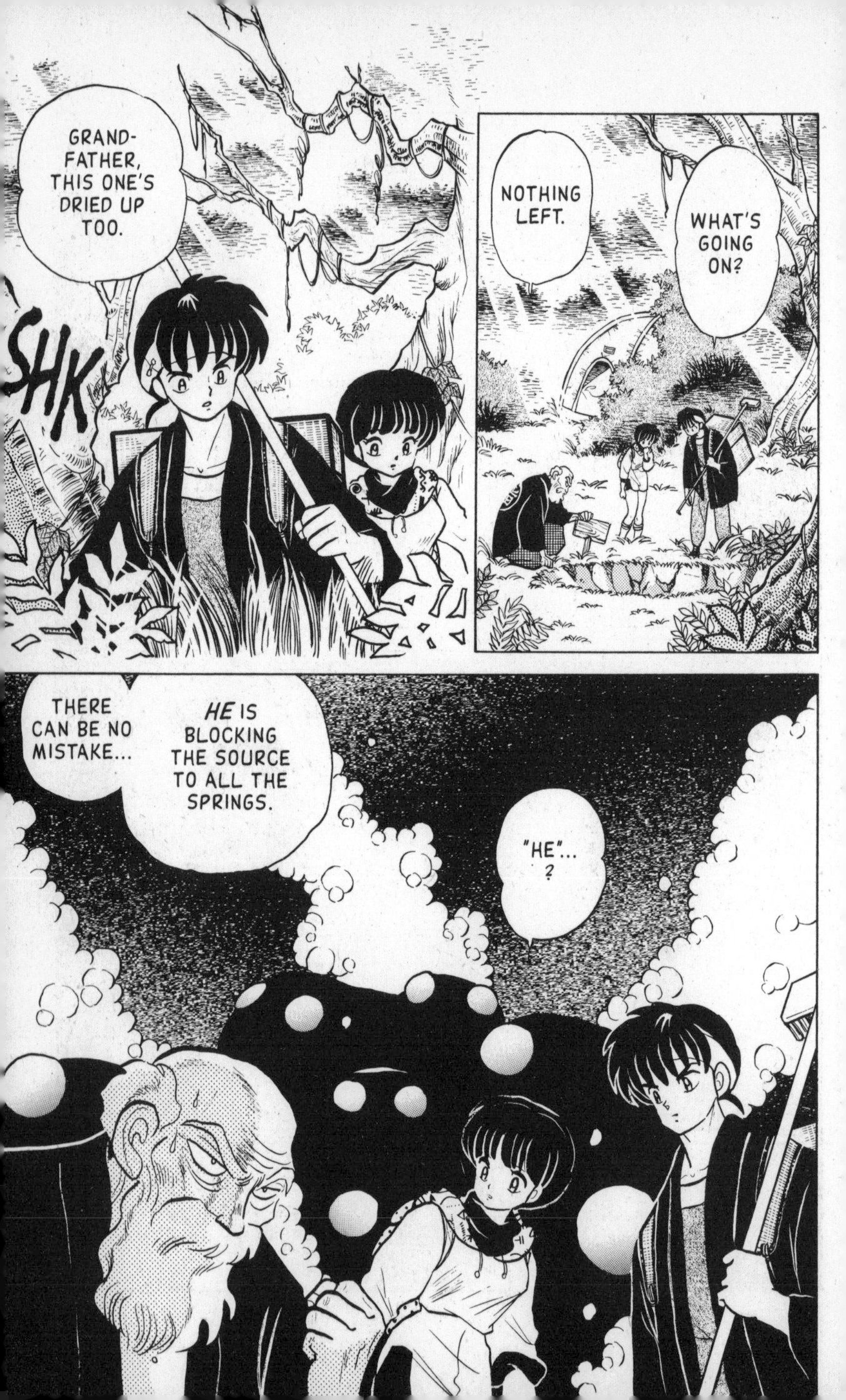
GRAND-FATHER, THIS ONE'S DRIED UP TOO.
SHK
NOTHING LEFT.
WHAT'S GOING ON?
THERE CAN BE NO MISTAKE...
HE IS BLOCKING THE SOURCE TO ALL THE SPRINGS.
"HE"...?

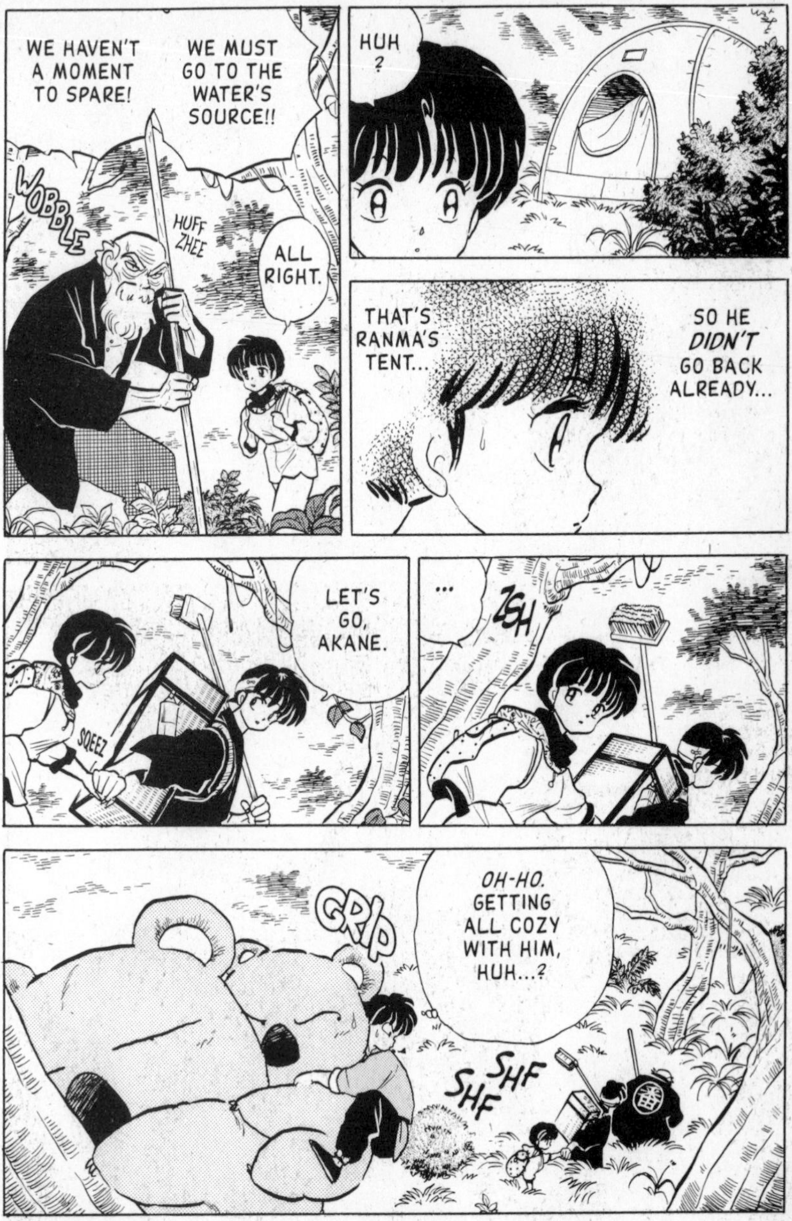
WE HAVEN'T A MOMENT TO SPARE!
WE MUST GO TO THE WATER'S SOURCE!!
WOBBLE
HUFF ZHEE
ALL RIGHT.
HUH ?
THAT'S RANMA'S TENT...
SO HE *DIDN'T* GO BACK ALREADY...
SQEEZ
LET'S GO, AKANE.
...
ZSH
GRIP
OH-HO. GETTING ALL COZY WITH HIM, HUH...?
SHF SHF

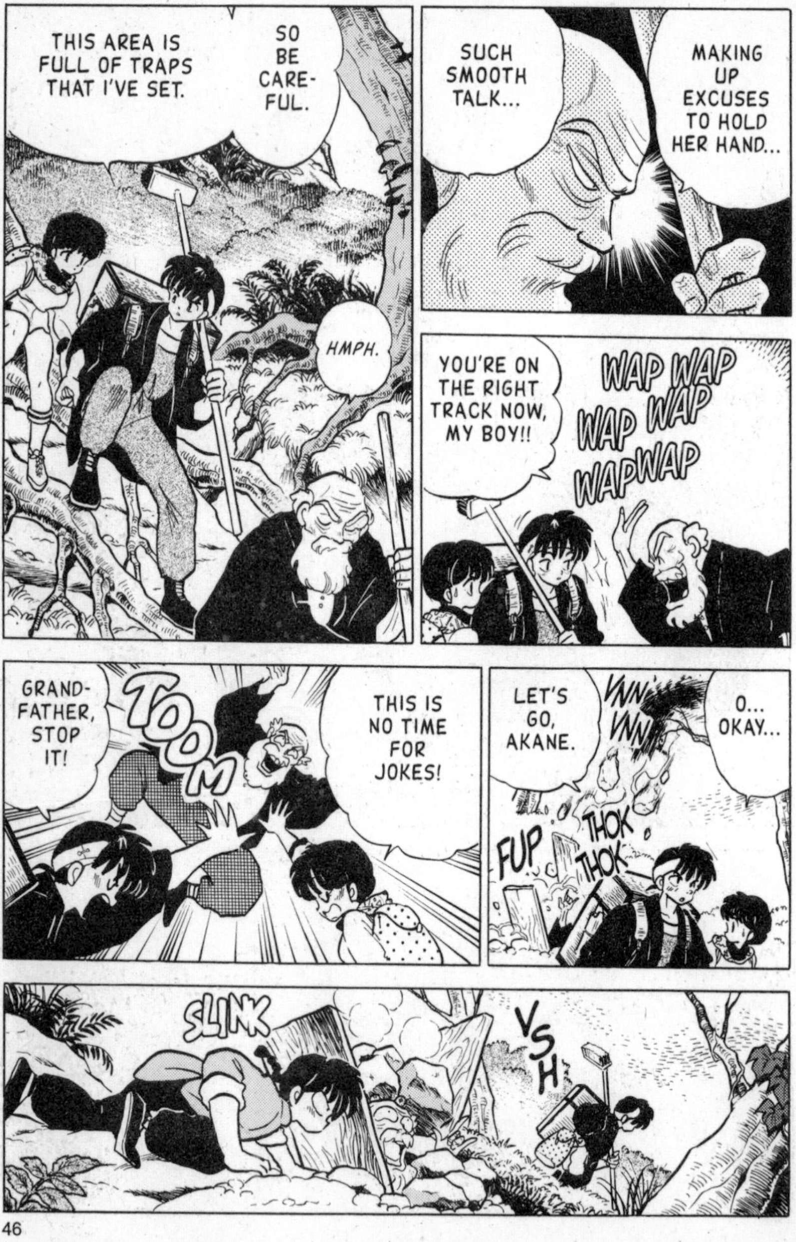
THIS AREA IS FULL OF TRAPS THAT I'VE SET.
SO BE CARE-FUL.
HMPH.
SUCH SMOOTH TALK...
MAKING UP EXCUSES TO HOLD HER HAND...
YOU'RE ON THE RIGHT TRACK NOW, MY BOY!!
WAP WAP WAP WAP WAPWAP
GRAND-FATHER, STOP IT!
TOOM
THIS IS NO TIME FOR JOKES!
LET'S GO, AKANE.
VNN VNN
O... OKAY...
FUP
THOK THOK
SLINK
VSH

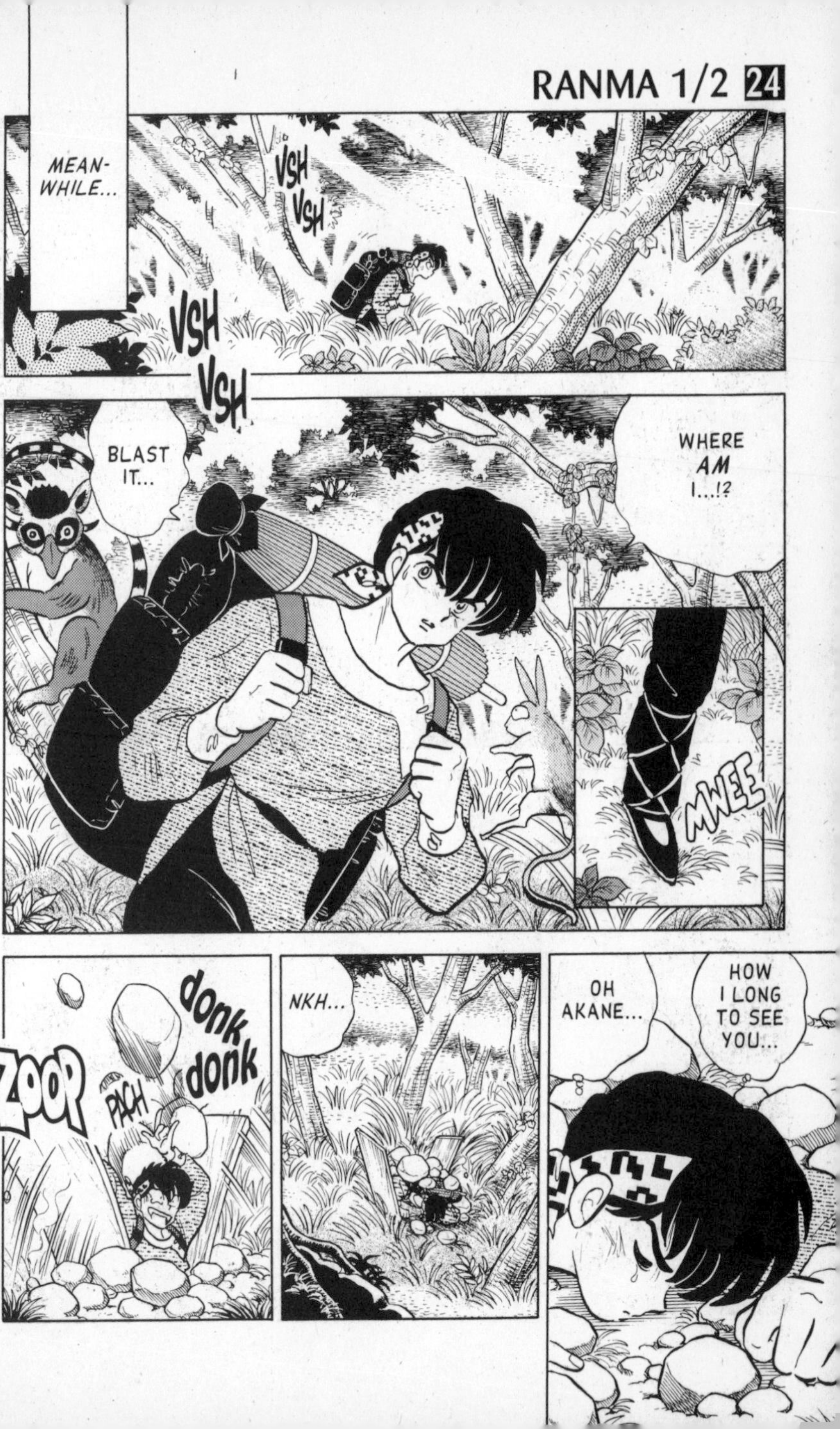
MEAN-WHILE...
VSH VSH
VSH VSH
BLAST IT...
WHERE AM I...!?
MWEE
ZOOP
donk donk
PACH
NKH...
OH AKANE...
HOW I LONG TO SEE YOU...

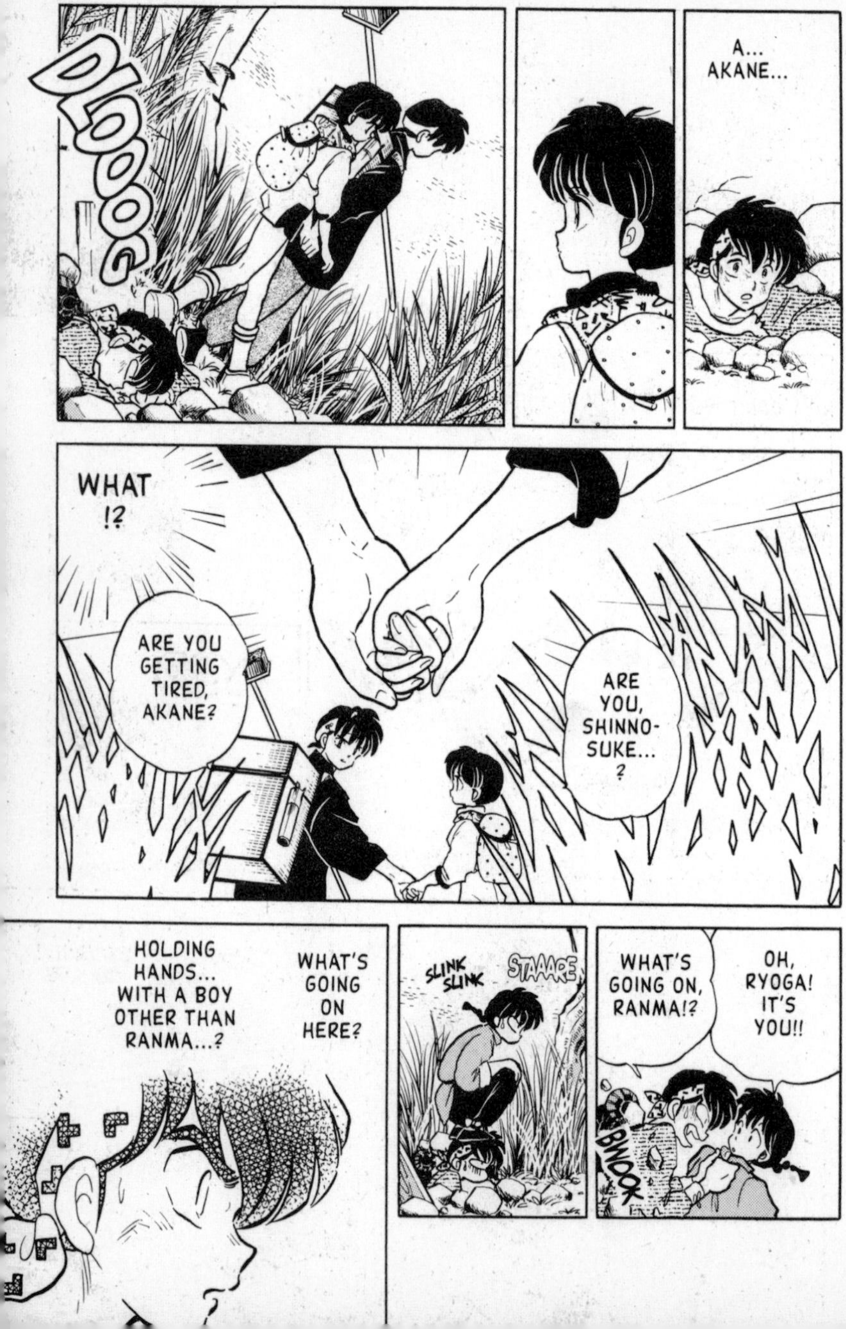
DLOOOG
A... AKANE...
WHAT !?
ARE YOU GETTING TIRED, AKANE?
ARE YOU, SHINNOSUKE...?
HOLDING HANDS... WITH A BOY OTHER THAN RANMA...?
WHAT'S GOING ON HERE?
SLINK SLINK
STAAARE
WHAT'S GOING ON, RANMA!?
OH, RYOGA! IT'S YOU!!
BWOOK

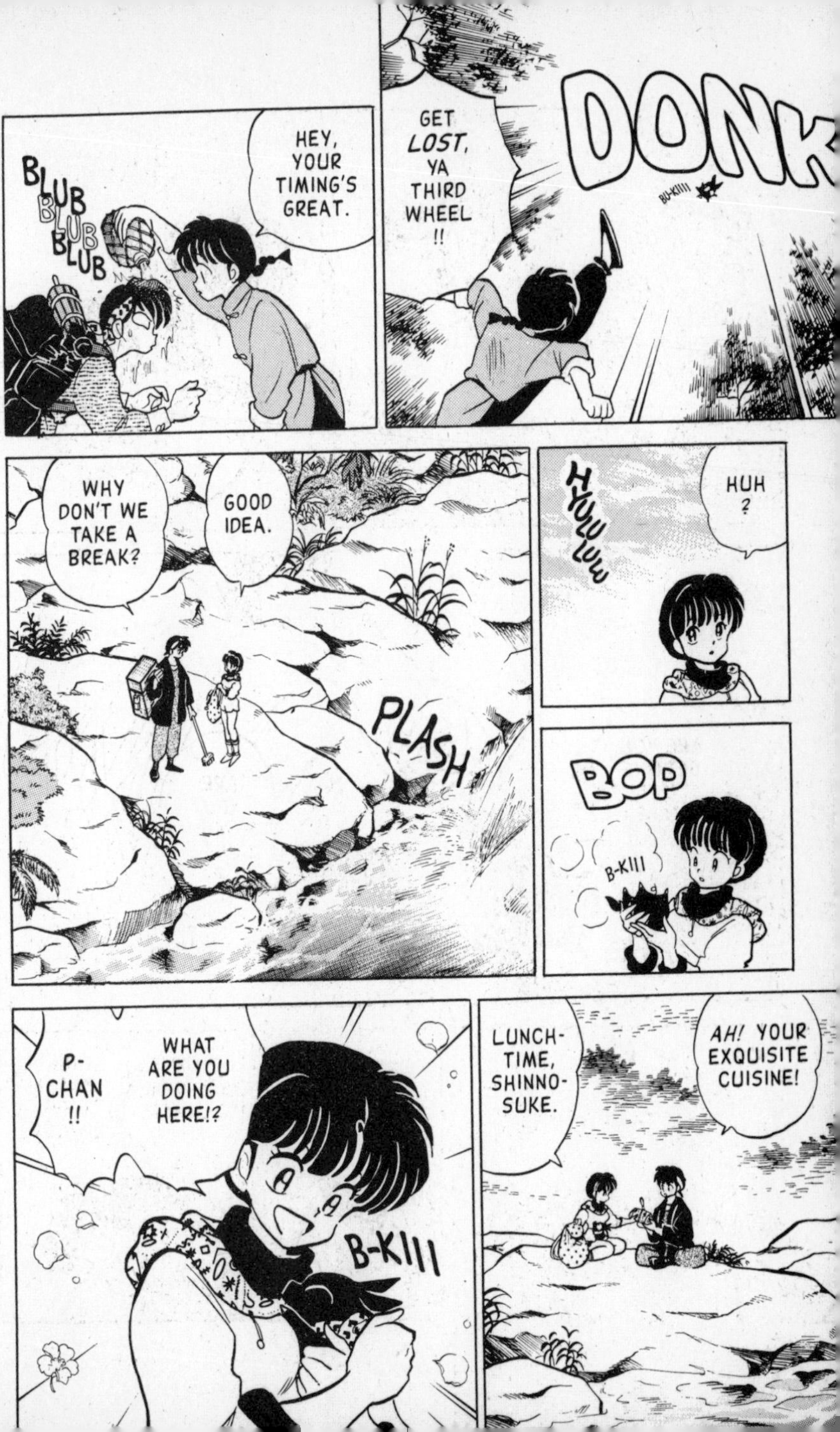
BLUB
BLUB
BLUB
HEY, YOUR TIMING'S GREAT.
GET LOST, YA THIRD WHEEL !!
DONK
BU-KIIII
WHY DON'T WE TAKE A BREAK?
GOOD IDEA.
PLASH
HYULULULU
HUH ?
BOP
B-KIII
P-CHAN !!
WHAT ARE YOU DOING HERE!?
B-KIII
LUNCH-TIME, SHINNO-SUKE.
AH! YOUR EXQUISITE CUISINE!

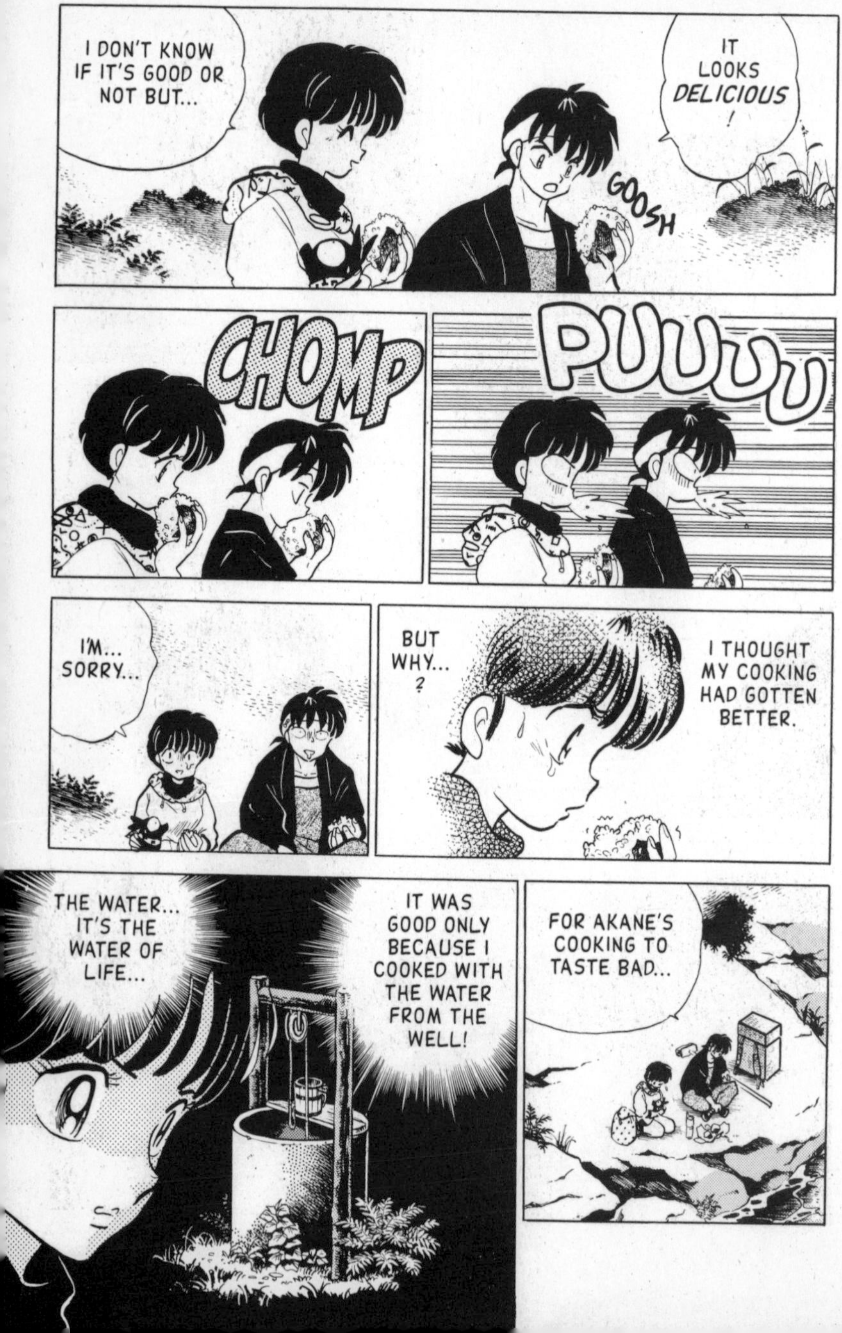
I DON'T KNOW IF IT'S GOOD OR NOT BUT...
IT LOOKS DELICIOUS!
GOOSH
CHOMP
PUUUU
I'M... SORRY...
BUT WHY...?
I THOUGHT MY COOKING HAD GOTTEN BETTER.
THE WATER... IT'S THE WATER OF LIFE...
IT WAS GOOD ONLY BECAUSE I COOKED WITH THE WATER FROM THE WELL!
FOR AKANE'S COOKING TO TASTE BAD...

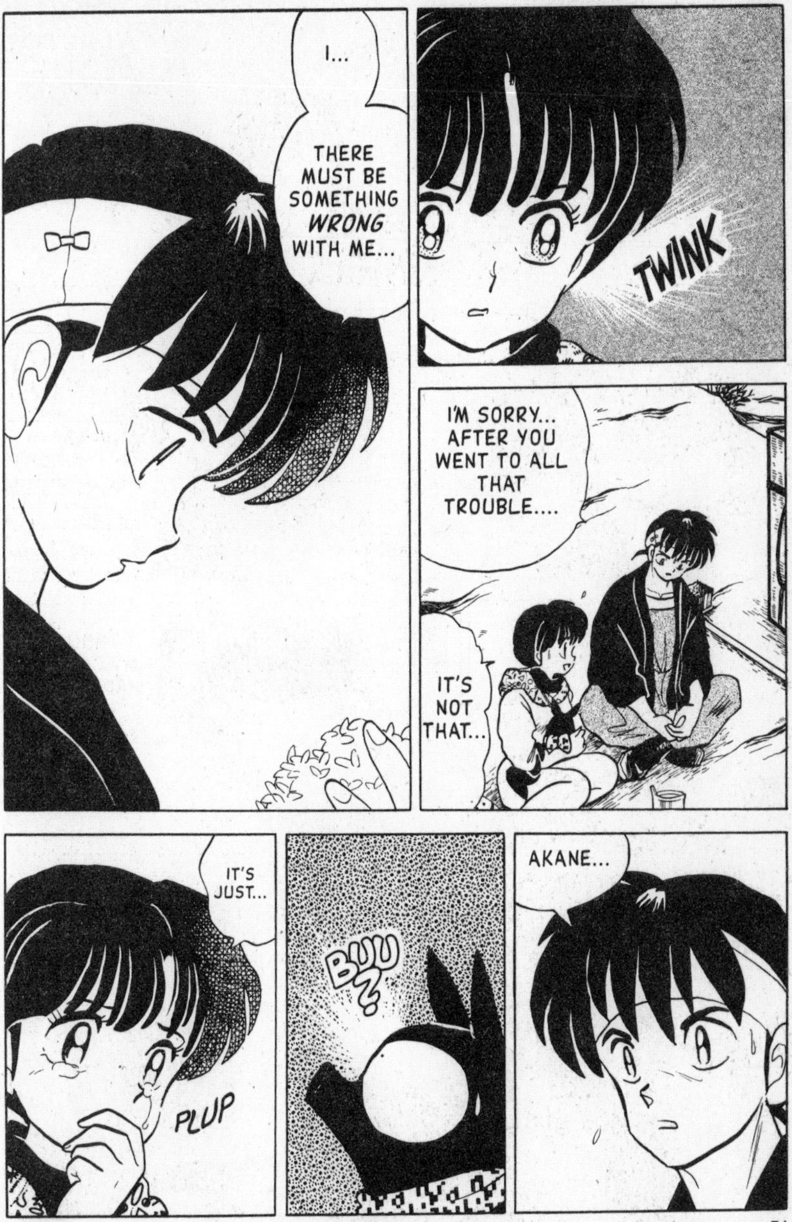
I...
THERE MUST BE SOMETHING *WRONG* WITH ME...
TWINK
I'M SORRY... AFTER YOU WENT TO ALL THAT TROUBLE....
IT'S NOT THAT...
IT'S JUST...
PLUP
BUU
?
AKANE...

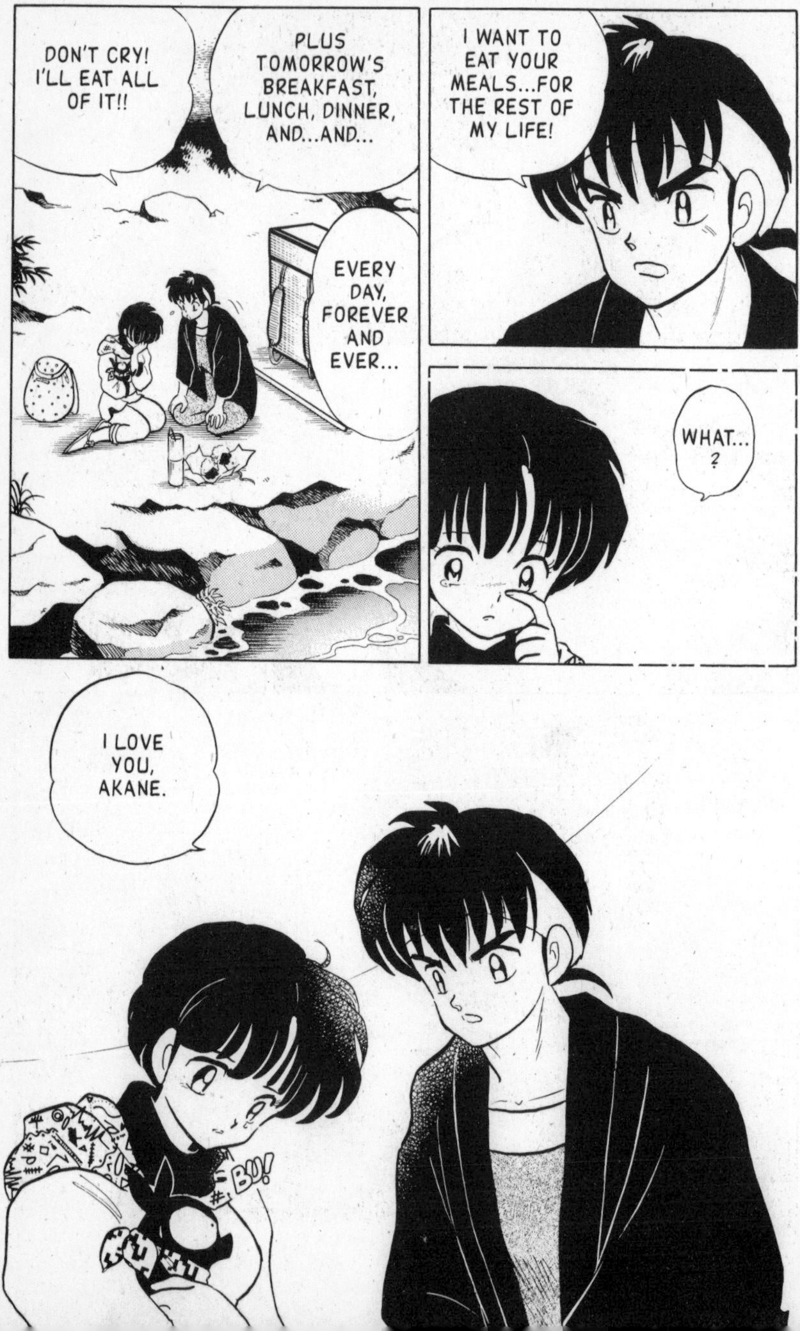
DON'T CRY! I'LL EAT ALL OF IT!!
PLUS TOMORROW'S BREAKFAST, LUNCH, DINNER, AND...AND...
EVERY DAY, FOREVER AND EVER...
I WANT TO EAT YOUR MEALS...FOR THE REST OF MY LIFE!
WHAT...?
I LOVE YOU, AKANE.
BU!

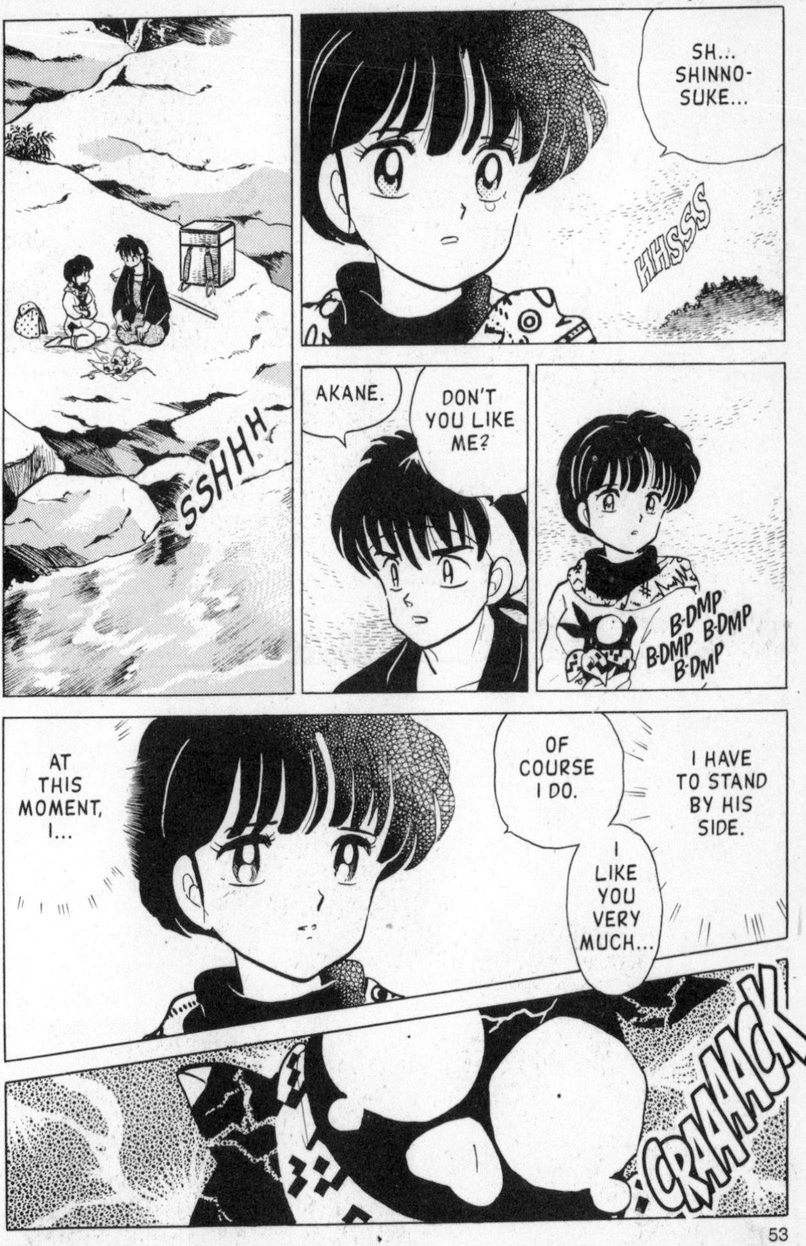
SSHHH
SH... SHINNO-SUKE...
HHSSS
AKANE.
DON'T YOU LIKE ME?
B-DMP B-DMP B-DMP B-DMP
AT THIS MOMENT, I...
OF COURSE I DO.
I LIKE YOU VERY MUCH...
I HAVE TO STAND BY HIS SIDE.
CRAAACK

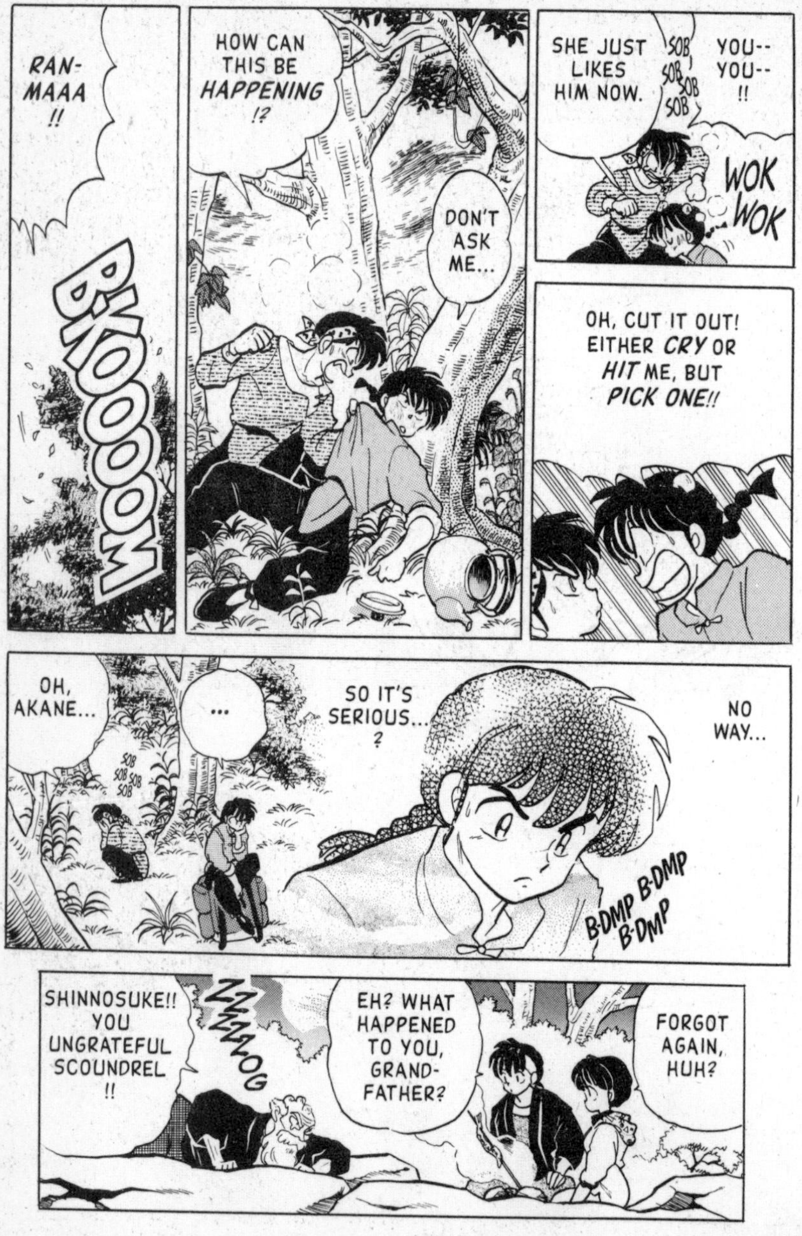
RAN-MAAA!!
BKOOOOM
HOW CAN THIS BE HAPPENING!?
DON'T ASK ME...
SHE JUST LIKES HIM NOW.
SOB, SOB SOB SOB SOB
YOU-- YOU--!!
WOK WOK
OH, CUT IT OUT! EITHER CRY OR HIT ME, BUT PICK ONE!!
OH, AKANE...
SOB SOB SOB SOB
...
SO IT'S SERIOUS...?
NO WAY...
B-DMP B-DMP B-DMP B-DMP
SHINNOSUKE!! YOU UNGRATEFUL SCOUNDREL!!
ZZZZZOG
EH? WHAT HAPPENED TO YOU, GRAND-FATHER?
FORGOT AGAIN, HUH?

Part 4

SEE YA, AKANE

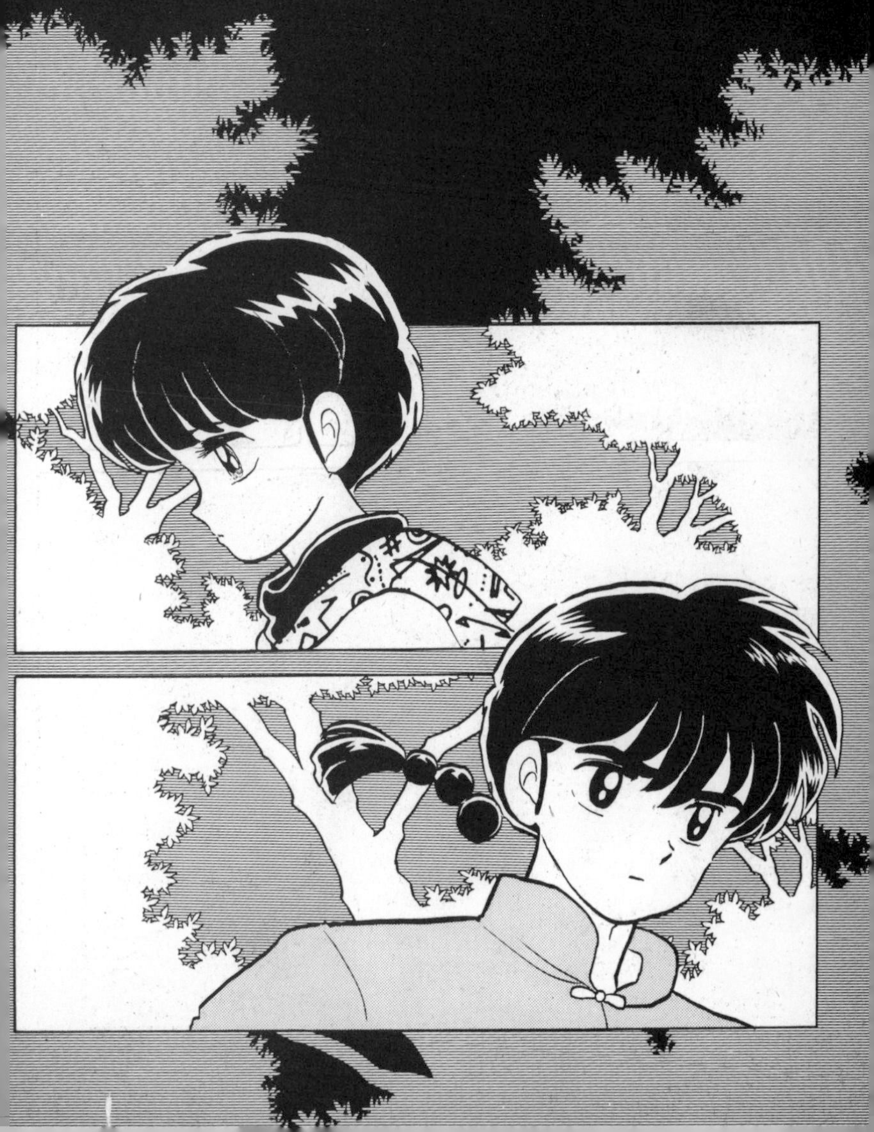

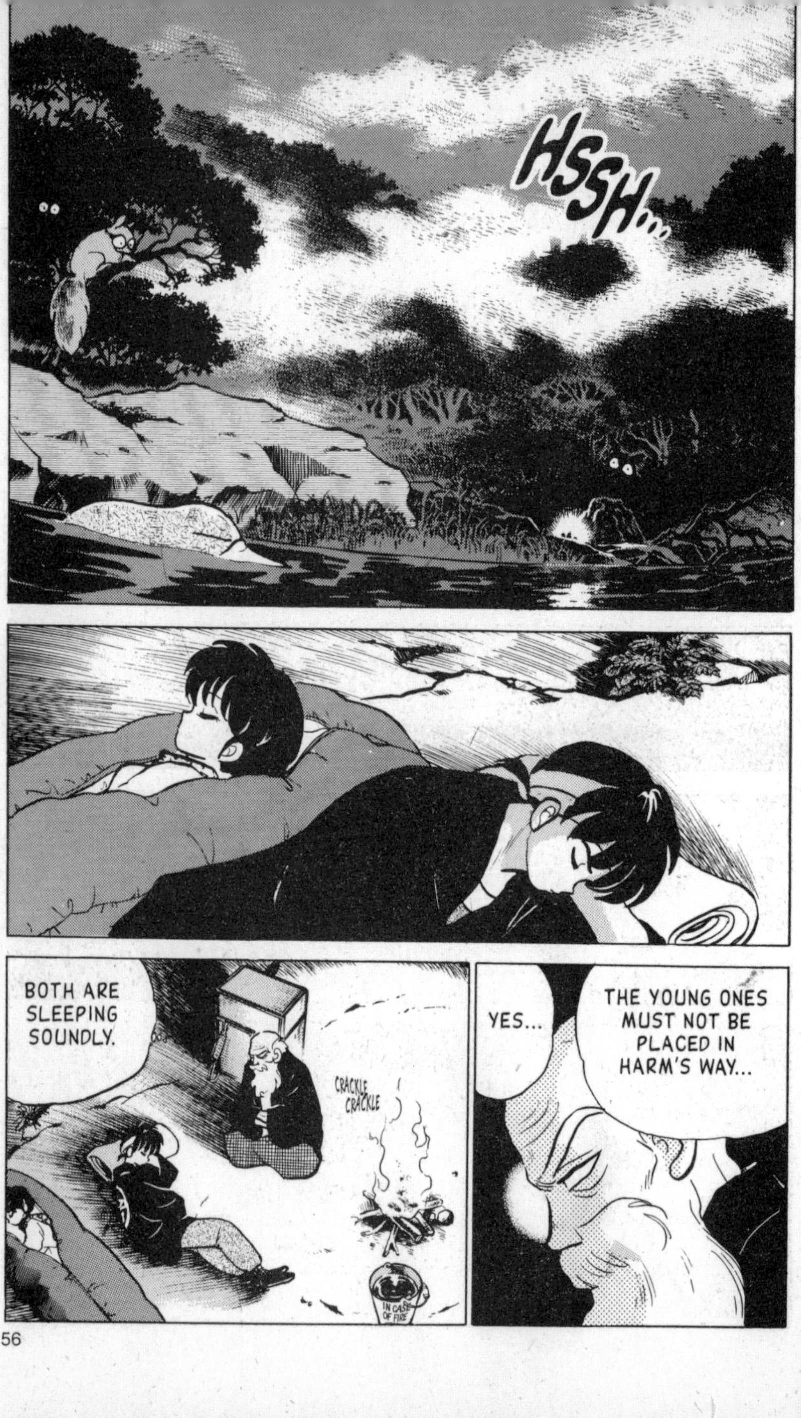
HSSH...
BOTH ARE SLEEPING SOUNDLY.
CRACKLE CRACKLE
IN CASE OF FIRE
YES...
THE YOUNG ONES MUST NOT BE PLACED IN HARM'S WAY...

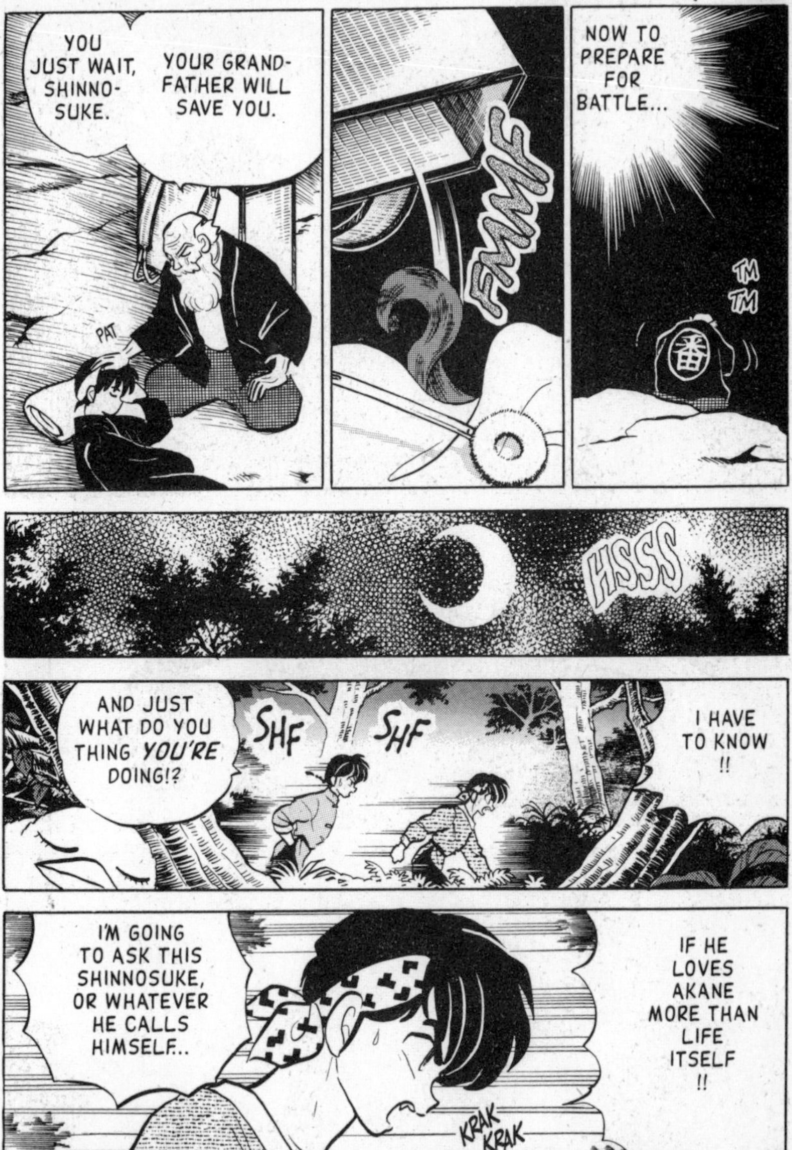
YOU JUST WAIT, SHINNO-SUKE.
YOUR GRAND-FATHER WILL SAVE YOU.
PAT
FMMF
NOW TO PREPARE FOR BATTLE...
TM TM
番
HSSS
AND JUST WHAT DO YOU THING *YOU'RE* DOING!?
SHF
SHF
I HAVE TO KNOW !!
I'M GOING TO ASK THIS SHINNOSUKE, OR WHATEVER HE CALLS HIMSELF...
KRAK KRAK
IF HE LOVES AKANE MORE THAN LIFE ITSELF !!

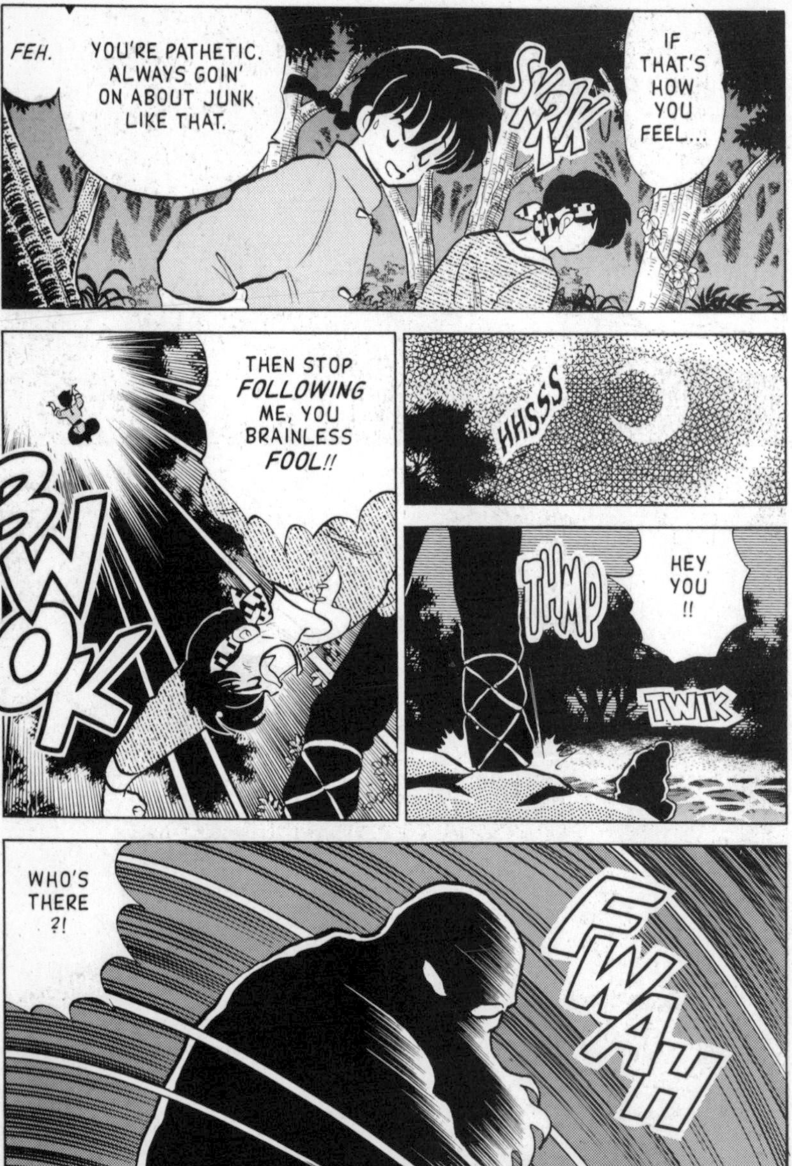
FEH.
YOU'RE PATHETIC. ALWAYS GOIN' ON ABOUT JUNK LIKE THAT.
IF THAT'S HOW YOU FEEL...
THEN STOP *FOLLOWING* ME, YOU BRAINLESS *FOOL!!*
BWOK
HHSSS
THMP
HEY YOU !!
TWIK
WHO'S THERE ?!
FWAH

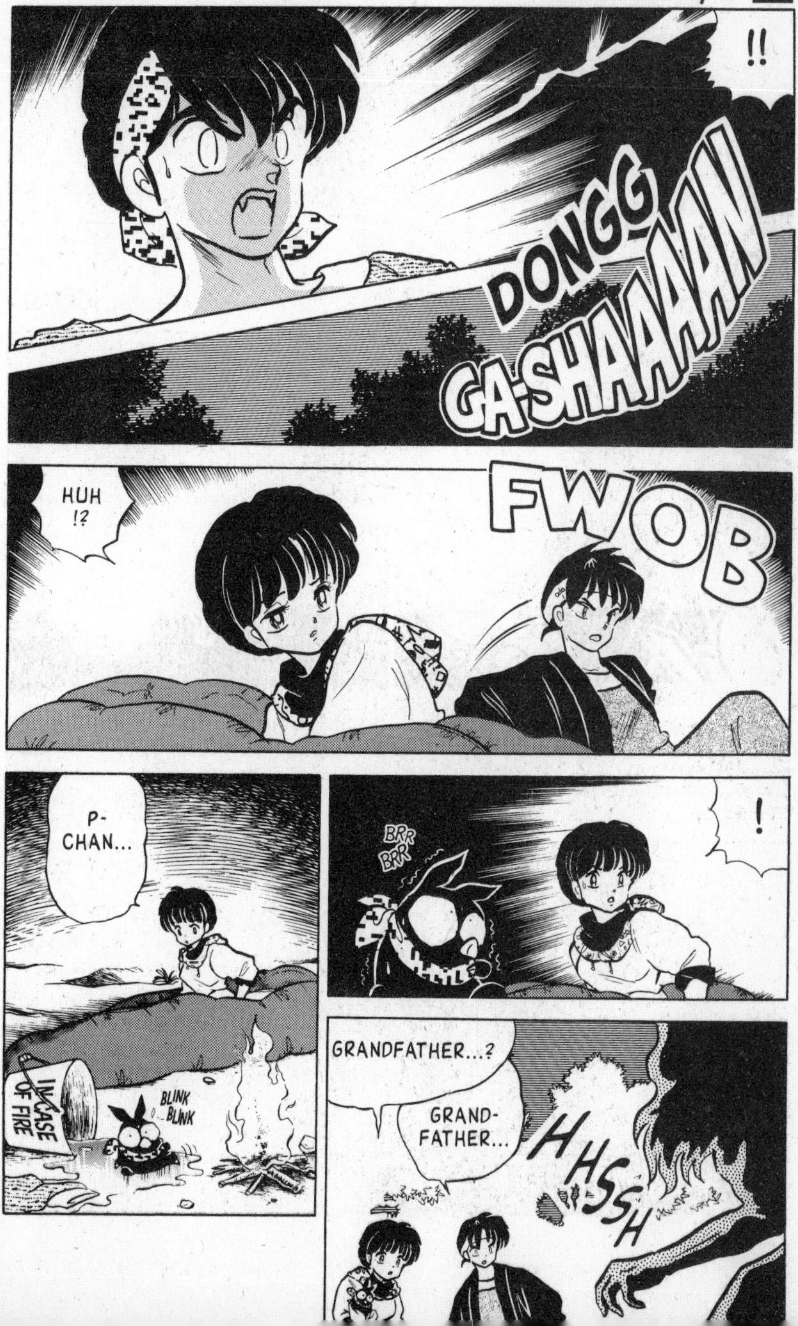
!!
DONGG
GA-SHAAAAAN
HUH !?
FWOB
P-CHAN...
IN CASE OF FIRE
BLINK BLINK
BRR BRR
!
GRANDFATHER...?
GRAND-FATHER...
HHSSH

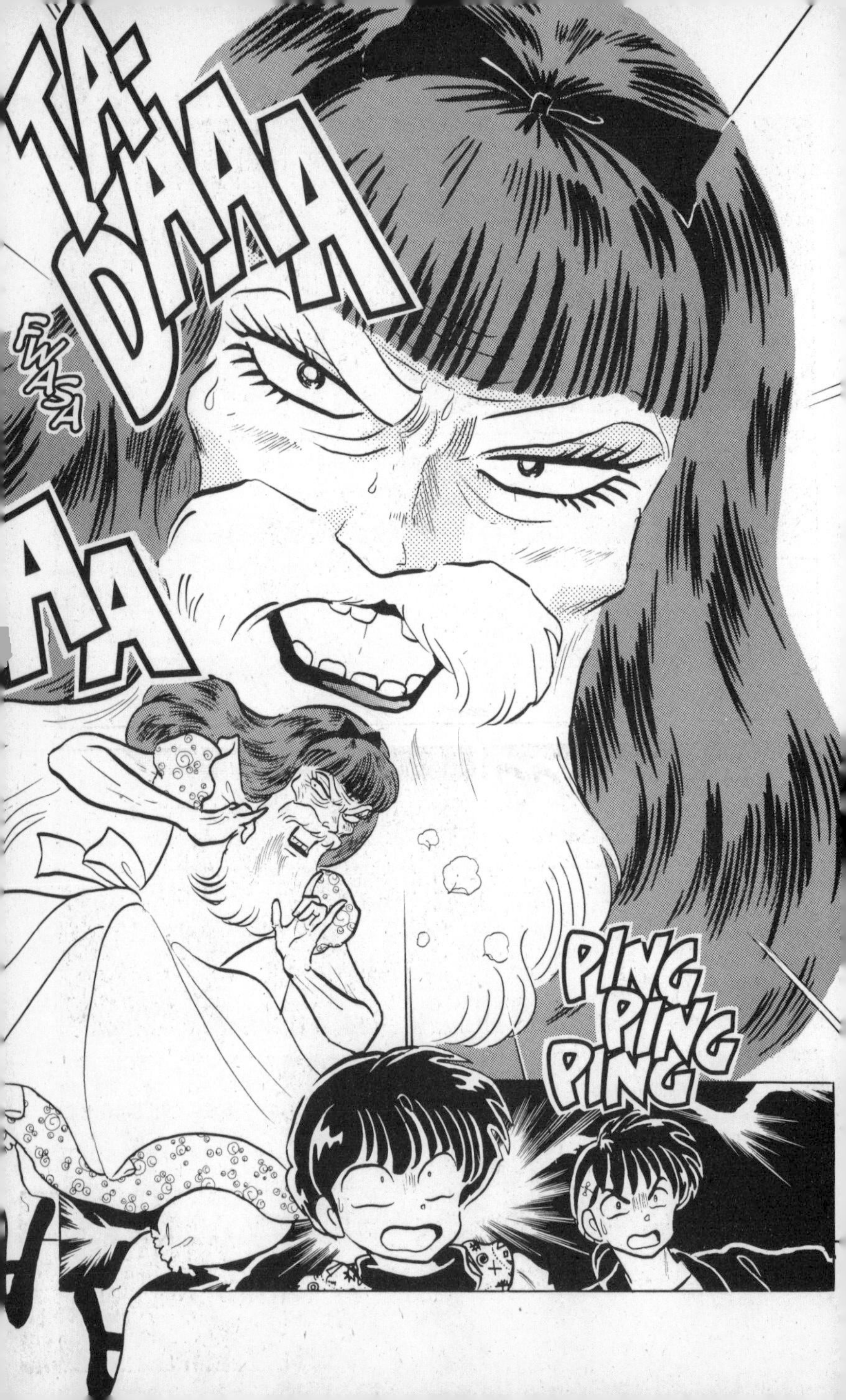

TA-DAAAA
FWASA
PING PING PING

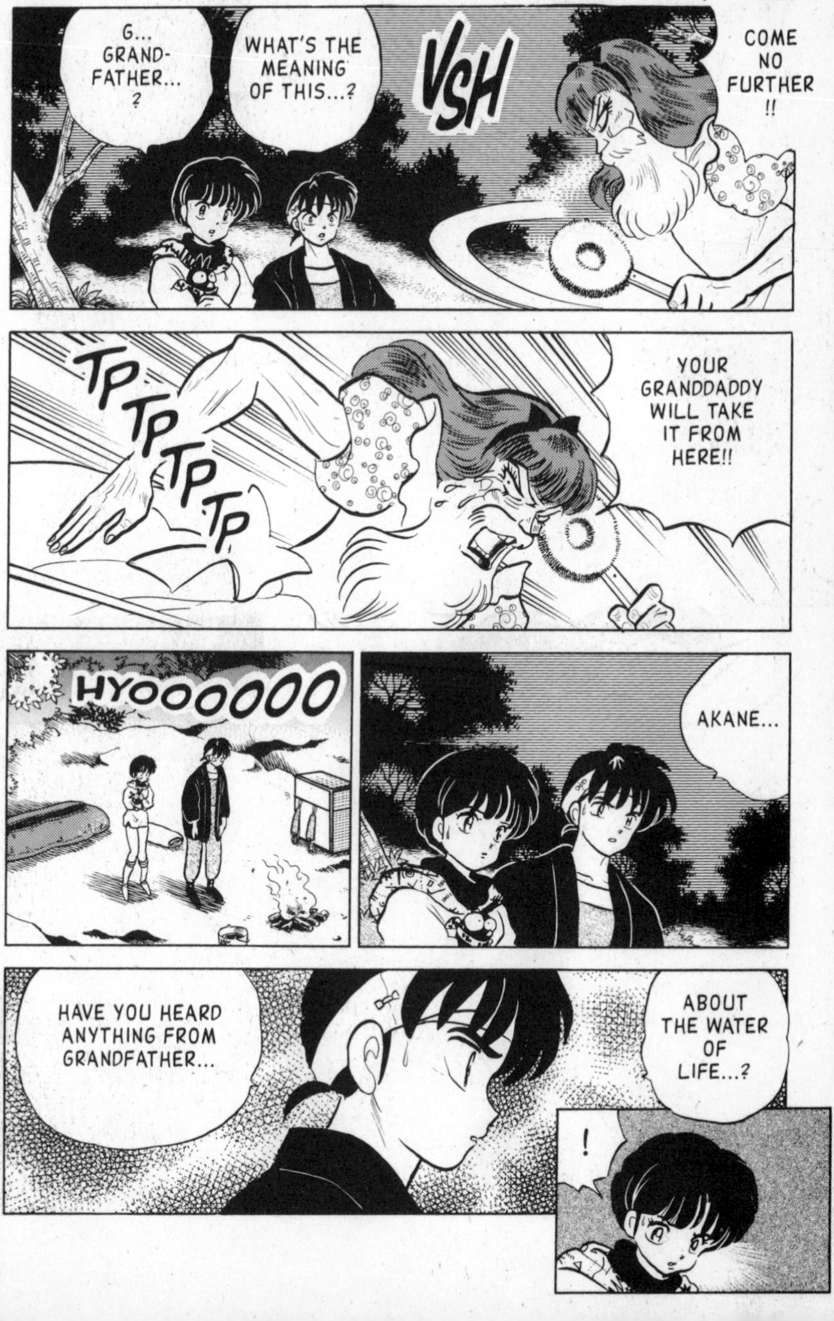
G... GRAND-FATHER... ?
WHAT'S THE MEANING OF THIS...?
VSH
COME NO FURTHER !!
TP TP TP TP TP
YOUR GRANDDADDY WILL TAKE IT FROM HERE!!
HYOOOOOO
AKANE...
HAVE YOU HEARD ANYTHING FROM GRANDFATHER...
ABOUT THE WATER OF LIFE...?
!

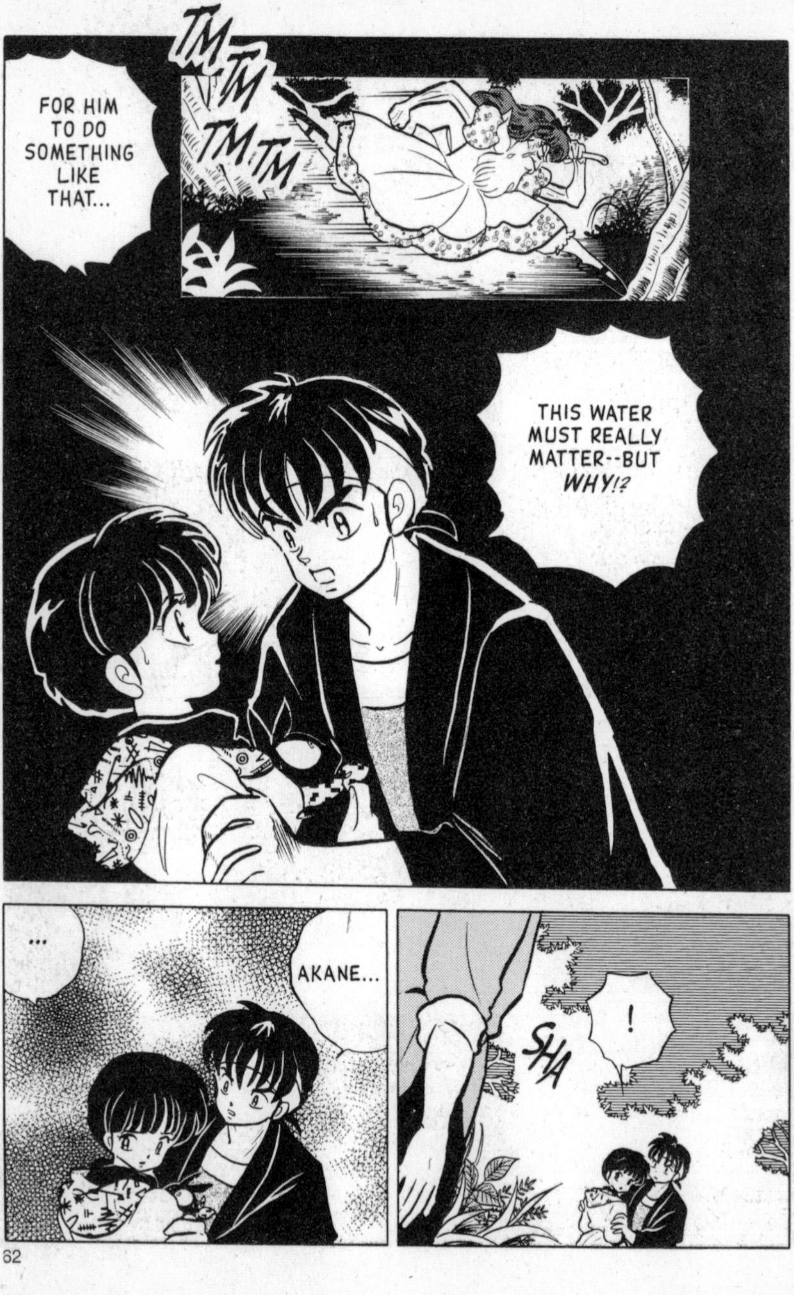

FOR HIM TO DO SOMETHING LIKE THAT...
TM-TM TM-TM
THIS WATER MUST REALLY MATTER--BUT WHY!?
...
AKANE...
SHA
!

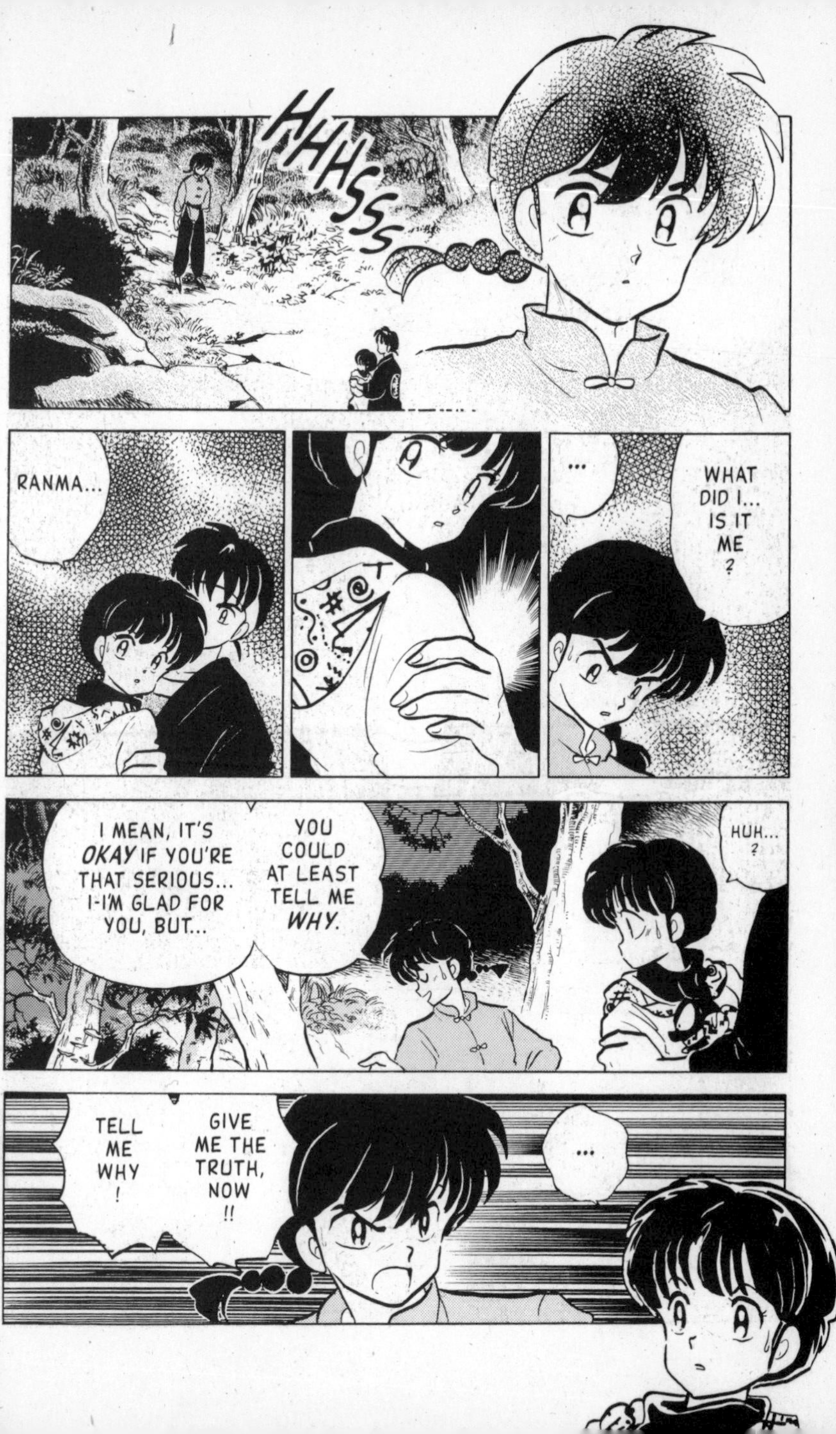
HHHSSS
RANMA...
...
WHAT DID I... IS IT ME ?
I MEAN, IT'S *OKAY* IF YOU'RE THAT SERIOUS... I-I'M GLAD FOR YOU, BUT...
YOU COULD AT LEAST TELL ME *WHY*.
HUH... ?
TELL ME WHY !
GIVE ME THE TRUTH, NOW !!
...

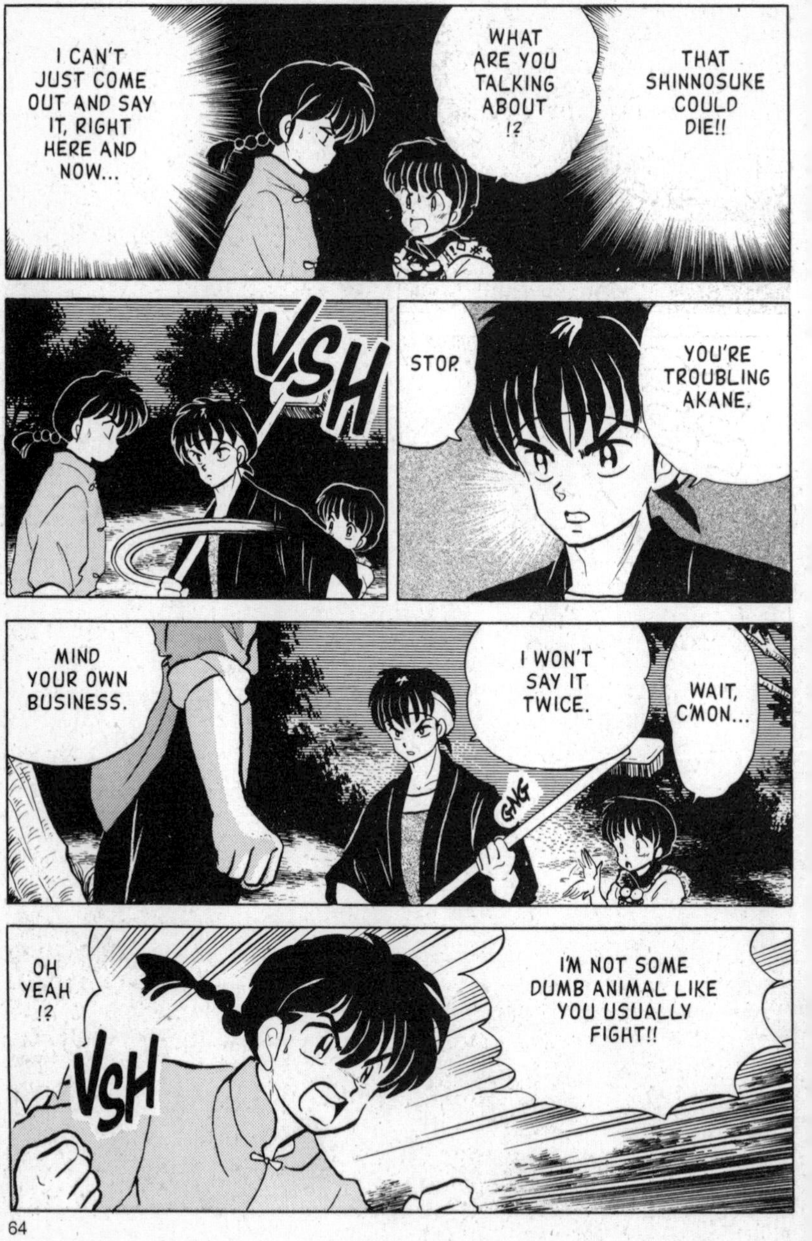
I CAN'T JUST COME OUT AND SAY IT, RIGHT HERE AND NOW...
WHAT ARE YOU TALKING ABOUT !?
THAT SHINNOSUKE COULD DIE!!
VSH
STOP.
YOU'RE TROUBLING AKANE.
MIND YOUR OWN BUSINESS.
I WON'T SAY IT TWICE.
GNG
WAIT, C'MON...
OH YEAH !?
VSH
I'M NOT SOME DUMB ANIMAL LIKE YOU USUALLY FIGHT!!

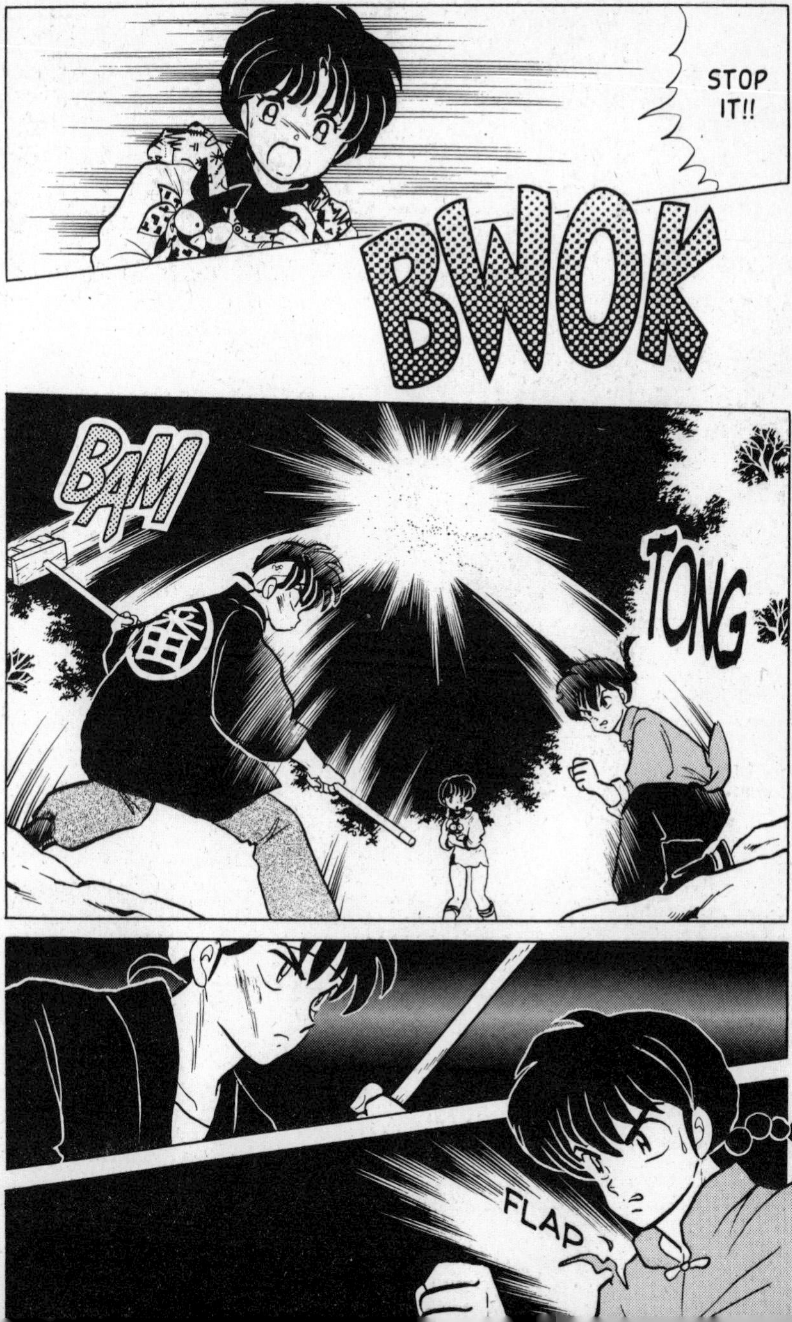
STOP IT!!
BWOK
BAM
TONG
FLAP

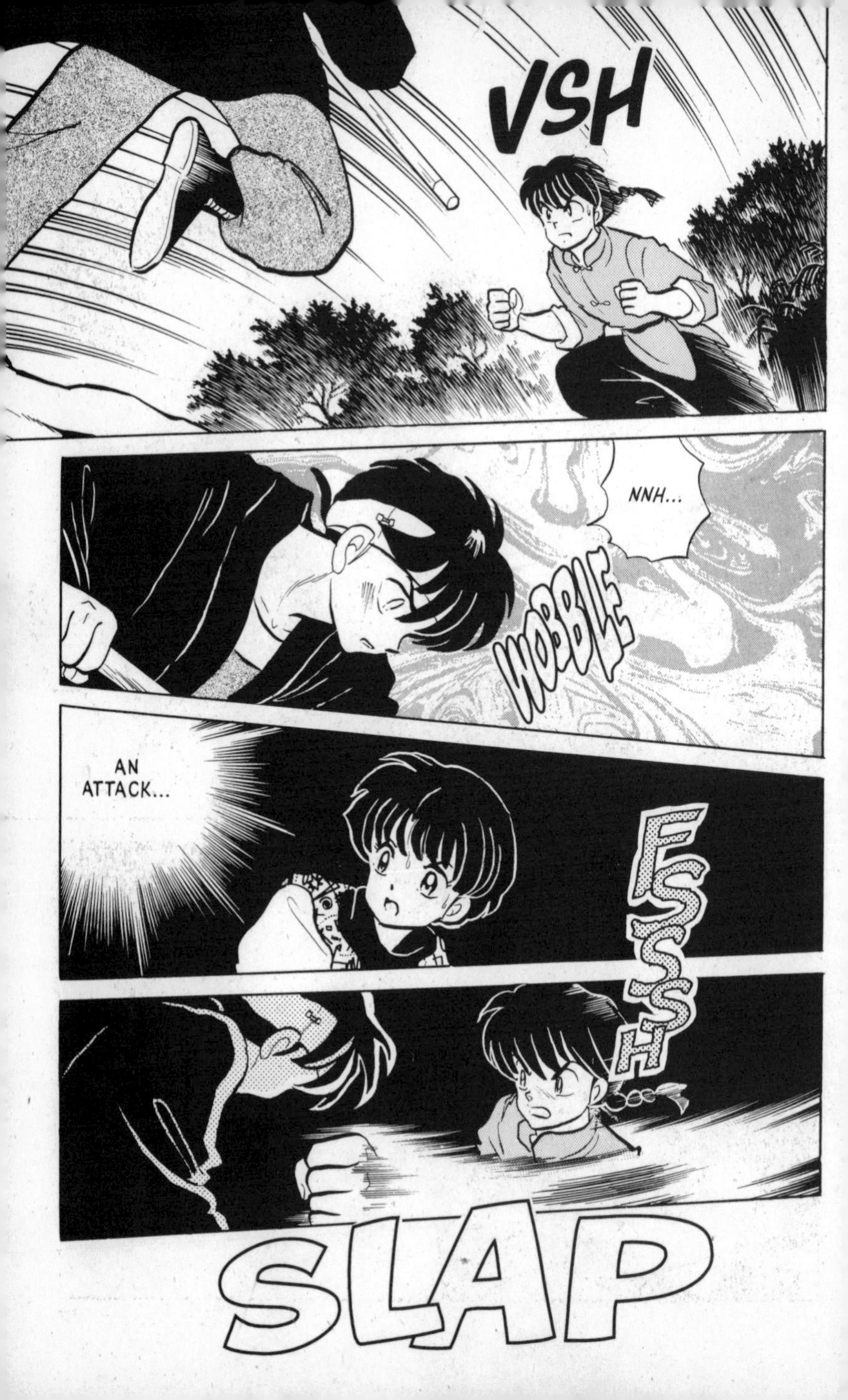
VSH
NNH...
WOBBLE
AN ATTACK...
FSSSH
SLAP

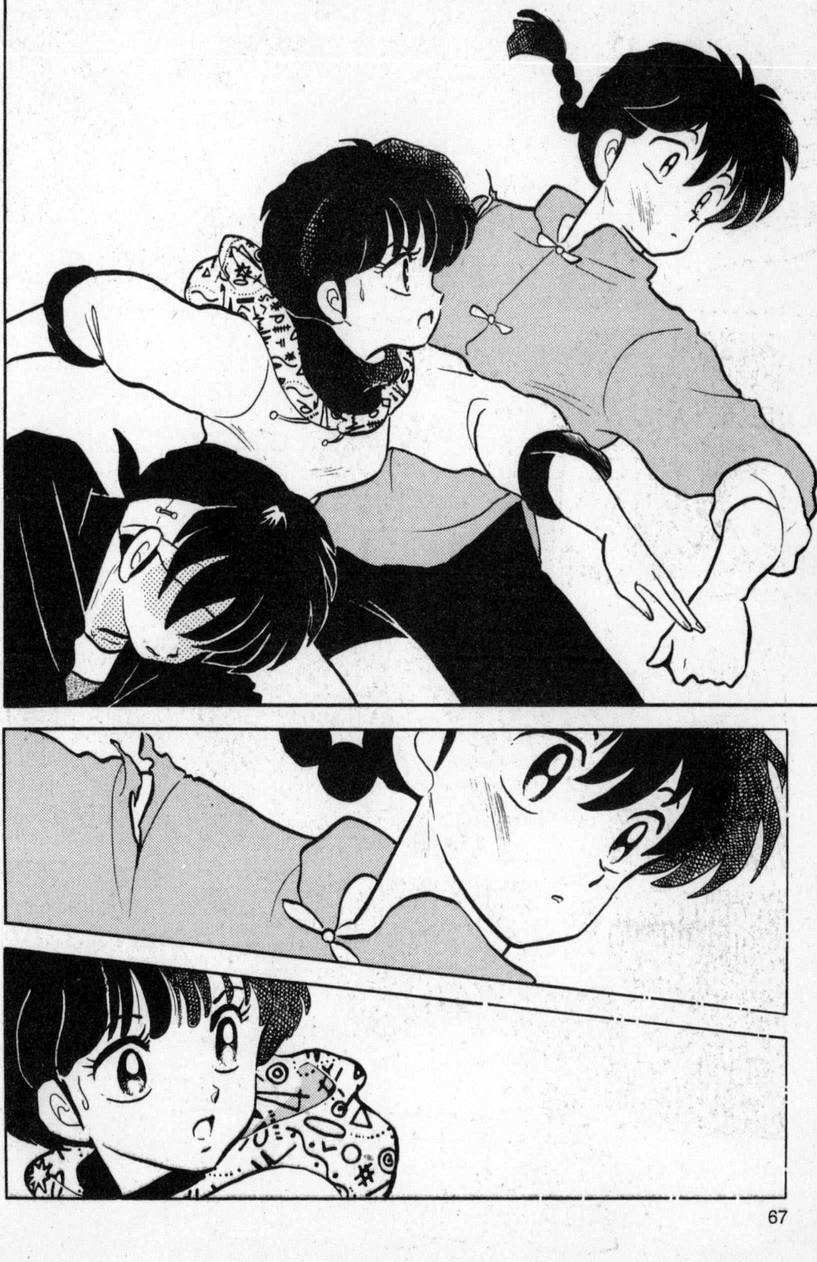

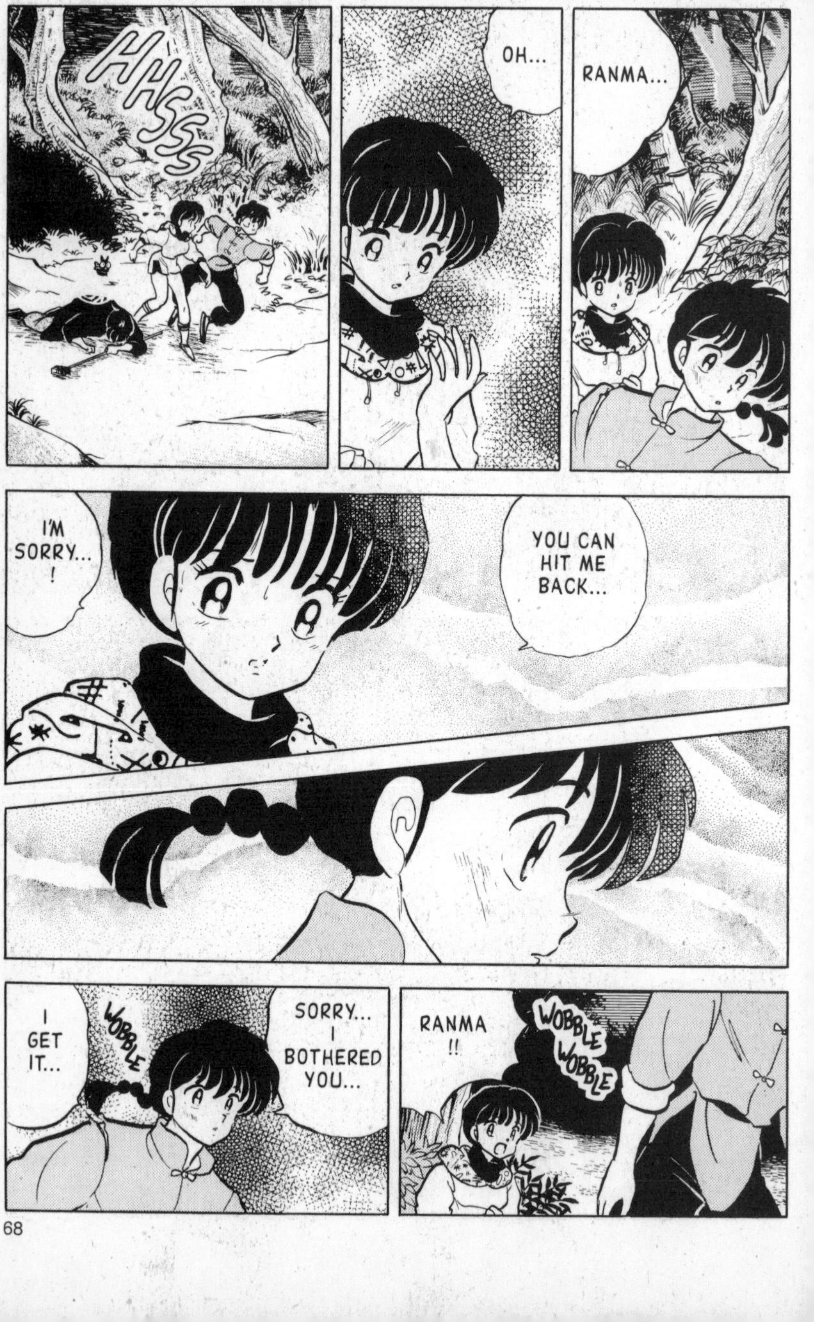
HHSSS
OH...
RANMA...
I'M SORRY... !
YOU CAN HIT ME BACK...
I GET IT...
WOBBLE
SORRY... I BOTHERED YOU...
RANMA !!
WOBBLE WOBBLE

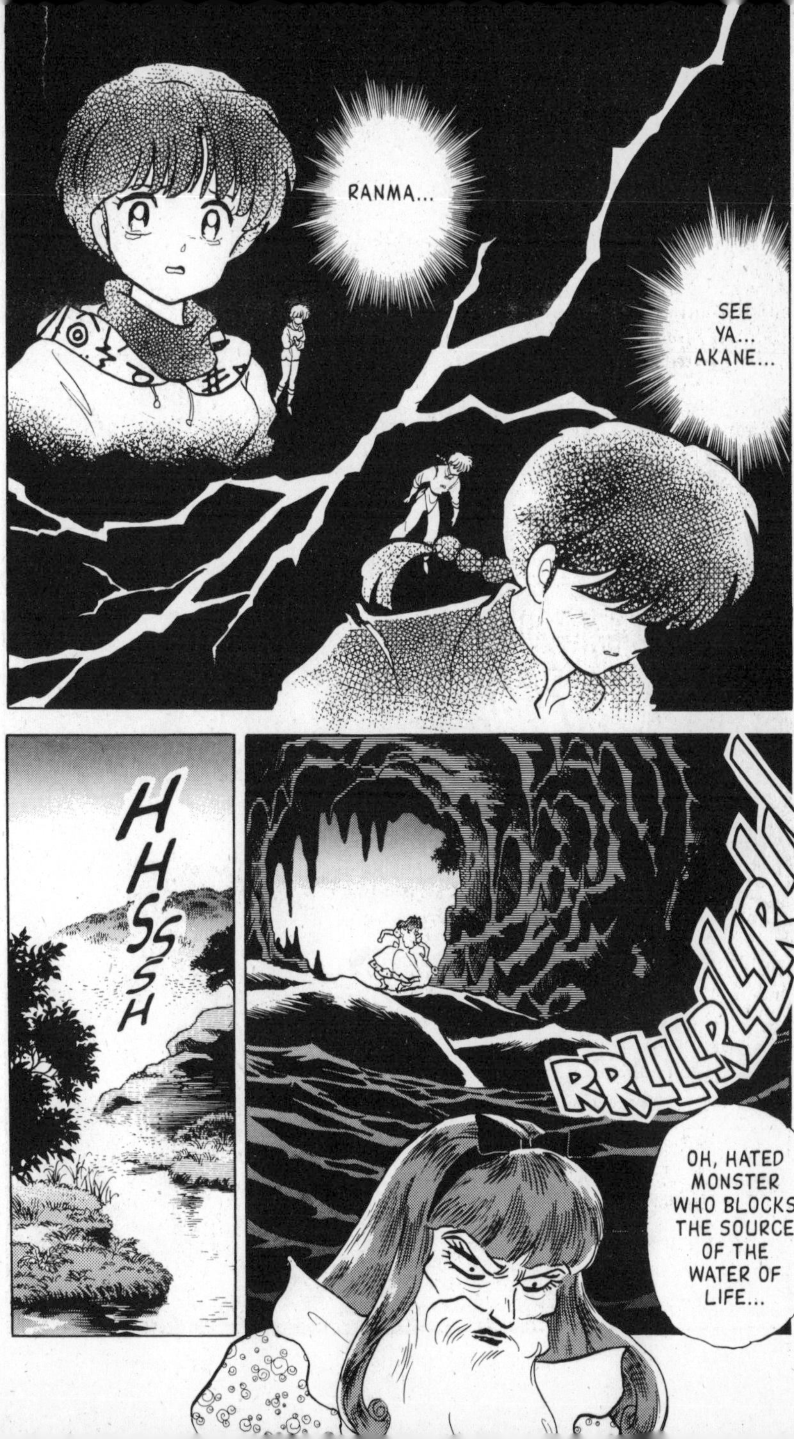
RANMA...
SEE YA... AKANE...
HHSSSH
RRLLLRLLRLL
OH, HATED MONSTER WHO BLOCKS THE SOURCE OF THE WATER OF LIFE...

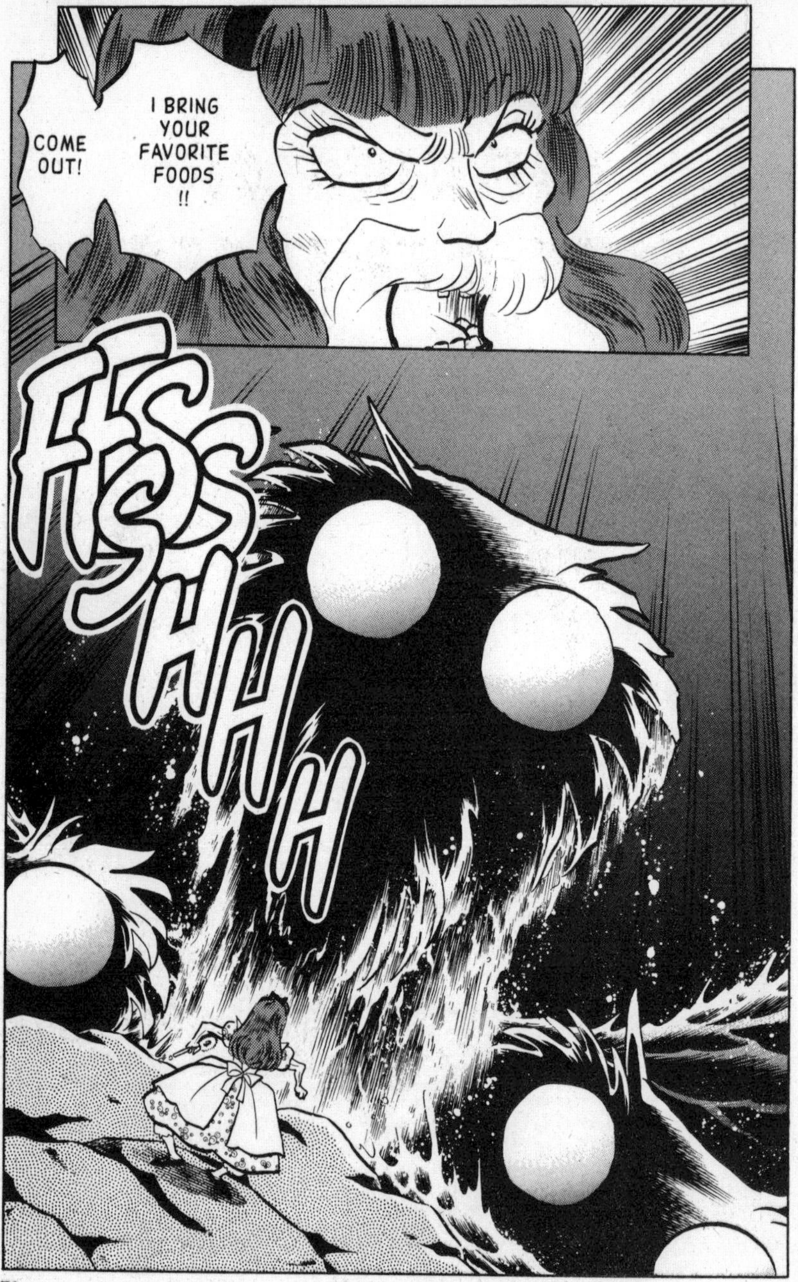
COME OUT!
I BRING YOUR FAVORITE FOODS !!
FSSSHHHH

Part 5

THE KING OF BEASTS EMERGES!!

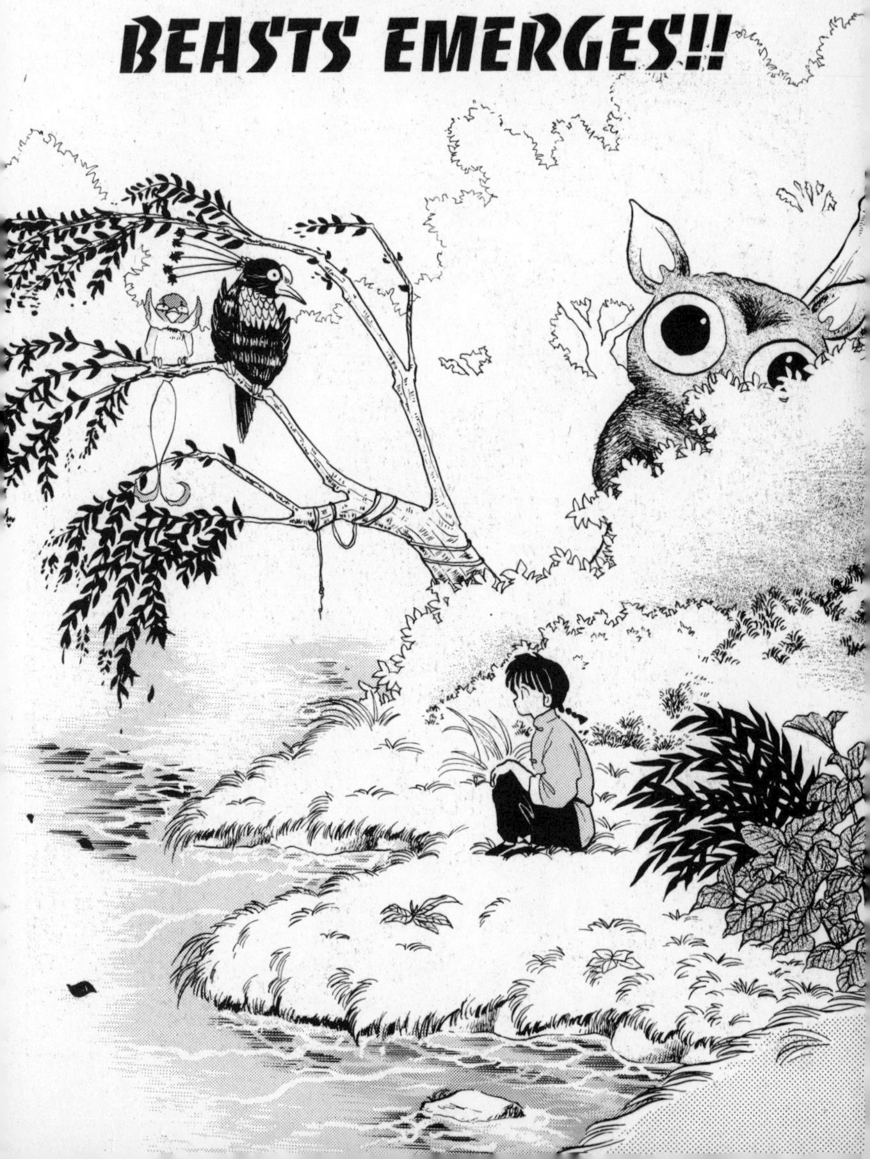

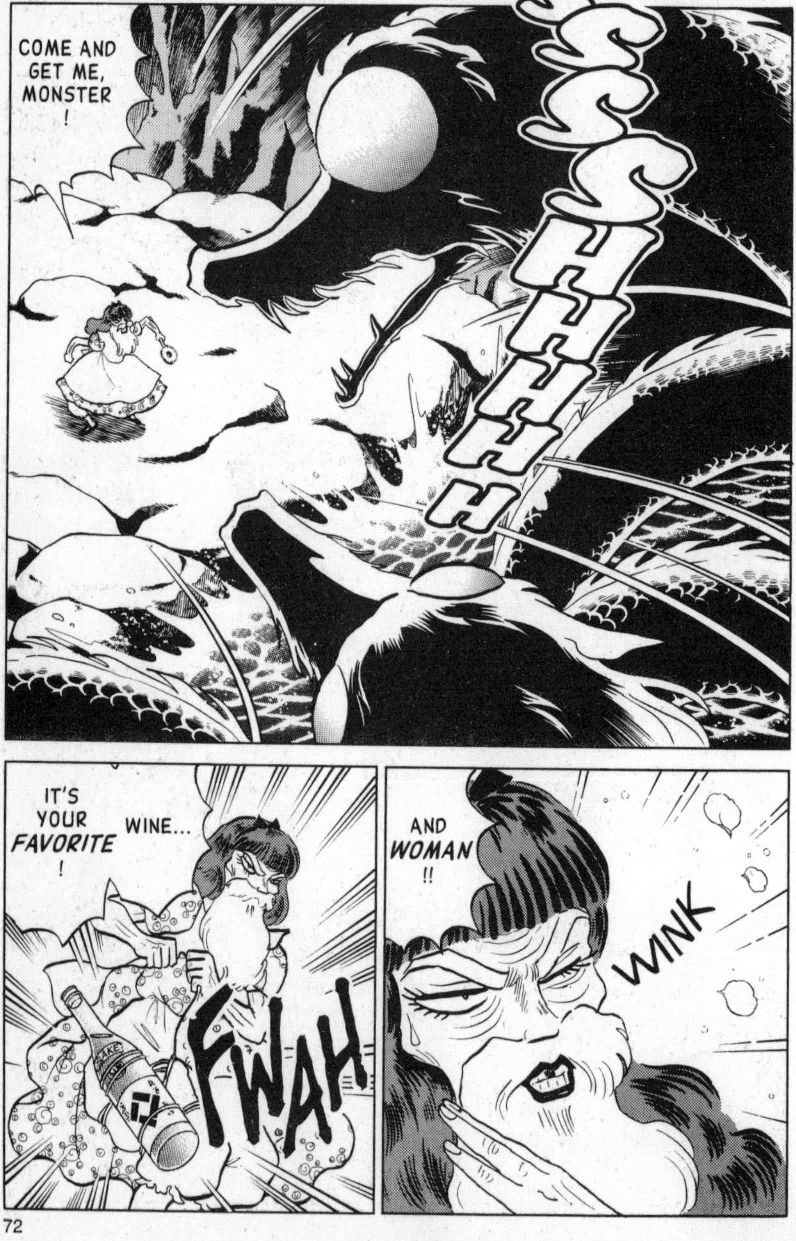
COME AND GET ME, MONSTER!
SSSSSHHHHHH
IT'S YOUR *FAVORITE* WINE...
FWAH
AND *WOMAN*!!
WINK

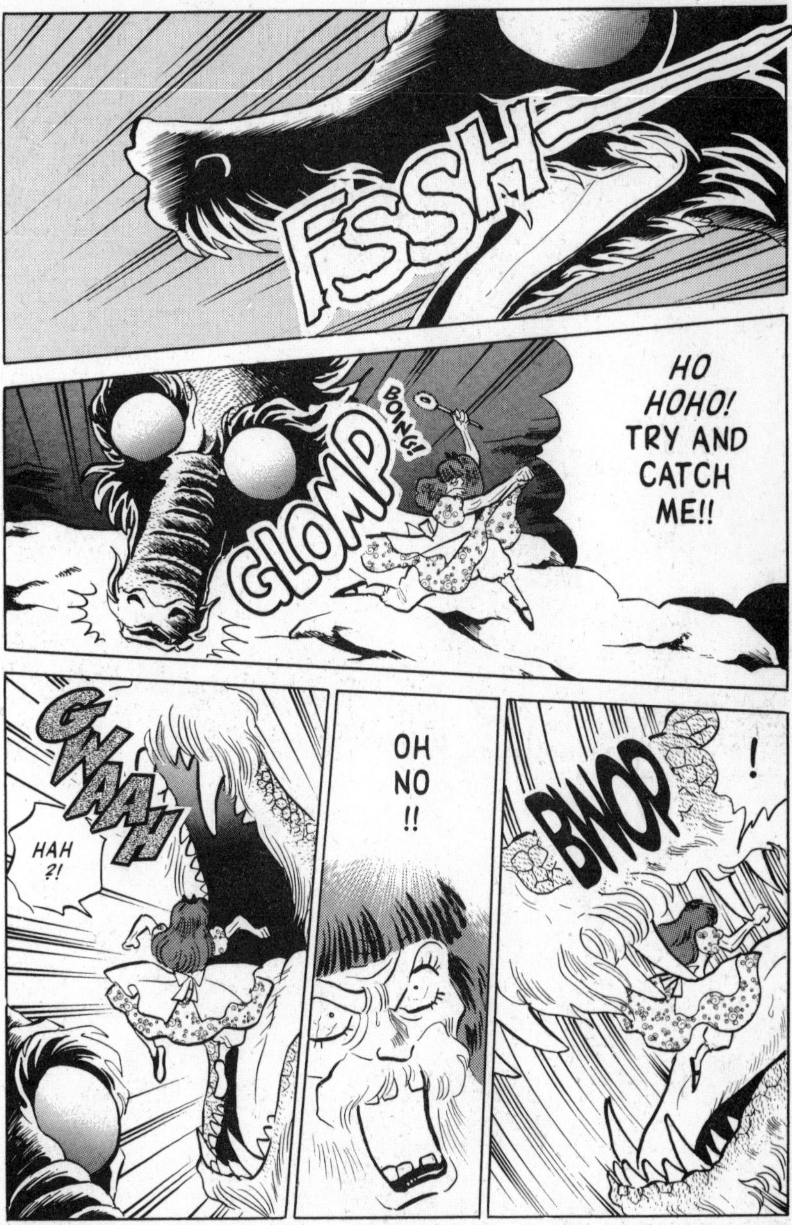
FSSH
GLOMP
BOING!
HO HOHO! TRY AND CATCH ME!!
GWAAAH
HAH ?!
OH NO !!
BWOP
!

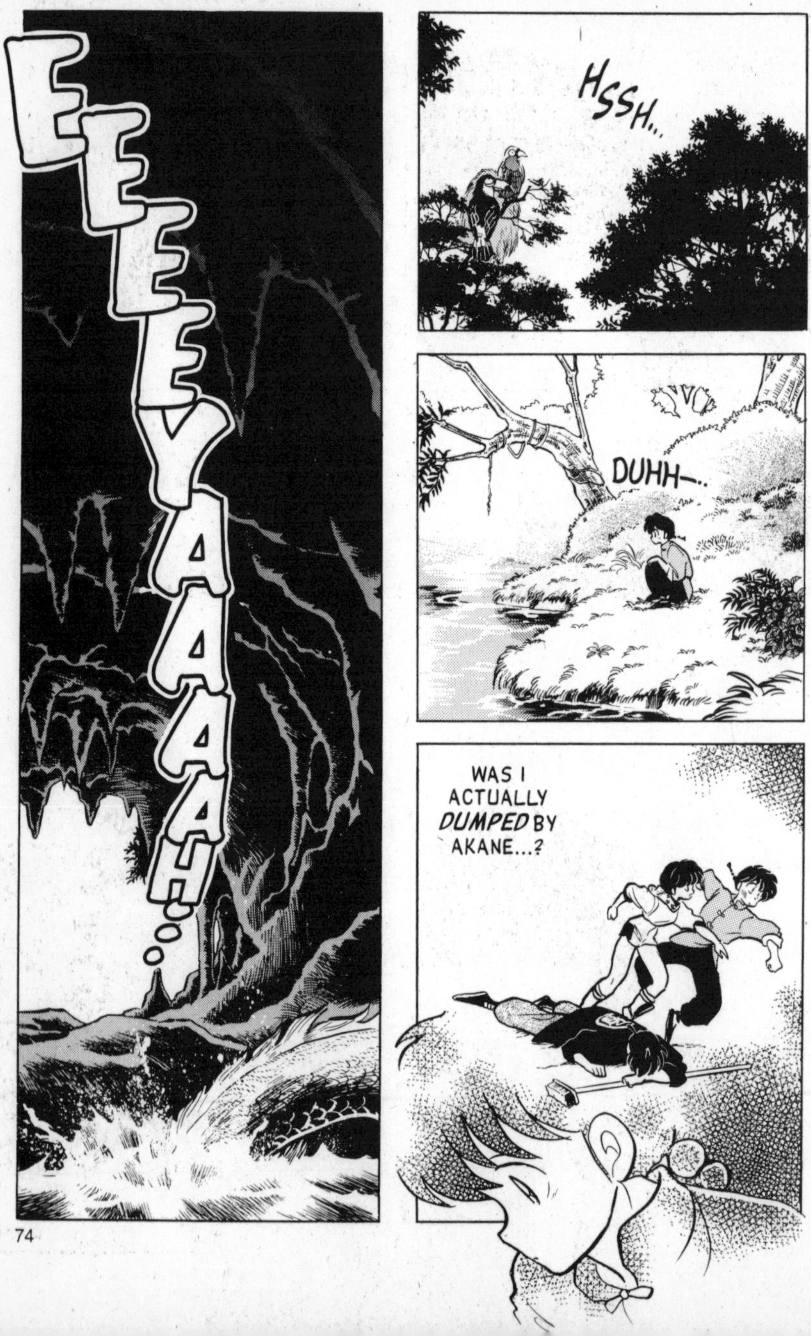
EEEEYAAAAH...
HSSH..
DUHH—..
WAS I ACTUALLY *DUMPED* BY AKANE...?

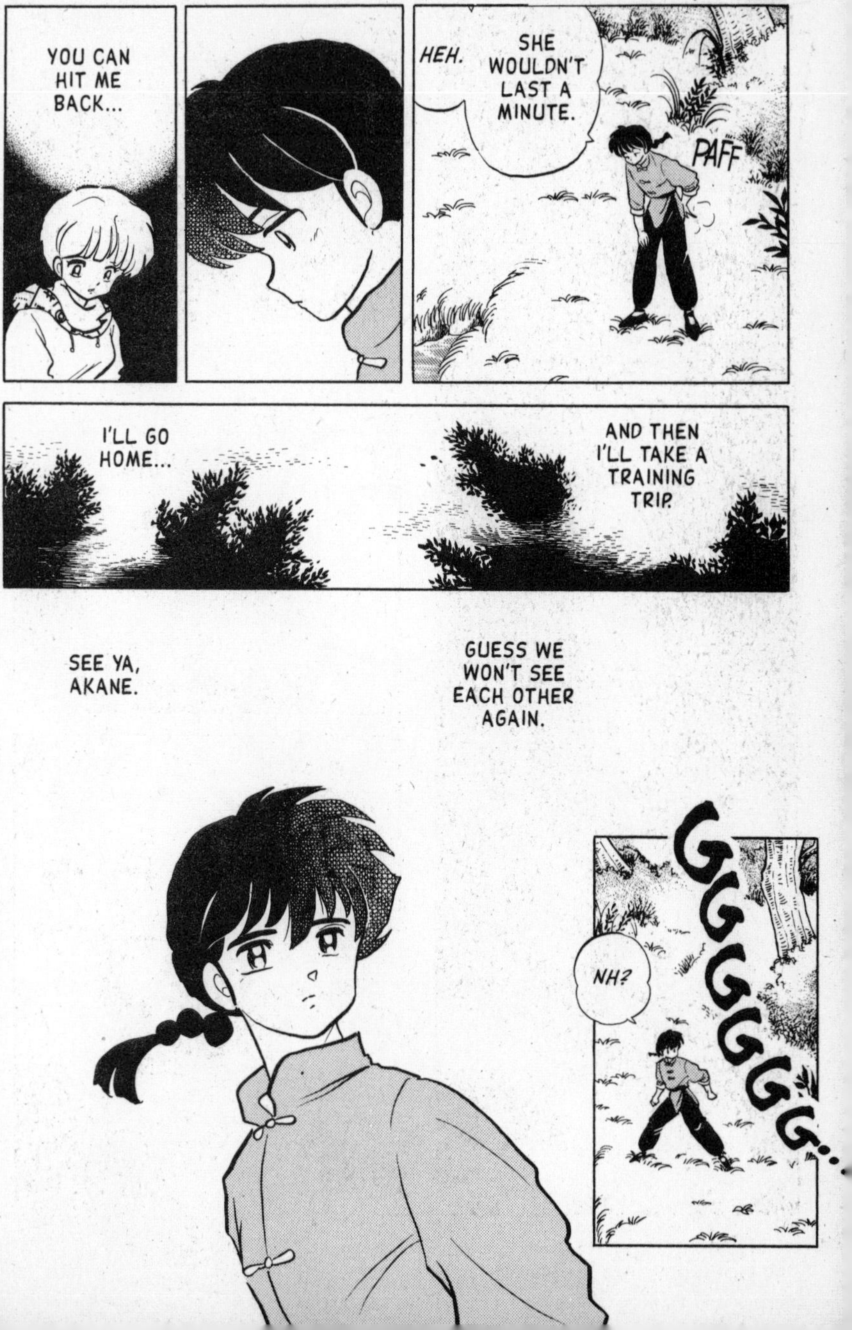
YOU CAN HIT ME BACK...
HEH.
SHE WOULDN'T LAST A MINUTE.
PAFF
I'LL GO HOME...
AND THEN I'LL TAKE A TRAINING TRIP.
SEE YA, AKANE.
GUESS WE WON'T SEE EACH OTHER AGAIN.
GGGGGG...
NH?

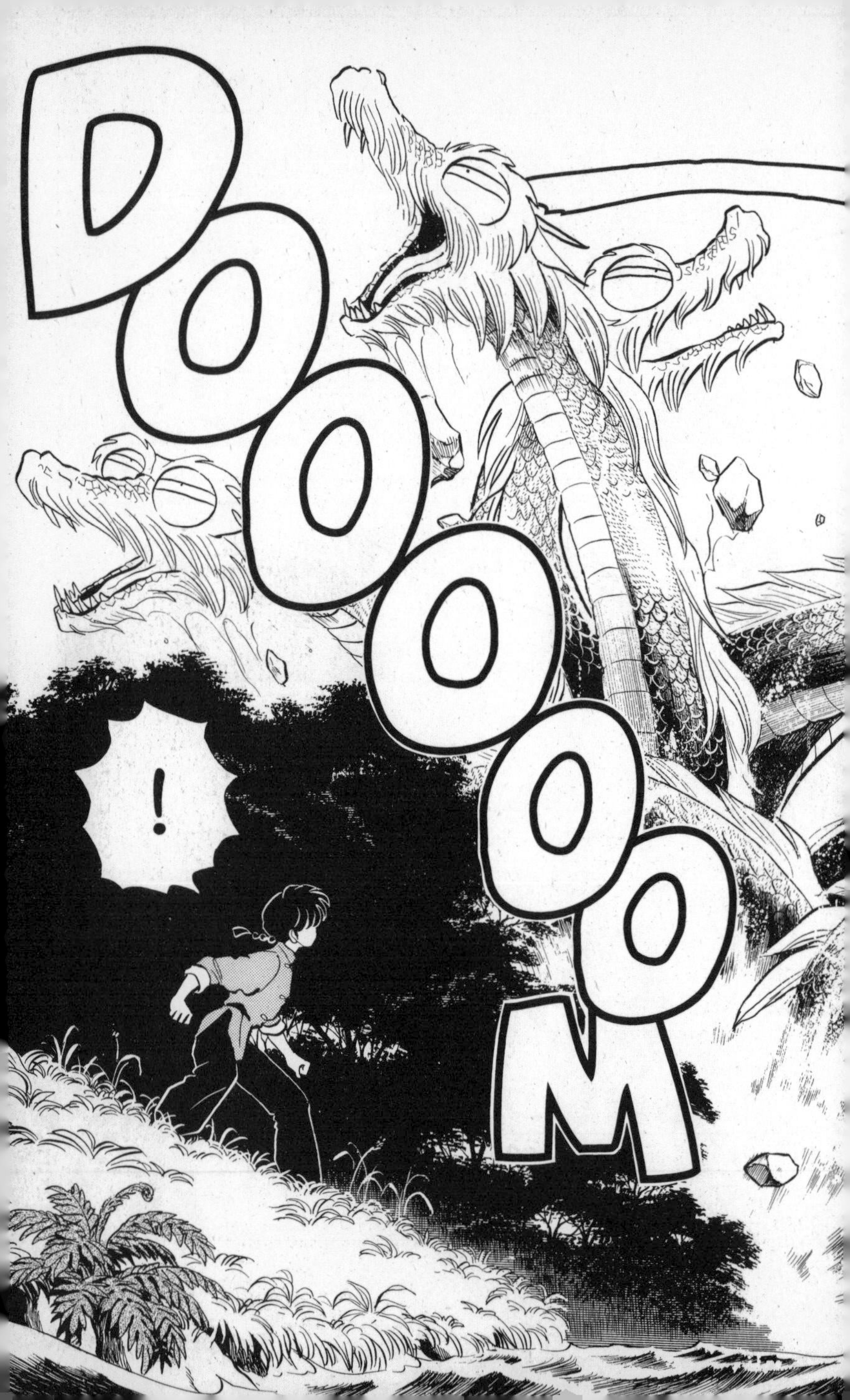
DOOOOOOOM
!

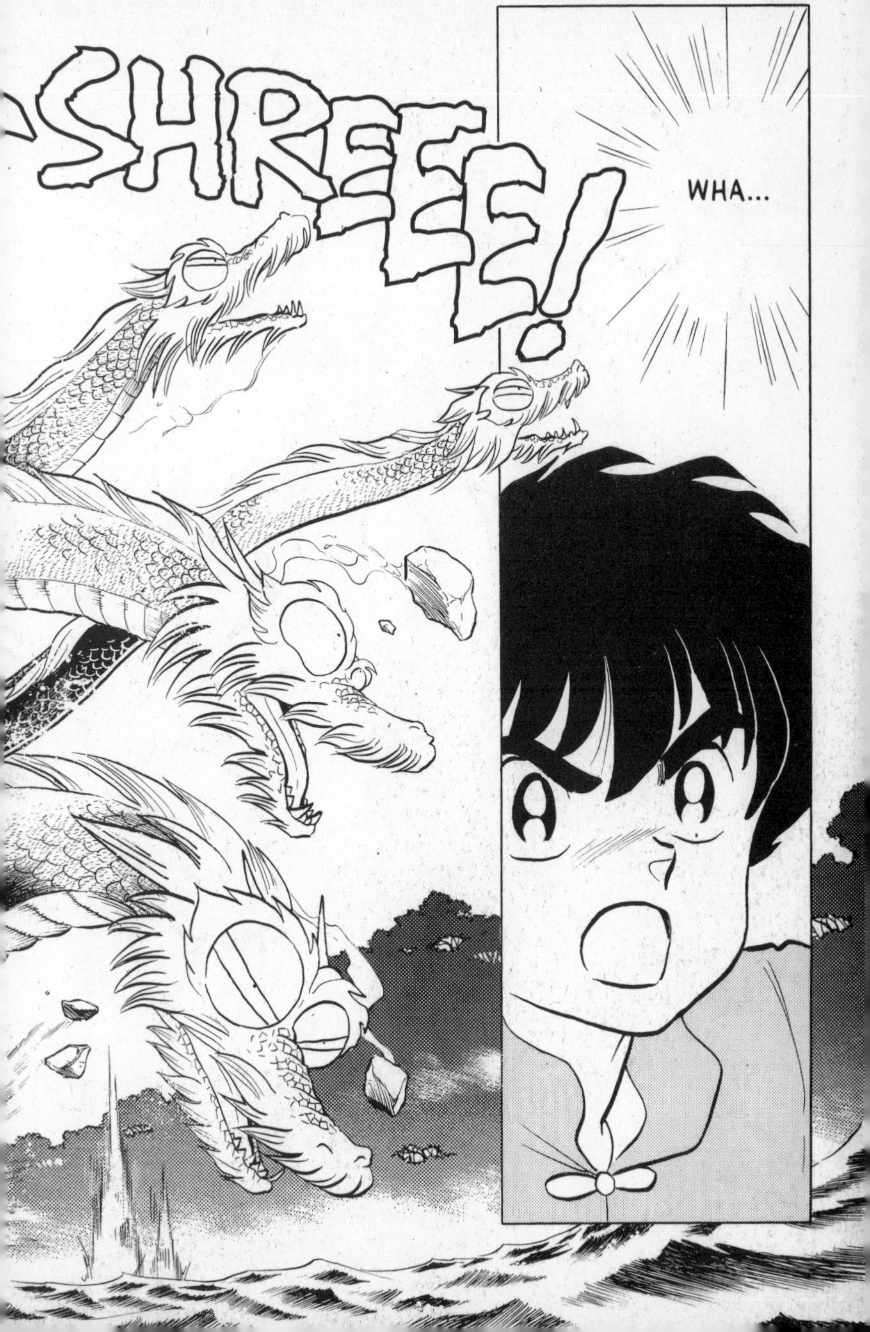
SHREEEE!
WHA...

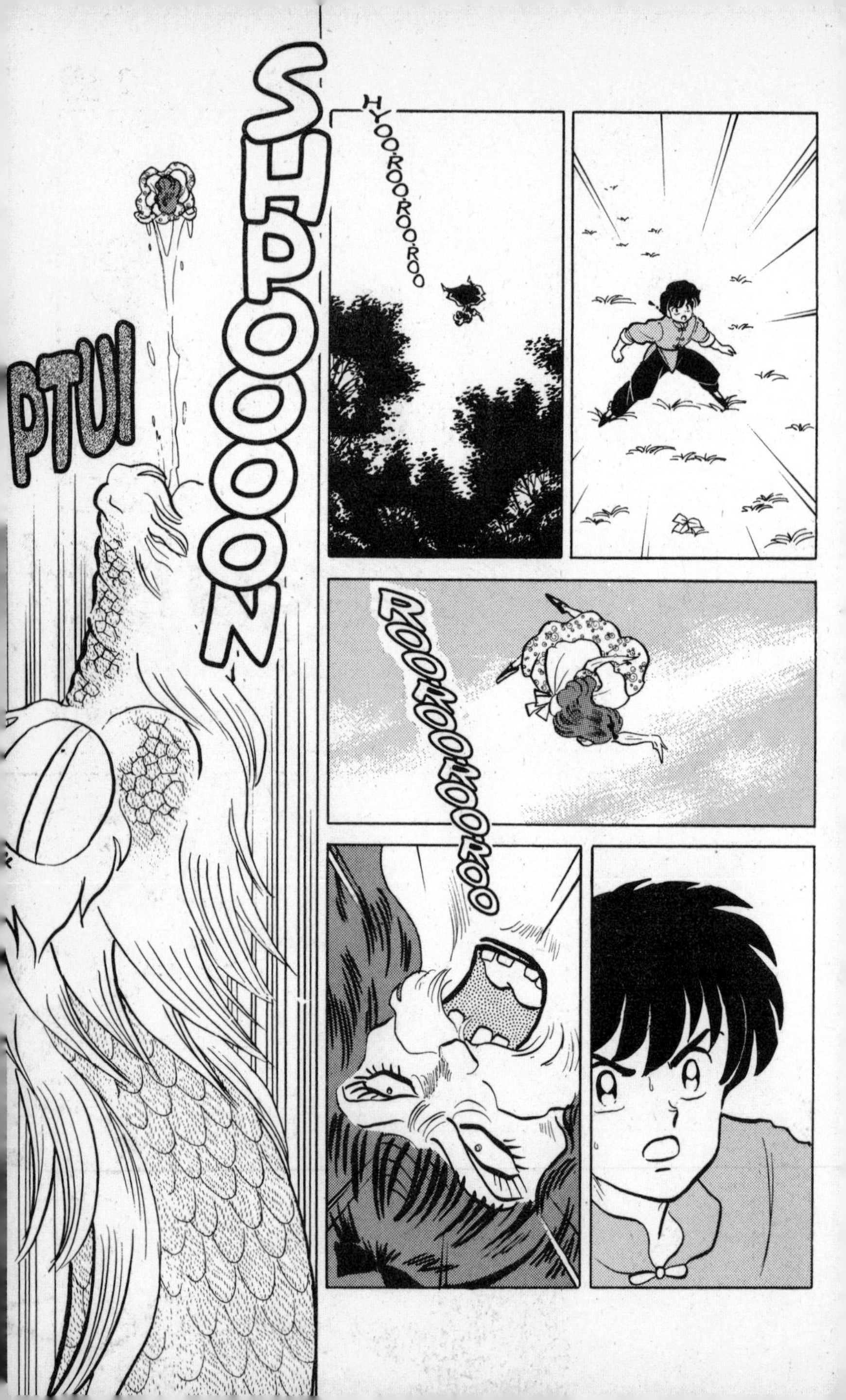
PTUI
SHPOOOOON
HYOO-ROO-ROO-ROO
ROO-ROO-ROO-ROO

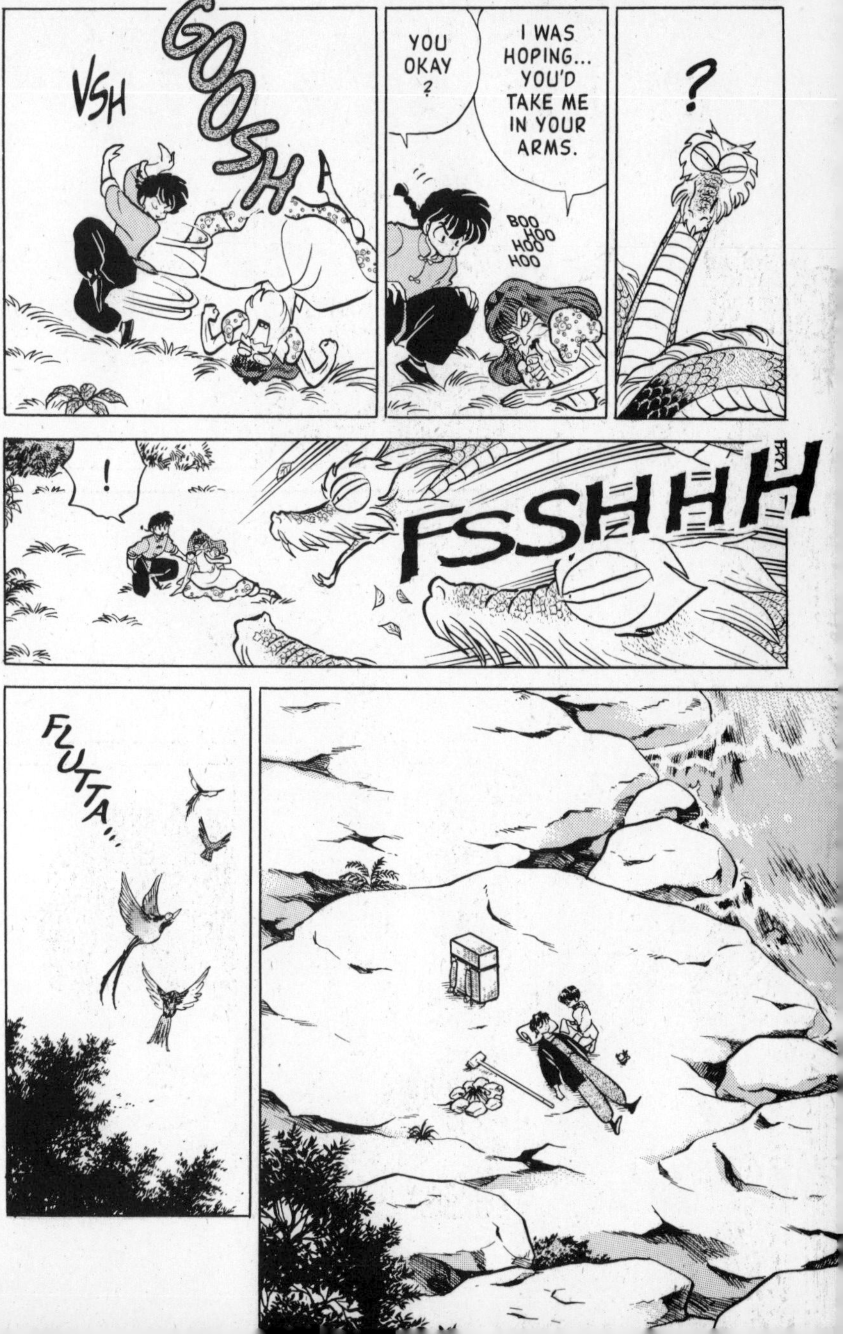
VSH
GOOSH
YOU OKAY ?
I WAS HOPING... YOU'D TAKE ME IN YOUR ARMS.
BOO HOO HOO HOO
?
!
FSSHHH
FLUTTA...

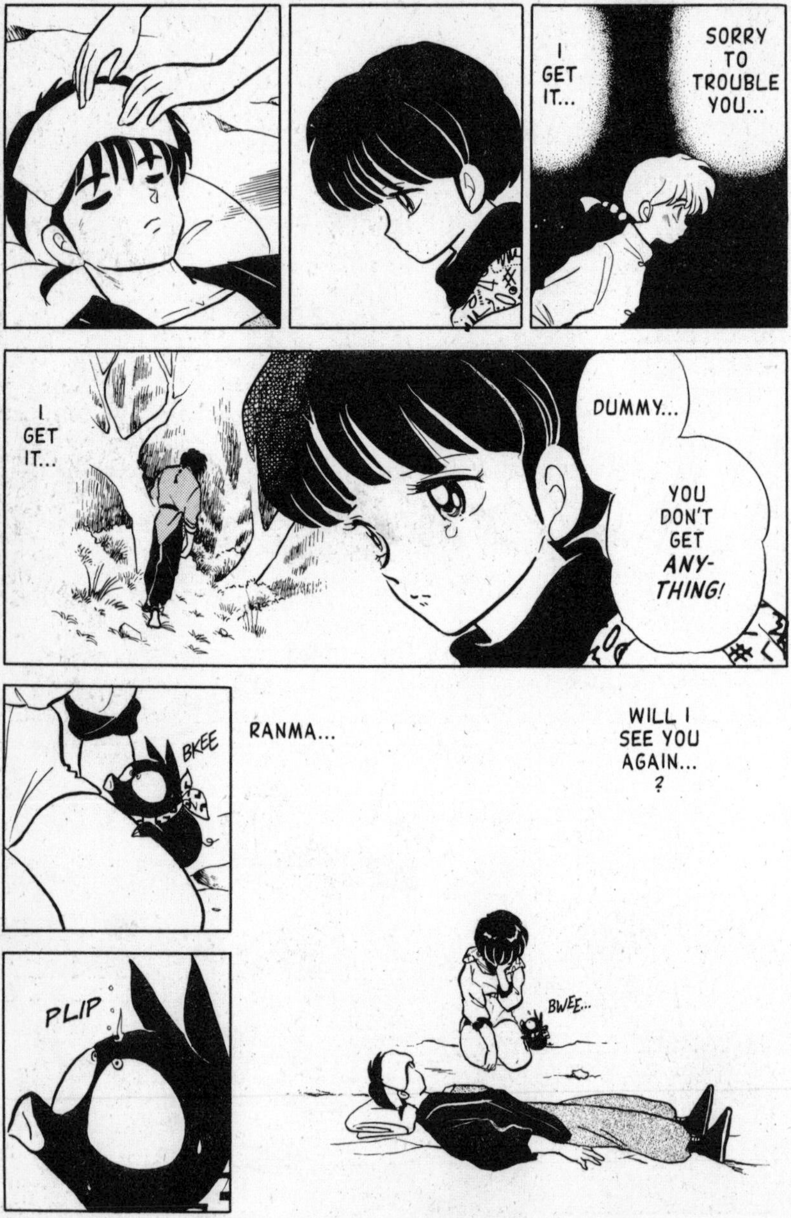
I GET IT...
SORRY TO TROUBLE YOU...
I GET IT...
DUMMY...
YOU DON'T GET *ANYTHING!*
BKEE
PLIP
RANMA...
WILL I SEE YOU AGAIN...?
BWEE...

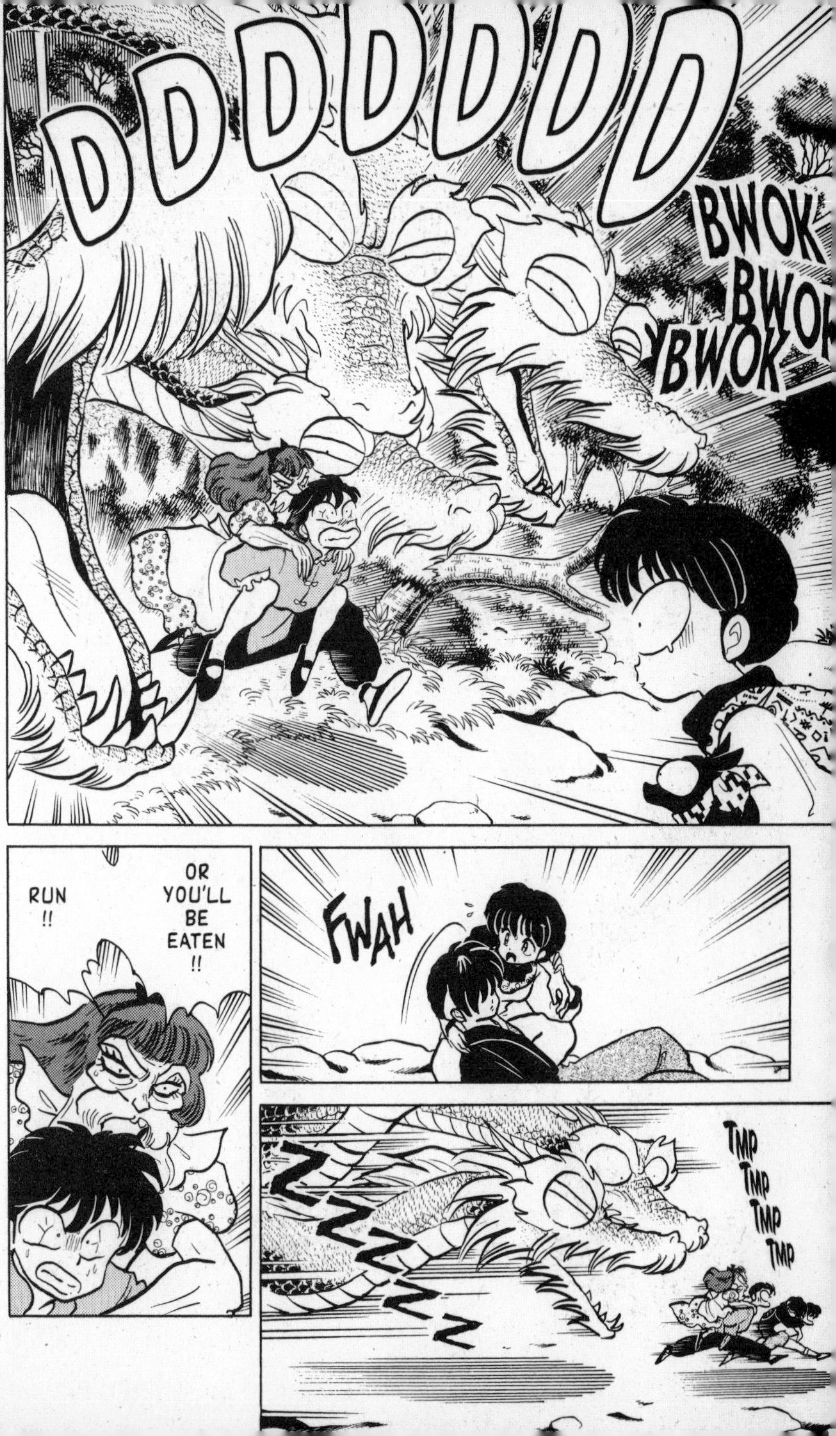
DDDDDDD
BWOK
BWOK
BWOK
RUN !!
OR YOU'LL BE EATEN !!
FWAH
TMP
TMP
TMP
TMP

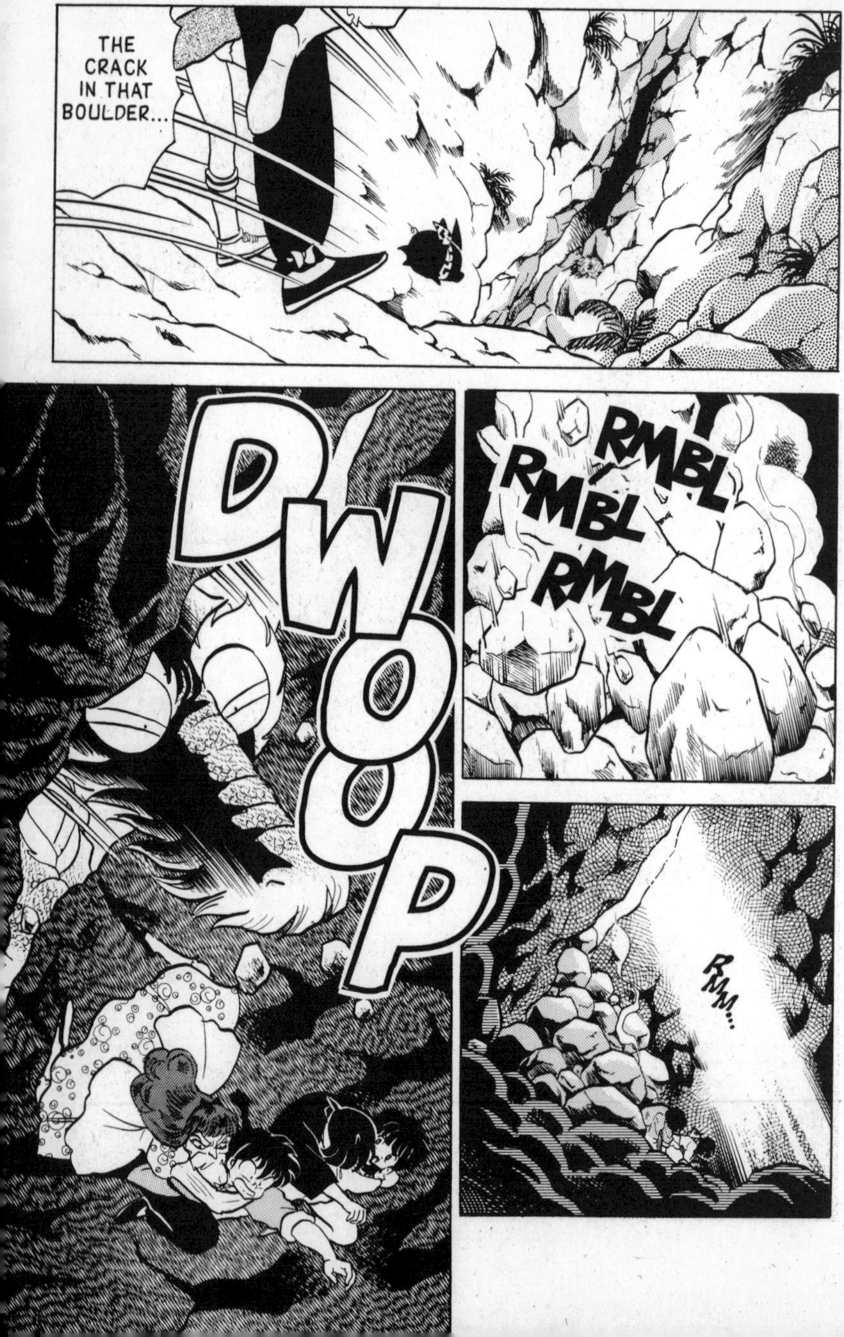
THE CRACK IN THAT BOULDER...
DWOOP
RMBL
RMBL
RMBL
RMBL
RMM...

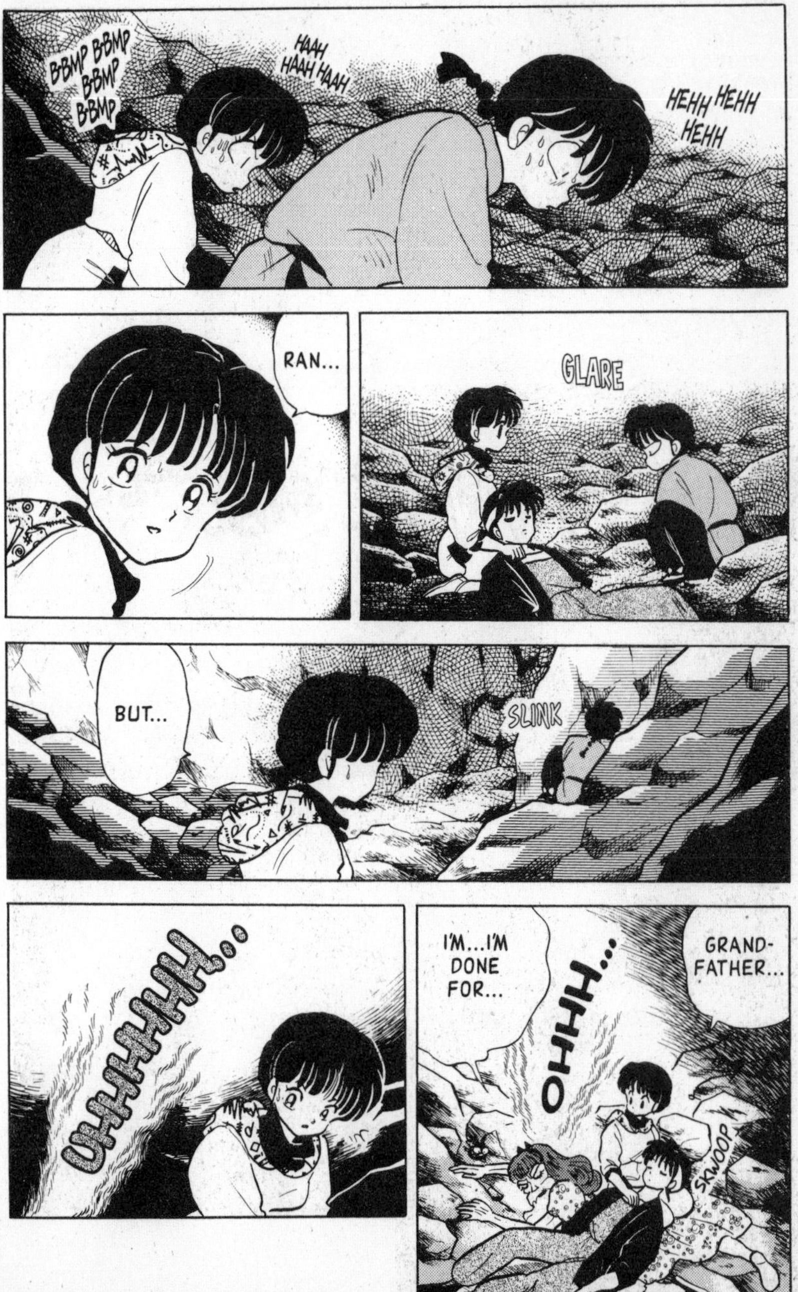
B-BMP B-BMP B-BMP B-BMP
HAAH HAAH HAAH
HEHH HEHH HEHH
RAN...
GLARE
BUT...
SLINK
UHHHHHH...
I'M...I'M DONE FOR...
OHHHH...
GRAND-FATHER...
SKWOOP

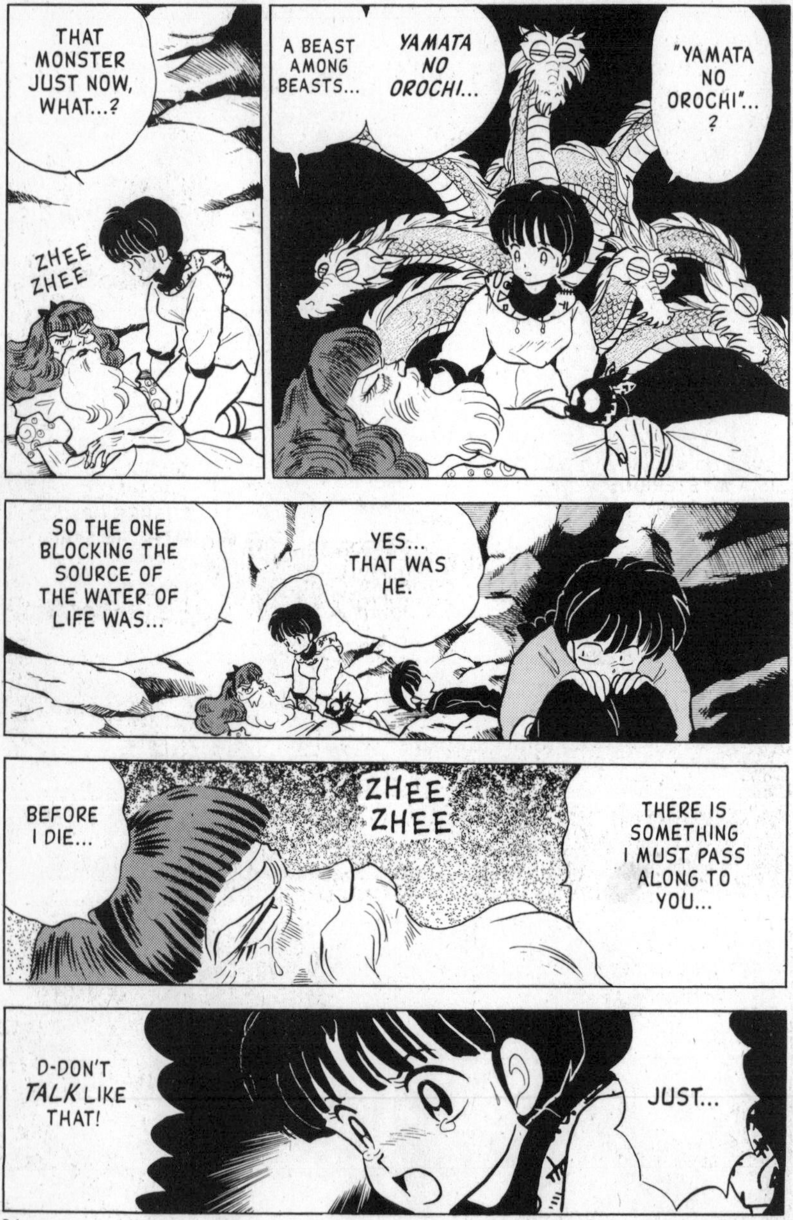
THAT MONSTER JUST NOW, WHAT...?
ZHEE ZHEE
A BEAST AMONG BEASTS...
YAMATA NO OROCHI...
"YAMATA NO OROCHI"...?
SO THE ONE BLOCKING THE SOURCE OF THE WATER OF LIFE WAS...
YES... THAT WAS HE.
BEFORE I DIE...
ZHEE ZHEE
THERE IS SOMETHING I MUST PASS ALONG TO YOU...
D-DON'T TALK LIKE THAT!
JUST...

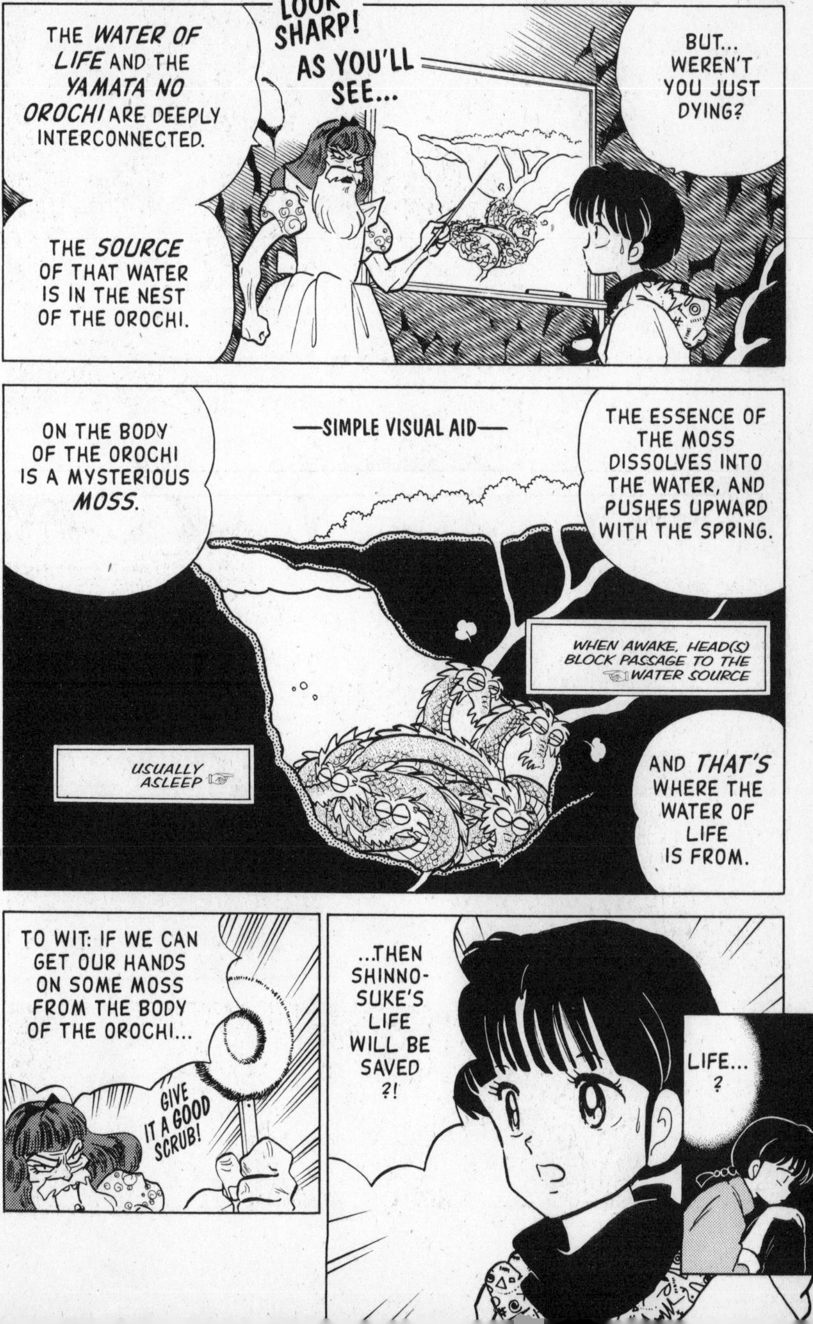
THE WATER OF LIFE AND THE YAMATA NO OROCHI ARE DEEPLY INTERCONNECTED.
LOOK SHARP!
AS YOU'LL SEE...
THE SOURCE OF THAT WATER IS IN THE NEST OF THE OROCHI.
BUT... WEREN'T YOU JUST DYING?
ON THE BODY OF THE OROCHI IS A MYSTERIOUS MOSS.
—SIMPLE VISUAL AID—
THE ESSENCE OF THE MOSS DISSOLVES INTO THE WATER, AND PUSHES UPWARD WITH THE SPRING.
WHEN AWAKE, HEAD(S) BLOCK PASSAGE TO THE WATER SOURCE
USUALLY ASLEEP
AND THAT'S WHERE THE WATER OF LIFE IS FROM.
TO WIT: IF WE CAN GET OUR HANDS ON SOME MOSS FROM THE BODY OF THE OROCHI...
GIVE IT A GOOD SCRUB!
...THEN SHINNO-SUKE'S LIFE WILL BE SAVED ?!
LIFE... ?

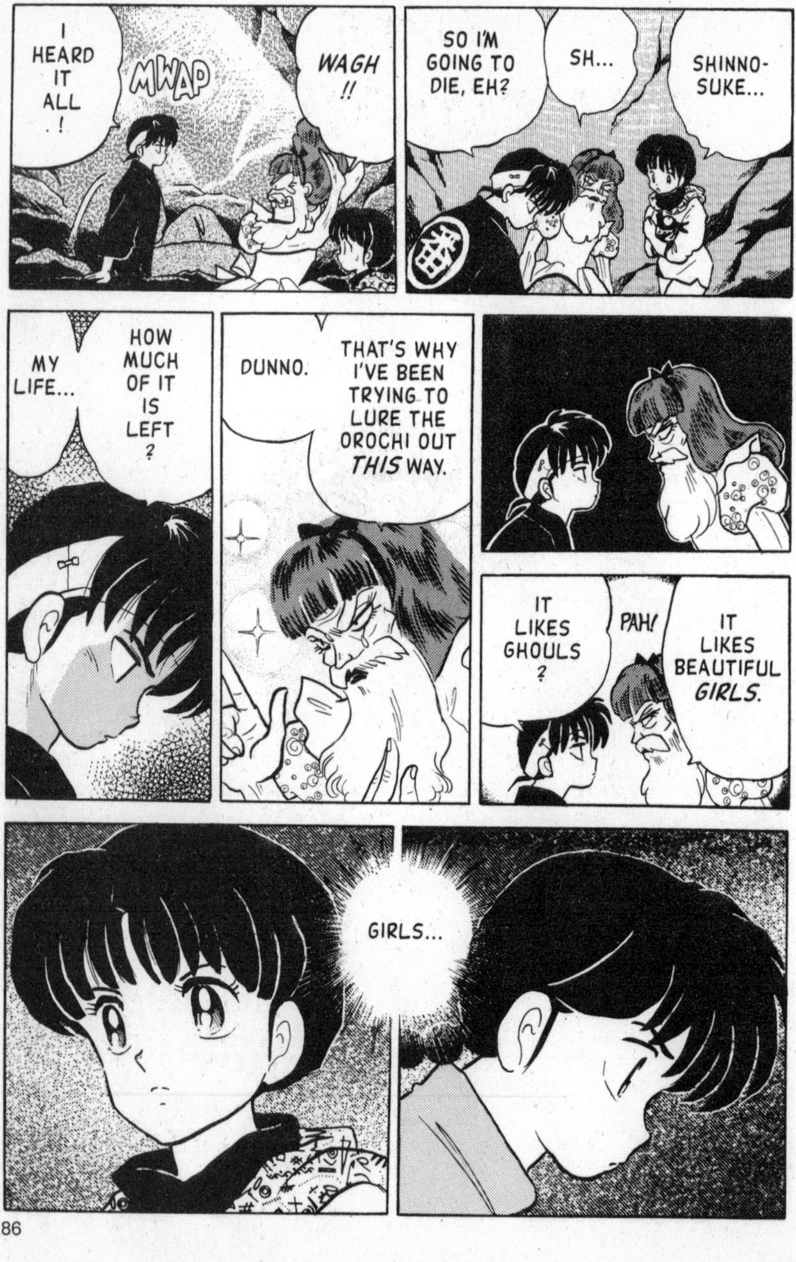
I HEARD IT ALL . !
MWAP
WAGH !!
SO I'M GOING TO DIE, EH?
SH...
SHINNO-SUKE...
MY LIFE...
HOW MUCH OF IT IS LEFT?
DUNNO.
THAT'S WHY I'VE BEEN TRYING TO LURE THE OROCHI OUT *THIS* WAY.
IT LIKES GHOULS?
PAH!
IT LIKES BEAUTIFUL *GIRLS*.
GIRLS...

Part 6

THE OROCHI AND ITS FURY

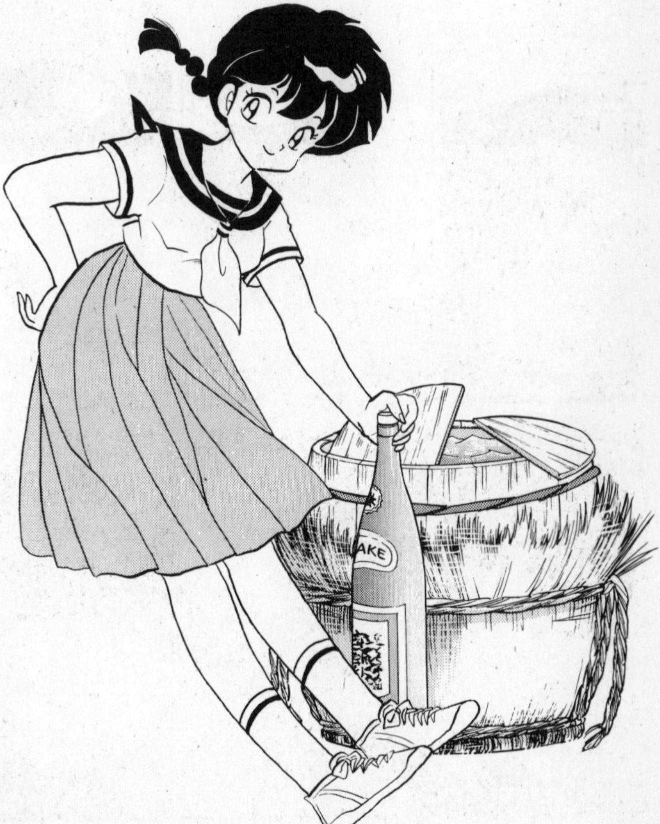
AKE

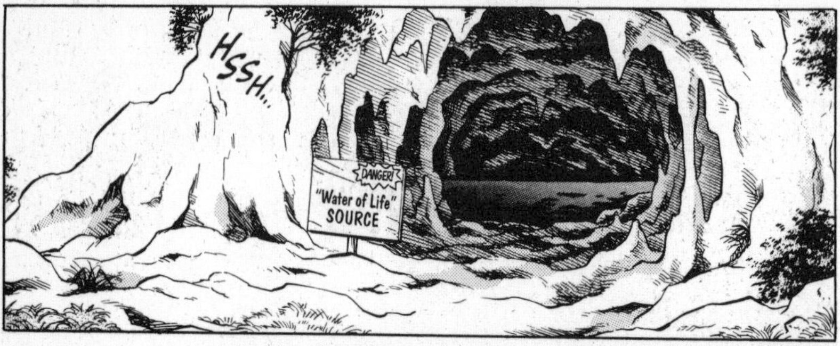
HSSH...
DANGER!
"Water of Life" SOURCE

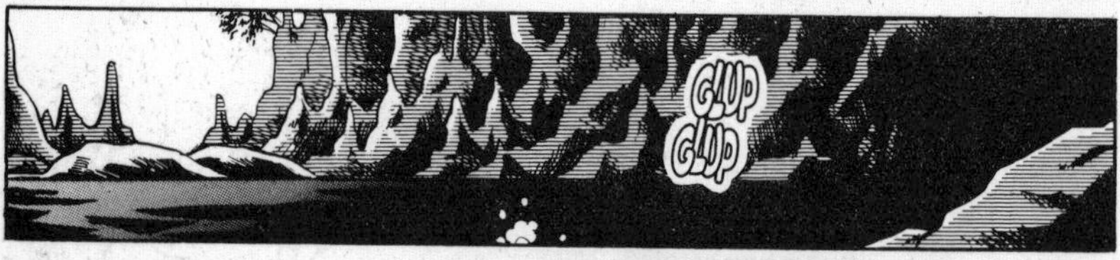
GLUP GLUP

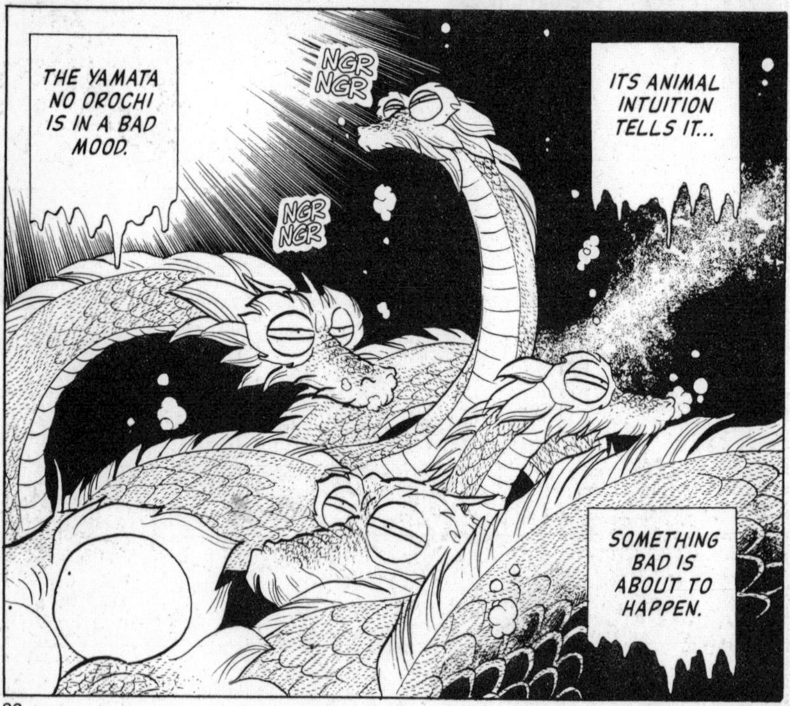
THE YAMATA NO OROCHI IS IN A BAD MOOD.
NGR NGR
NGR NGR
ITS ANIMAL INTUITION TELLS IT...
SOMETHING BAD IS ABOUT TO HAPPEN.

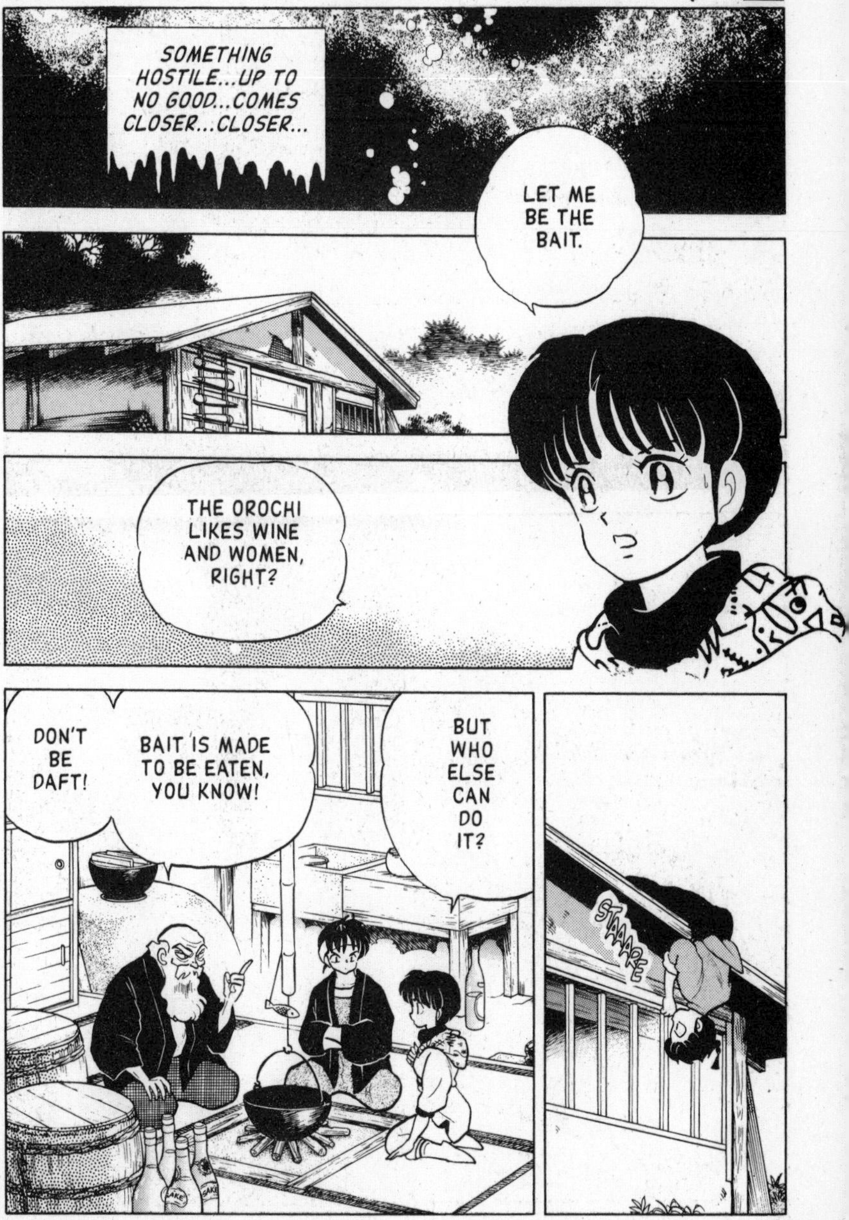
SOMETHING HOSTILE...UP TO NO GOOD...COMES CLOSER...CLOSER...
LET ME BE THE BAIT.
THE OROCHI LIKES WINE AND WOMEN, RIGHT?
DON'T BE DAFT!
BAIT IS MADE TO BE EATEN, YOU KNOW!
BUT WHO ELSE CAN DO IT?
STAAARE
SAKE
SAKE

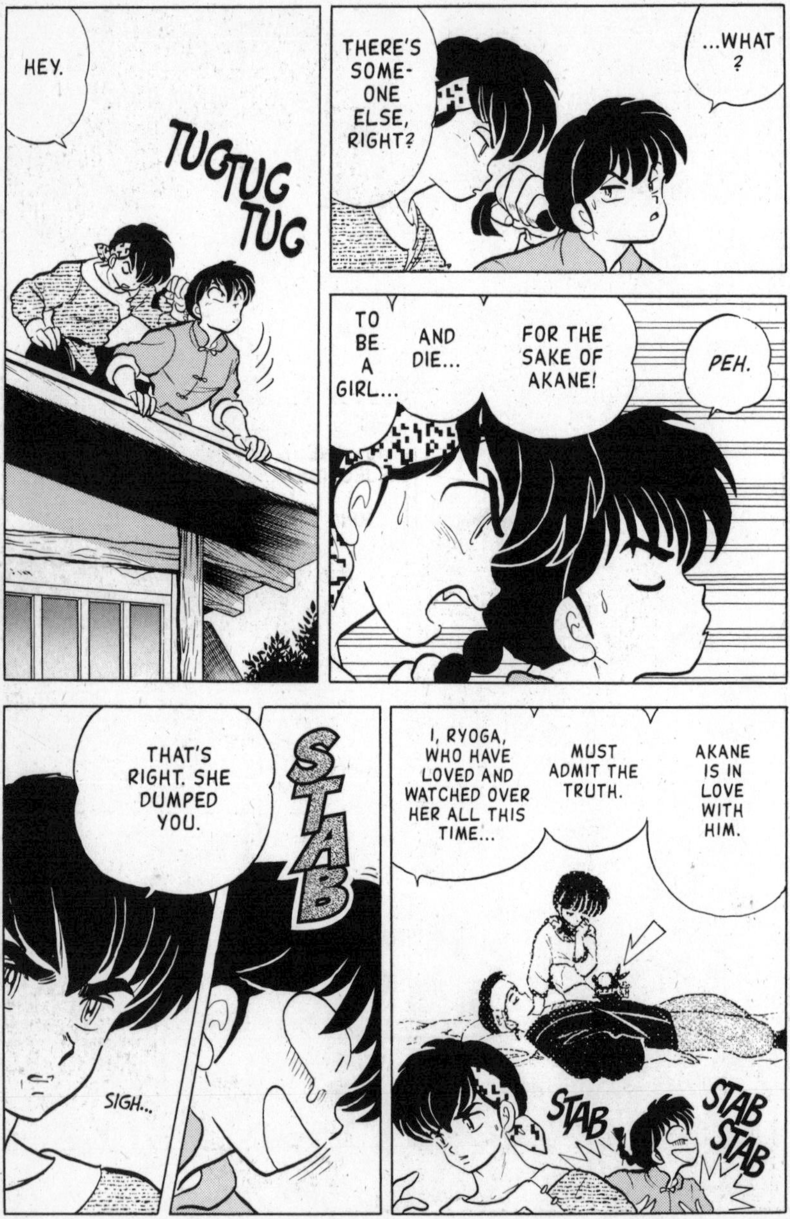
HEY.
TUGTUG TUG
THERE'S SOME-ONE ELSE, RIGHT?
...WHAT?
TO BE A GIRL...
AND DIE...
FOR THE SAKE OF AKANE!
PEH.
THAT'S RIGHT. SHE DUMPED YOU.
STAB
SIGH...
I, RYOGA, WHO HAVE LOVED AND WATCHED OVER HER ALL THIS TIME...
MUST ADMIT THE TRUTH.
AKANE IS IN LOVE WITH HIM.
STAB
STAB STAB

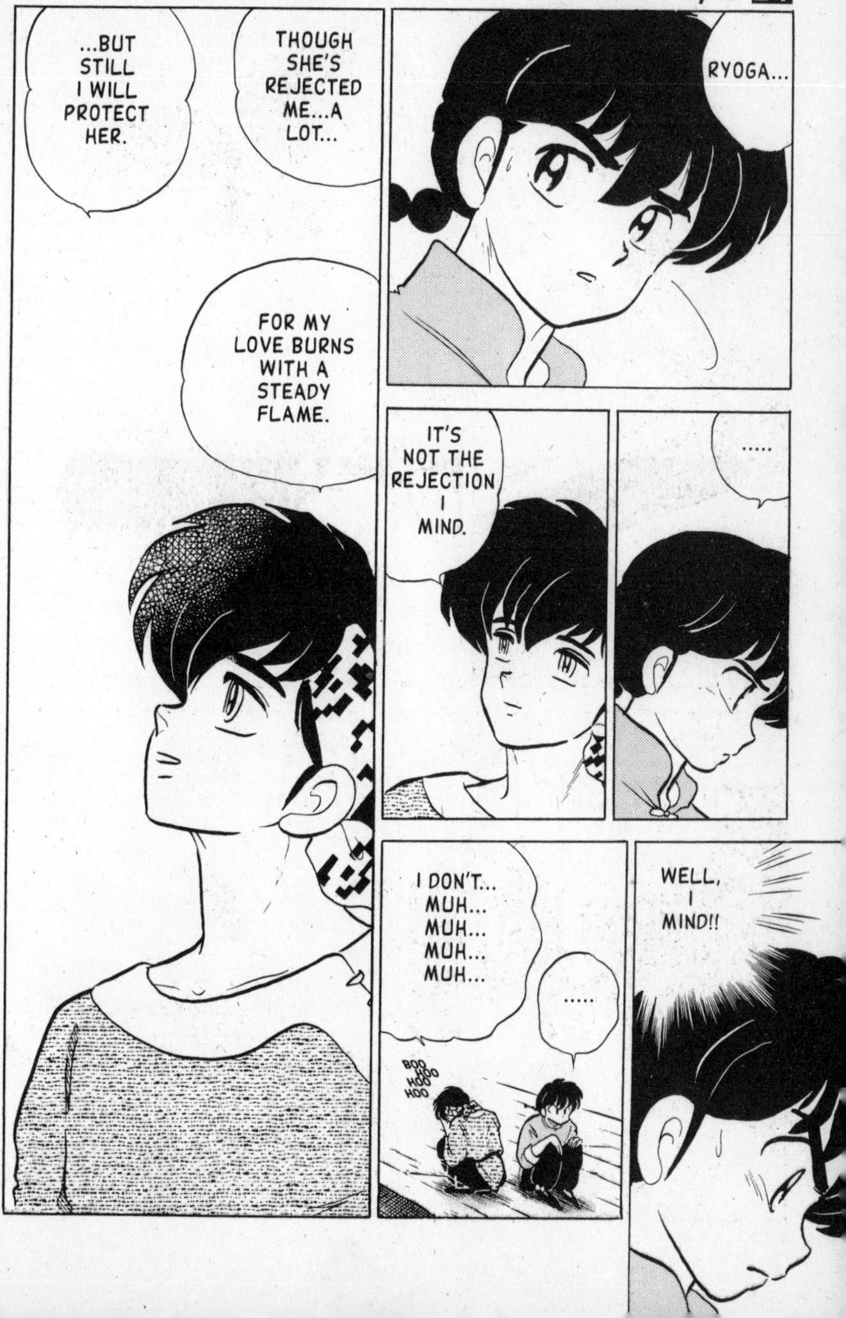
...BUT STILL I WILL PROTECT HER.
THOUGH SHE'S REJECTED ME...A LOT...
FOR MY LOVE BURNS WITH A STEADY FLAME.
RYOGA...
IT'S NOT THE REJECTION I MIND.
.....
I DON'T... MUH... MUH... MUH... MUH...
.....
BOO HOO HOO HOO
WELL, I MIND!!

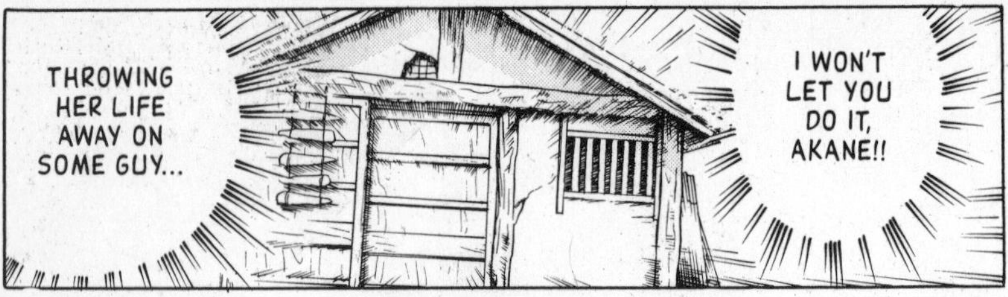
THROWING HER LIFE AWAY ON SOME GUY...
I WON'T LET YOU DO IT, AKANE!!
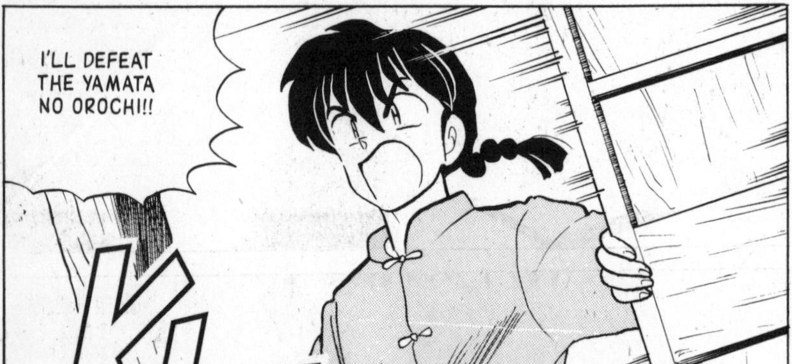
I'LL DEFEAT THE YAMATA NO OROCHI!!
KLATATT
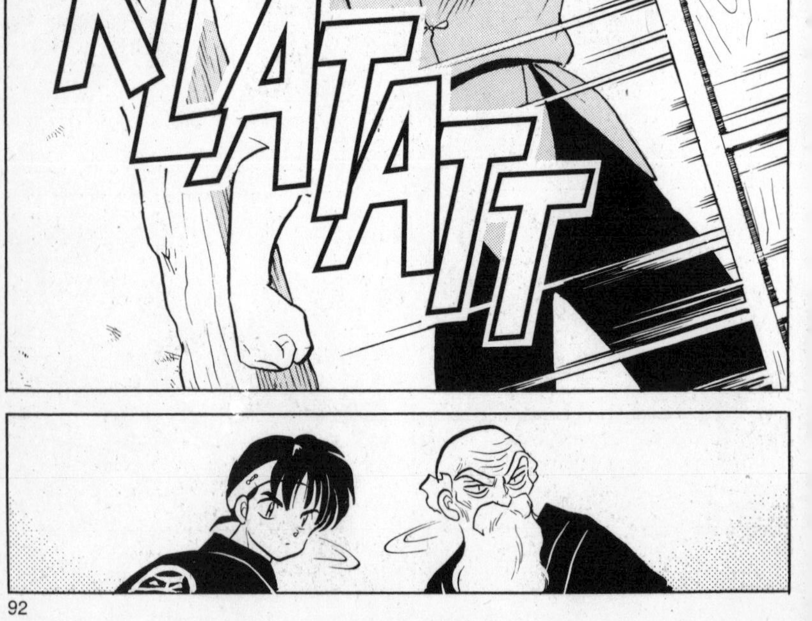

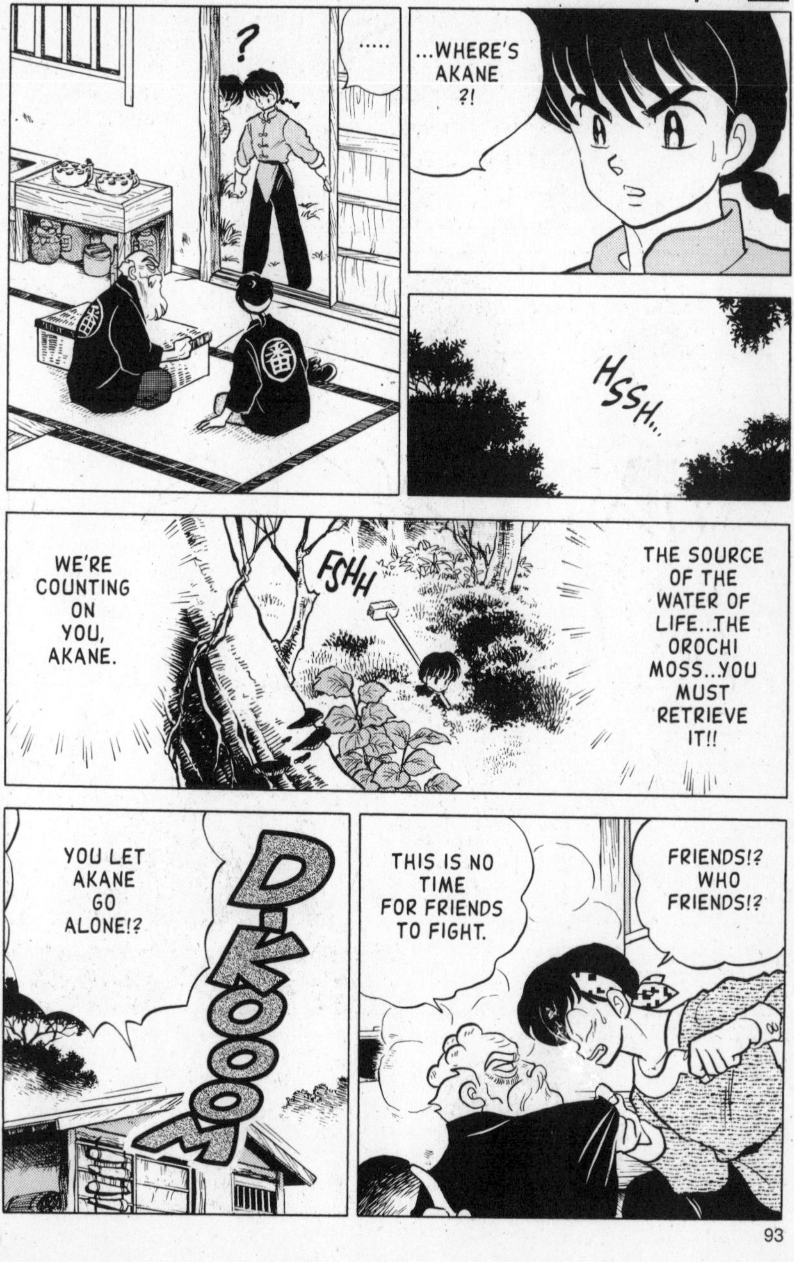
?
.....
...WHERE'S AKANE ?!
HSSH...
WE'RE COUNTING ON YOU, AKANE.
FSHH
THE SOURCE OF THE WATER OF LIFE...THE OROCHI MOSS...YOU MUST RETRIEVE IT!!
YOU LET AKANE GO ALONE!?
D-KOOOOM
THIS IS NO TIME FOR FRIENDS TO FIGHT.
FRIENDS!? WHO FRIENDS!?

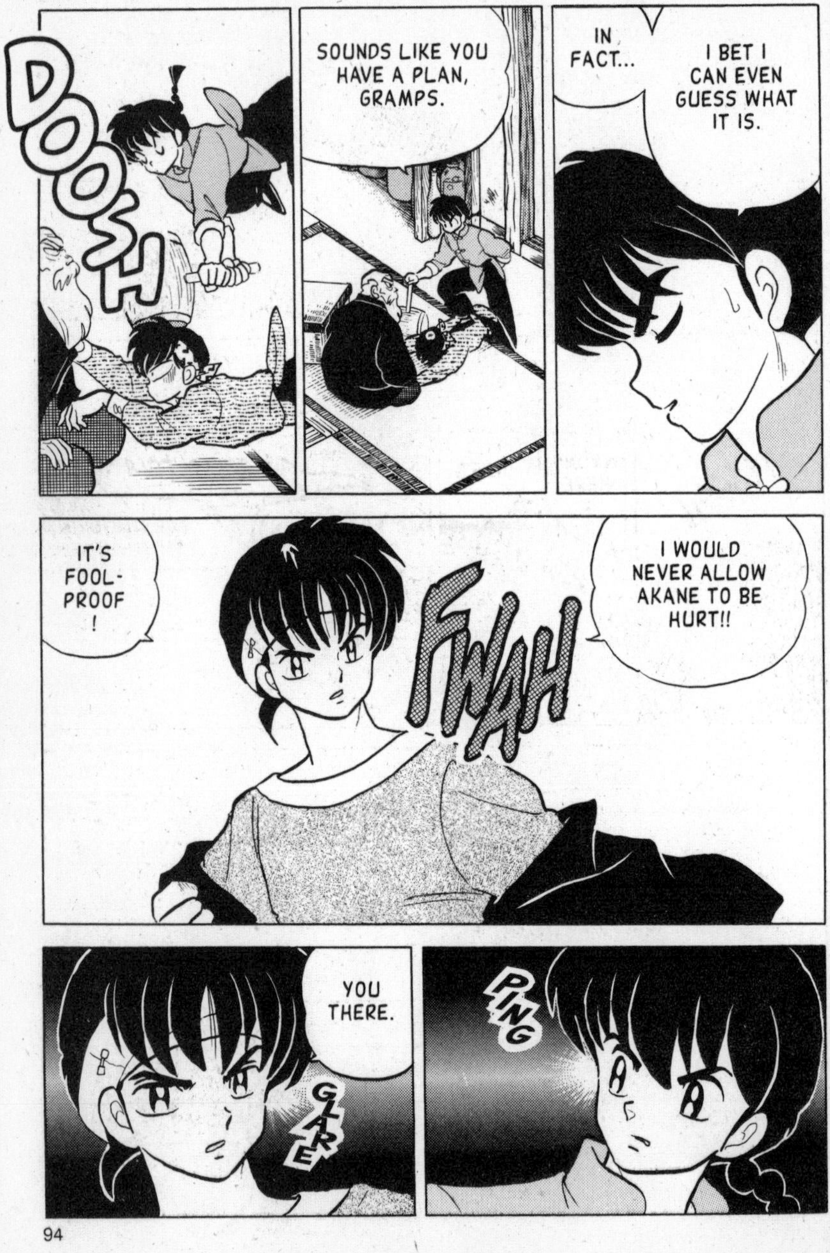
DOOSH
SOUNDS LIKE YOU HAVE A PLAN, GRAMPS.
IN FACT...
I BET I CAN EVEN GUESS WHAT IT IS.
IT'S FOOL-PROOF!
FWAH
I WOULD NEVER ALLOW AKANE TO BE HURT!!
YOU THERE.
GLARE
PING

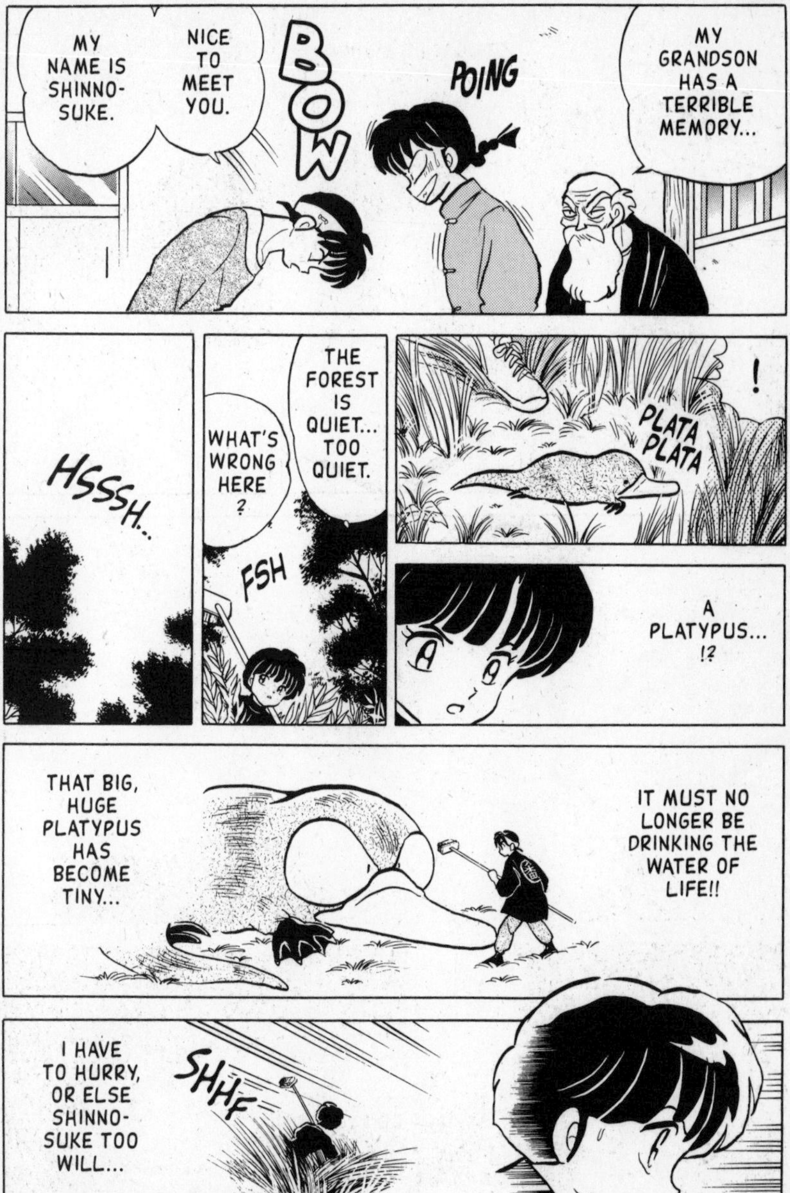
MY NAME IS SHINNO-SUKE.
NICE TO MEET YOU.
BOW
POING
MY GRANDSON HAS A TERRIBLE MEMORY...
HSSSH...
THE FOREST IS QUIET... TOO QUIET.
WHAT'S WRONG HERE ?
FSH
!
PLATA PLATA
A PLATYPUS... !?
THAT BIG, HUGE PLATYPUS HAS BECOME TINY...
IT MUST NO LONGER BE DRINKING THE WATER OF LIFE!!
I HAVE TO HURRY, OR ELSE SHINNO-SUKE TOO WILL...
SHHF

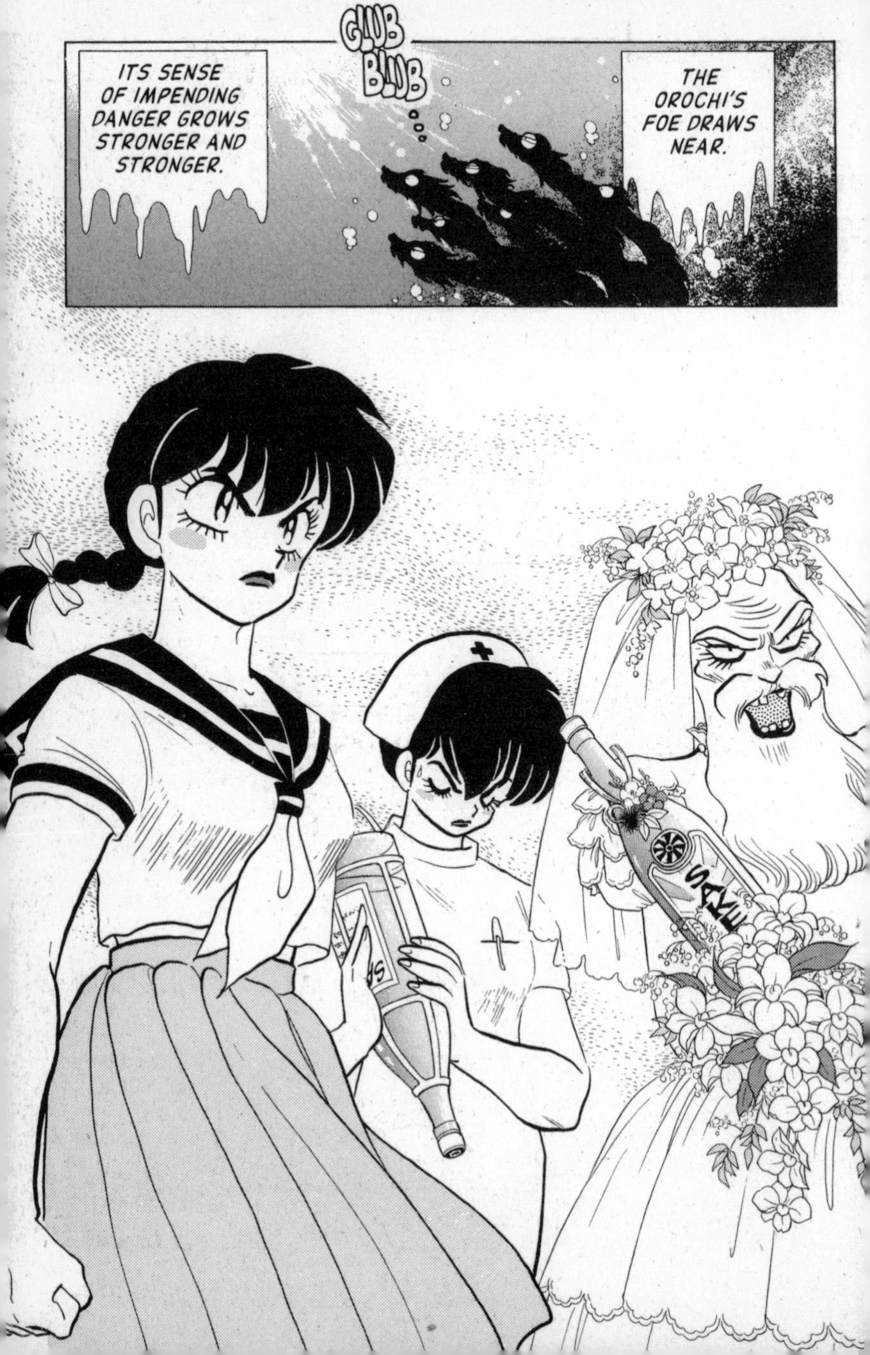
ITS SENSE OF IMPENDING DANGER GROWS STRONGER AND STRONGER.
GLUB BLUB
THE OROCHI'S FOE DRAWS NEAR.
SAKE

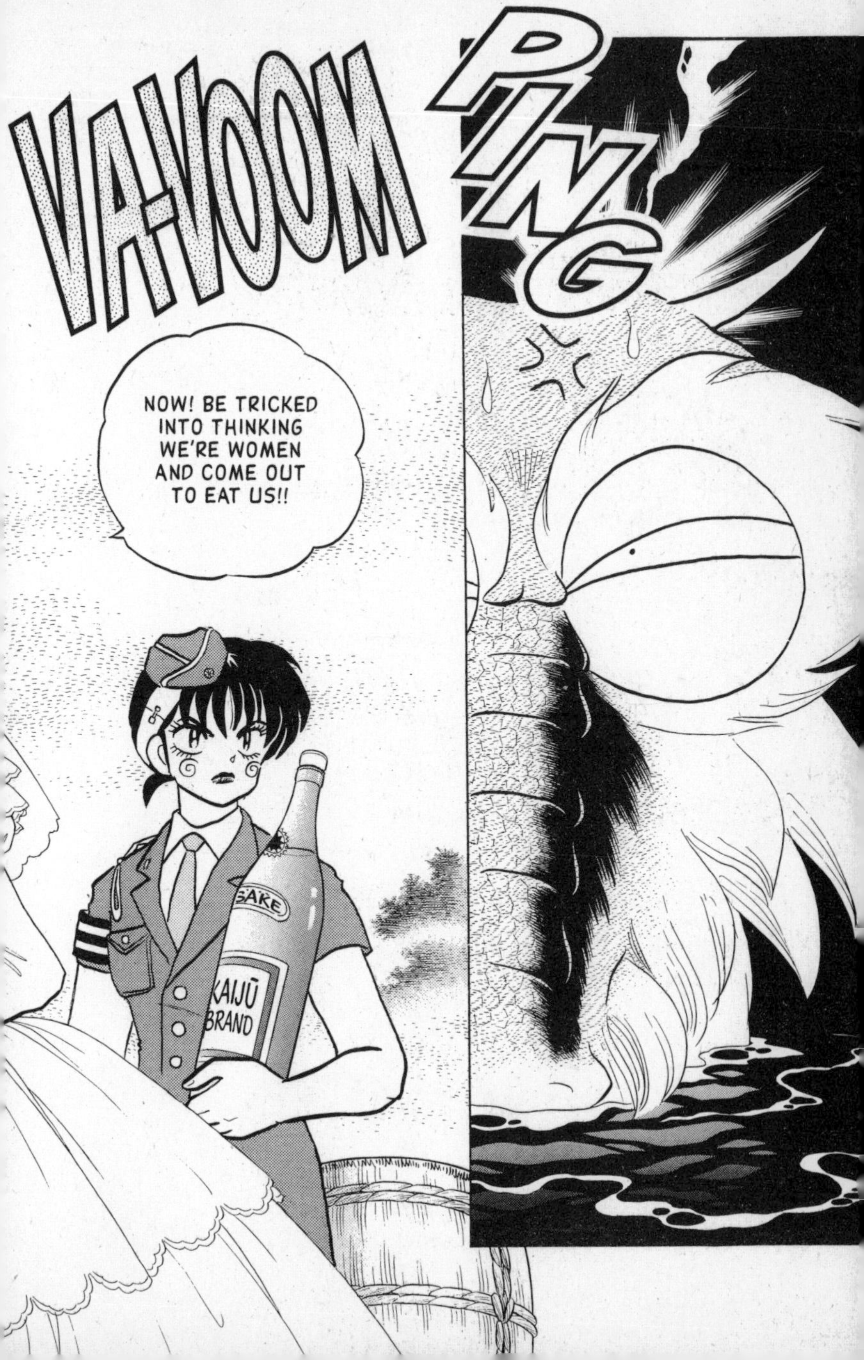
VA-VOOM
NOW! BE TRICKED INTO THINKING WE'RE WOMEN AND COME OUT TO EAT US!!
SAKE
KAIJŪ BRAND
PING

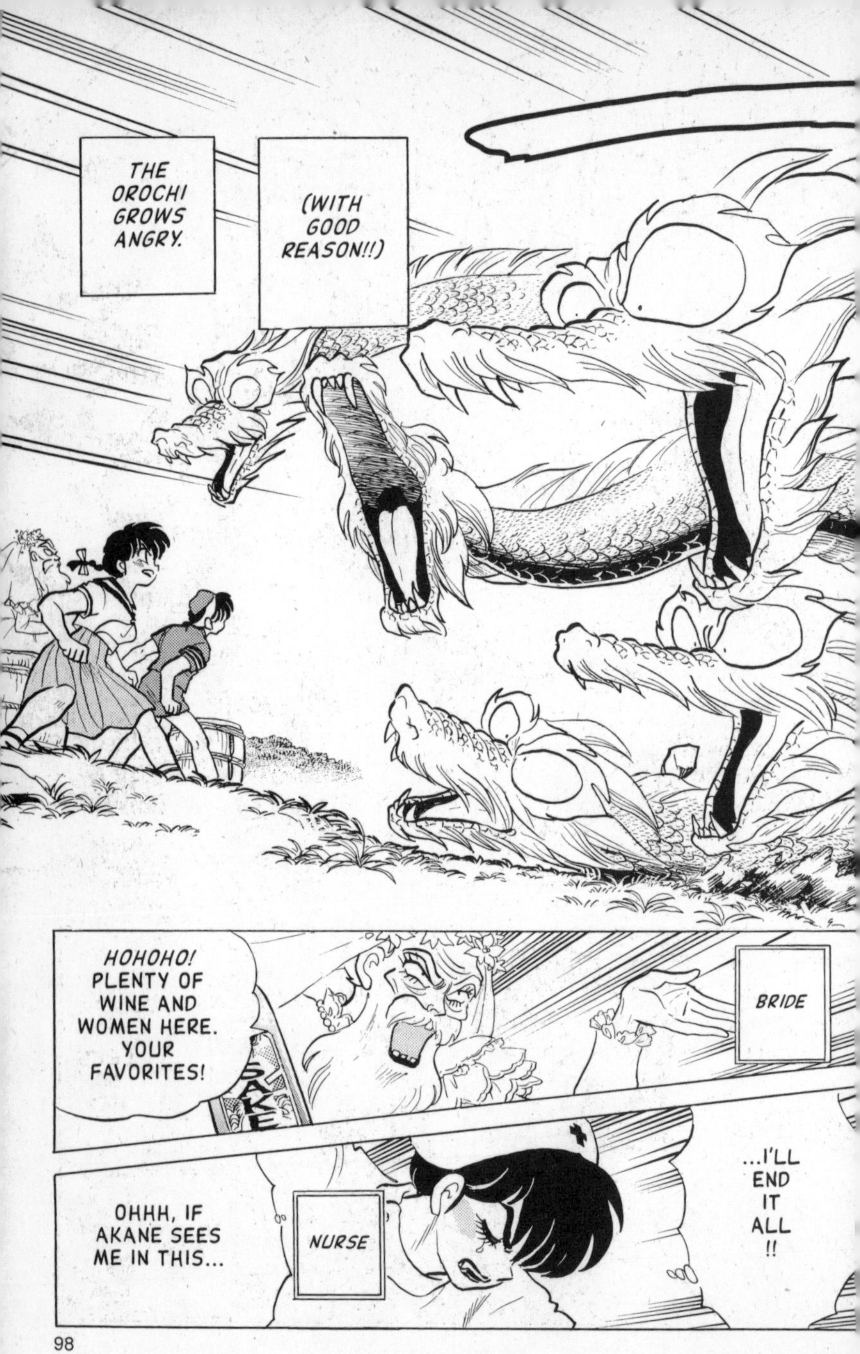
THE OROCHI GROWS ANGRY.
(WITH GOOD REASON!!)
HOHOHO! PLENTY OF WINE AND WOMEN HERE. YOUR FAVORITES!
SAKE
BRIDE
OHHH, IF AKANE SEES ME IN THIS...
NURSE
...I'LL END IT ALL !!

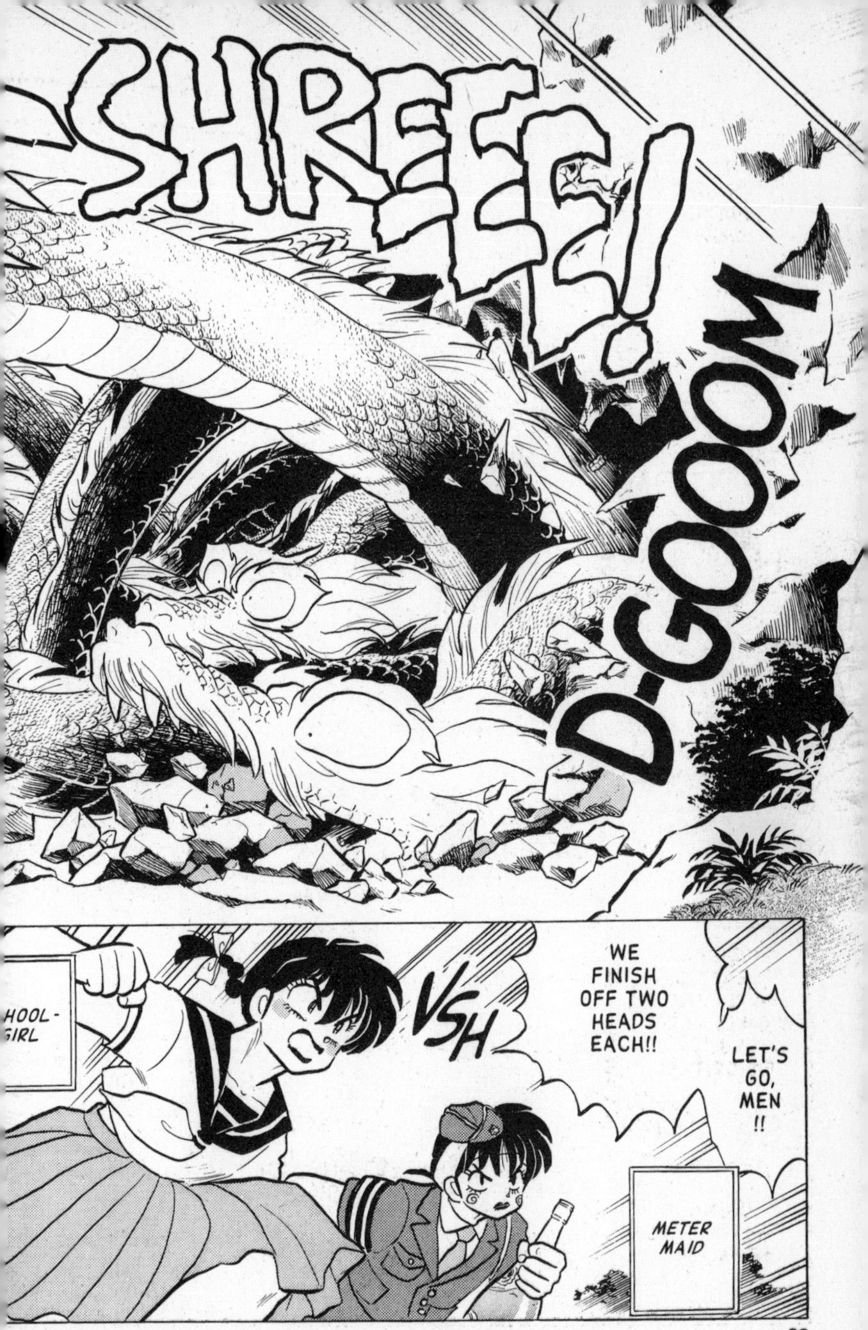
SHREEE!
D-GOOOM
HOOL-GIRL
VSH
WE FINISH OFF TWO HEADS EACH!!
LET'S GO, MEN !!
METER MAID

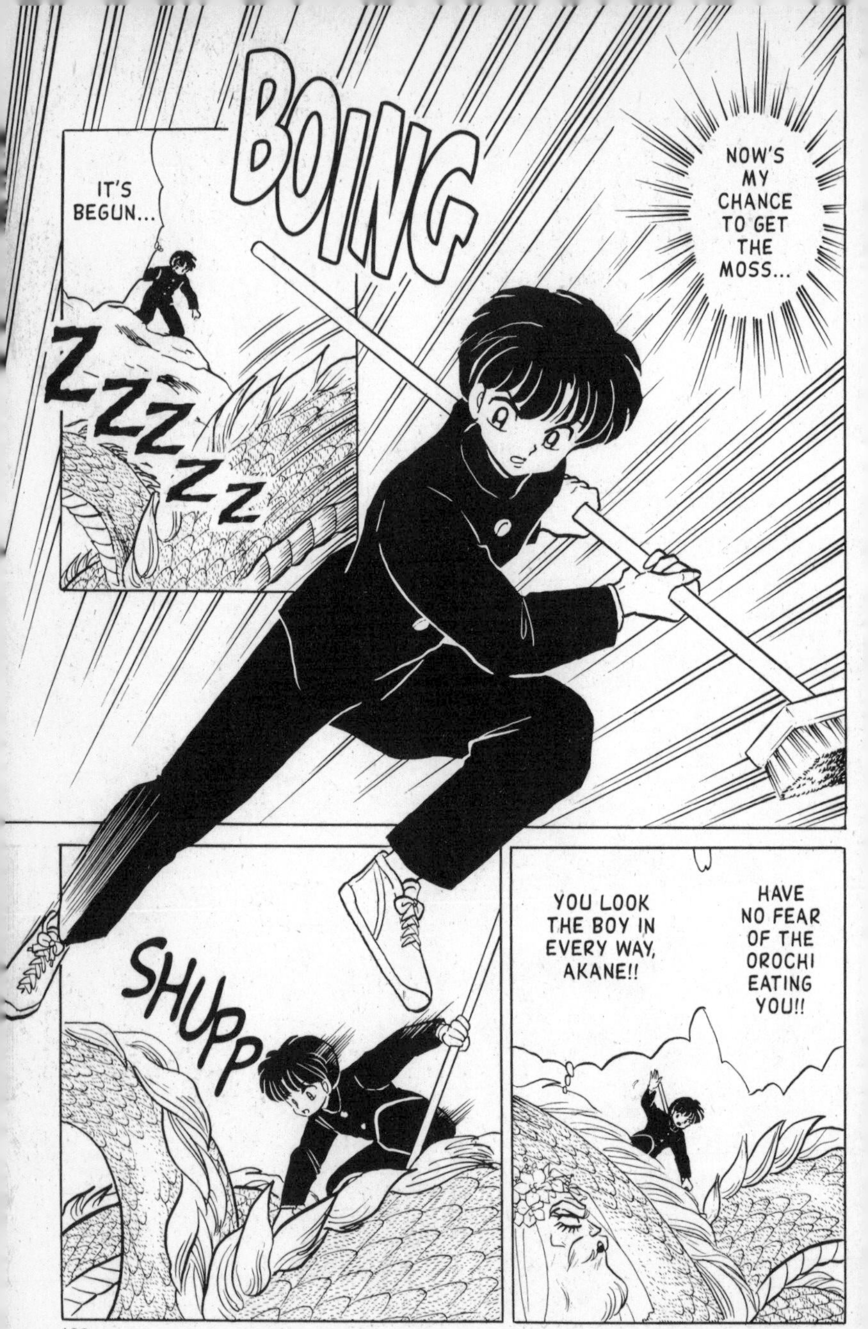
IT'S BEGUN...
ZZZZZZ
BOING
NOW'S MY CHANCE TO GET THE MOSS...
SHUPP
YOU LOOK THE BOY IN EVERY WAY, AKANE!!
HAVE NO FEAR OF THE OROCHI EATING YOU!!

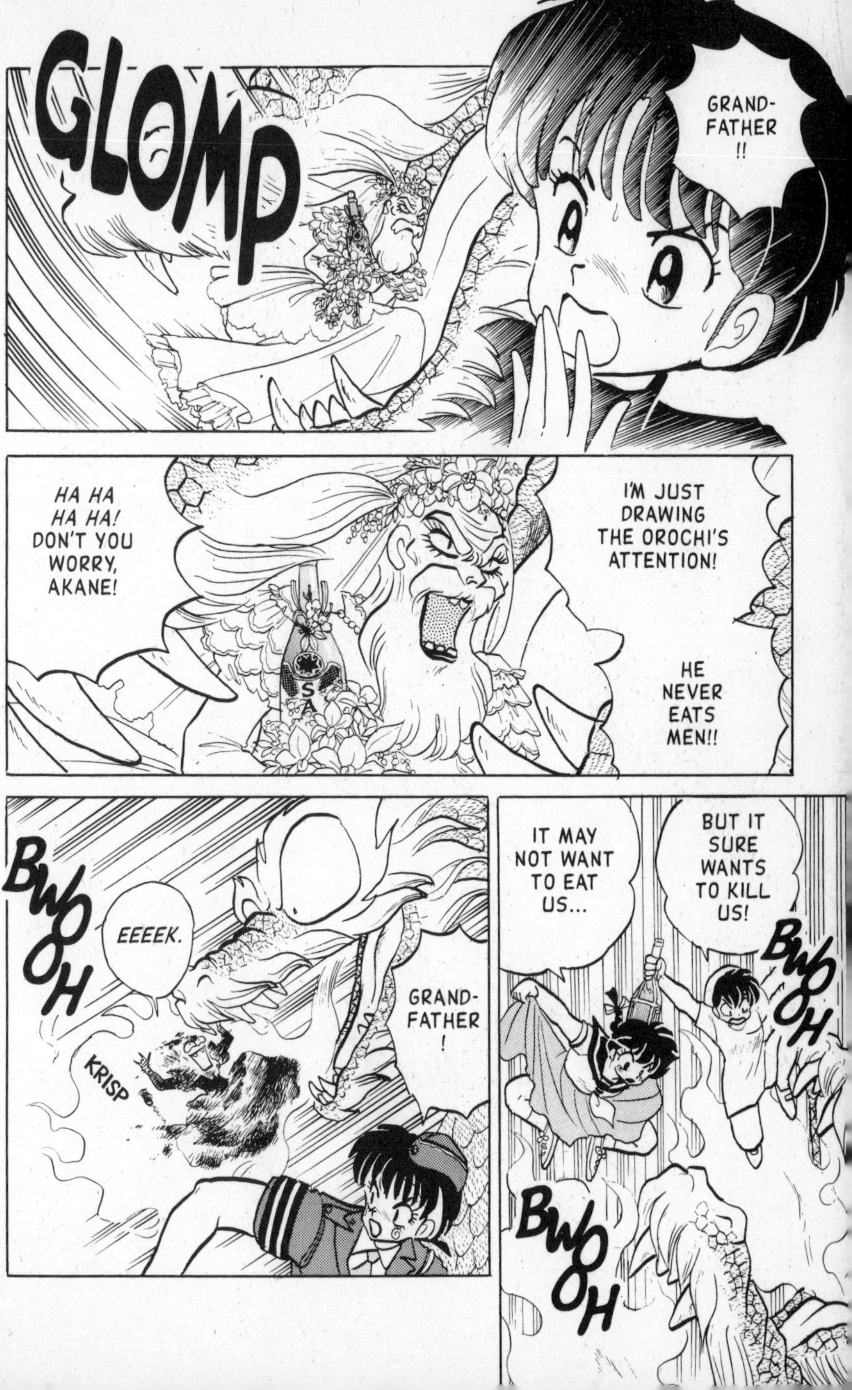
GLOMP
GRAND-FATHER !!
HA HA HA HA! DON'T YOU WORRY, AKANE!
I'M JUST DRAWING THE OROCHI'S ATTENTION!
HE NEVER EATS MEN!!
BWOOH
EEEEK.
KRISP
GRAND-FATHER !
IT MAY NOT WANT TO EAT US...
BUT IT SURE WANTS TO KILL US!
BWOOH
BWOOH

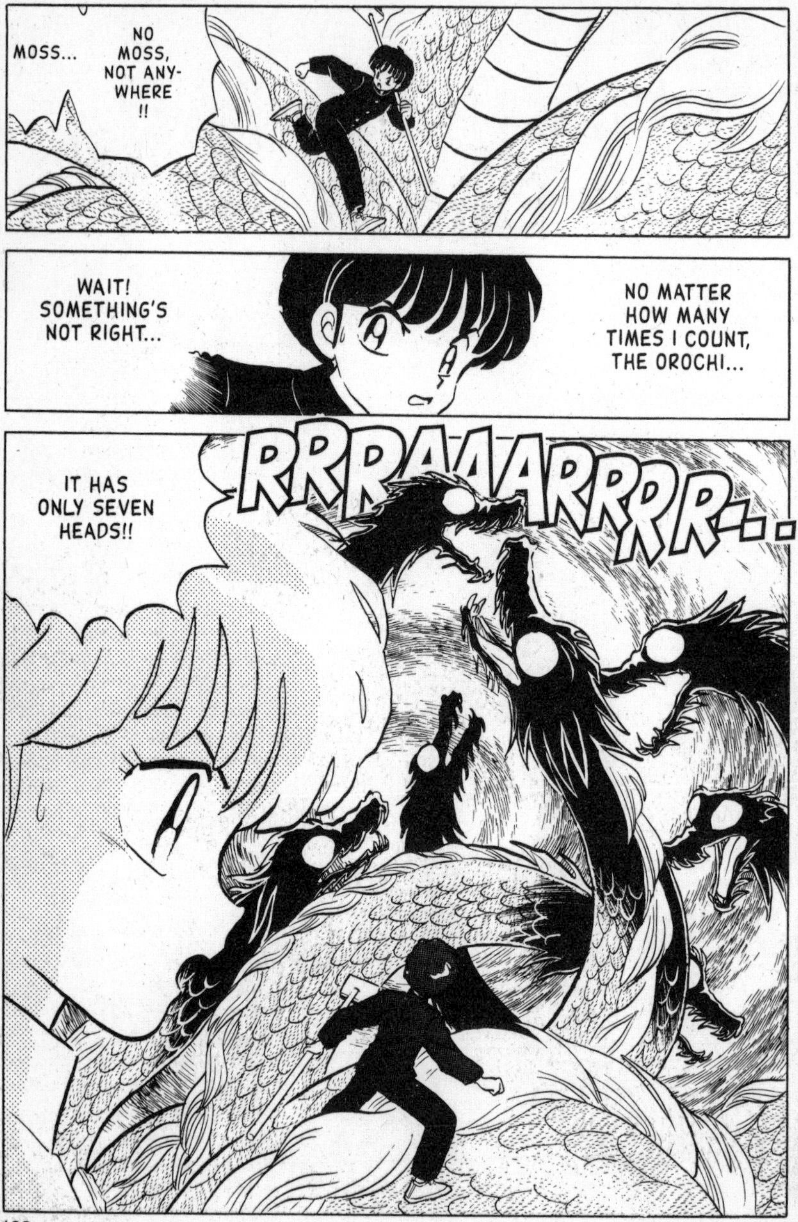
MOSS...
NO MOSS, NOT ANYWHERE !!
WAIT! SOMETHING'S NOT RIGHT...
NO MATTER HOW MANY TIMES I COUNT, THE OROCHI...
IT HAS ONLY SEVEN HEADS!!
RRRAAARRRRR...

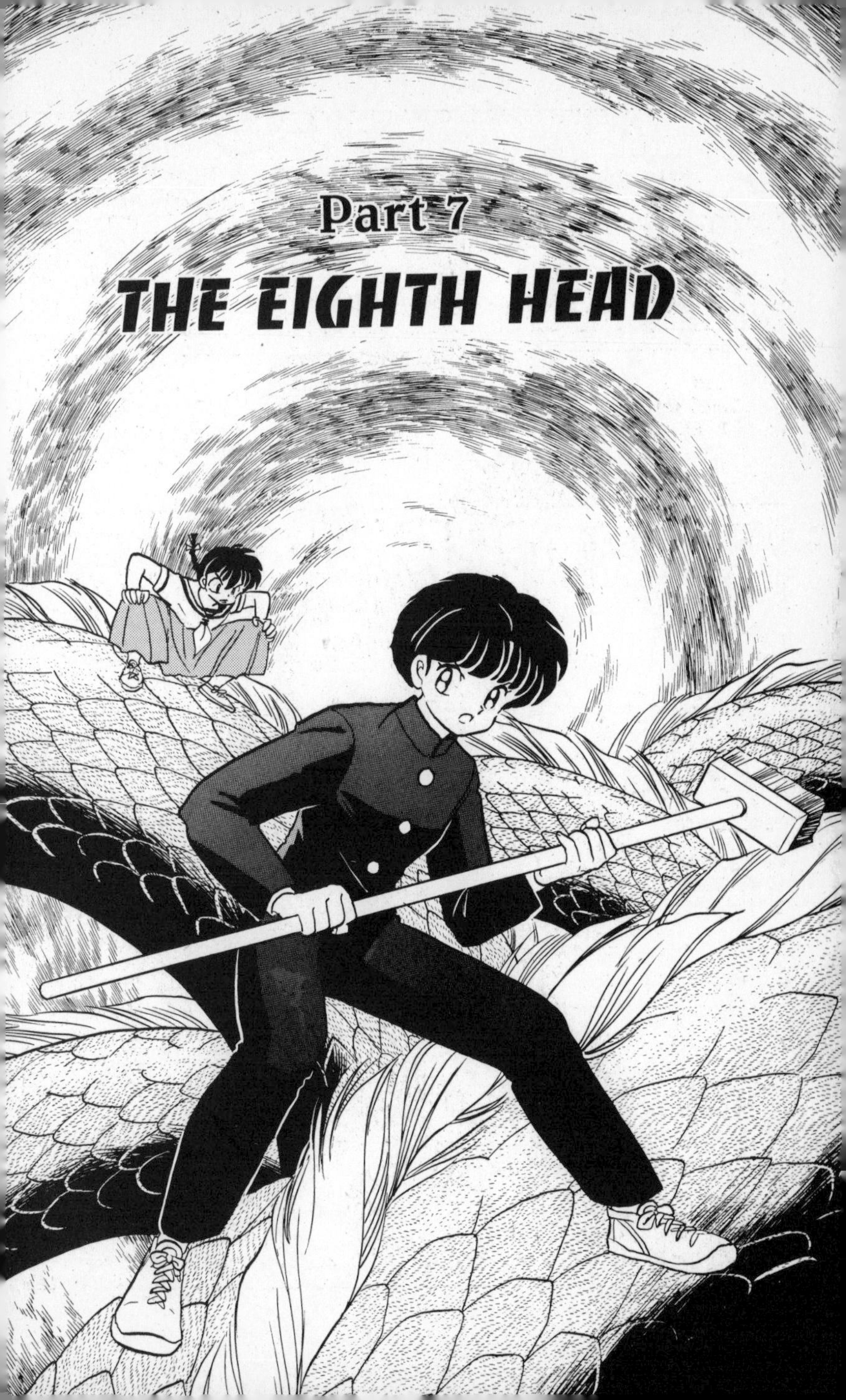
Part 7
THE EIGHTH HEAD

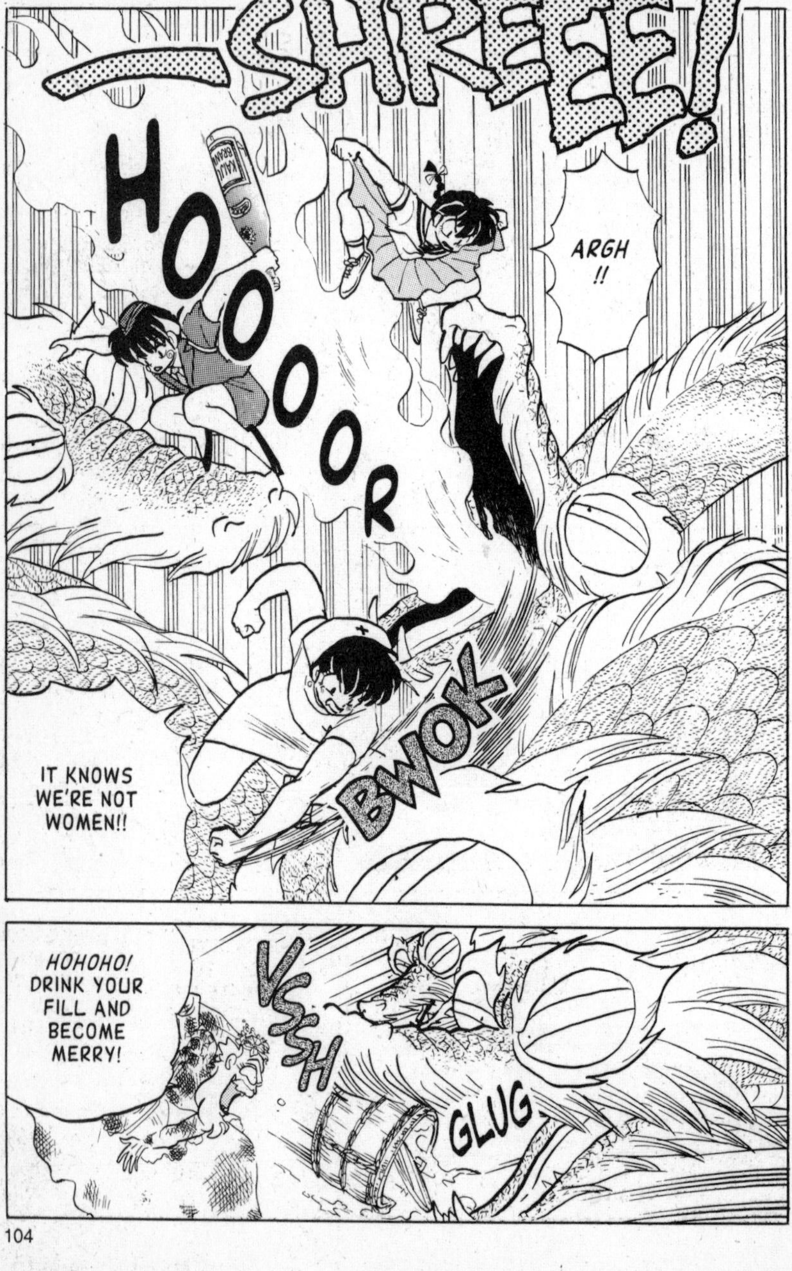
SHREEE!
HOOOOOR
ARGH !!
BWOK
IT KNOWS WE'RE NOT WOMEN!!
HOHOHO! DRINK YOUR FILL AND BECOME MERRY!
VSSH
GLUG

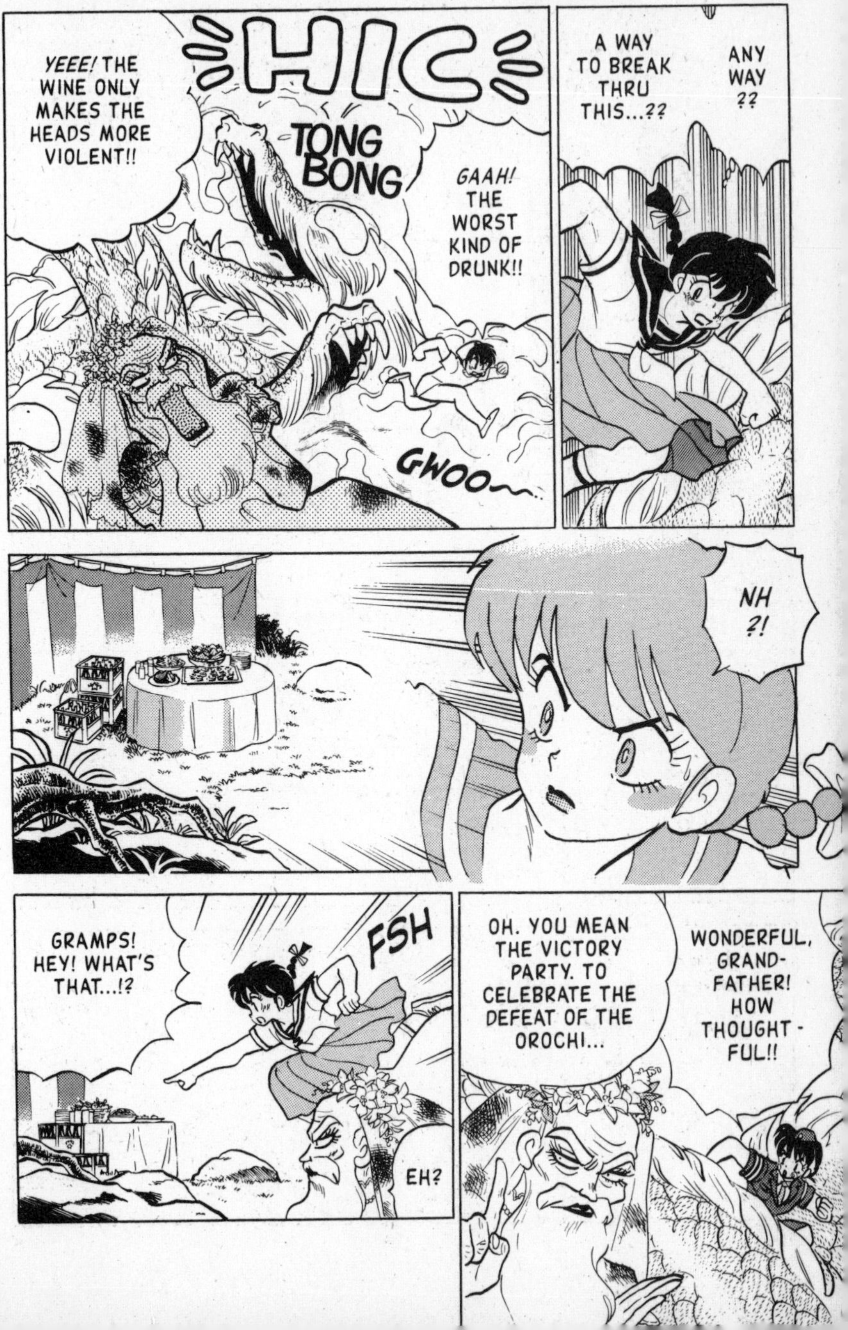
HIC
YEEE! THE WINE ONLY MAKES THE HEADS MORE VIOLENT!!
TONG BONG
GAAH! THE WORST KIND OF DRUNK!!
GWOO~
A WAY TO BREAK THRU THIS...??
ANY WAY ??
NH ?!
GRAMPS! HEY! WHAT'S THAT...!?
FSH
EH?
OH. YOU MEAN THE VICTORY PARTY. TO CELEBRATE THE DEFEAT OF THE OROCHI...
WONDERFUL, GRAND-FATHER! HOW THOUGHT-FUL!!

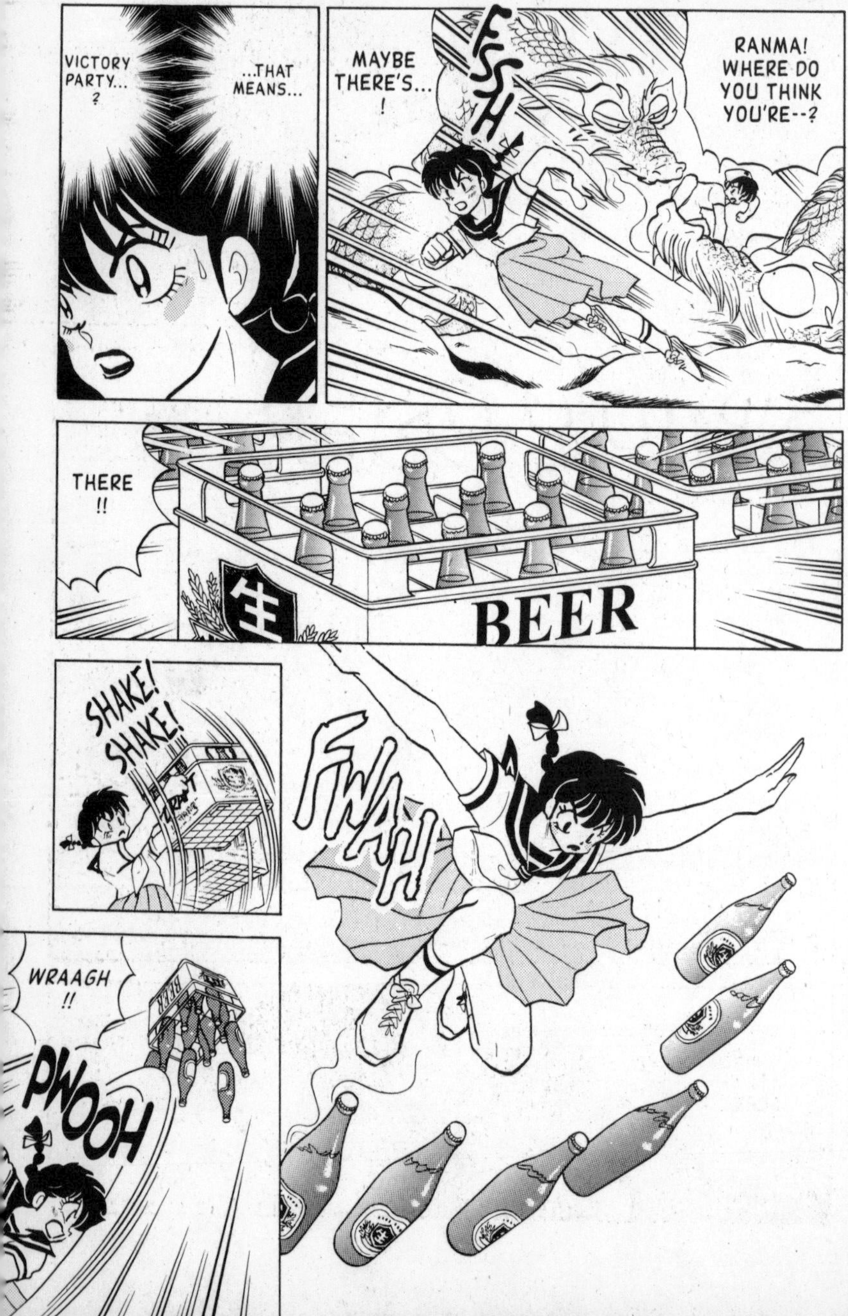
VICTORY PARTY...?
...THAT MEANS...
MAYBE THERE'S...!
FSSH
RANMA! WHERE DO YOU THINK YOU'RE--?
THERE!!
生
BEER
SHAKE! SHAKE!
FWAH
WRAAGH!!
PWOOH

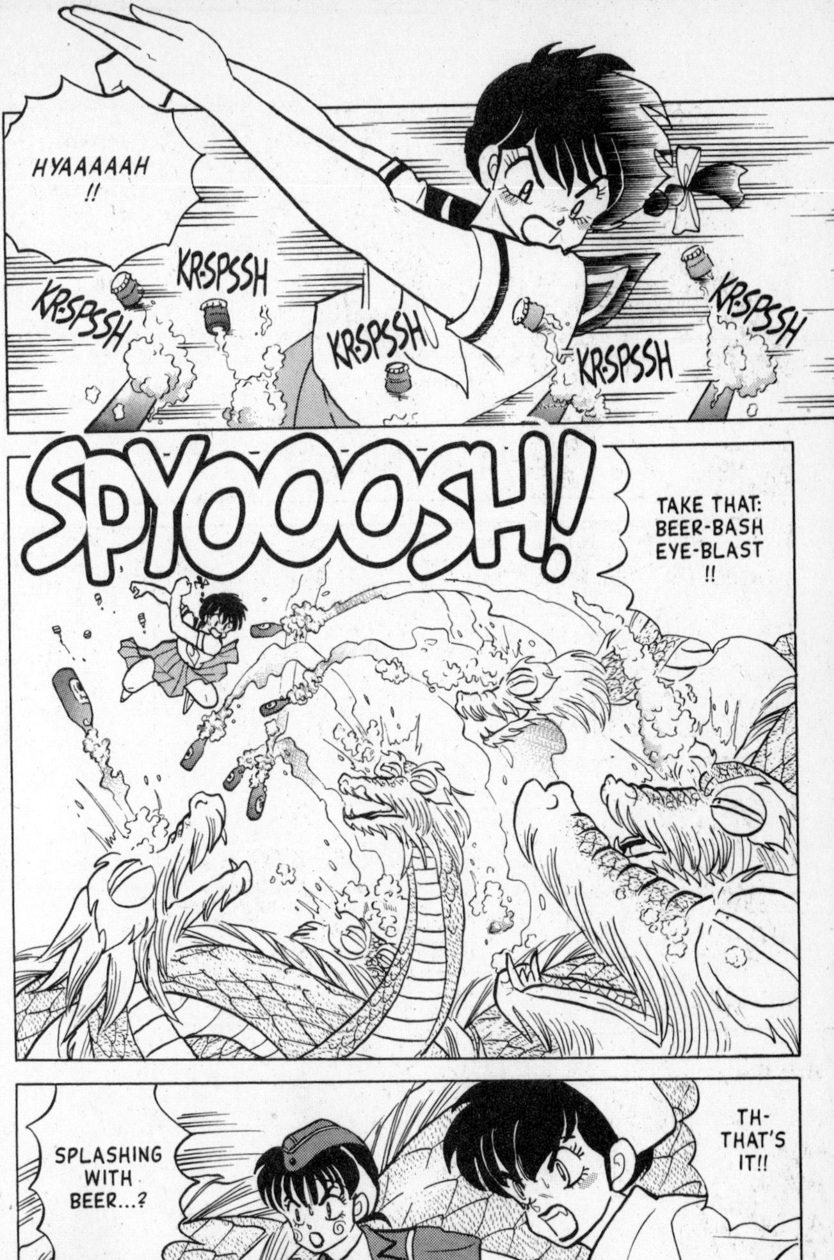
HYAAAAAH !!
KR-SPSSH
KR-SPSSH
KR-SPSSH
KR-SPSSH
KR-SPSSH
SPYOOOSH!
TAKE THAT: BEER-BASH EYE-BLAST !!
SPLASHING WITH BEER...?
TH- THAT'S IT!!

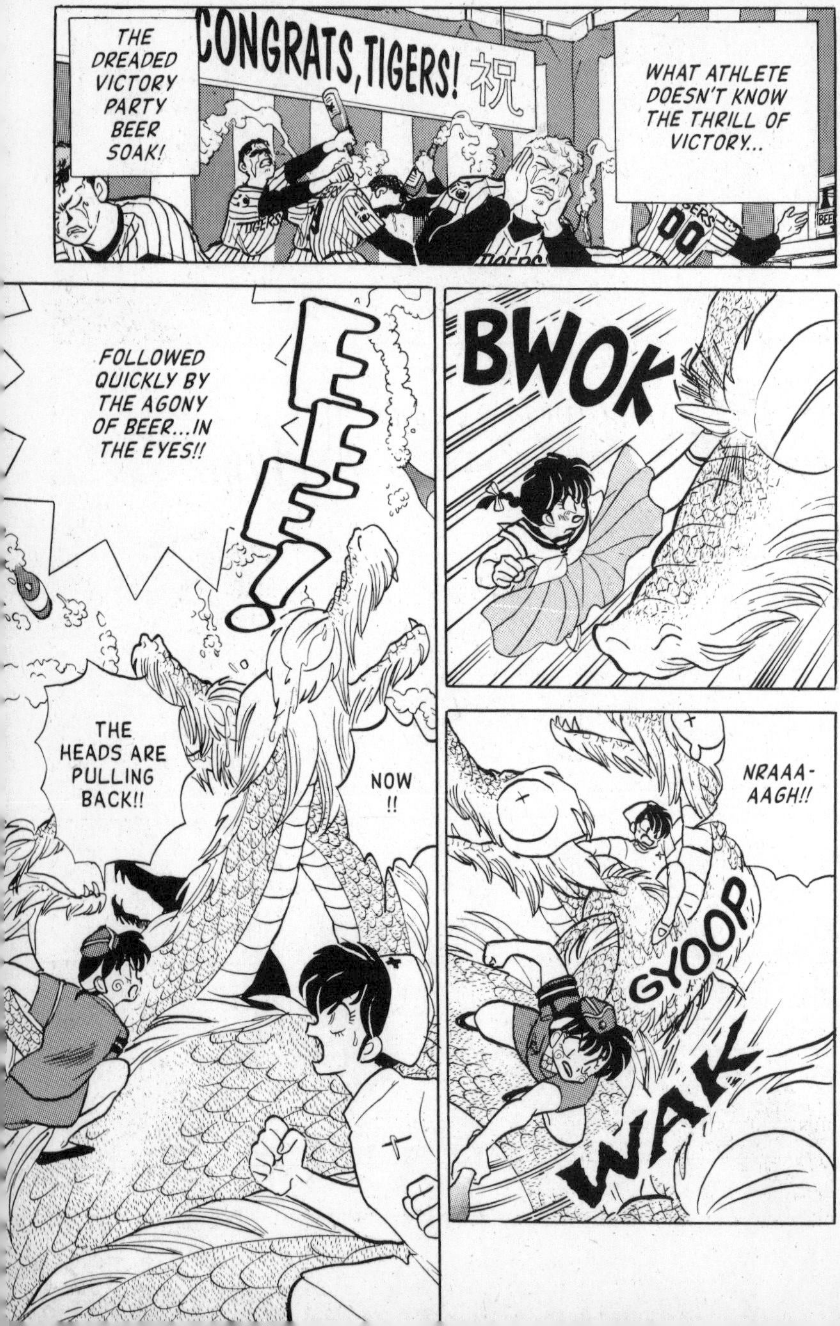
THE DREADED VICTORY PARTY BEER SOAK!
CONGRATS, TIGERS! 祝
WHAT ATHLETE DOESN'T KNOW THE THRILL OF VICTORY...
FOLLOWED QUICKLY BY THE AGONY OF BEER...IN THE EYES!!
EEEE!
THE HEADS ARE PULLING BACK!!
NOW !!
BWOK
NRAAA-AAGH!!
GYOOP
WAK

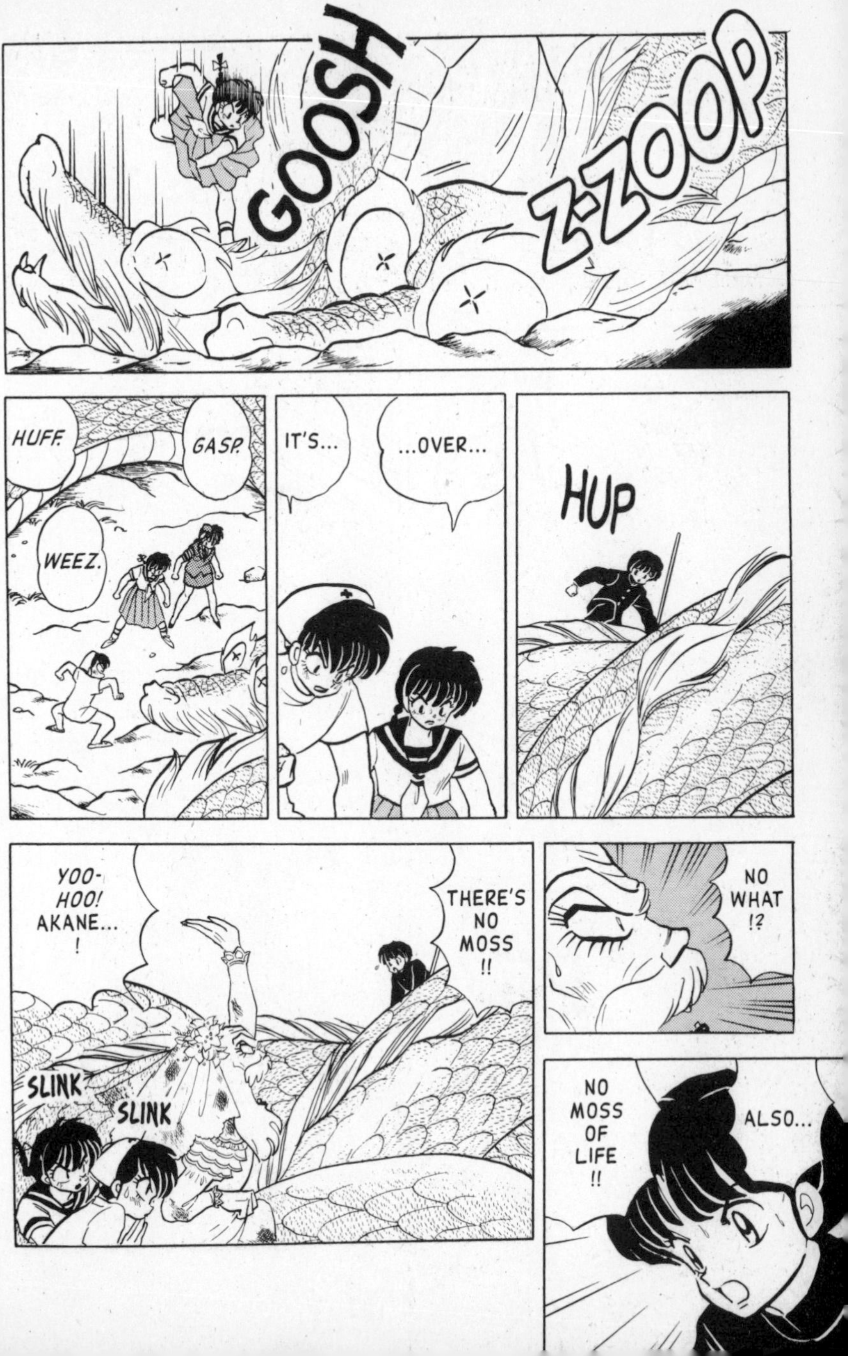
GOOSH
Z-ZOOP
HUFF.
GASP.
WEEZ.
IT'S...
...OVER...
HUP
YOO-HOO! AKANE... !
THERE'S NO MOSS !!
SLINK
SLINK
NO WHAT !?
NO MOSS OF LIFE !!
ALSO...

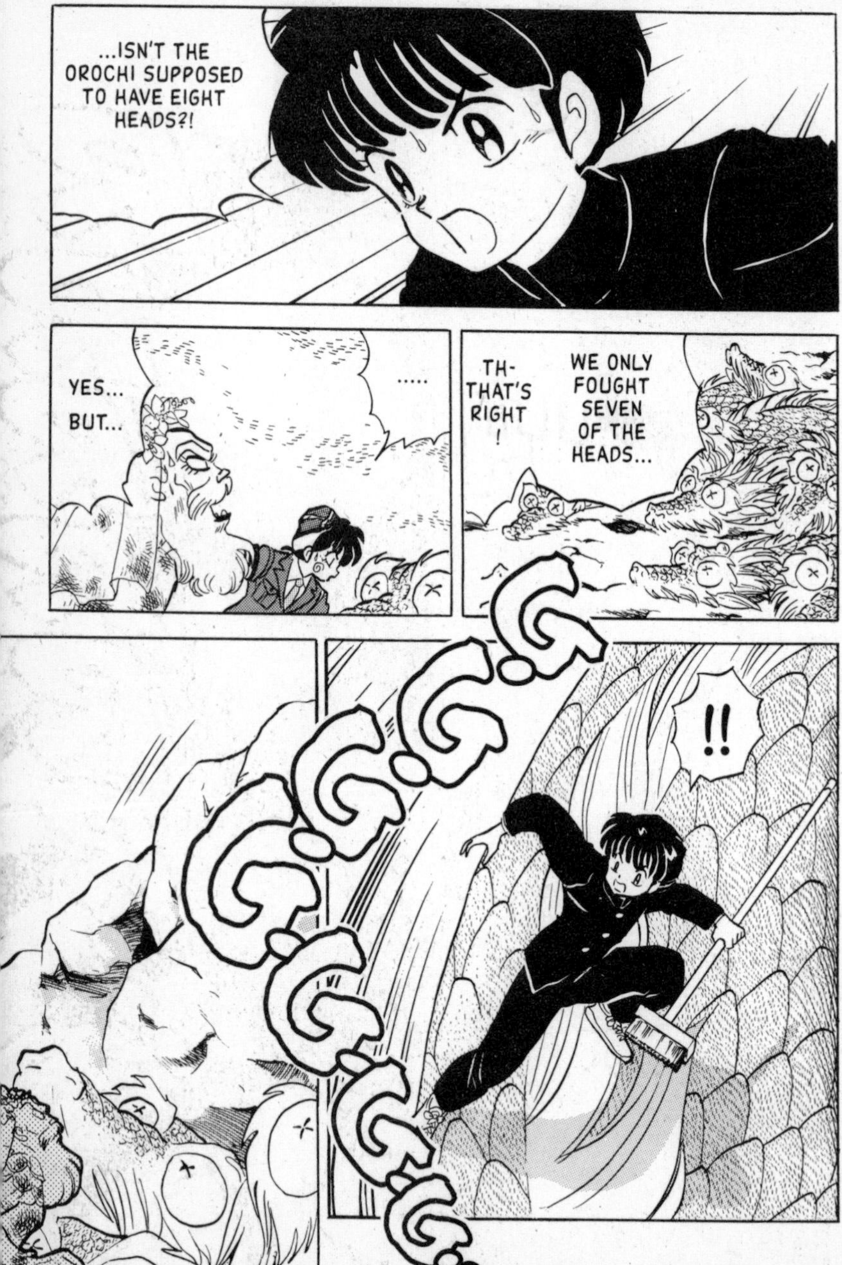
...ISN'T THE OROCHI SUPPOSED TO HAVE EIGHT HEADS?!
YES... BUT...
.....
WE ONLY FOUGHT SEVEN OF THE HEADS...
TH-THAT'S RIGHT!
!!

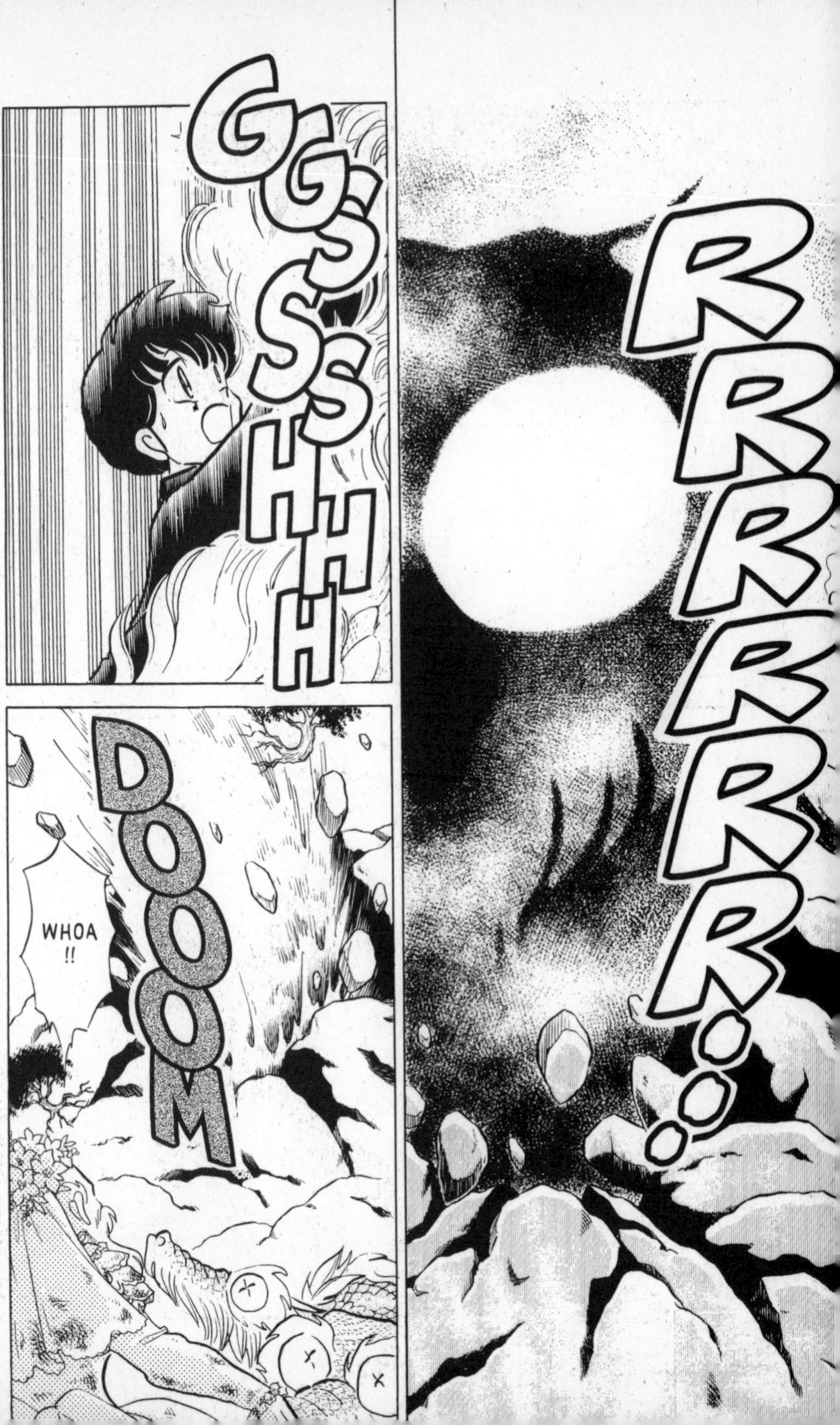
RRRRRRR...
GGSSHHHH
DOOOOM
WHOA !!

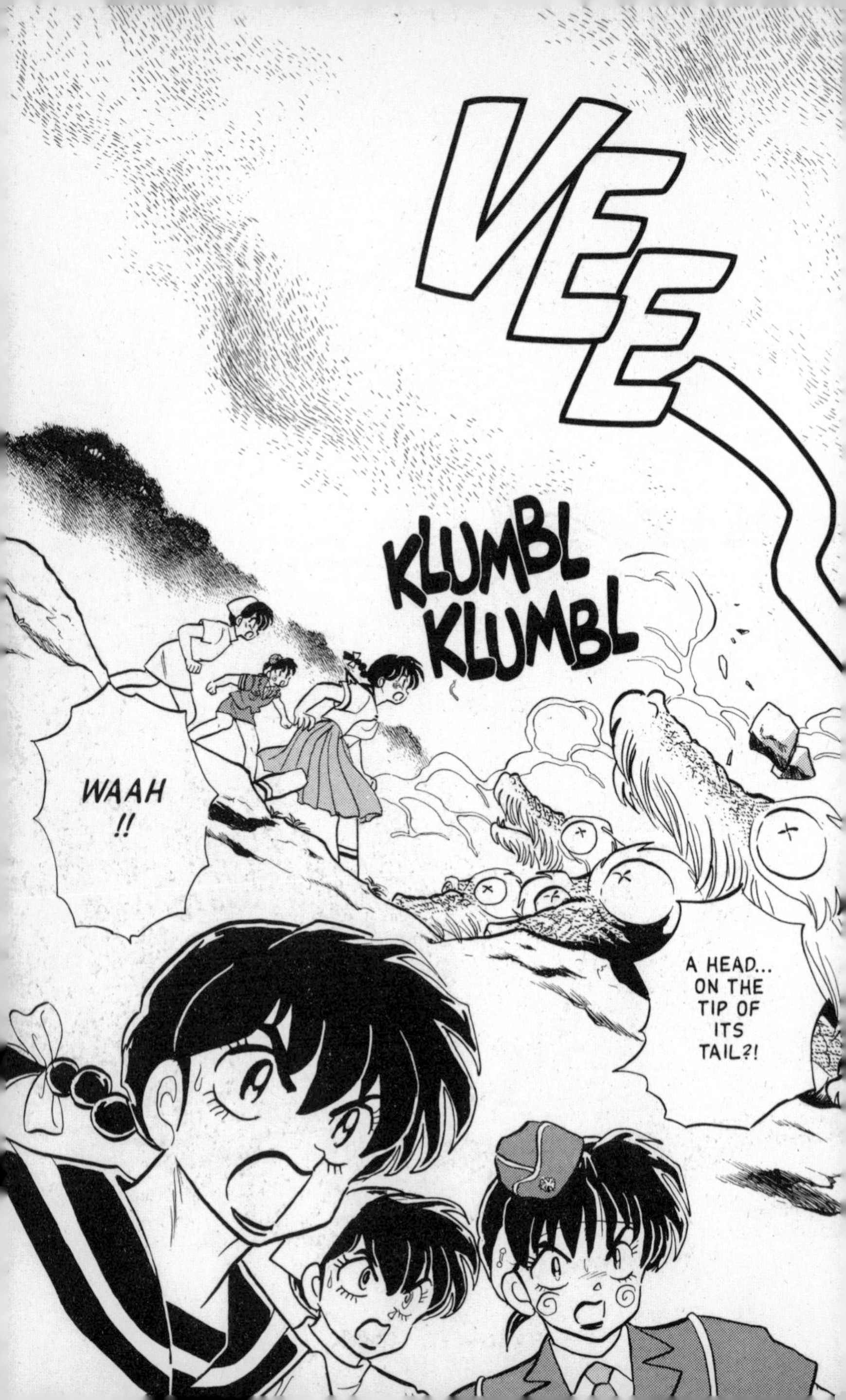
VEEE
KLUMBL KLUMBL
WAAH !!
A HEAD... ON THE TIP OF ITS TAIL?!

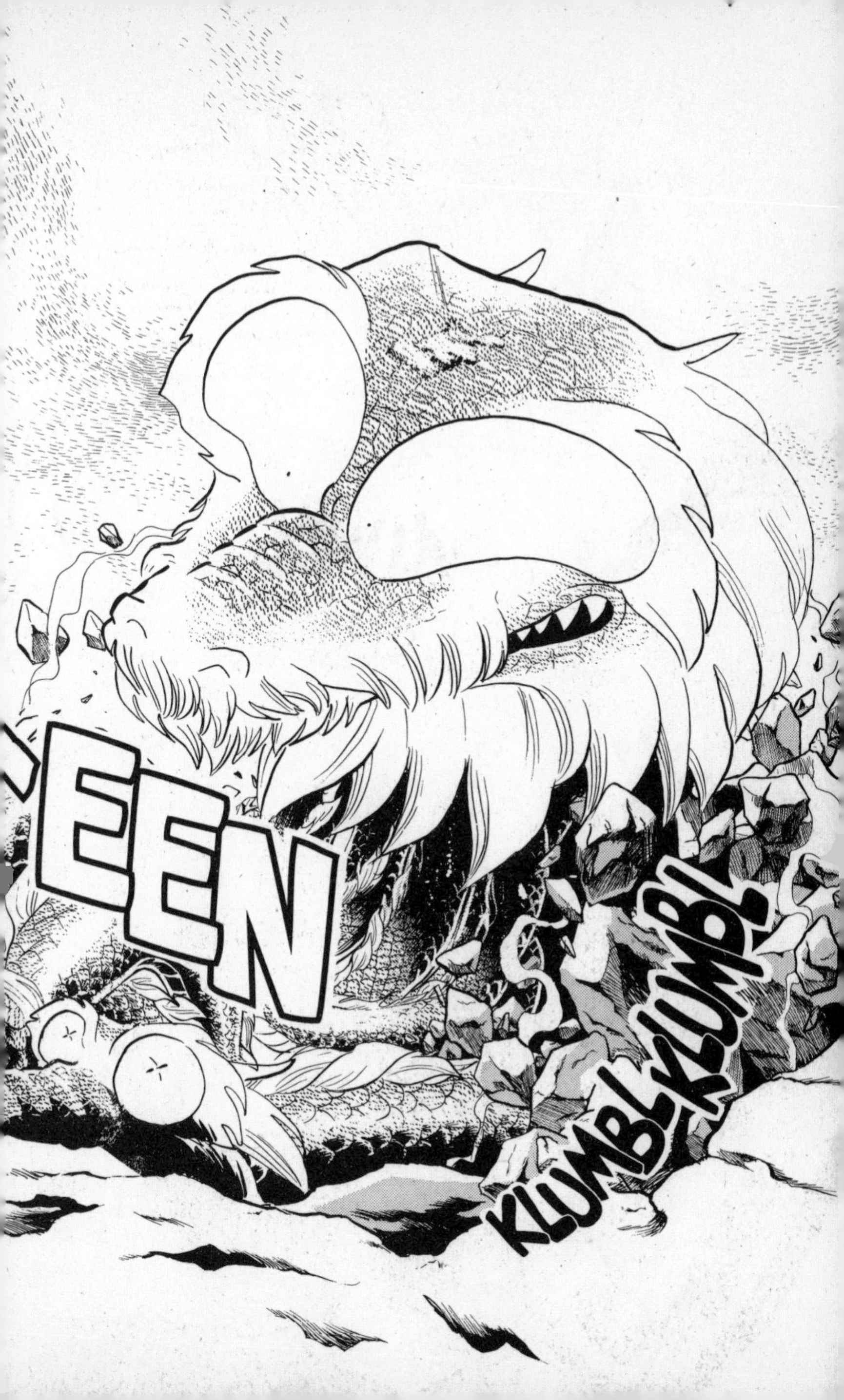
EEN
KLUMBL KLUMBL

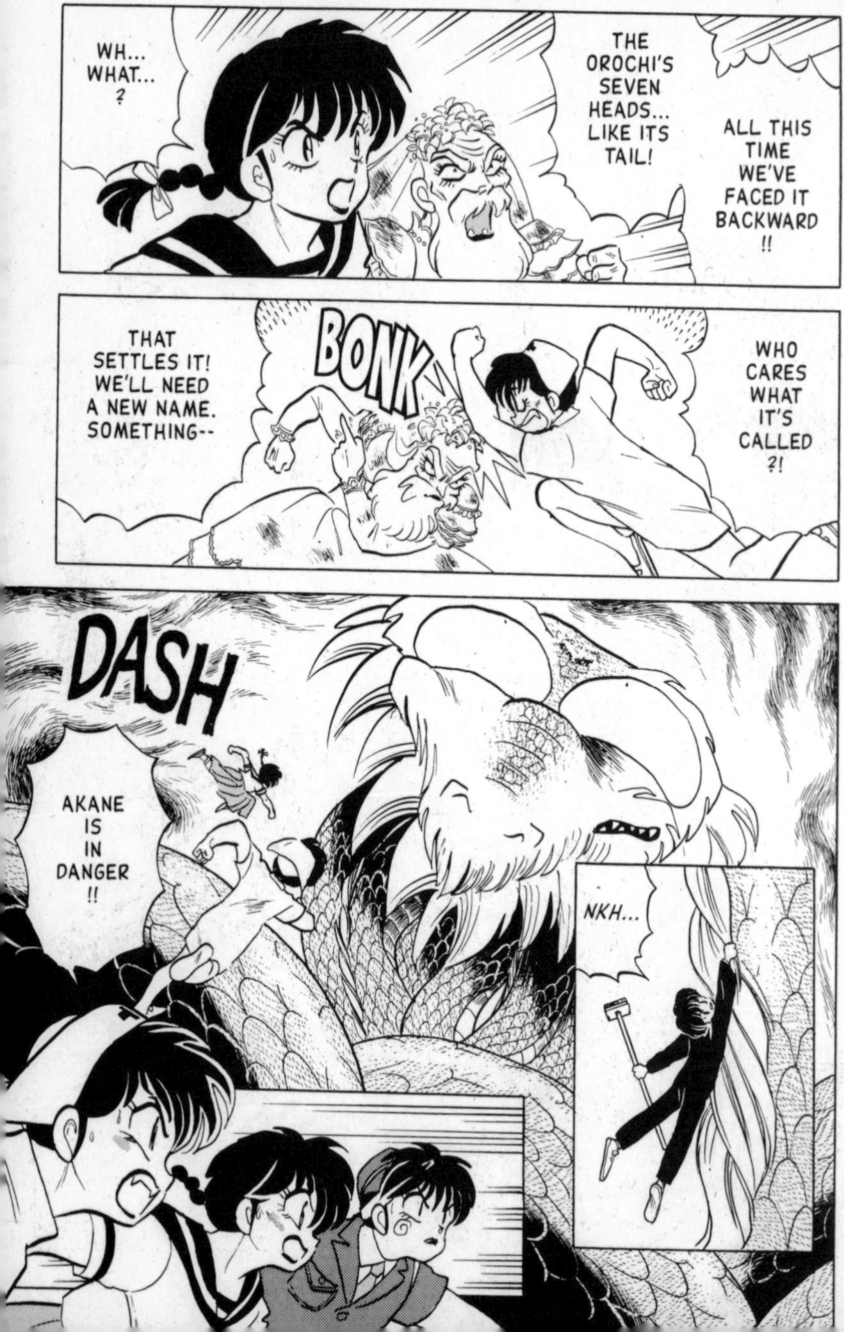
WH... WHAT... ?
THE OROCHI'S SEVEN HEADS... LIKE ITS TAIL!
ALL THIS TIME WE'VE FACED IT BACKWARD !!
THAT SETTLES IT! WE'LL NEED A NEW NAME. SOMETHING--
BONK
WHO CARES WHAT IT'S CALLED ?!
DASH
AKANE IS IN DANGER !!
NKH...

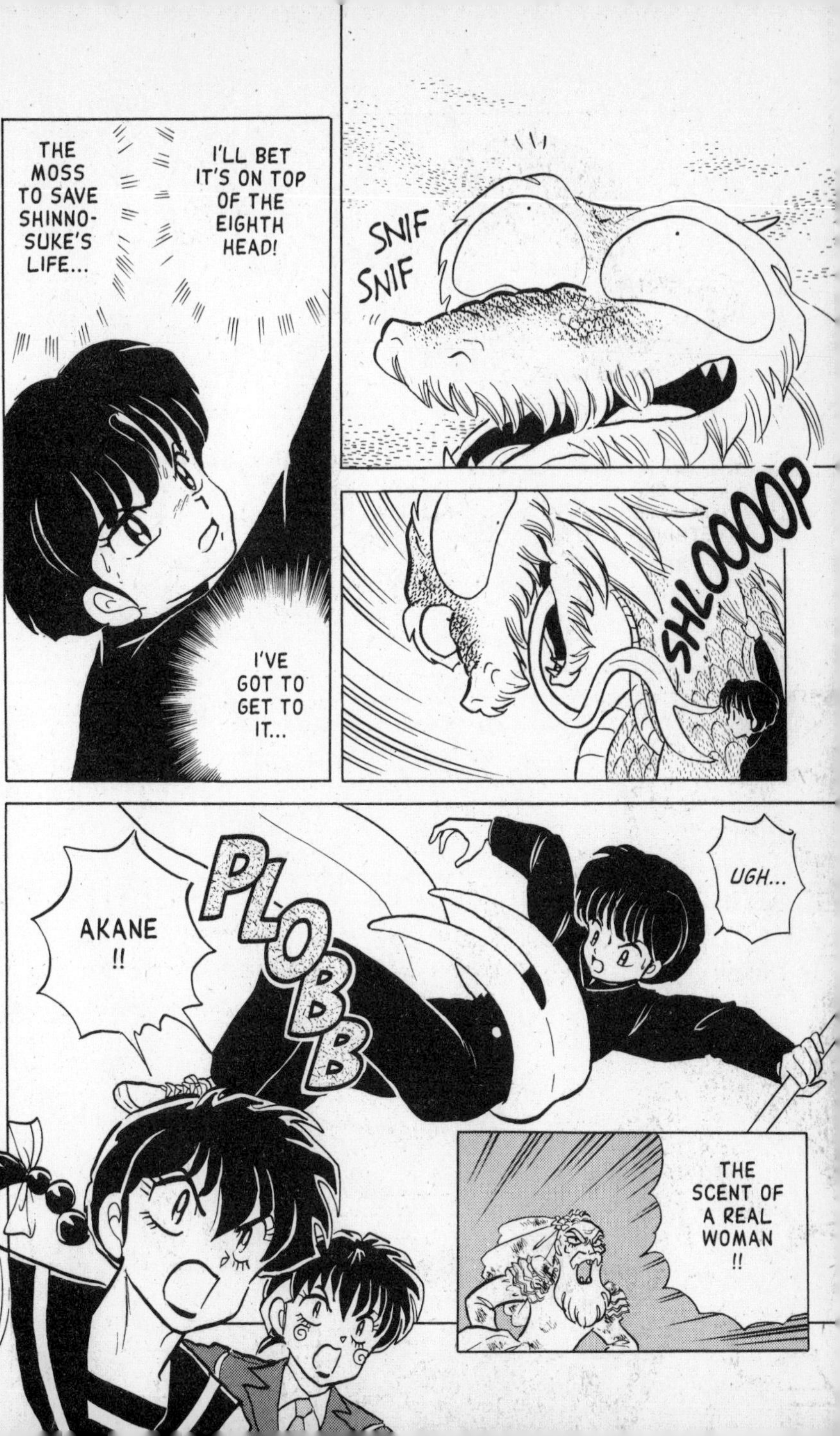
THE MOSS TO SAVE SHINNOSUKE'S LIFE...
I'LL BET IT'S ON TOP OF THE EIGHTH HEAD!
I'VE GOT TO GET TO IT...
SNIF SNIF
SHLOOOOP
AKANE !!
PLOBB
UGH...
THE SCENT OF A REAL WOMAN !!

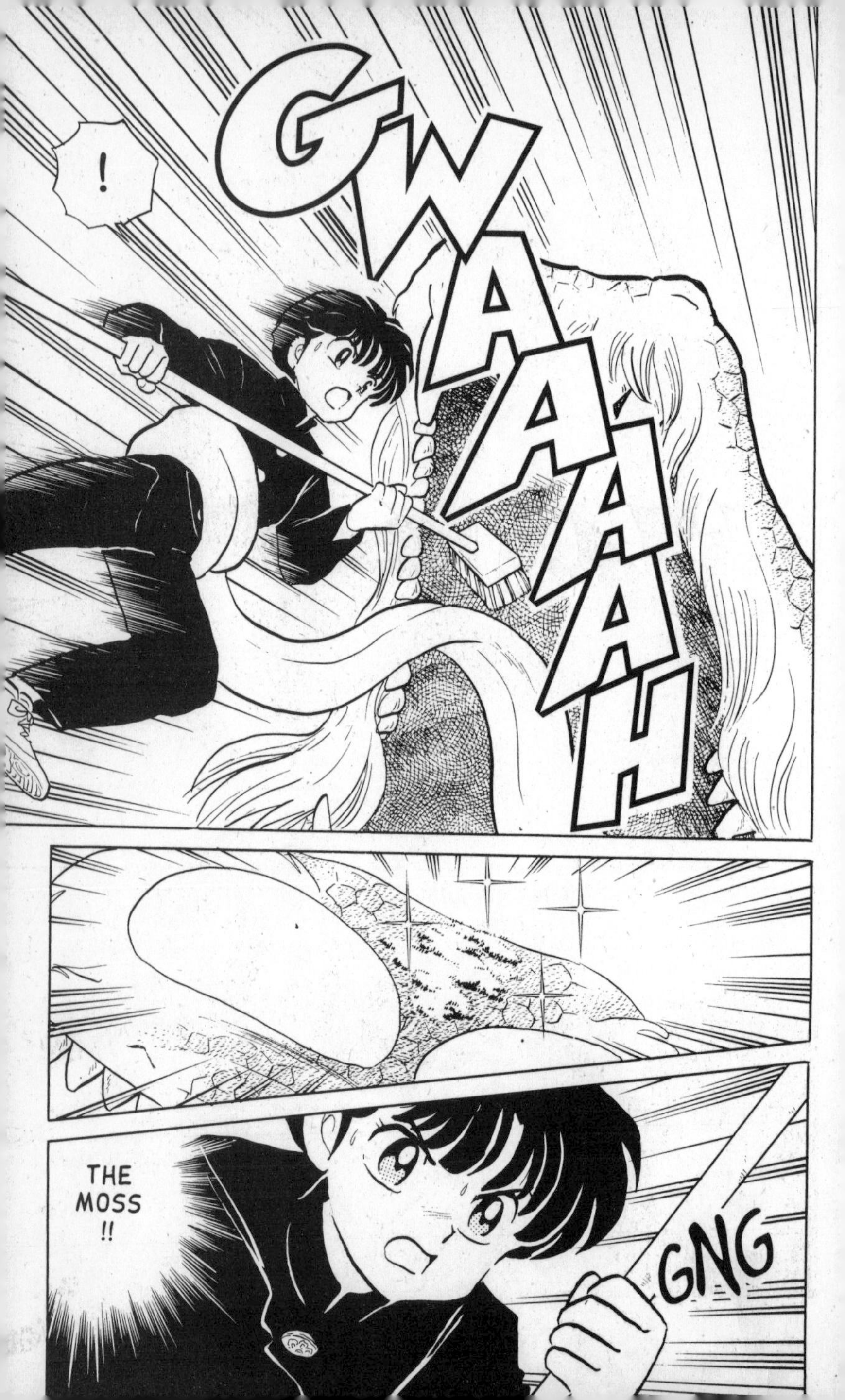
!
GWAAAAAH
THE MOSS !!
GNG

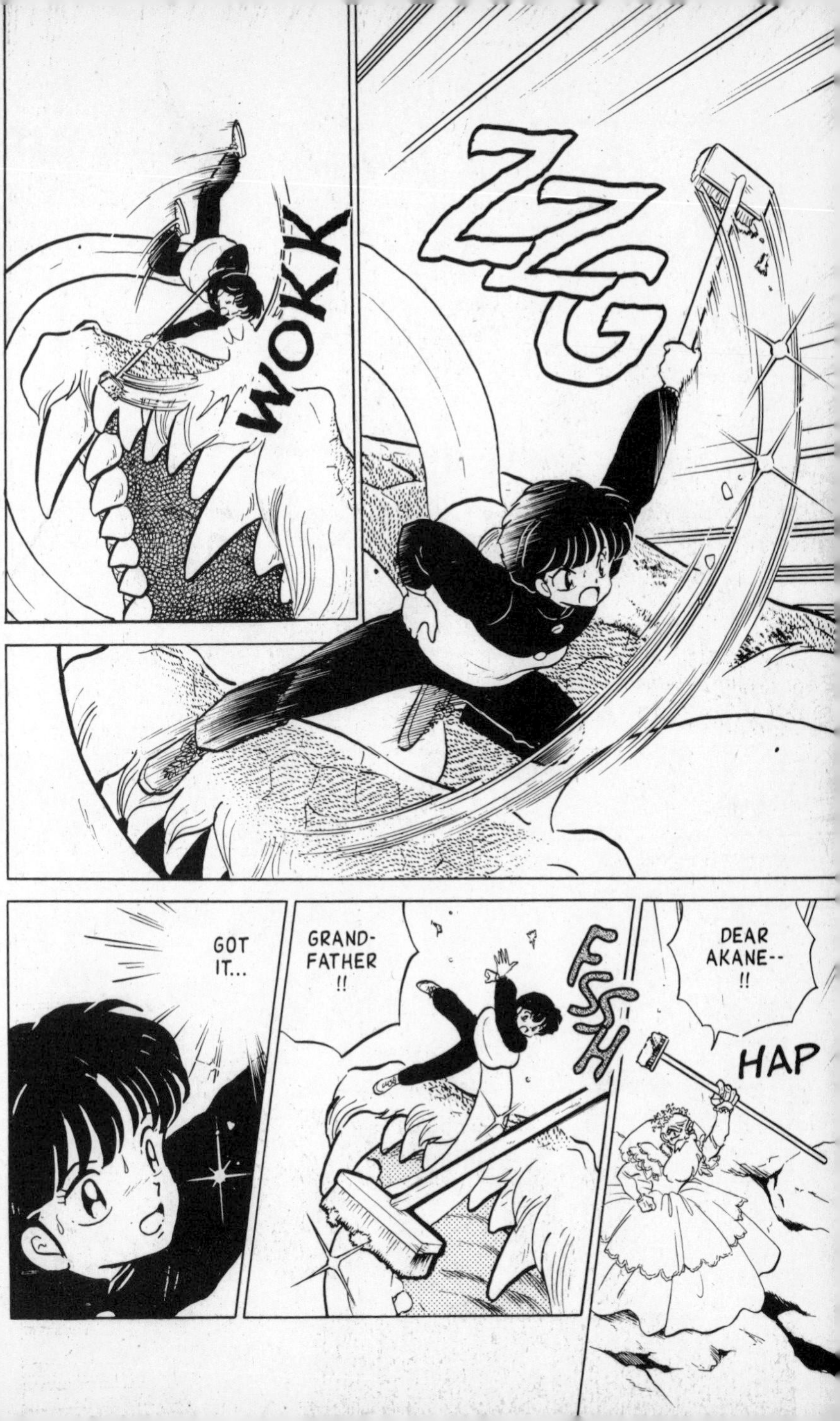
WOKK
ZZG
GOT IT...
GRAND-FATHER !!
ESSH
DEAR AKANE-- !!
HAP

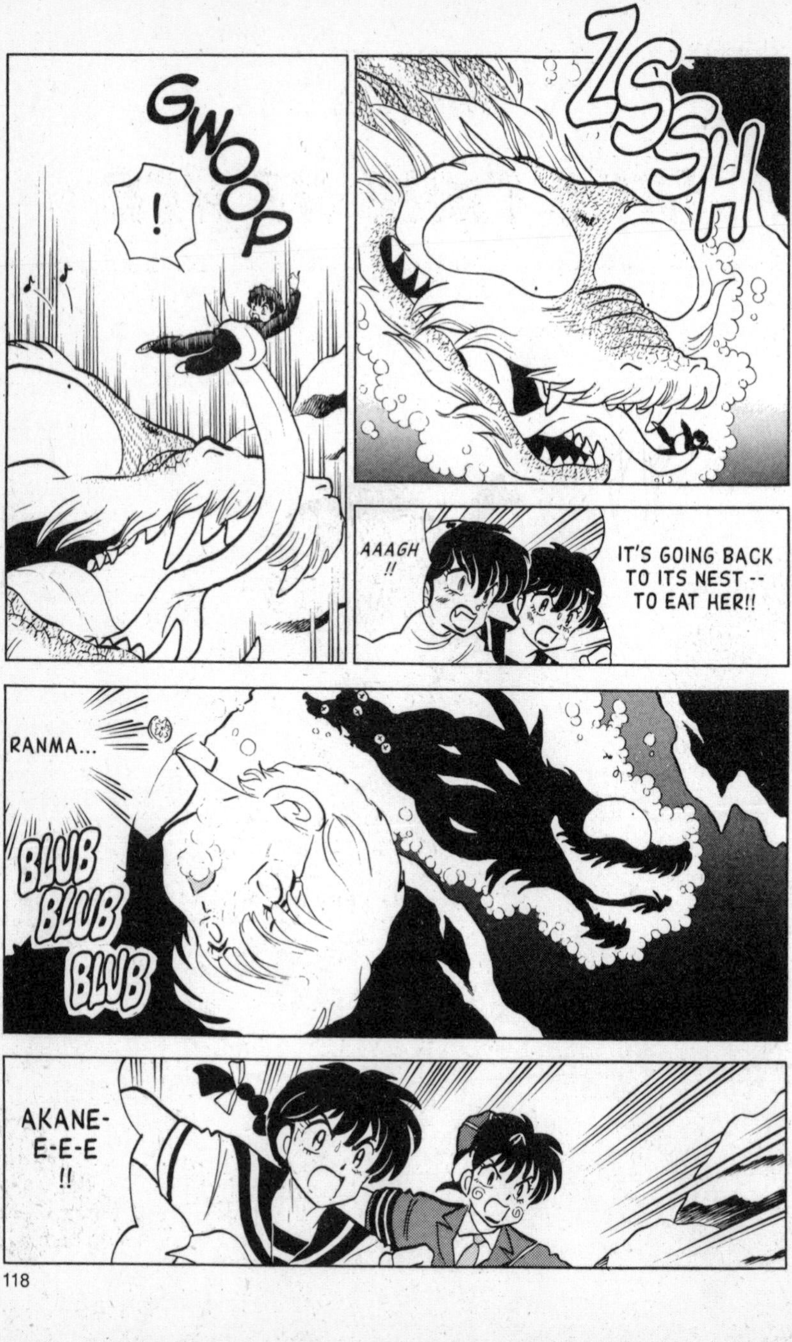
GWOOP
!
ZSSH
AAAGH !!
IT'S GOING BACK TO ITS NEST -- TO EAT HER!!
RANMA...
BLUB BLUB BLUB
AKANE-E-E-E !!

Part 8
TAKE CARE OF HER

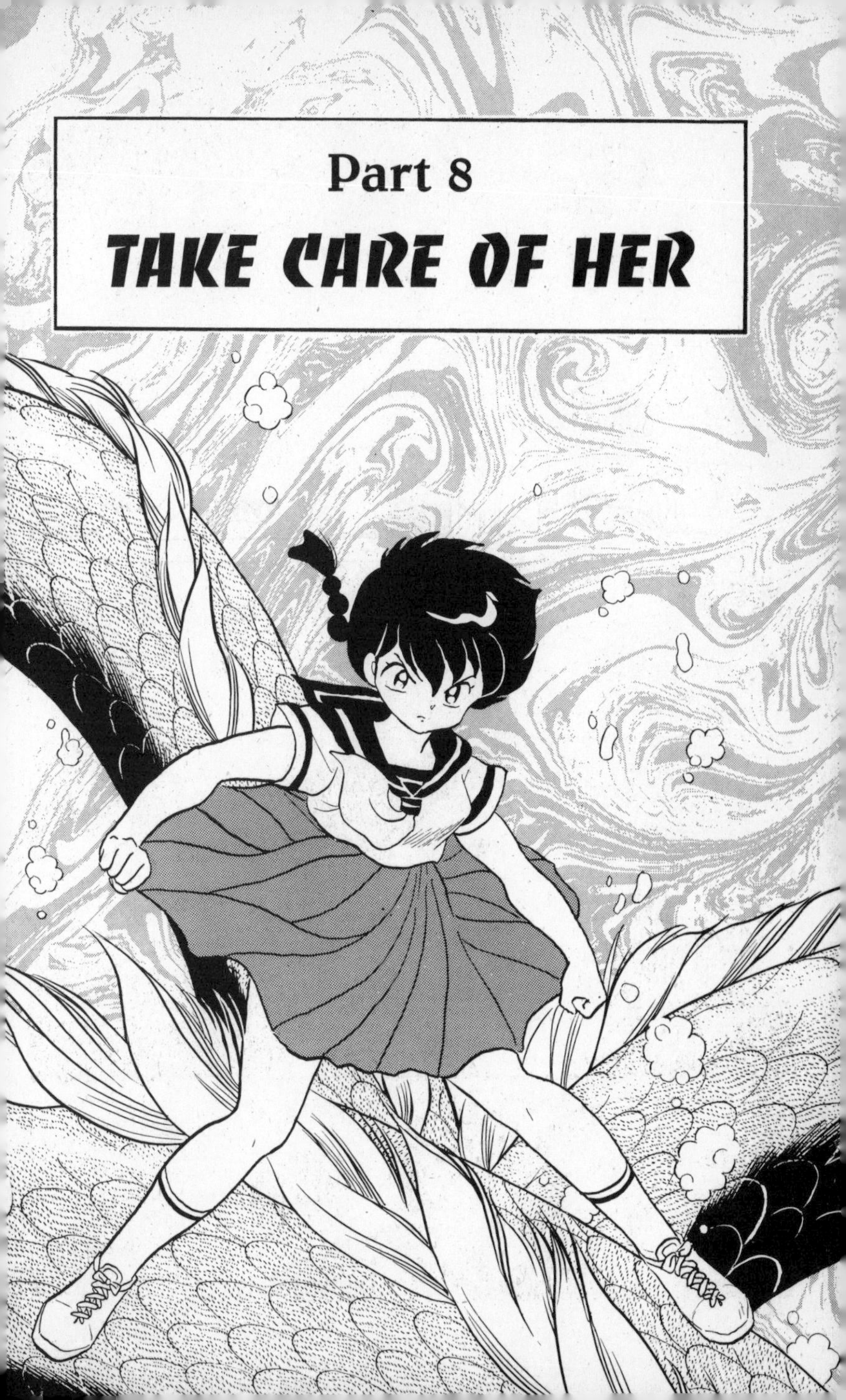

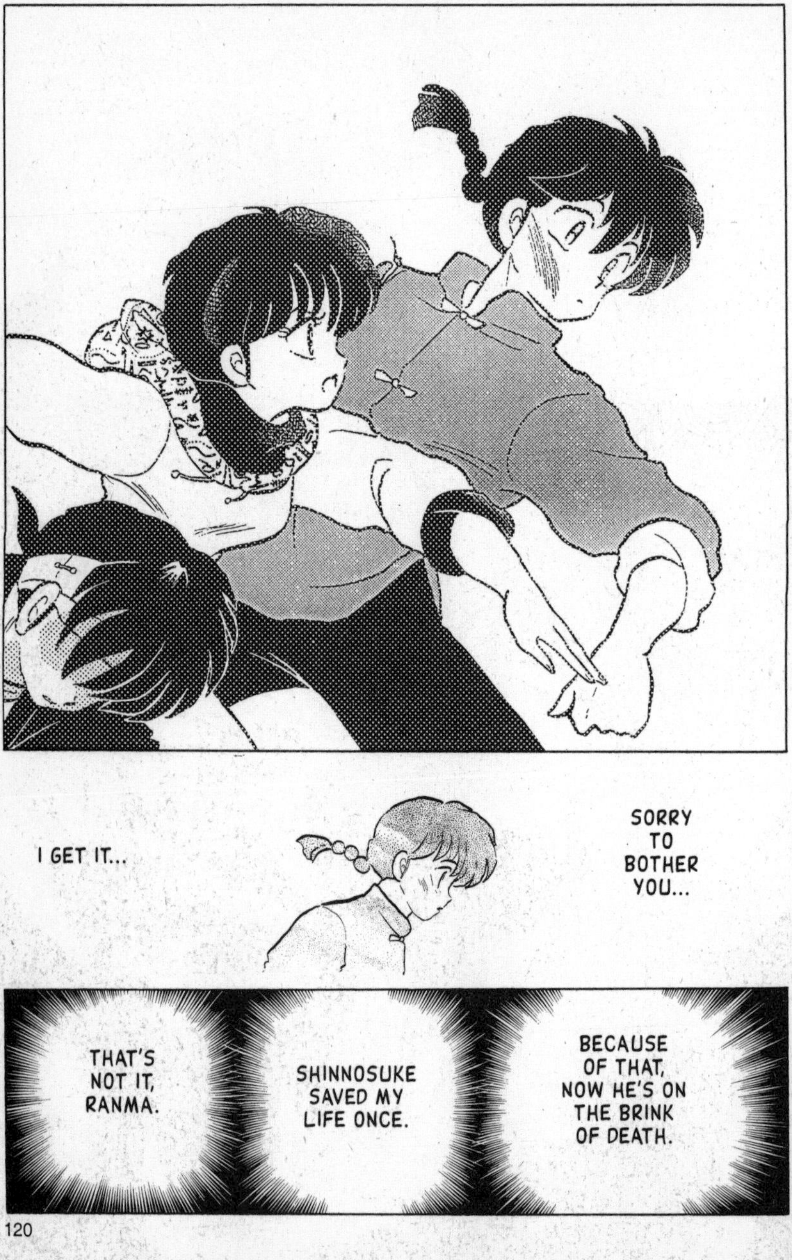
I GET IT...
SORRY TO BOTHER YOU...
THAT'S NOT IT, RANMA.
SHINNOSUKE SAVED MY LIFE ONCE.
BECAUSE OF THAT, NOW HE'S ON THE BRINK OF DEATH.

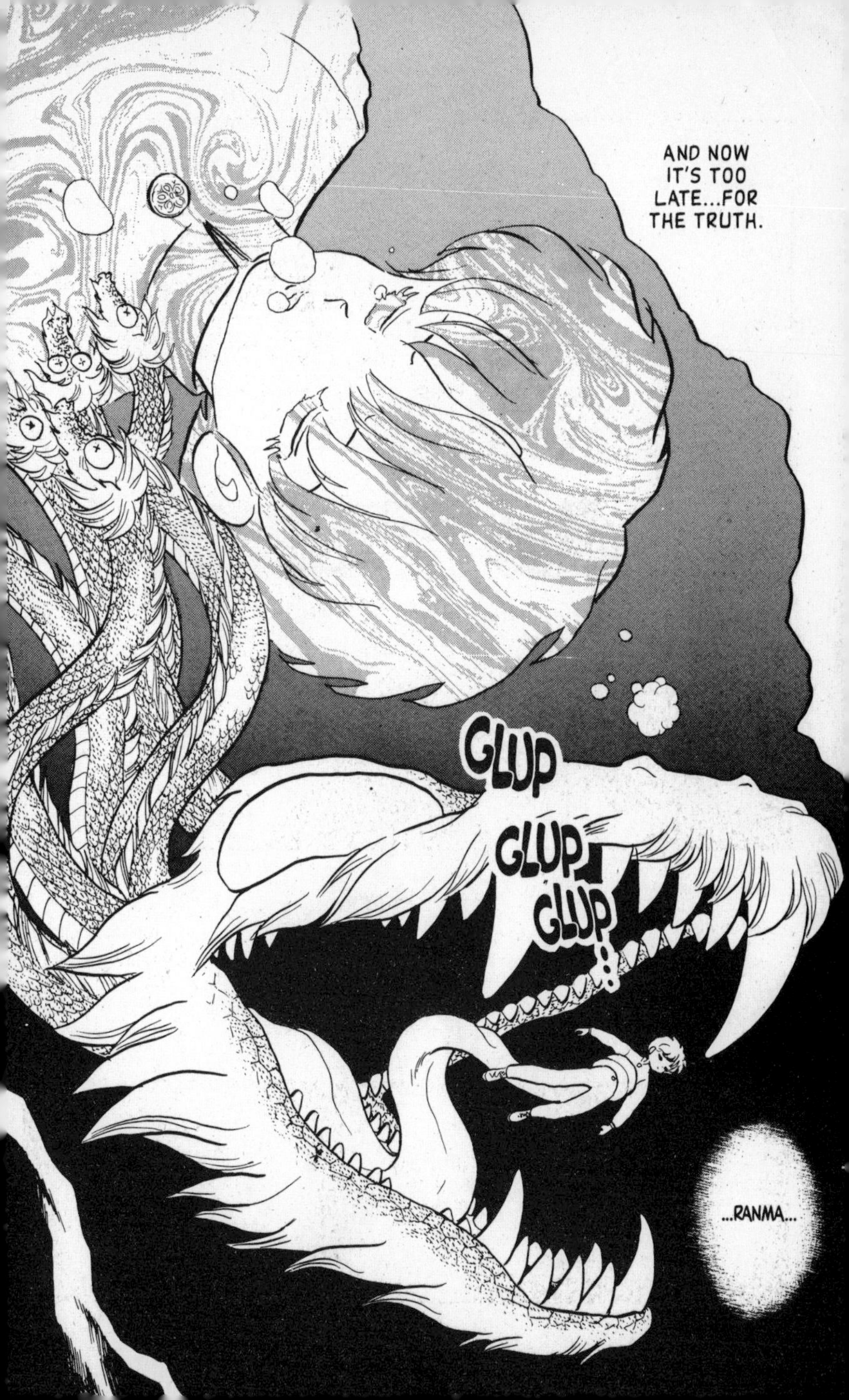
AND NOW IT'S TOO LATE...FOR THE TRUTH.
GLUP
GLUP
GLUP...
...RANMA...

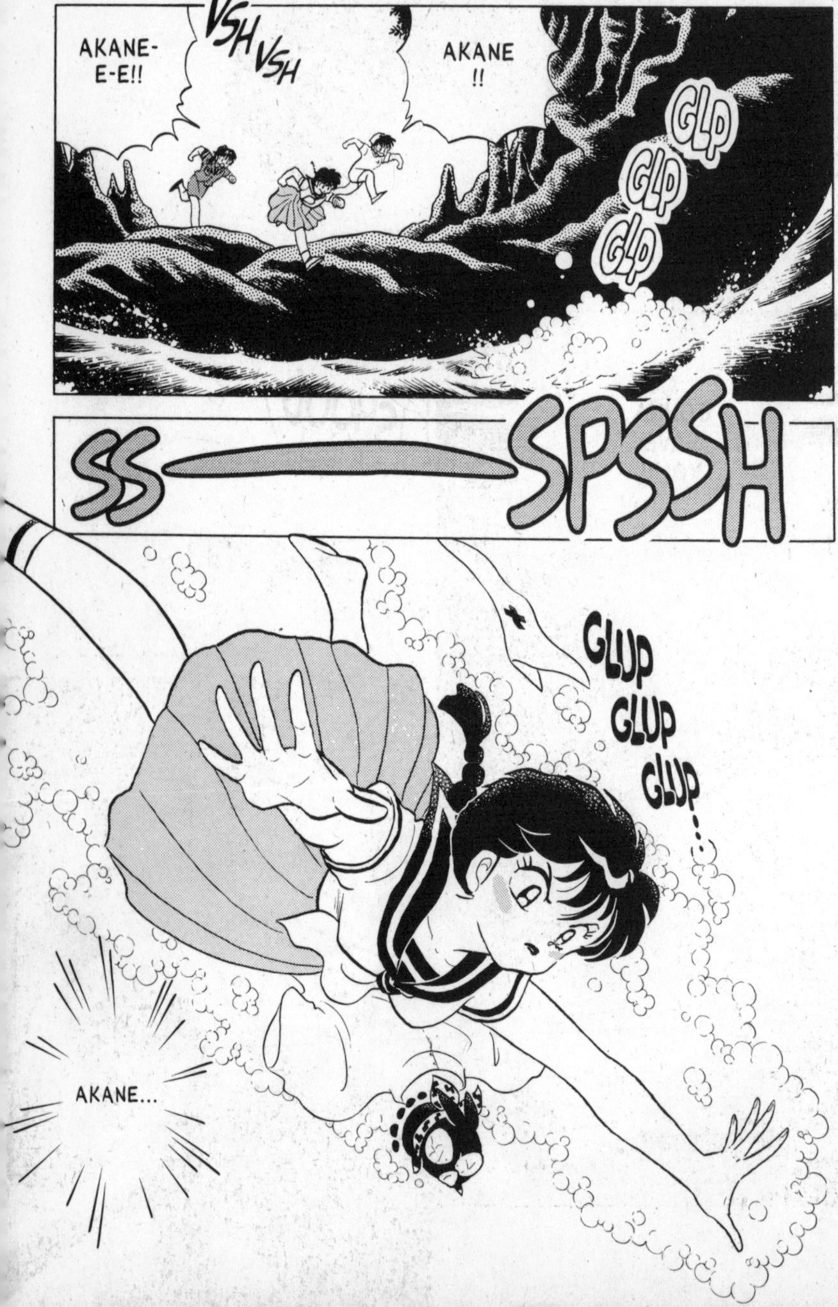

AKANE-
E-E!!
VSH VSH
AKANE
!!
GLP
GLP
GLP
SS——SPSSH
GLUP
GLUP
GLUP...
AKANE...

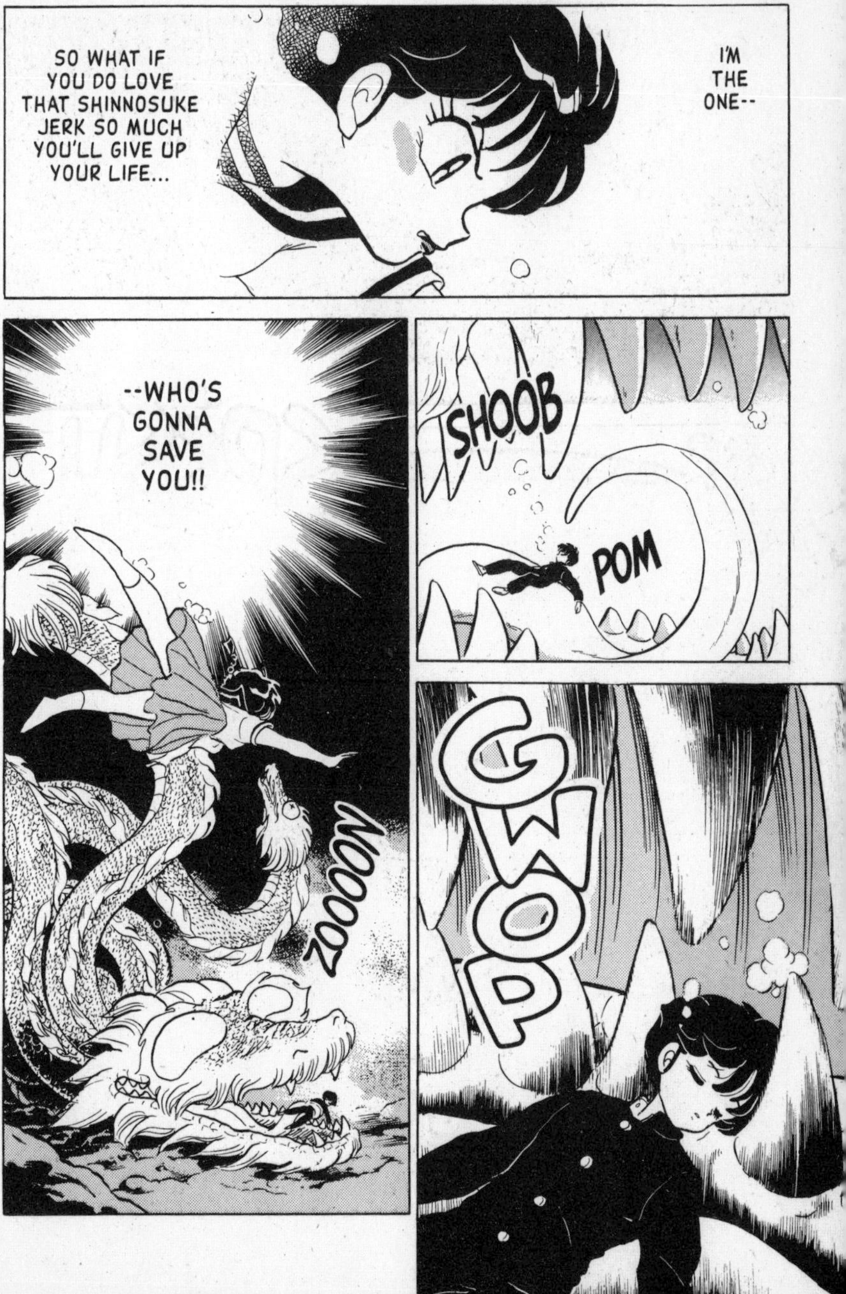
SO WHAT IF YOU DO LOVE THAT SHINNOSUKE JERK SO MUCH YOU'LL GIVE UP YOUR LIFE...
I'M THE ONE--
--WHO'S GONNA SAVE YOU!!
ZOOOOON
SHOOB
POM
GWOP

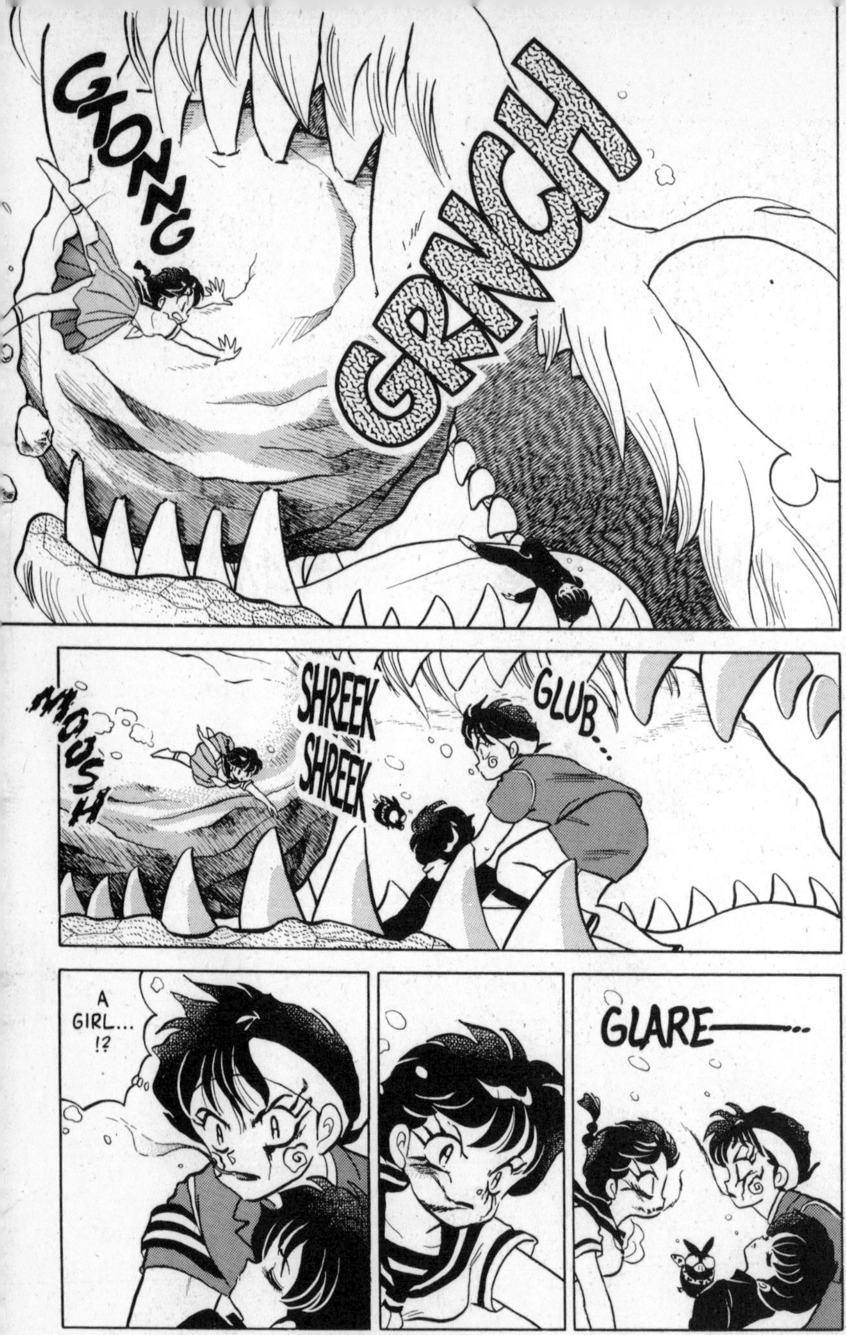
GONNG
GRNCH
MOOSH
SHREEK
SHREEK
GLUB...
A GIRL... !?
GLARE———...

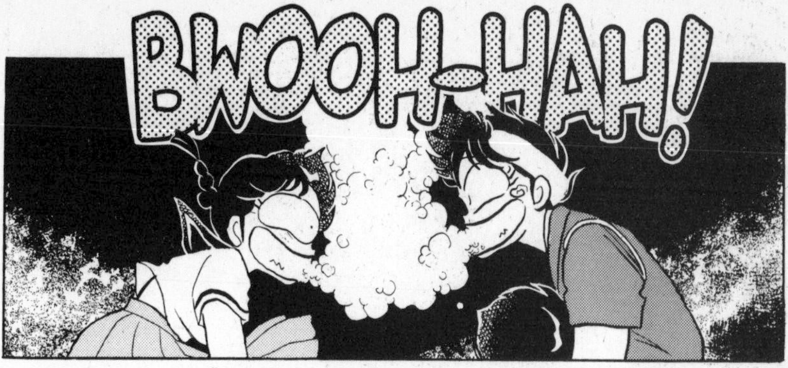
BWOOH-HAH!

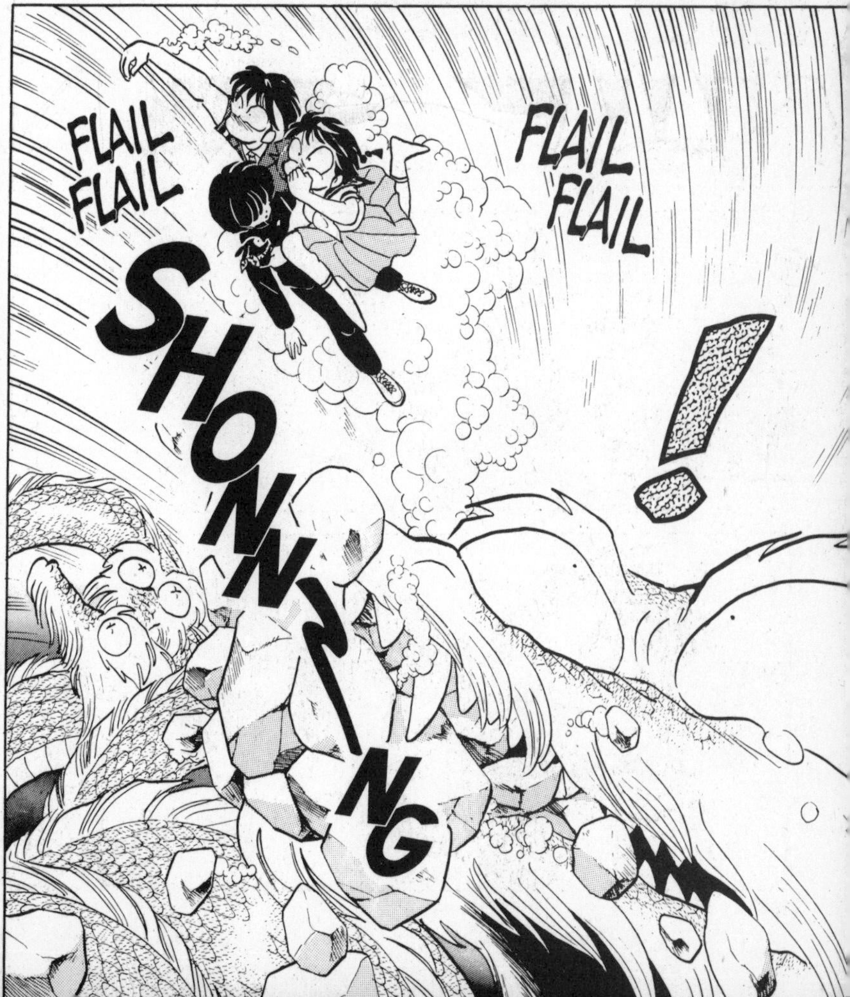
FLAIL
FLAIL
FLAIL
FLAIL
SHONNNNG
!

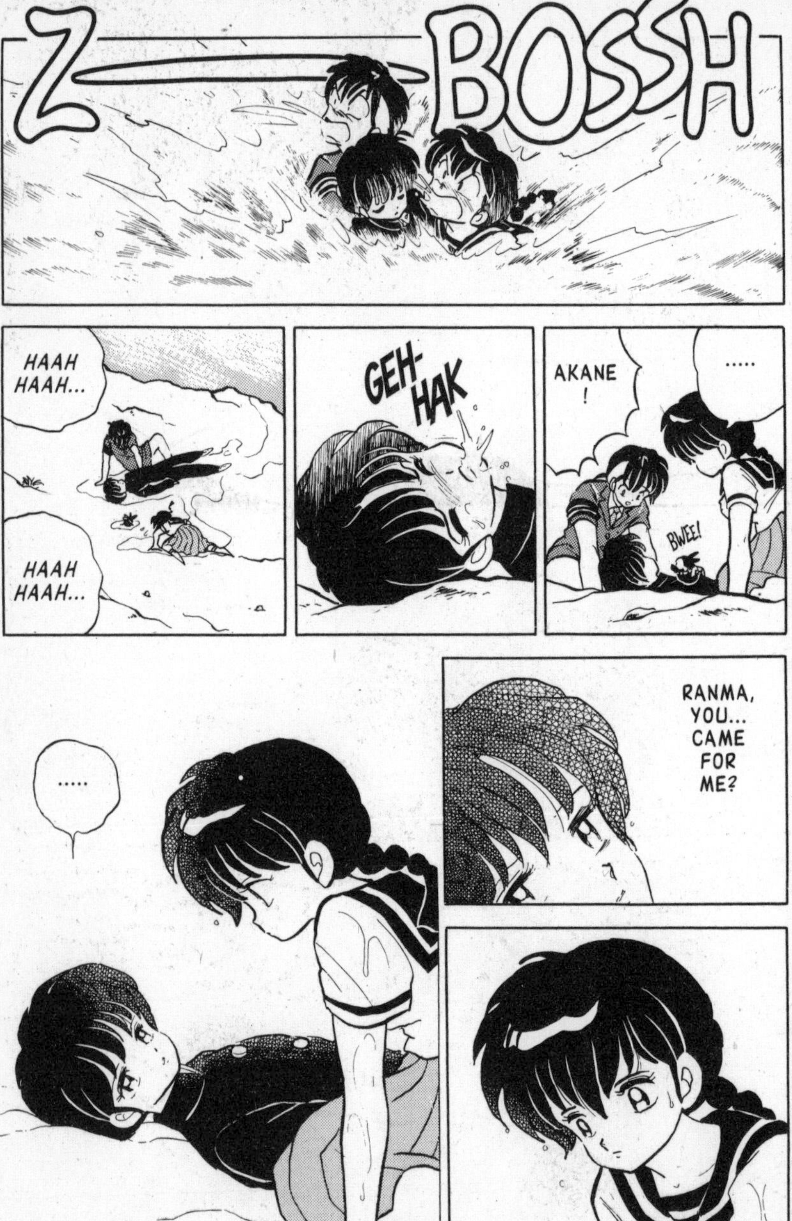
Z——BOSSH
HAAH HAAH...
HAAH HAAH...
GEH-HAK
AKANE!
.....
BWEE!
.....
RANMA, YOU... CAME FOR ME?

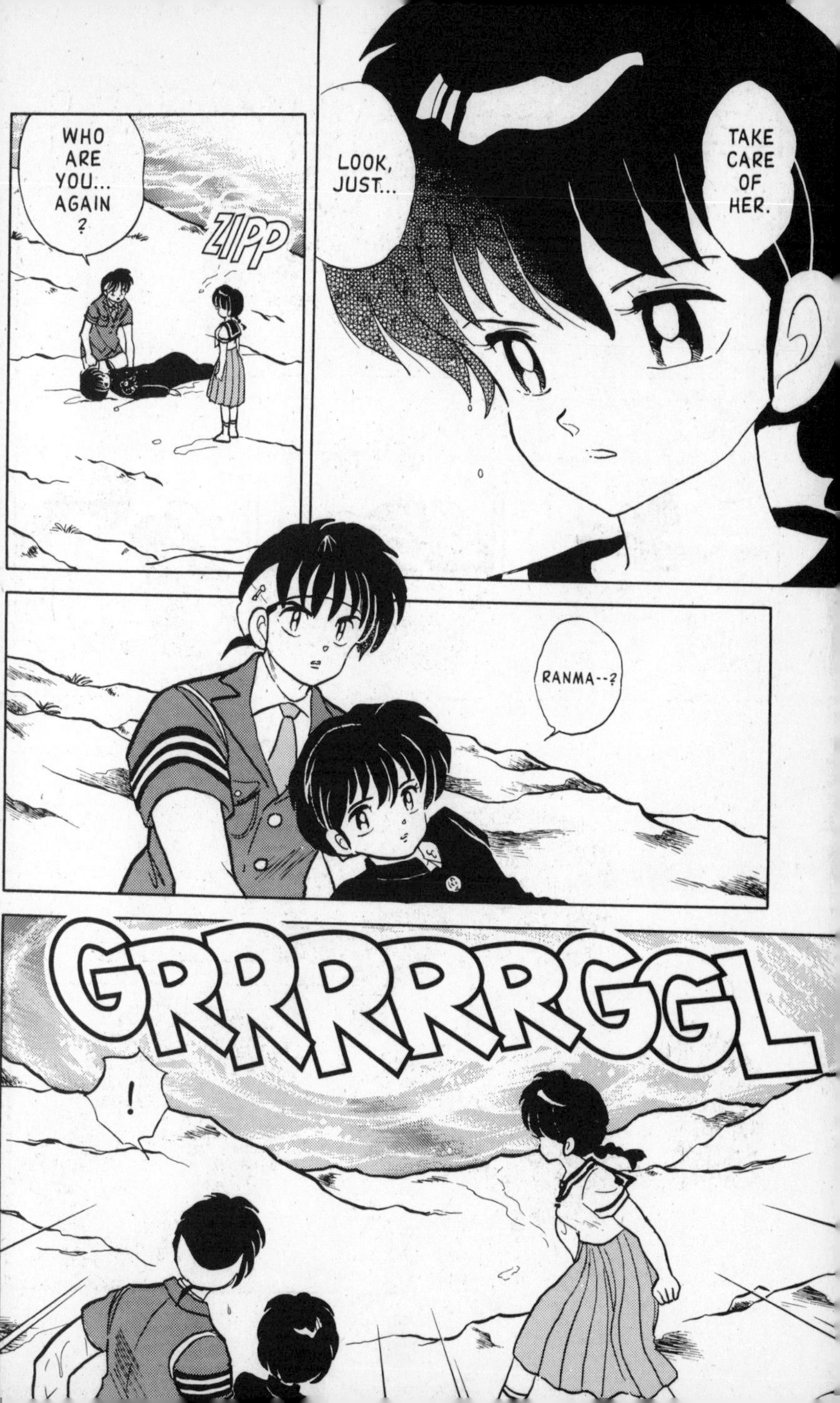
WHO ARE YOU... AGAIN ?
ZIPP
LOOK, JUST...
TAKE CARE OF HER.
RANMA--?
GRRRRRGGL
!

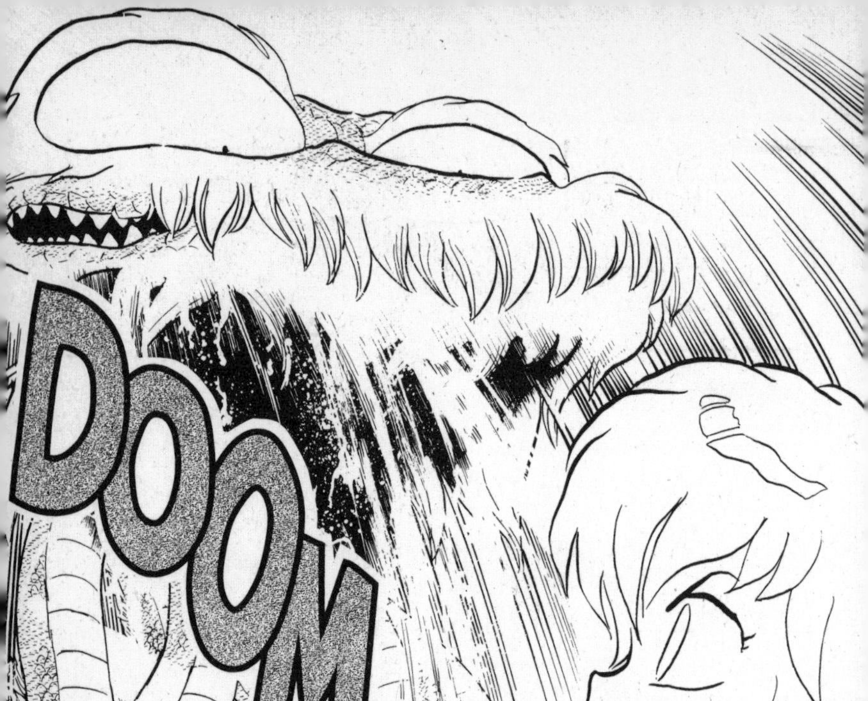
DOOOM

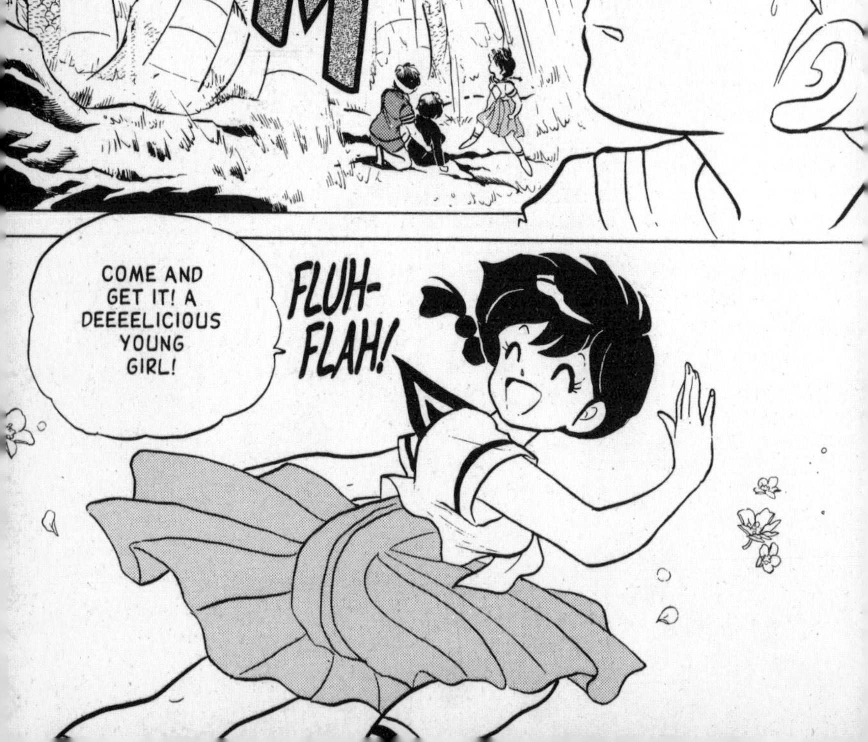
COME AND GET IT! A DEEEELICIOUS YOUNG GIRL!
FLUH-FLAH!

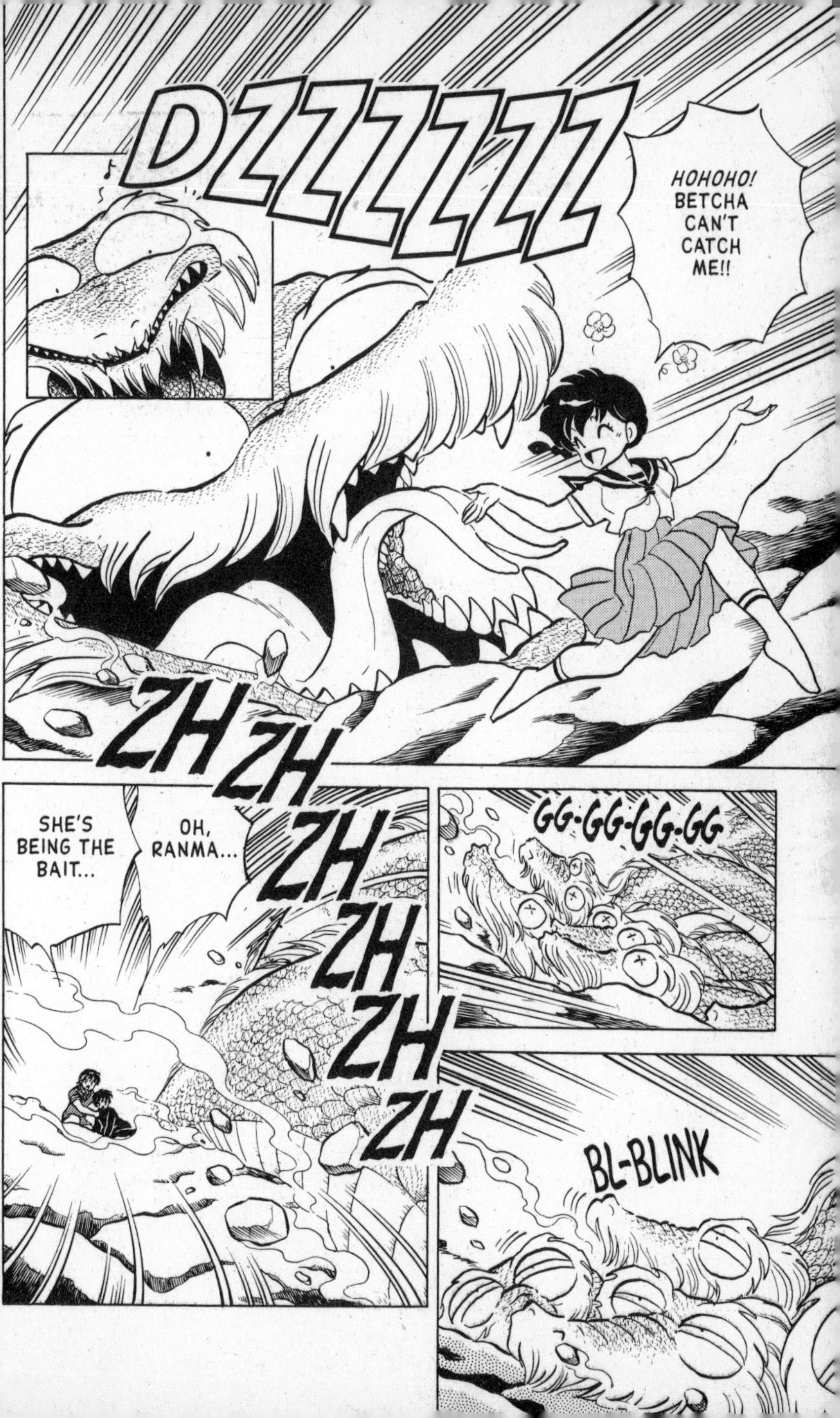
DZZZZZZZ
HOHOHO! BETCHA CAN'T CATCH ME!!
ZH ZH ZH ZH ZH ZH
SHE'S BEING THE BAIT...
OH, RANMA...
GG-GG-GG-GG
BL-BLINK

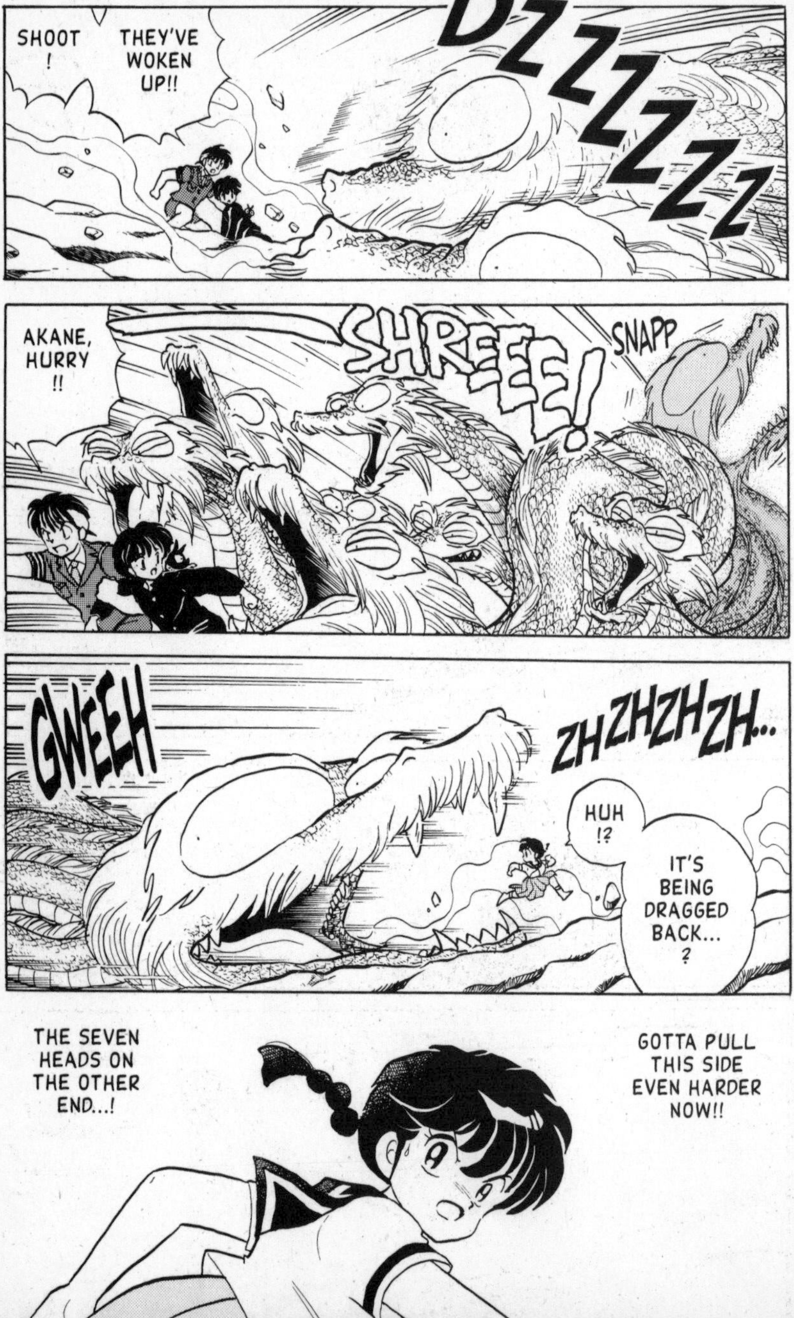
SHOOT !
THEY'VE WOKEN UP!!
DZZZZZZ
AKANE, HURRY !!
SHREEE!
SNAPP
GWEEH
ZHZHZHZH...
HUH !?
IT'S BEING DRAGGED BACK... ?
THE SEVEN HEADS ON THE OTHER END...!
GOTTA PULL THIS SIDE EVEN HARDER NOW!!

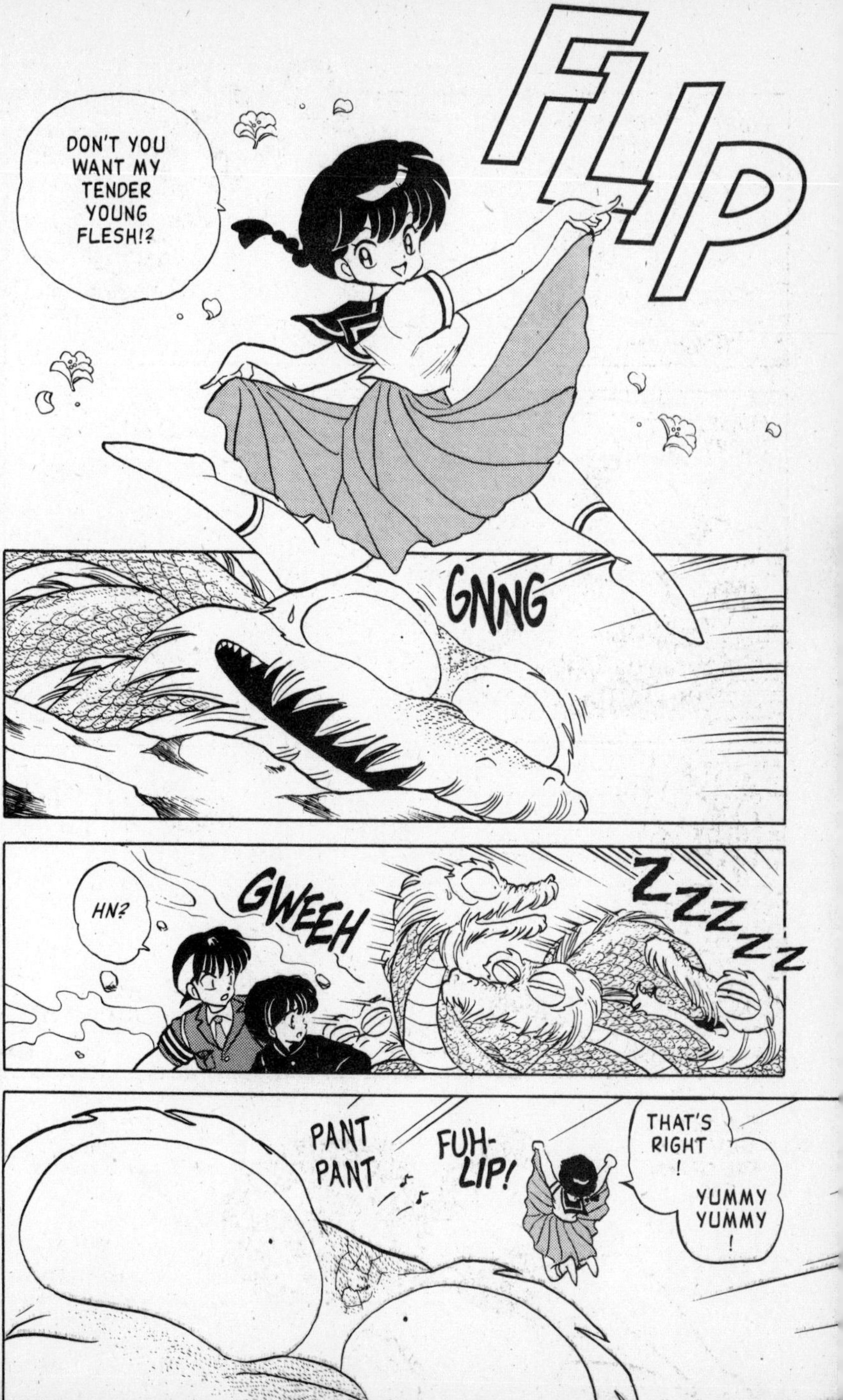
DON'T YOU WANT MY TENDER YOUNG FLESH!?
FLIP
GNNG
HN?
GWEEH
ZZZZZ
PANT PANT
FUH-LIP!
THAT'S RIGHT!
YUMMY YUMMY!

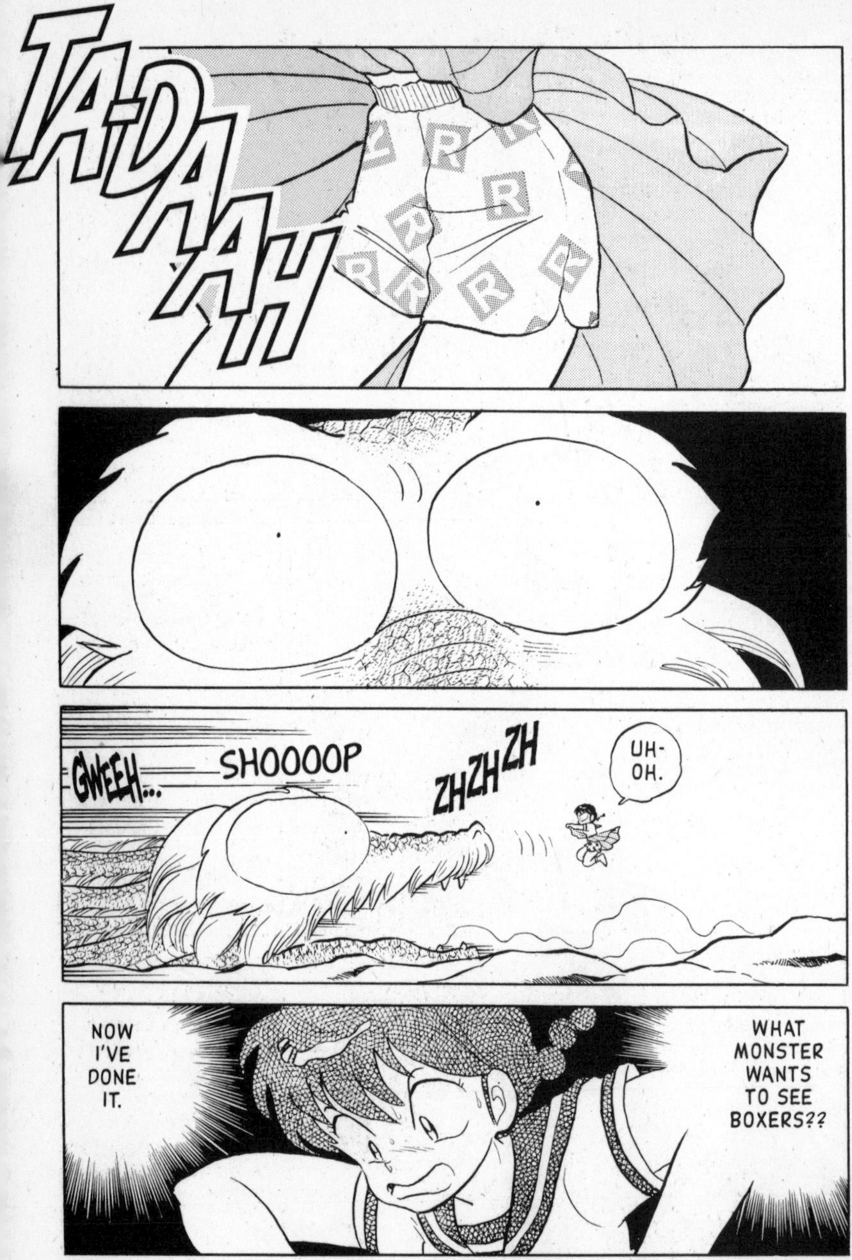
TA-DA-AH
GWEEH...
SHOOOOP
ZHZHZH
UH-OH.
NOW I'VE DONE IT.
WHAT MONSTER WANTS TO SEE BOXERS??

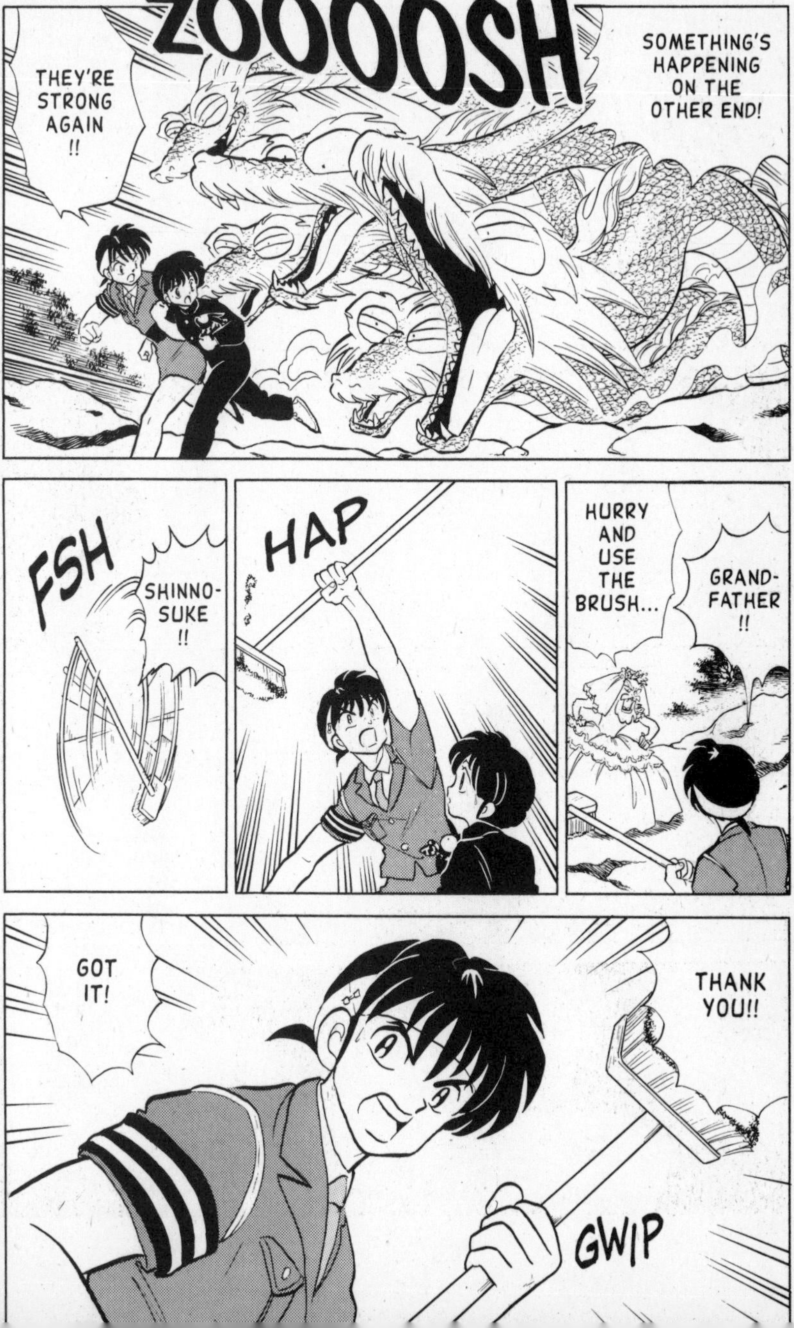
THEY'RE STRONG AGAIN !!
ZOOOOSH
SOMETHING'S HAPPENING ON THE OTHER END!
FSH
SHINNO-SUKE !!
HAP
HURRY AND USE THE BRUSH...
GRAND-FATHER !!
GOT IT!
THANK YOU!!
GWIP

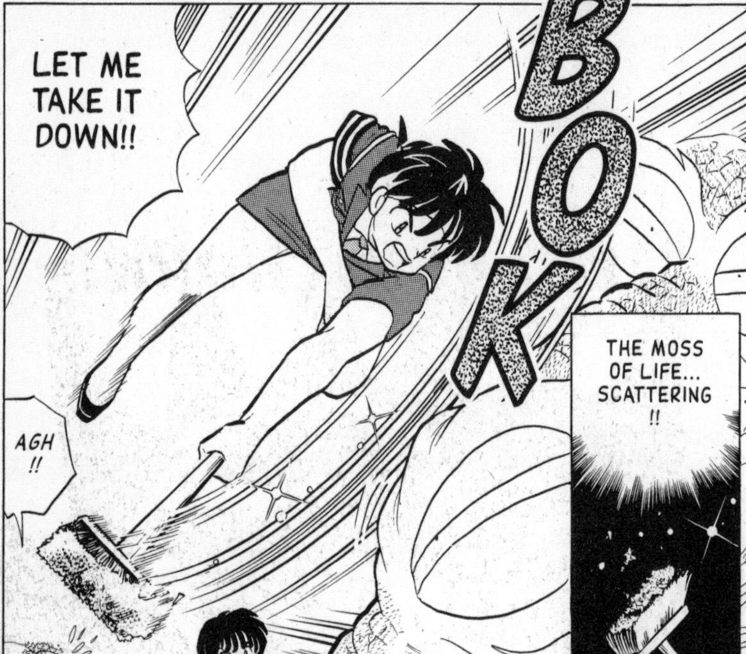
LET ME TAKE IT DOWN!!
BOK
AGH !!
THE MOSS OF LIFE... SCATTERING !!

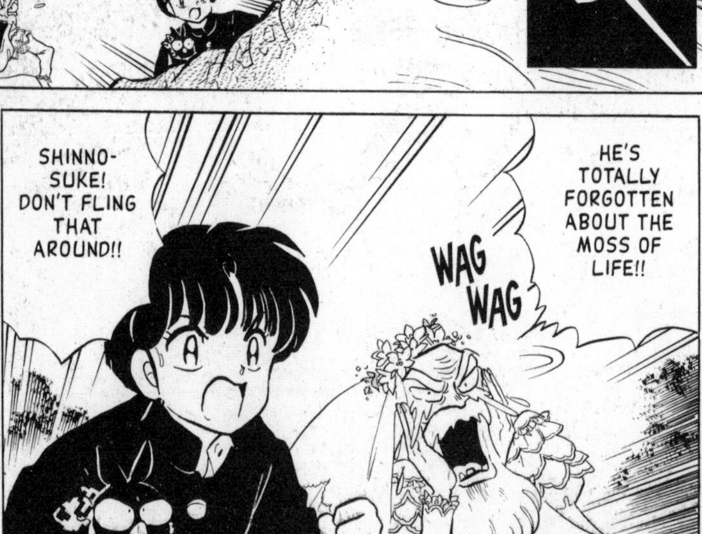
SHINNO-SUKE! DON'T FLING THAT AROUND!!
WAG WAG
HE'S TOTALLY FORGOTTEN ABOUT THE MOSS OF LIFE!!

Part 9
BLOW YOUR HORN!!

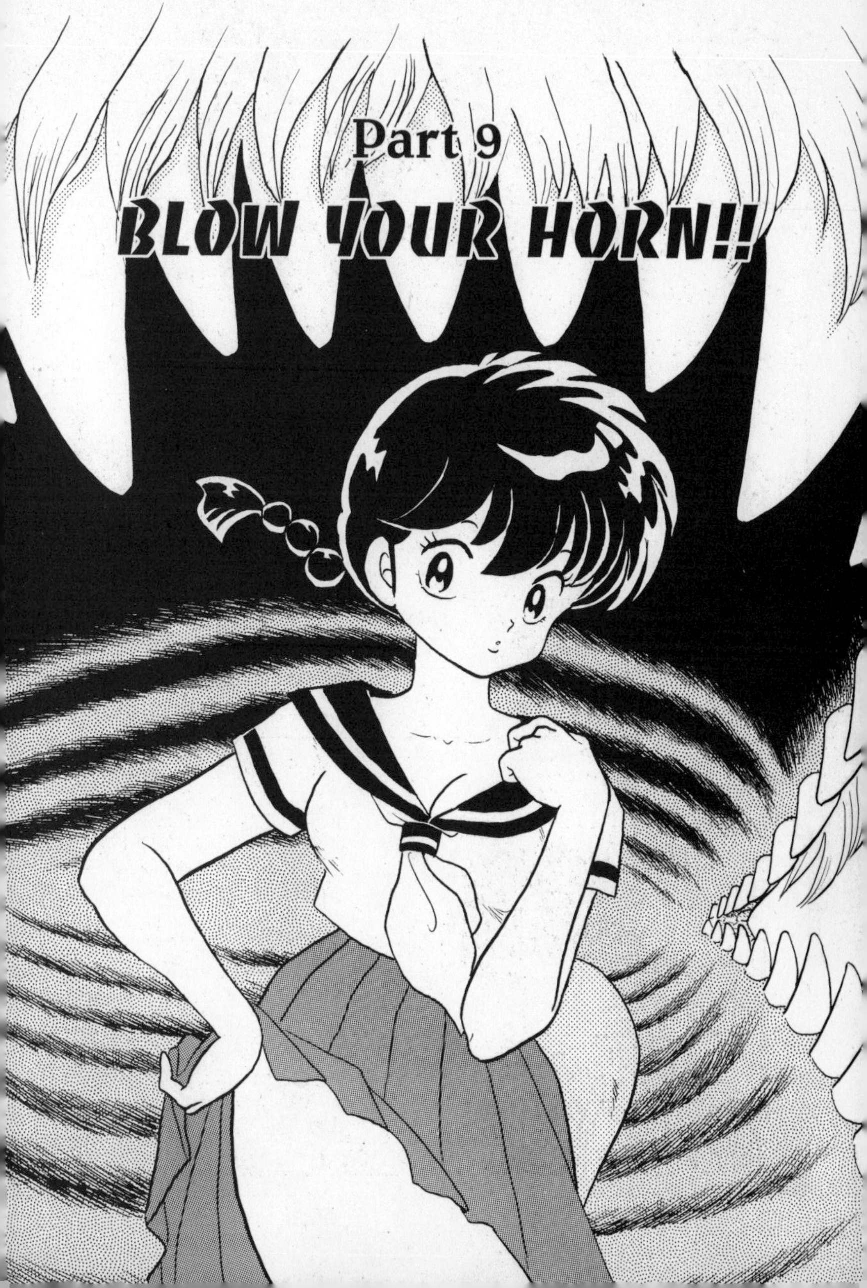

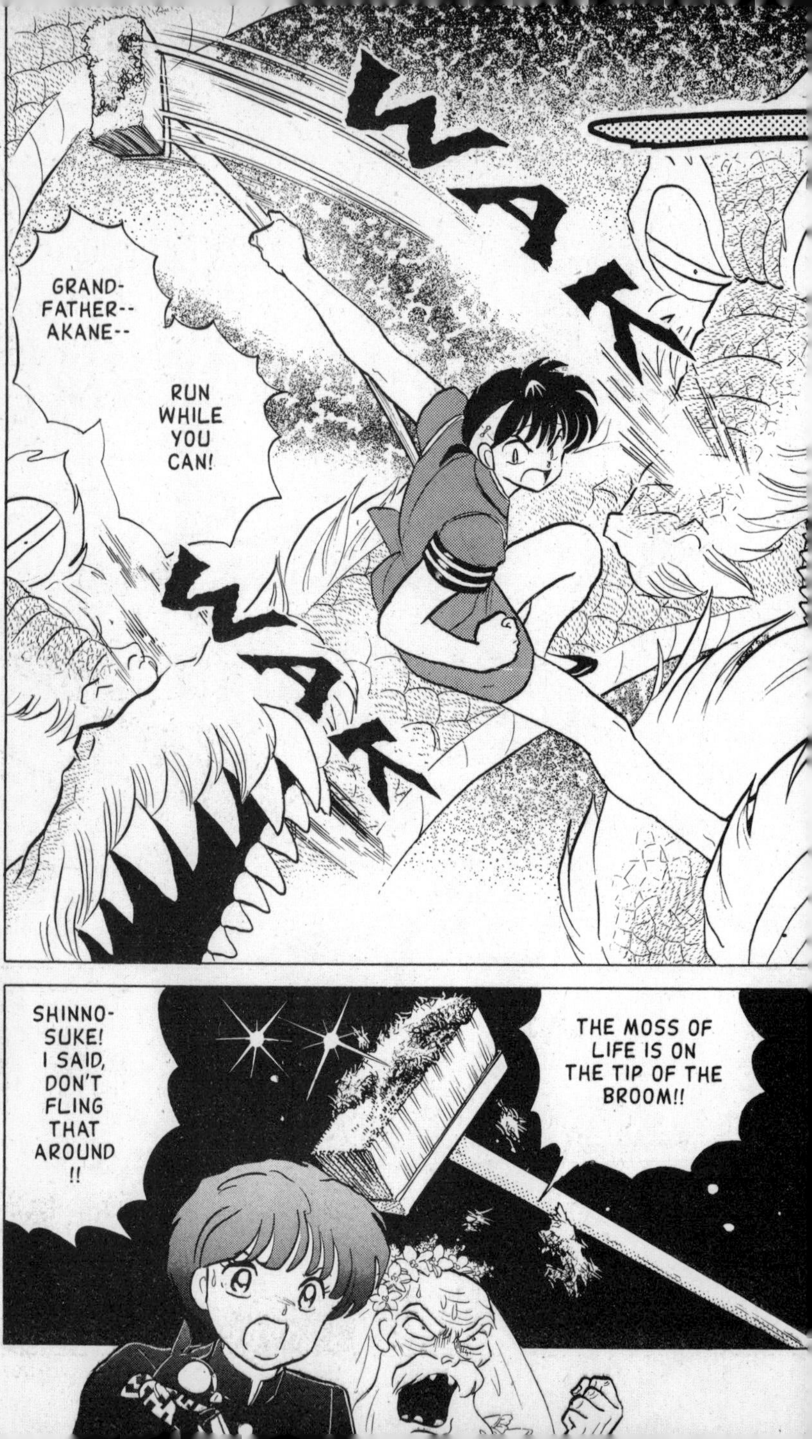
WAK
GRAND-FATHER-- AKANE--
RUN WHILE YOU CAN!
WAK
SHINNO-SUKE! I SAID, DON'T FLING THAT AROUND !!
THE MOSS OF LIFE IS ON THE TIP OF THE BROOM!!

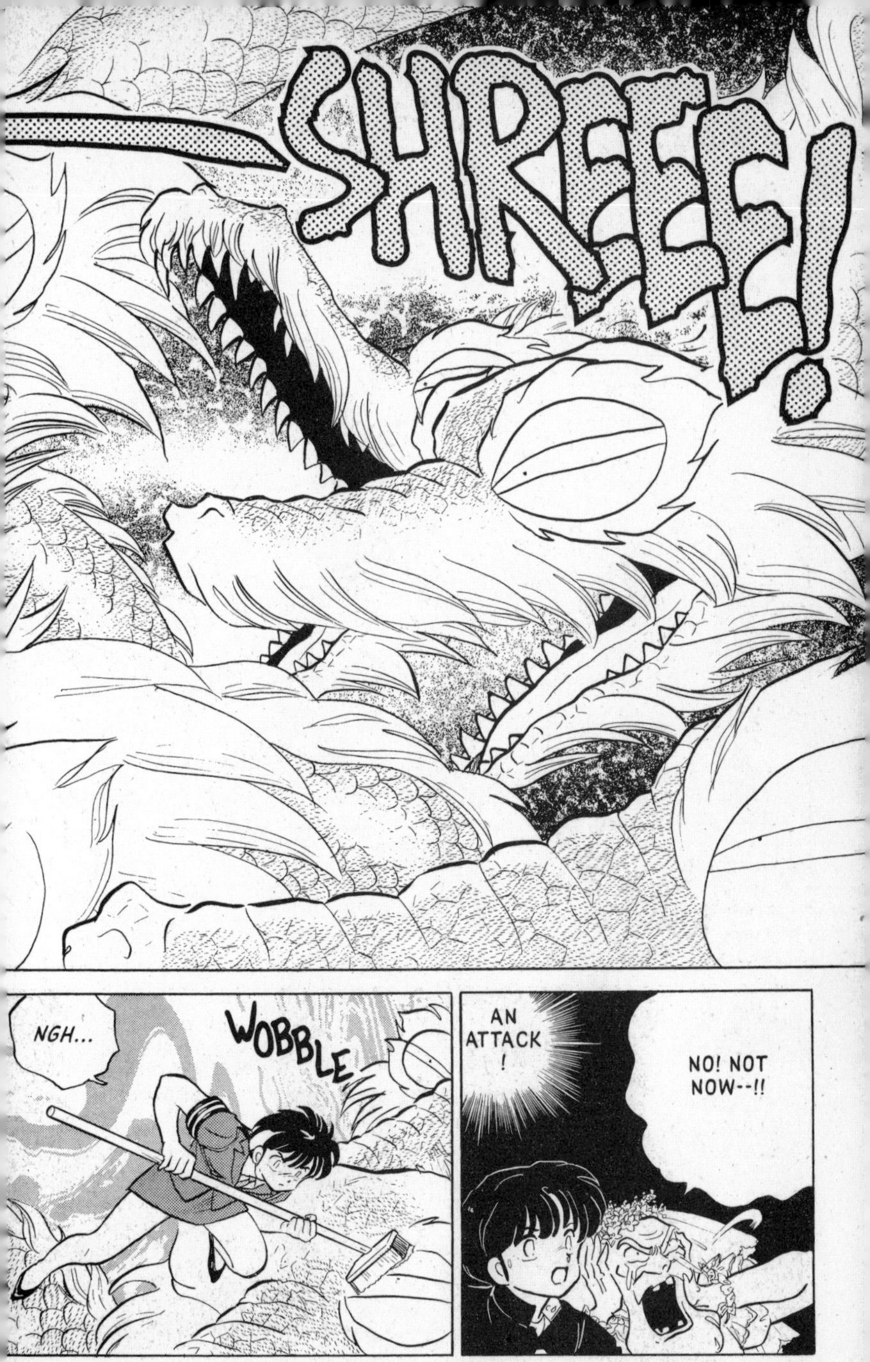
SHREEE!!
NGH...
WOBBLE
AN ATTACK!
NO! NOT NOW--!!

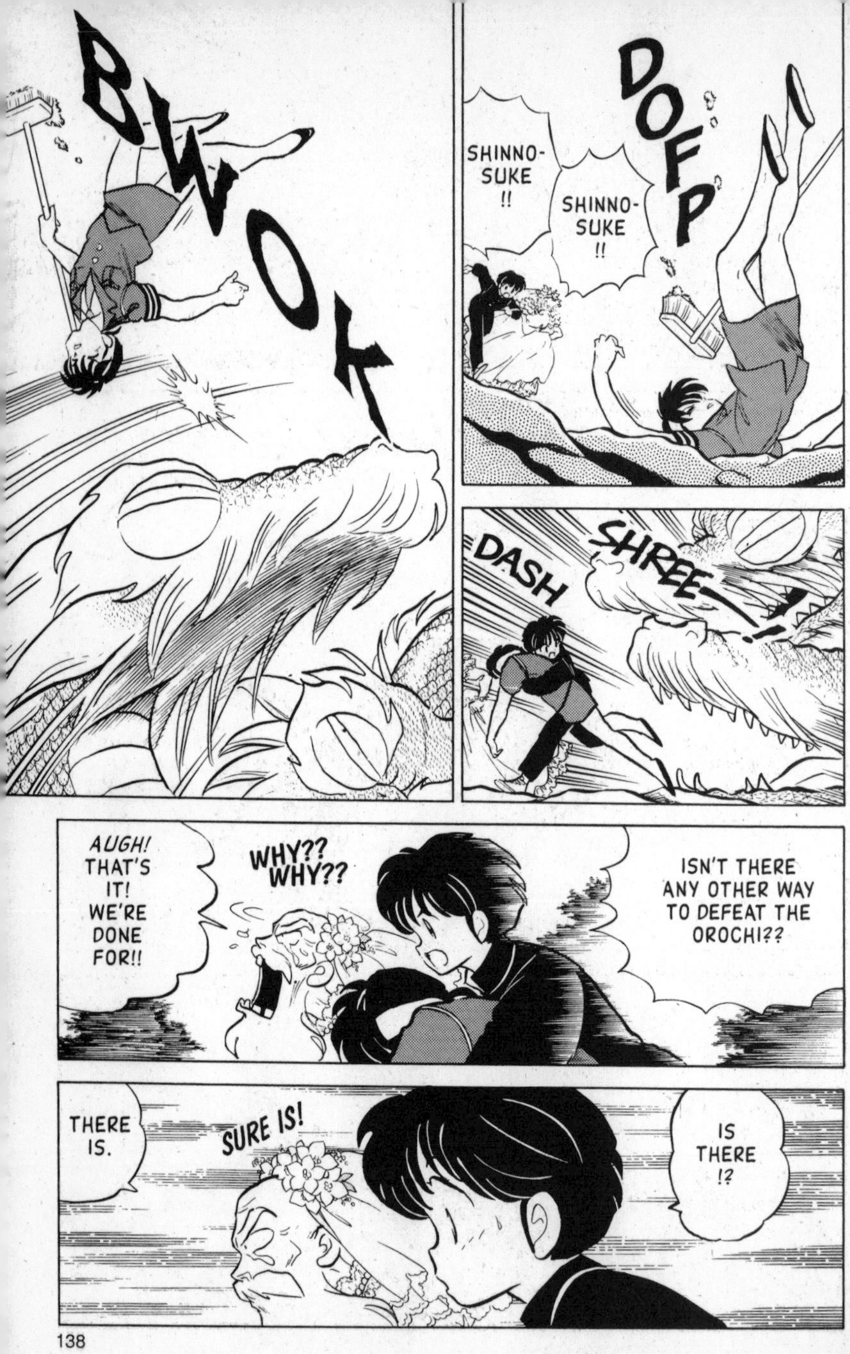
BWOK
SHINNO-SUKE !!
SHINNO-SUKE !!
DOFP
DASH
SHREE—!!
AUGH! THAT'S IT! WE'RE DONE FOR!!
WHY?? WHY??
ISN'T THERE ANY OTHER WAY TO DEFEAT THE OROCHI??
THERE IS.
SURE IS!
IS THERE !?

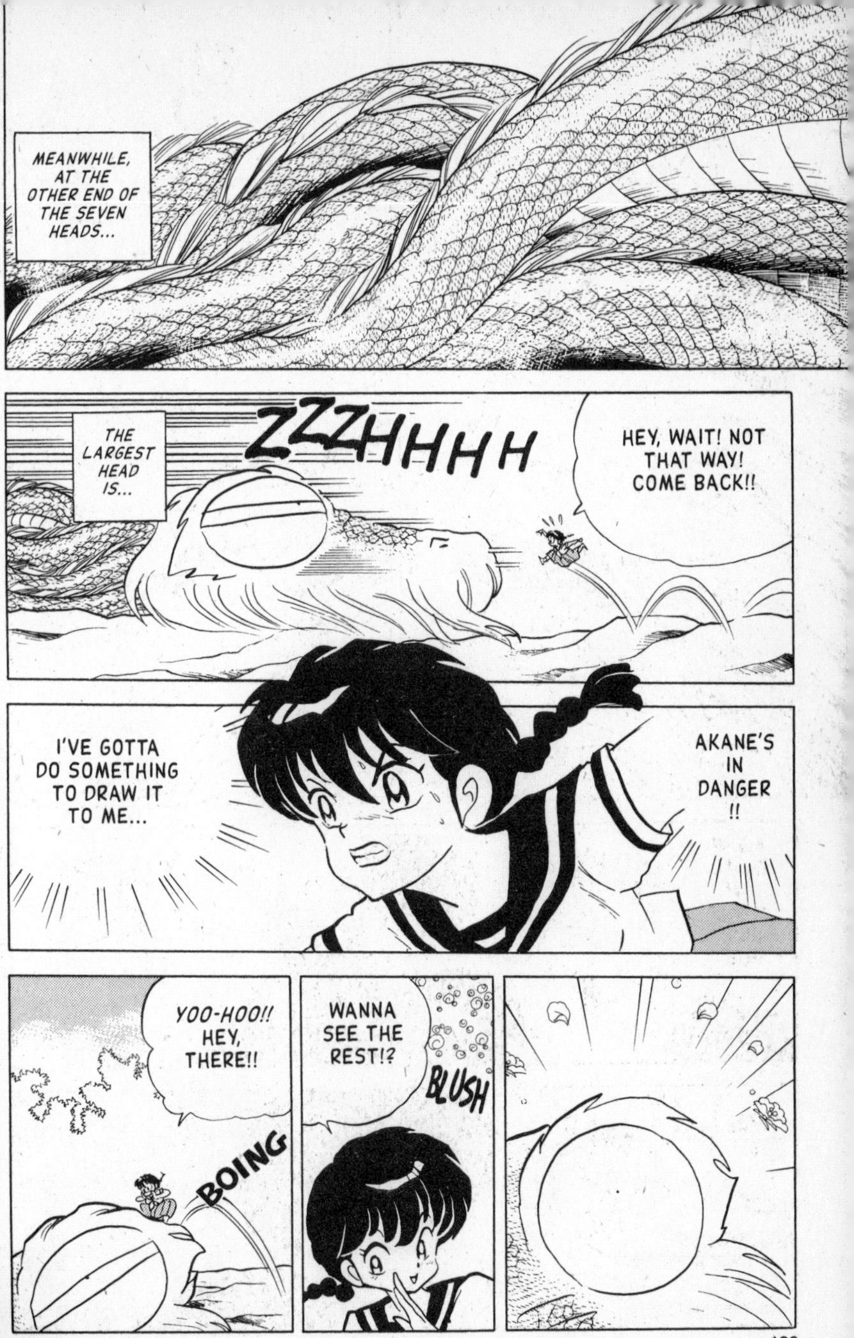
MEANWHILE, AT THE OTHER END OF THE SEVEN HEADS...
THE LARGEST HEAD IS...
ZZZHHHHH
HEY, WAIT! NOT THAT WAY! COME BACK!!
I'VE GOTTA DO SOMETHING TO DRAW IT TO ME...
AKANE'S IN DANGER !!
YOO-HOO!! HEY, THERE!!
BOING
WANNA SEE THE REST!?
BLUSH

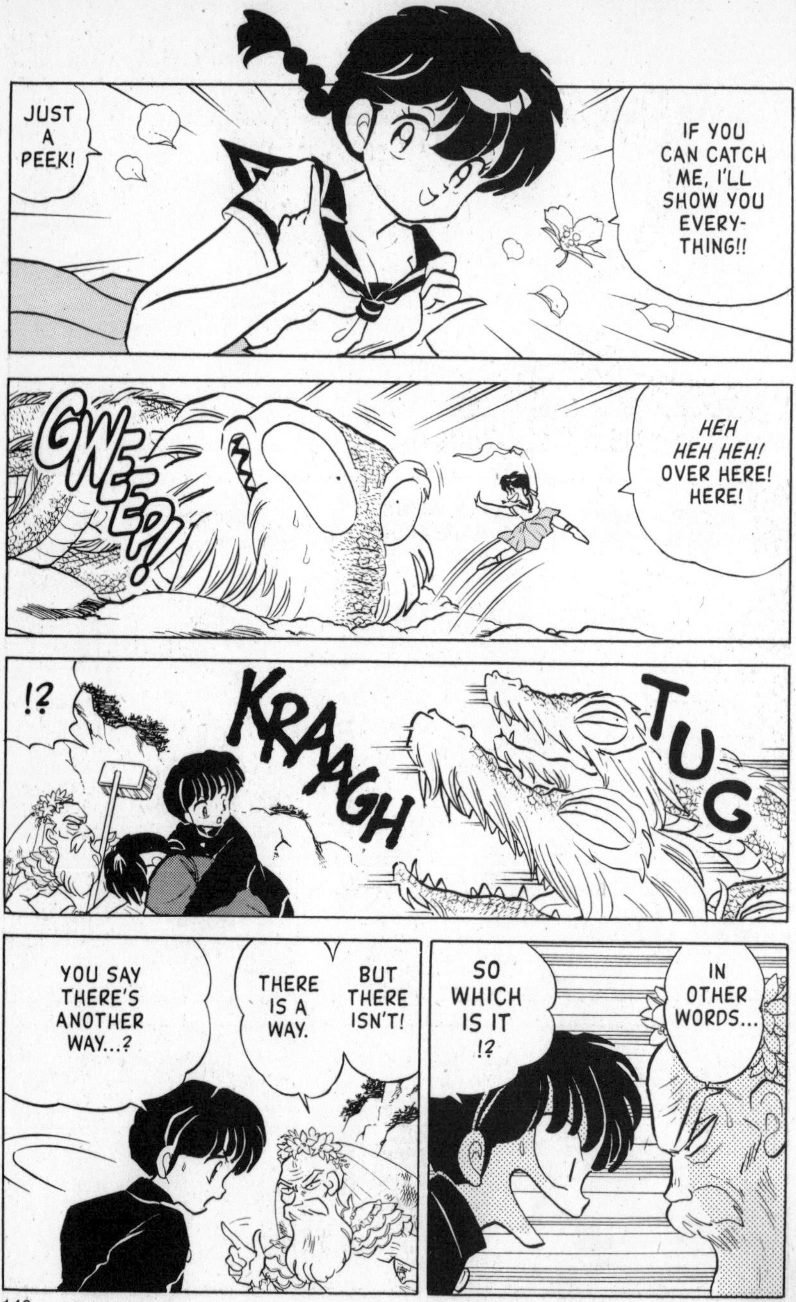
JUST A PEEK!
IF YOU CAN CATCH ME, I'LL SHOW YOU EVERY-THING!!
GWEEP!
HEH HEH HEH! OVER HERE! HERE!
!?
KRAAAGH
TUG
YOU SAY THERE'S ANOTHER WAY...?
THERE IS A WAY. BUT THERE ISN'T!
SO WHICH IS IT !?
IN OTHER WORDS...

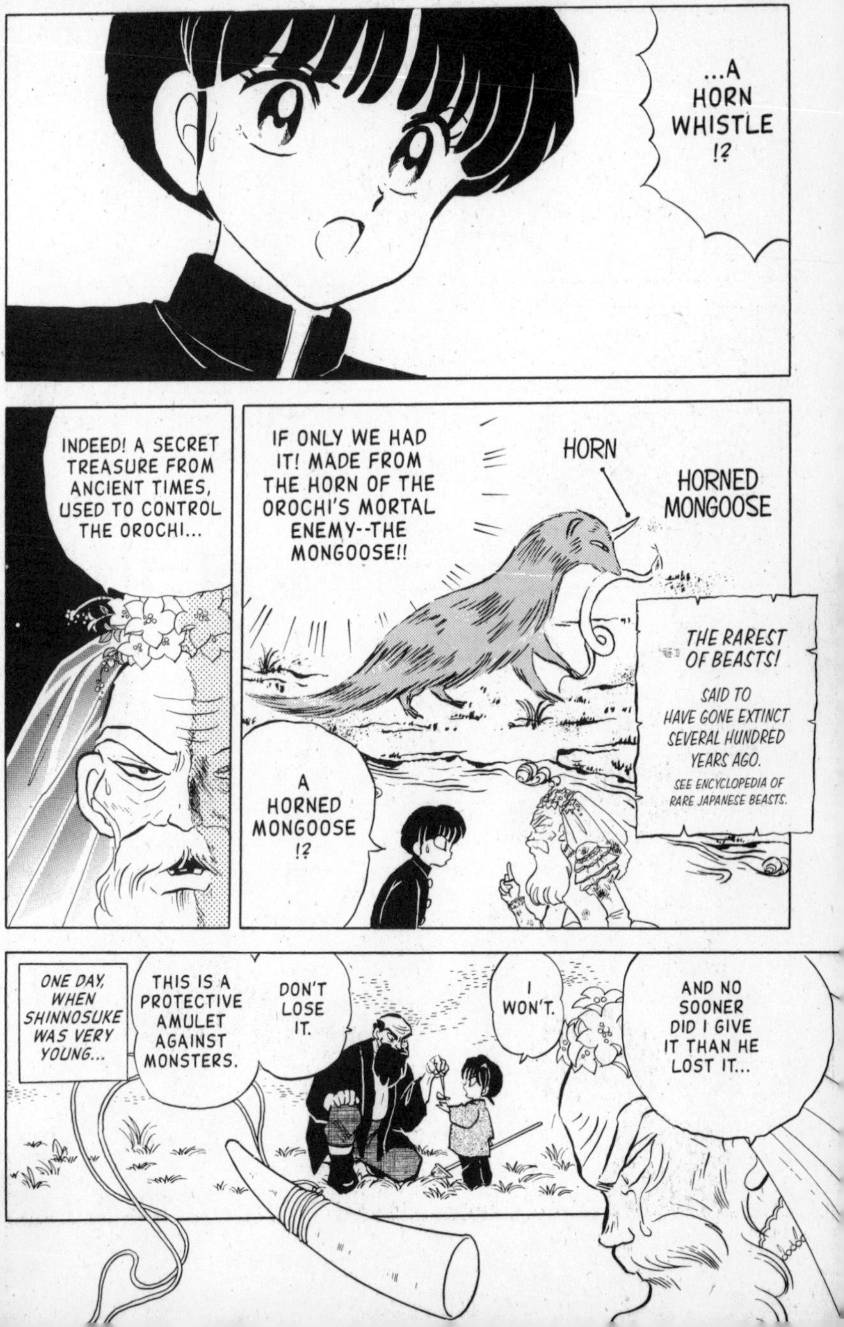
...A HORN WHISTLE !?
INDEED! A SECRET TREASURE FROM ANCIENT TIMES, USED TO CONTROL THE OROCHI...
IF ONLY WE HAD IT! MADE FROM THE HORN OF THE OROCHI'S MORTAL ENEMY--THE MONGOOSE!!
HORN
HORNED MONGOOSE
THE RAREST OF BEASTS!
SAID TO HAVE GONE EXTINCT SEVERAL HUNDRED YEARS AGO.
SEE ENCYCLOPEDIA OF RARE JAPANESE BEASTS.
A HORNED MONGOOSE !?
ONE DAY, WHEN SHINNOSUKE WAS VERY YOUNG...
THIS IS A PROTECTIVE AMULET AGAINST MONSTERS.
DON'T LOSE IT.
I WON'T.
AND NO SOONER DID I GIVE IT THAN HE LOST IT...

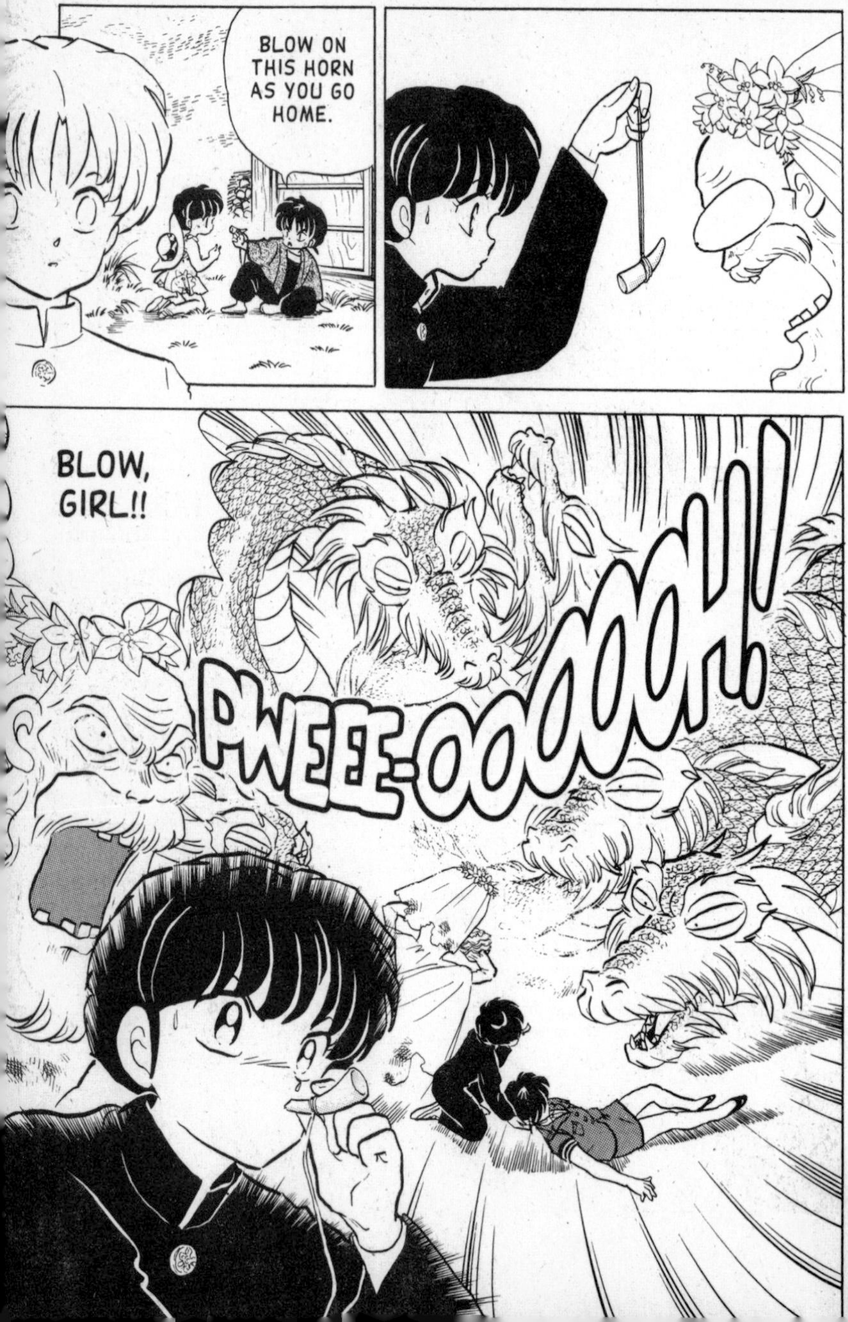
BLOW ON THIS HORN AS YOU GO HOME.
BLOW, GIRL!!
PWEEE-OOOOOH!

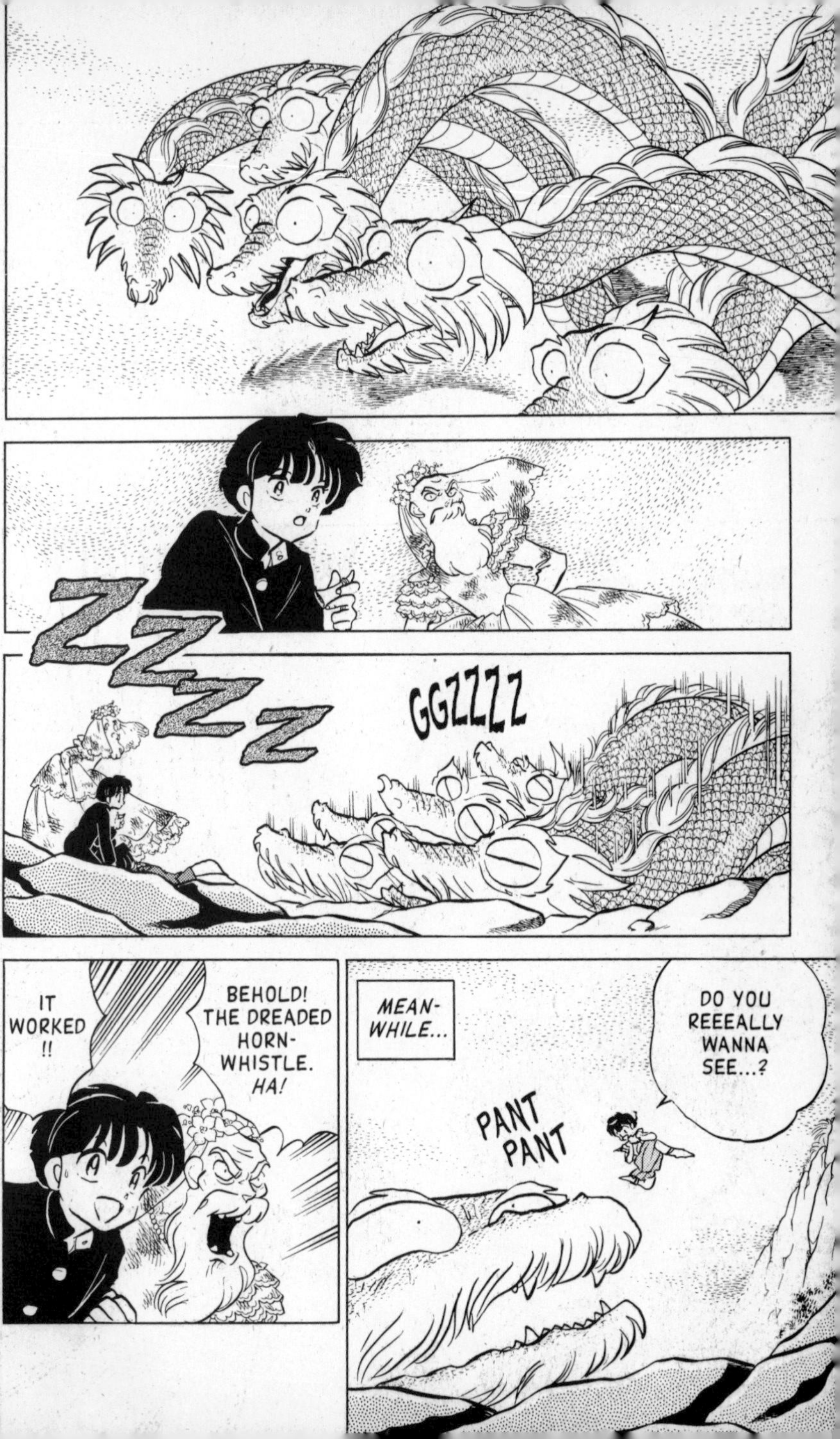
ZZZZZ
GGZZZZ
IT WORKED !!
BEHOLD! THE DREADED HORN-WHISTLE. HA!
MEAN-WHILE...
PANT PANT
DO YOU REEEALLY WANNA SEE...?

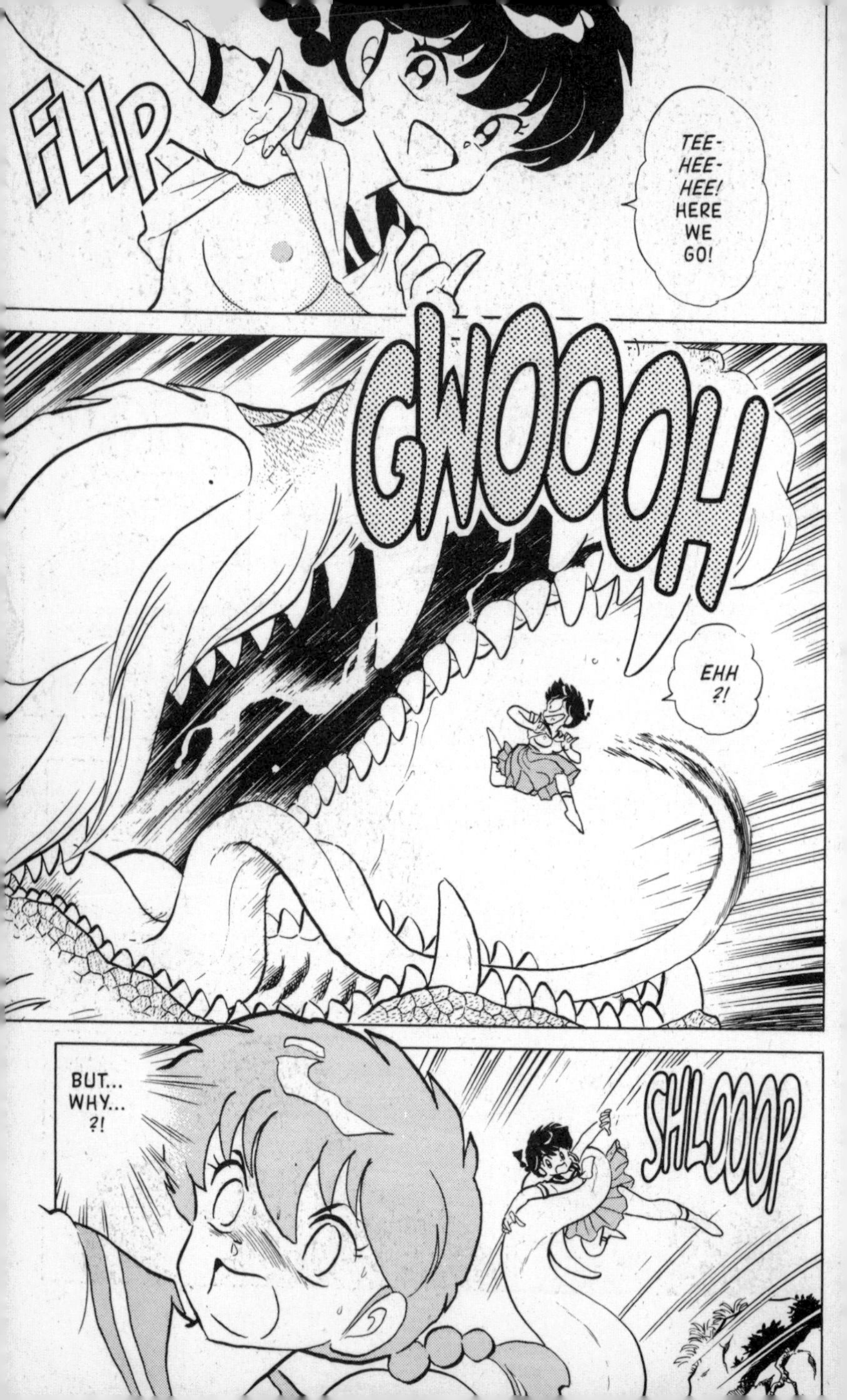
FLIP
TEE-HEE-HEE! HERE WE GO!
GWOOOH
EHH ?!
BUT... WHY... ?!
SHLOOP

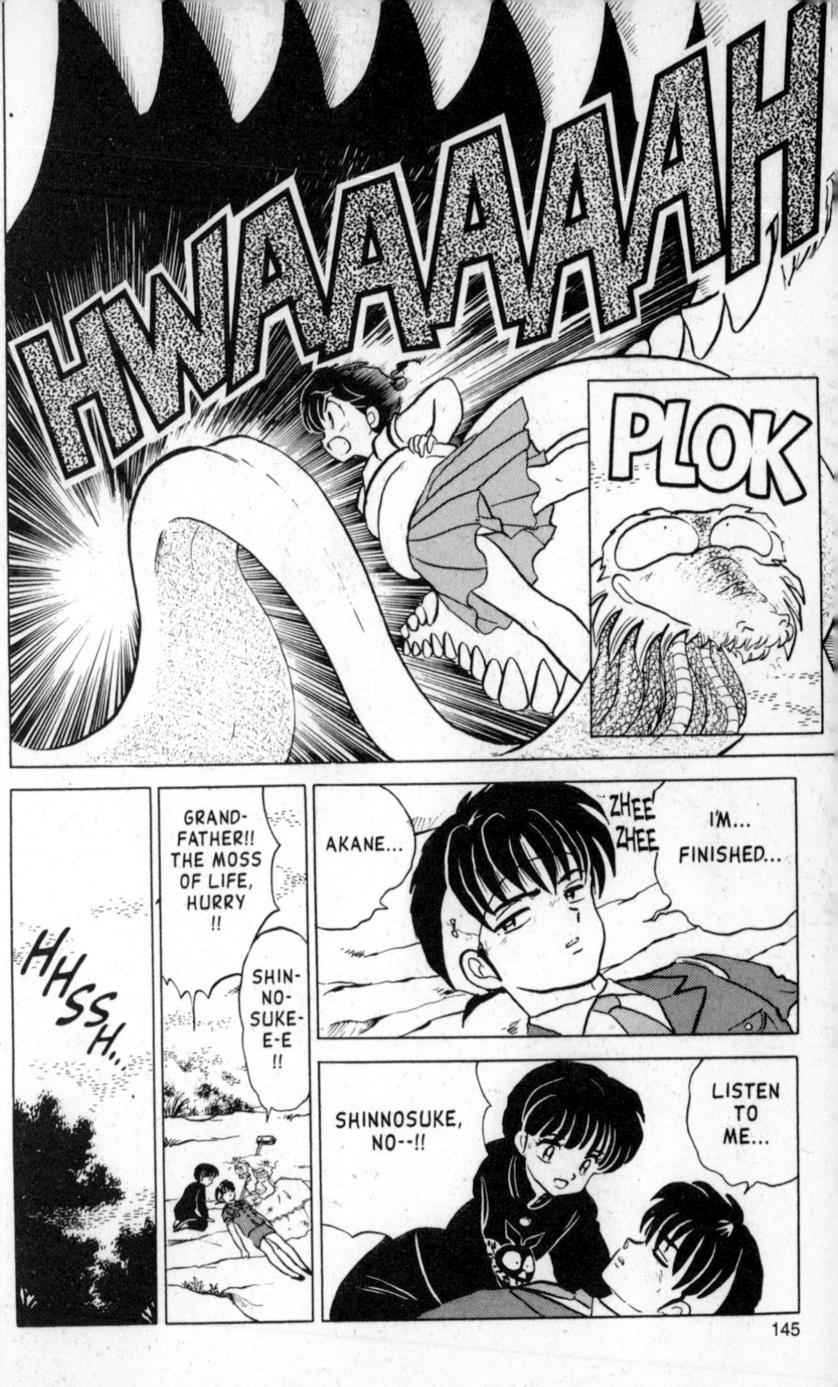
HWAAAAAH
PLOK
HHSSH...
GRAND-FATHER!! THE MOSS OF LIFE, HURRY !!
SHIN-NO-SUKE-E-E !!
AKANE...
ZHEE ZHEE
I'M... FINISHED...
SHINNOSUKE, NO--!!
LISTEN TO ME...

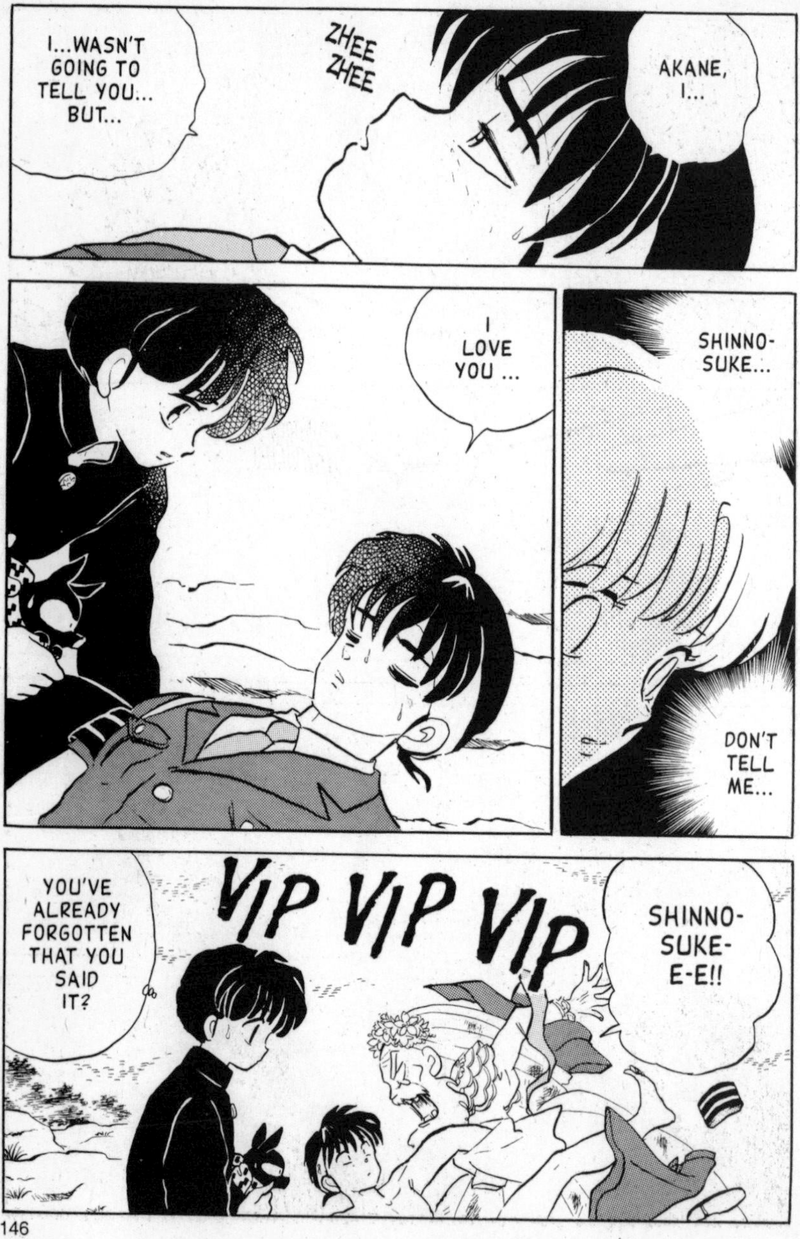
I...WASN'T GOING TO TELL YOU... BUT...
ZHEE ZHEE
AKANE, I...
I LOVE YOU ...
SHINNO-SUKE...
DON'T TELL ME...
YOU'VE ALREADY FORGOTTEN THAT YOU SAID IT?
VIP VIP VIP
SHINNO-SUKE-E-E!!

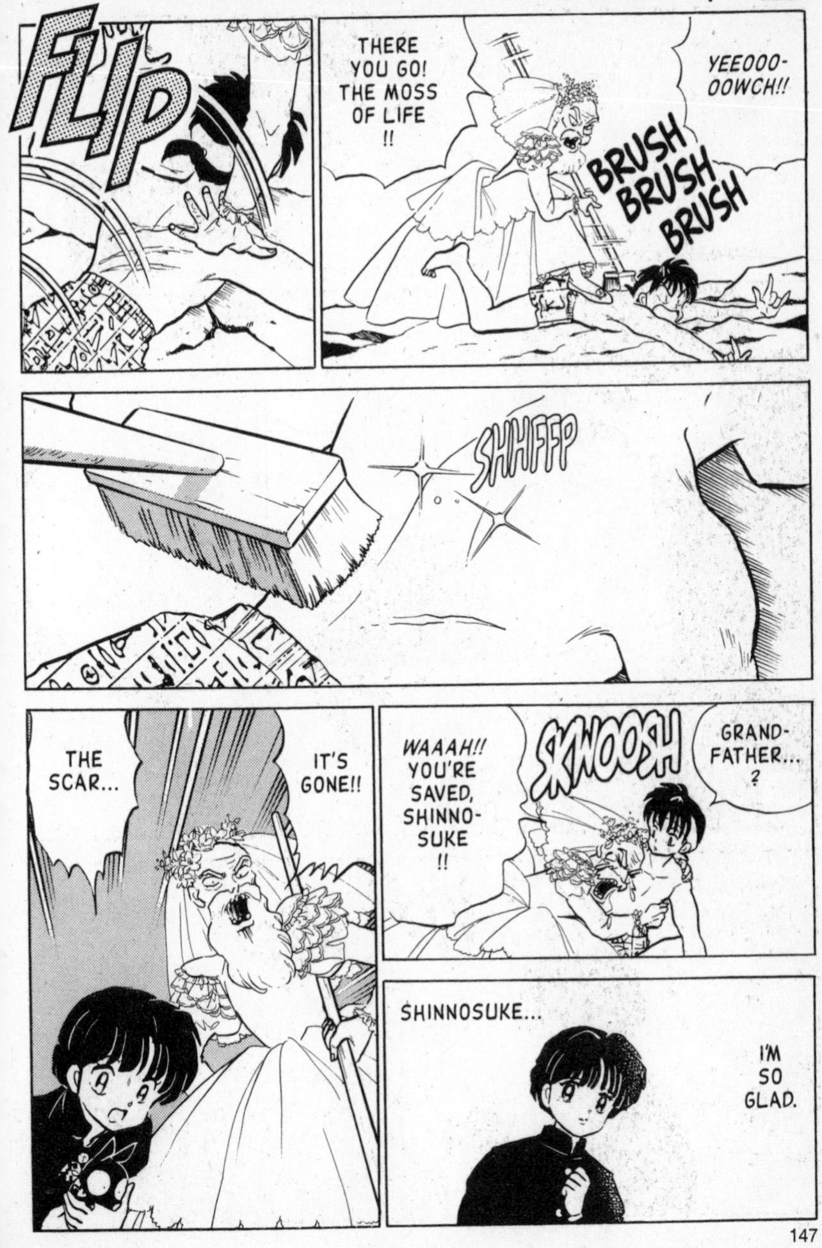
FLIP
THERE YOU GO! THE MOSS OF LIFE !!
YEEOOO-OOWCH!!
BRUSH BRUSH BRUSH
SHHFFP
THE SCAR...
IT'S GONE!!
WAAAH!! YOU'RE SAVED, SHINNO-SUKE !!
SKWOOSH
GRAND-FATHER... ?
SHINNOSUKE...
I'M SO GLAD.

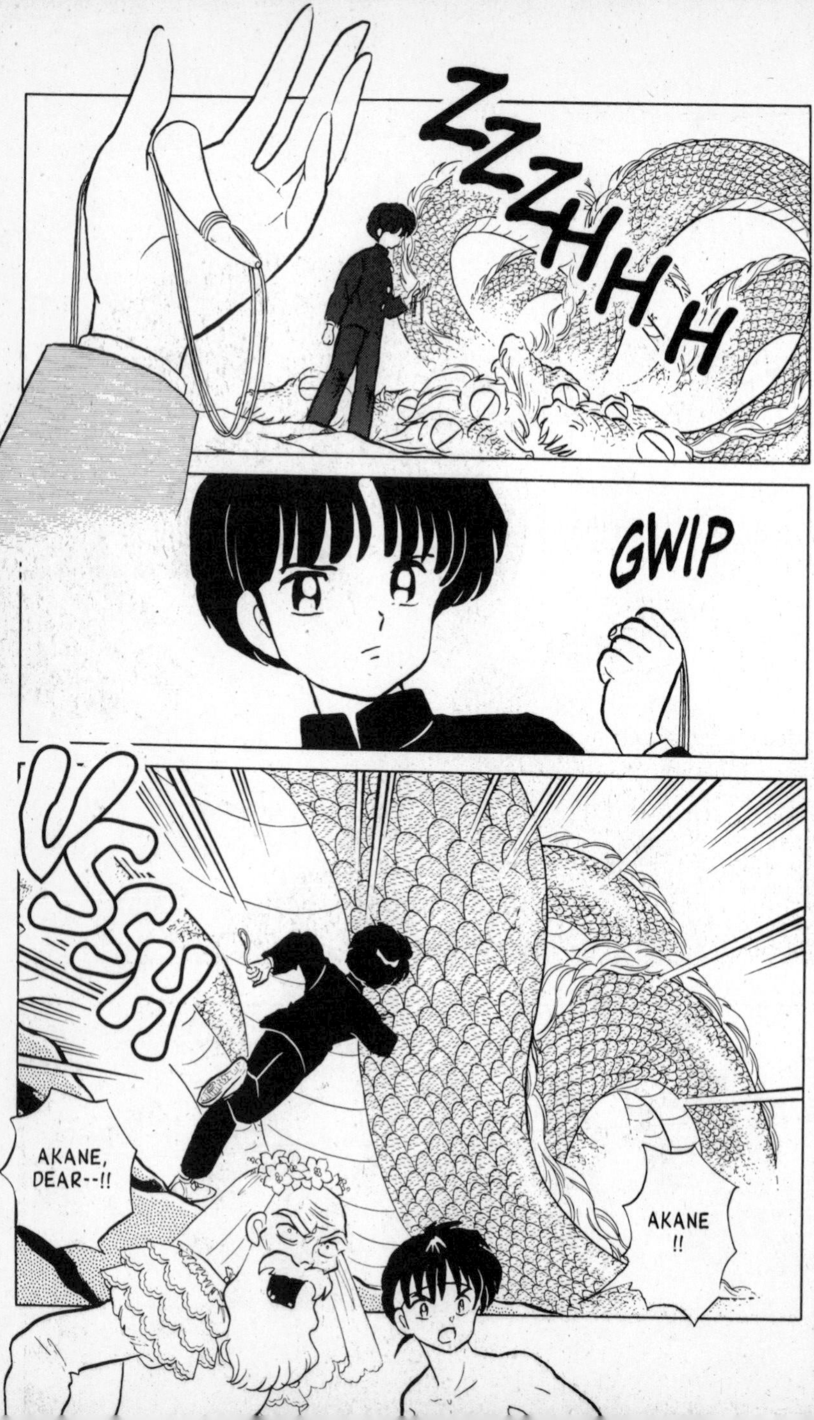

ZZZHHHH
GWIP
VSSSH
AKANE, DEAR--!!
AKANE !!

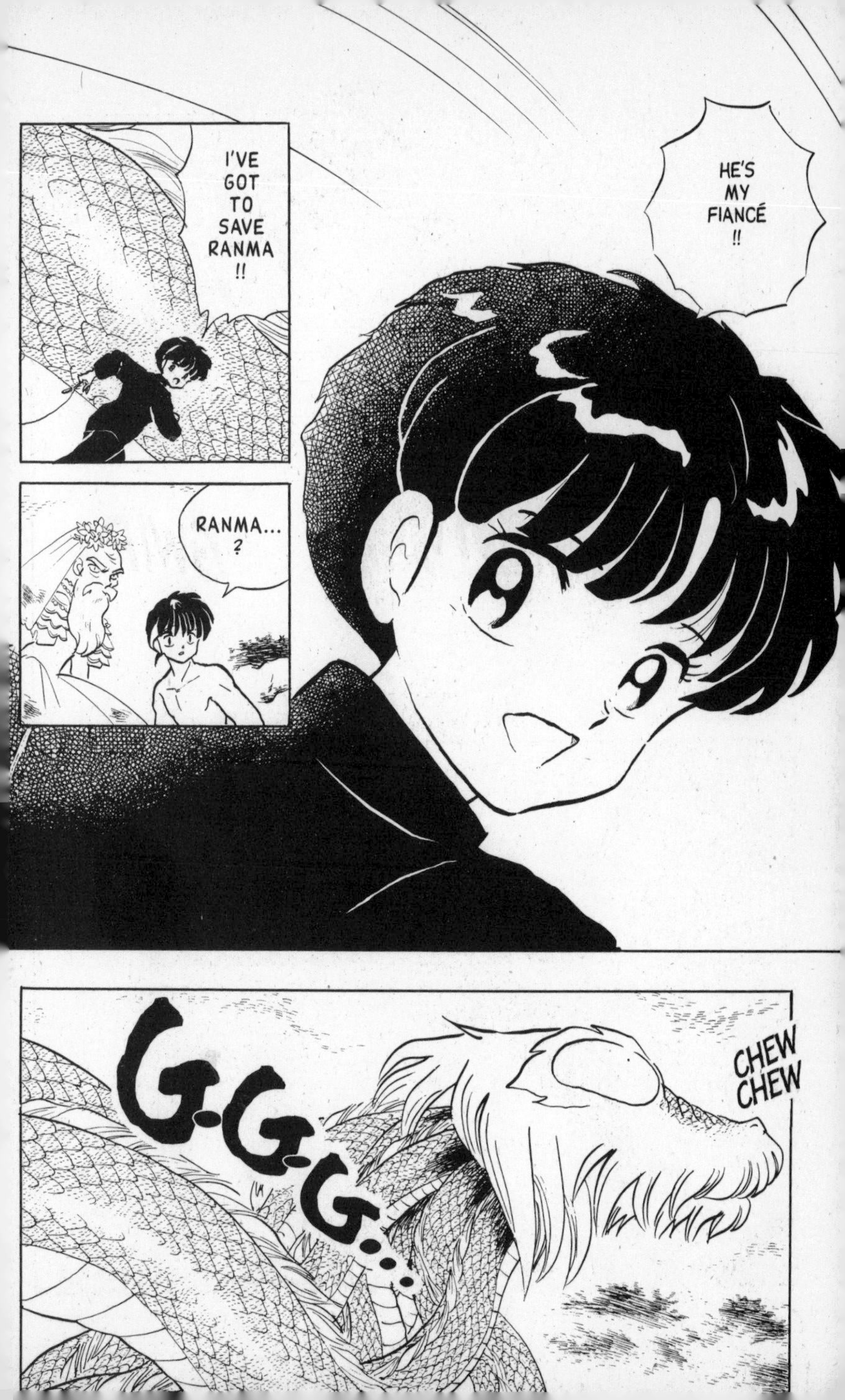
I'VE GOT TO SAVE RANMA !!
RANMA... ?
HE'S MY FIANCÉ !!
G-G-G...
CHEW CHEW

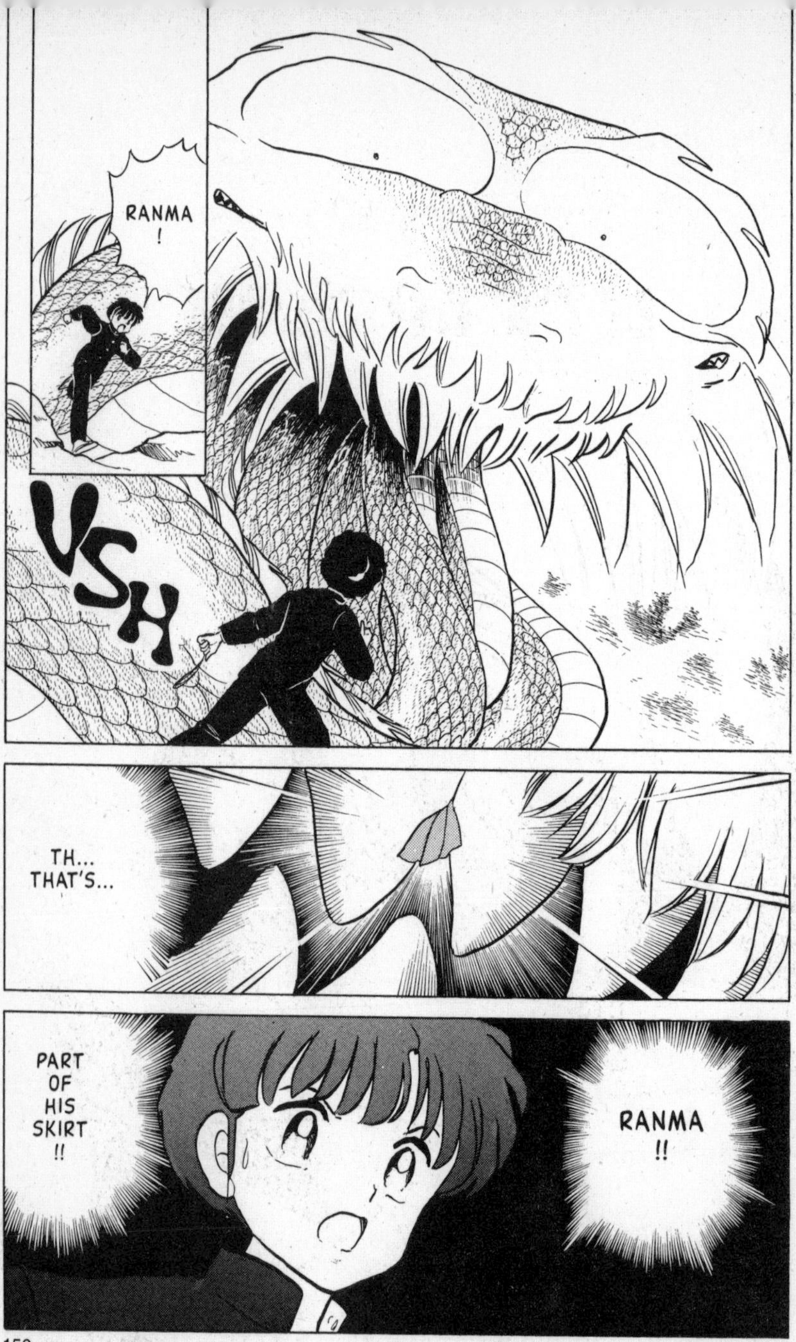
RANMA !
VSH
TH... THAT'S...
PART OF HIS SKIRT !!
RANMA !!

Part 10

LET'S GO HOME

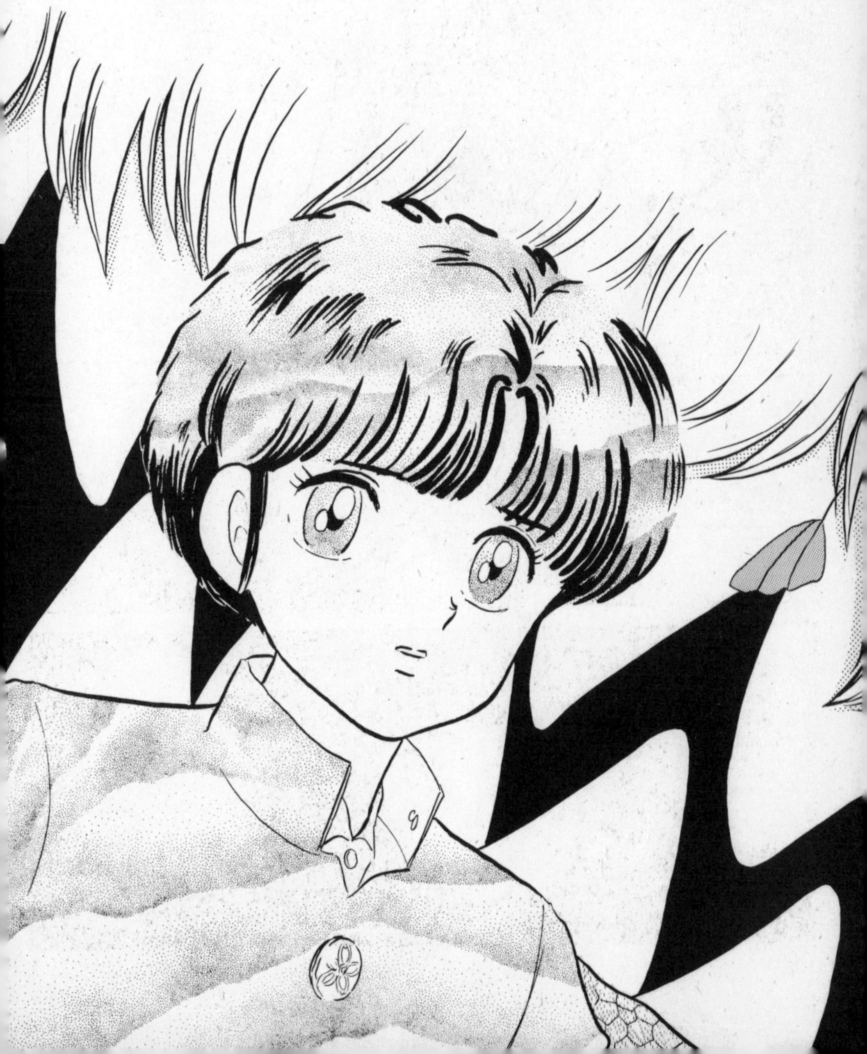

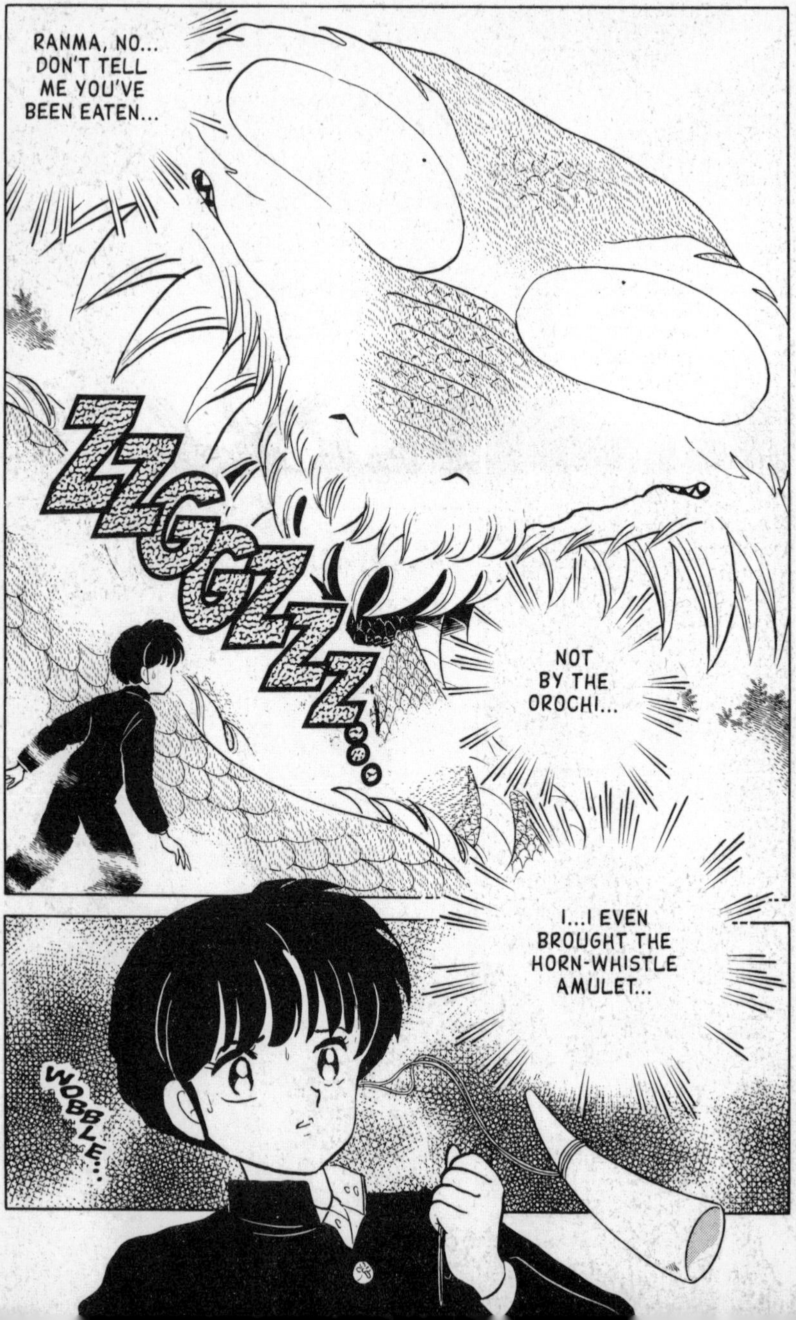
RANMA, NO... DON'T TELL ME YOU'VE BEEN EATEN...
ZZGGZZZ...
NOT BY THE OROCHI...
WOBBLE...
I...I EVEN BROUGHT THE HORN-WHISTLE AMULET...

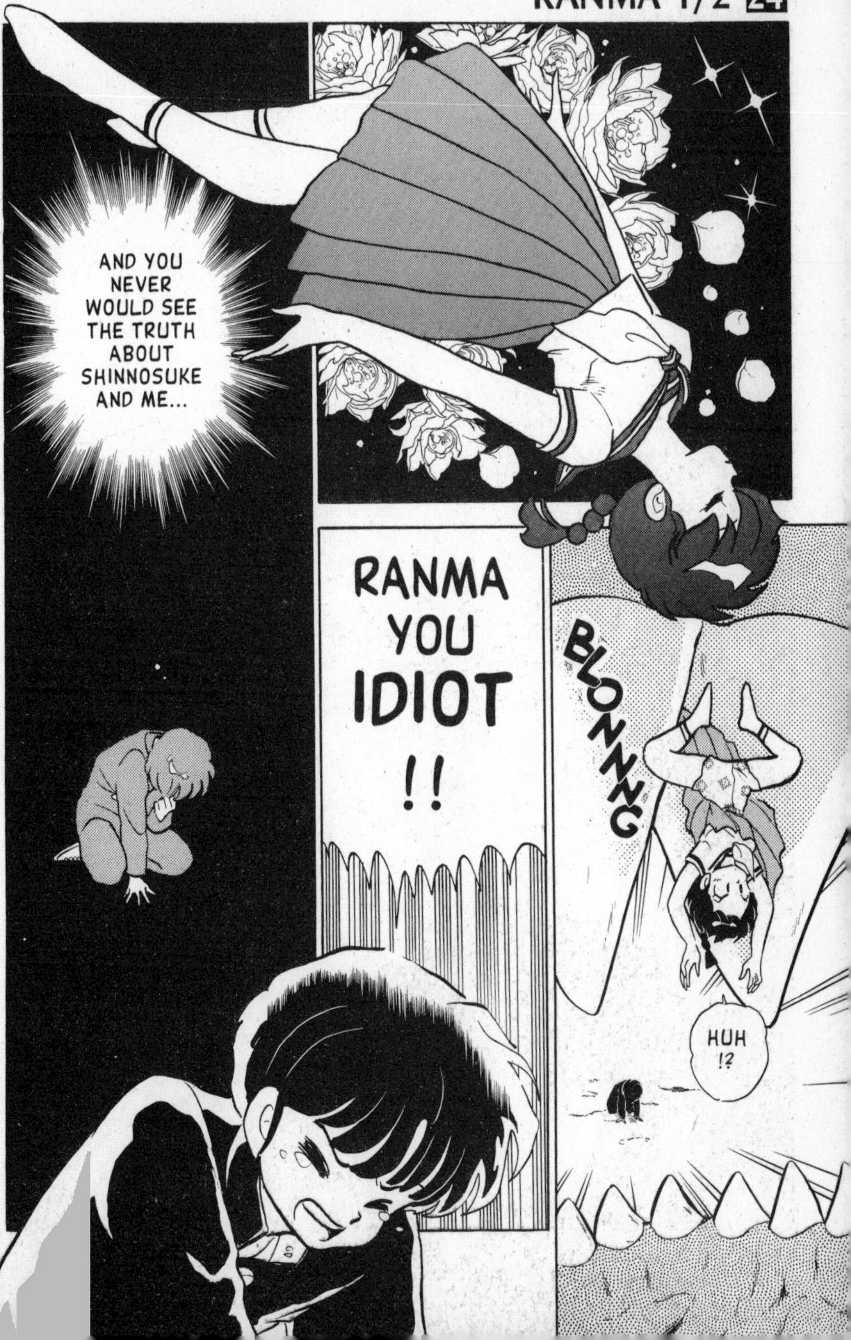
AND YOU NEVER WOULD SEE THE TRUTH ABOUT SHINNOSUKE AND ME...
RANMA YOU IDIOT !!
BLONNNG
HUH !?

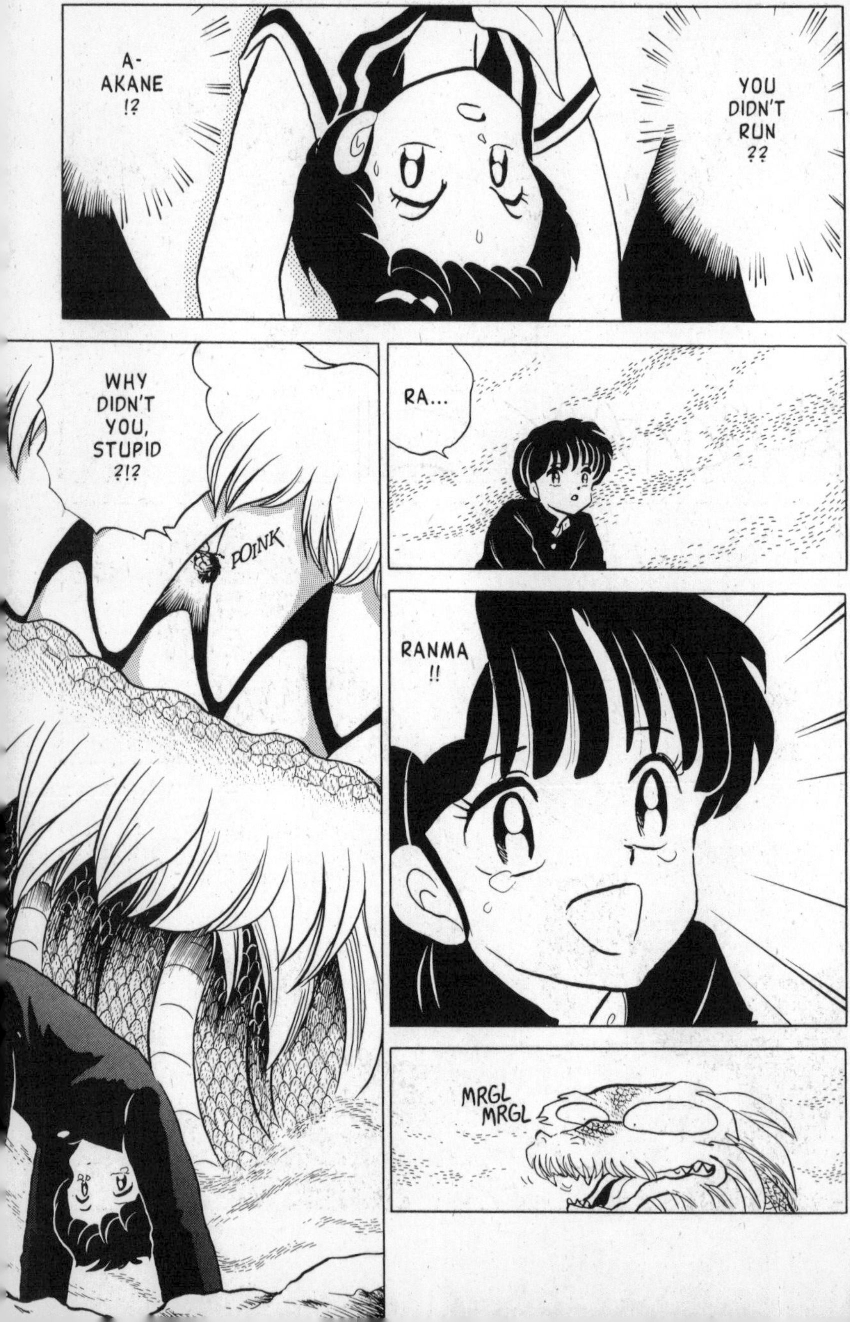
A-
AKANE
!?
YOU
DIDN'T
RUN
??
WHY
DIDN'T
YOU,
STUPID
?!?
POINK
RA...
RANMA
!!
MRGL
MRGL

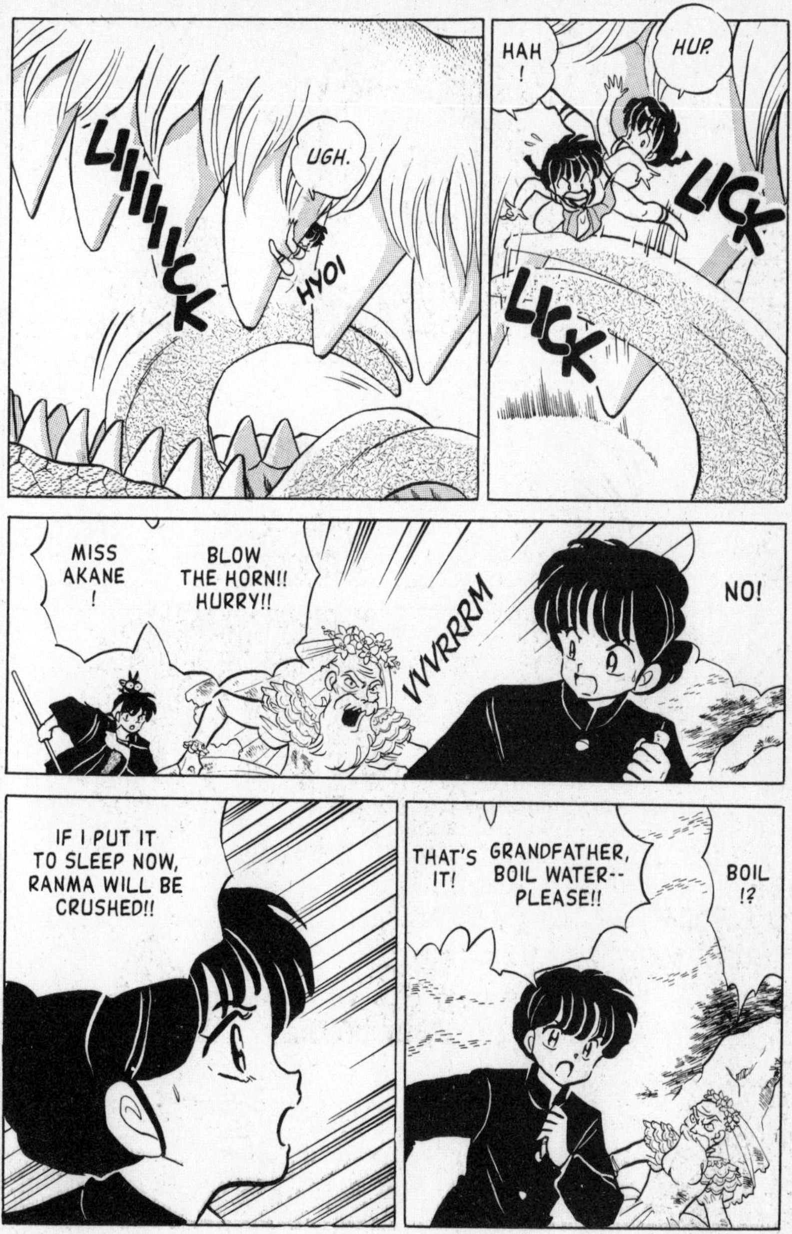
LIIIIICK
UGH.
HYOI
HAH !
HUP.
LICK
LICK
MISS AKANE !
BLOW THE HORN!! HURRY!!
VVVRRRM
NO!
IF I PUT IT TO SLEEP NOW, RANMA WILL BE CRUSHED!!
THAT'S IT!
GRANDFATHER, BOIL WATER-- PLEASE!!
BOIL !?

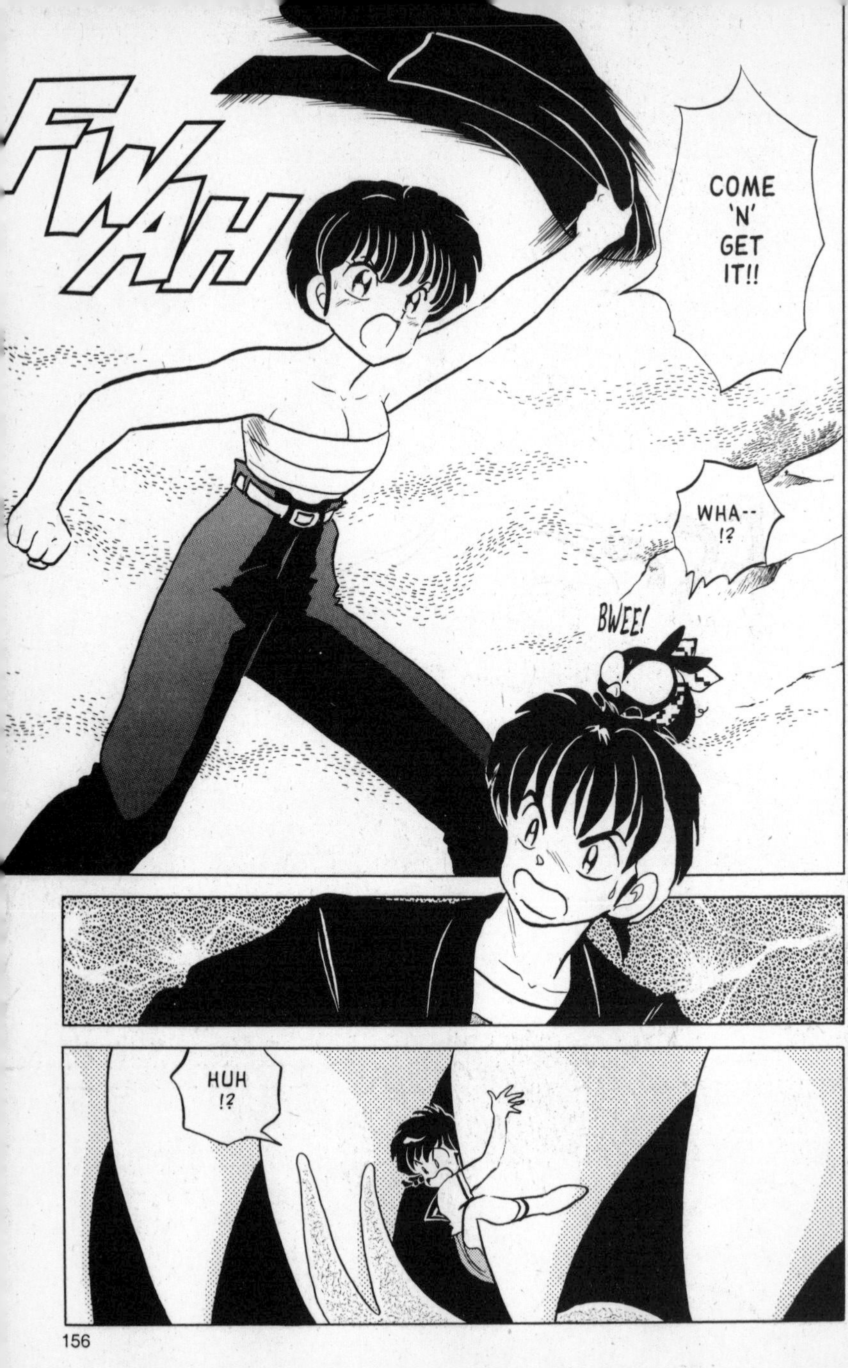
FWAH
COME 'N' GET IT!!
WHA--!?
BWEE!
HUH!?

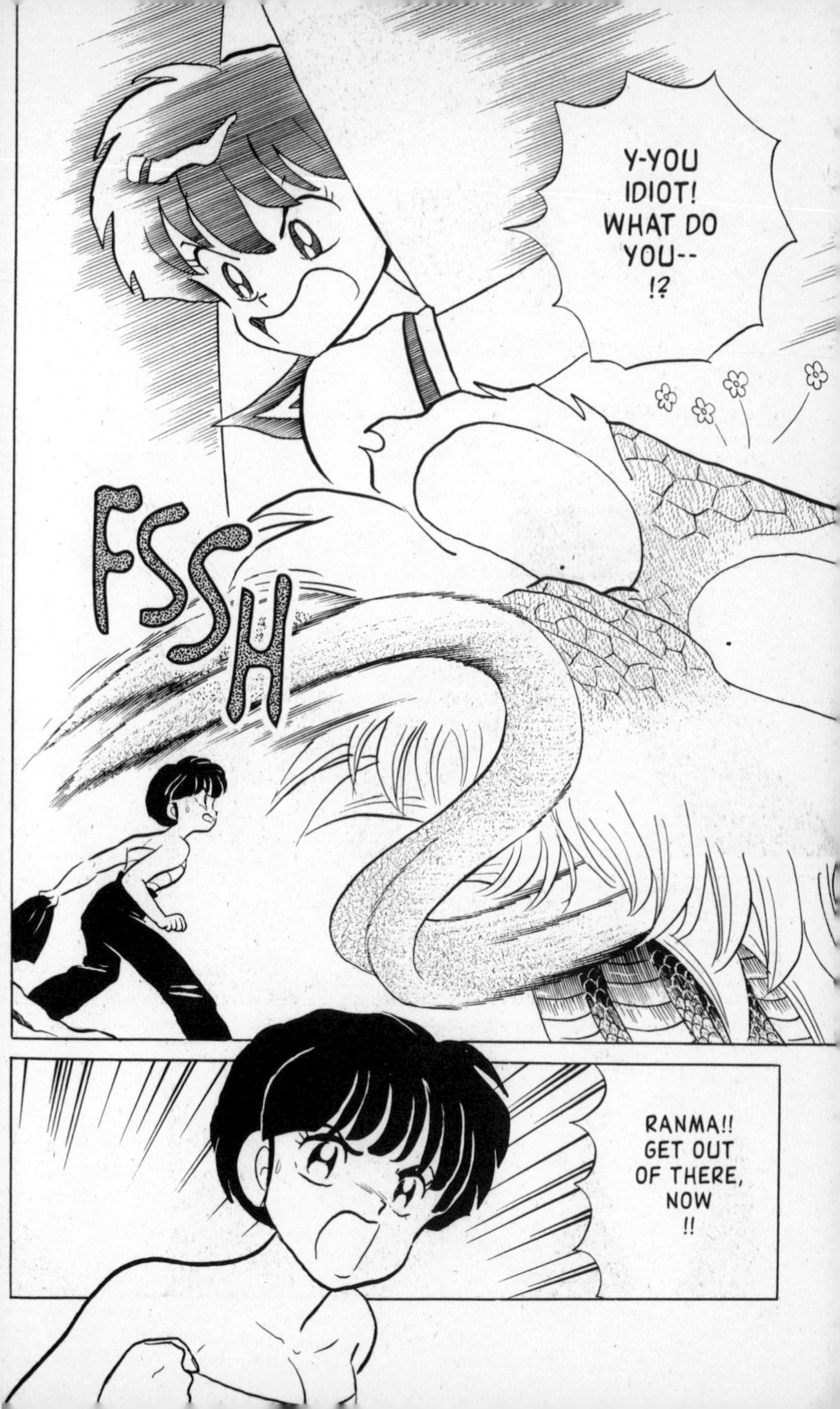
Y-YOU IDIOT! WHAT DO YOU-- !?
FSSH
RANMA!! GET OUT OF THERE, NOW !!

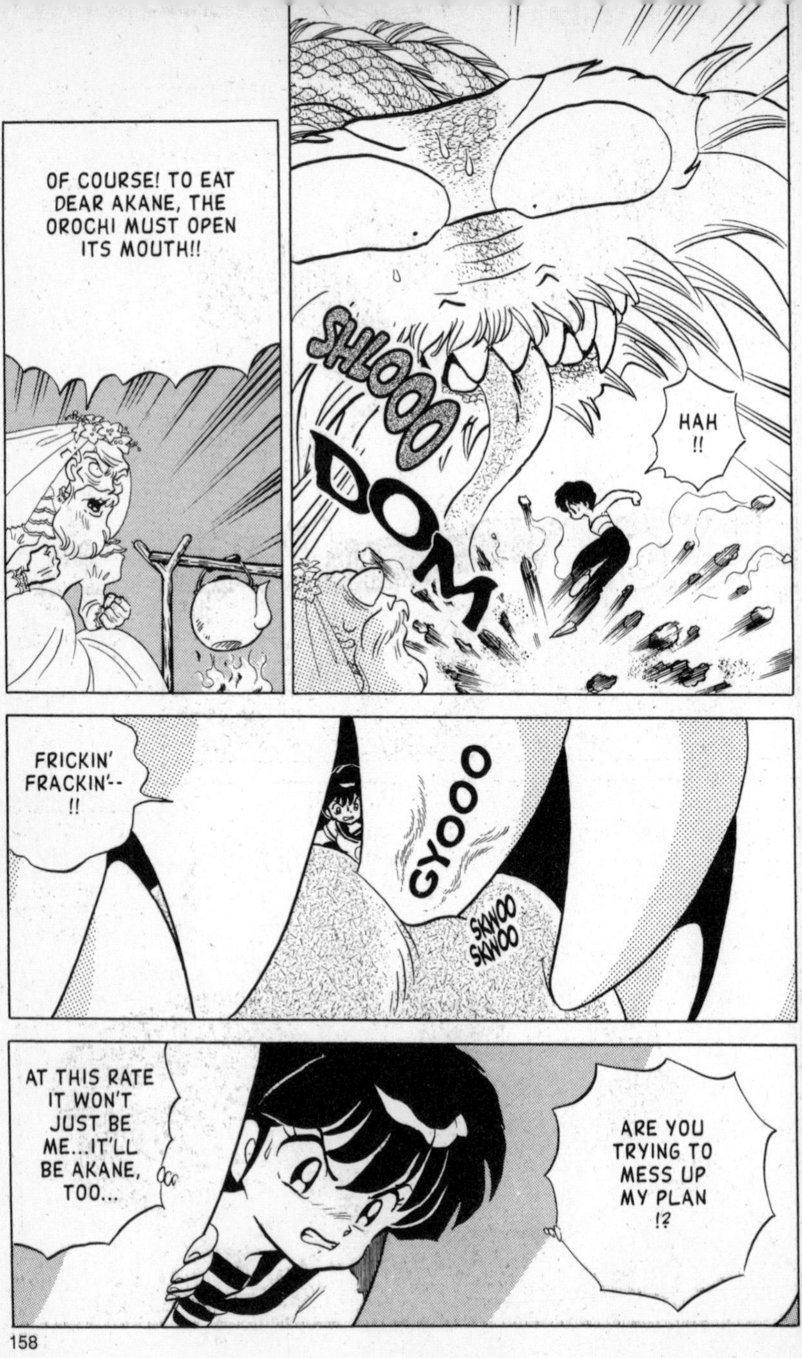

OF COURSE! TO EAT DEAR AKANE, THE OROCHI MUST OPEN ITS MOUTH!!
SHLOOO
DOM
HAH !!
FRICKIN' FRACKIN'-- !!
GYOOO
SKWOO SKWOO
AT THIS RATE IT WON'T JUST BE ME...IT'LL BE AKANE, TOO...
ARE YOU TRYING TO MESS UP MY PLAN !?

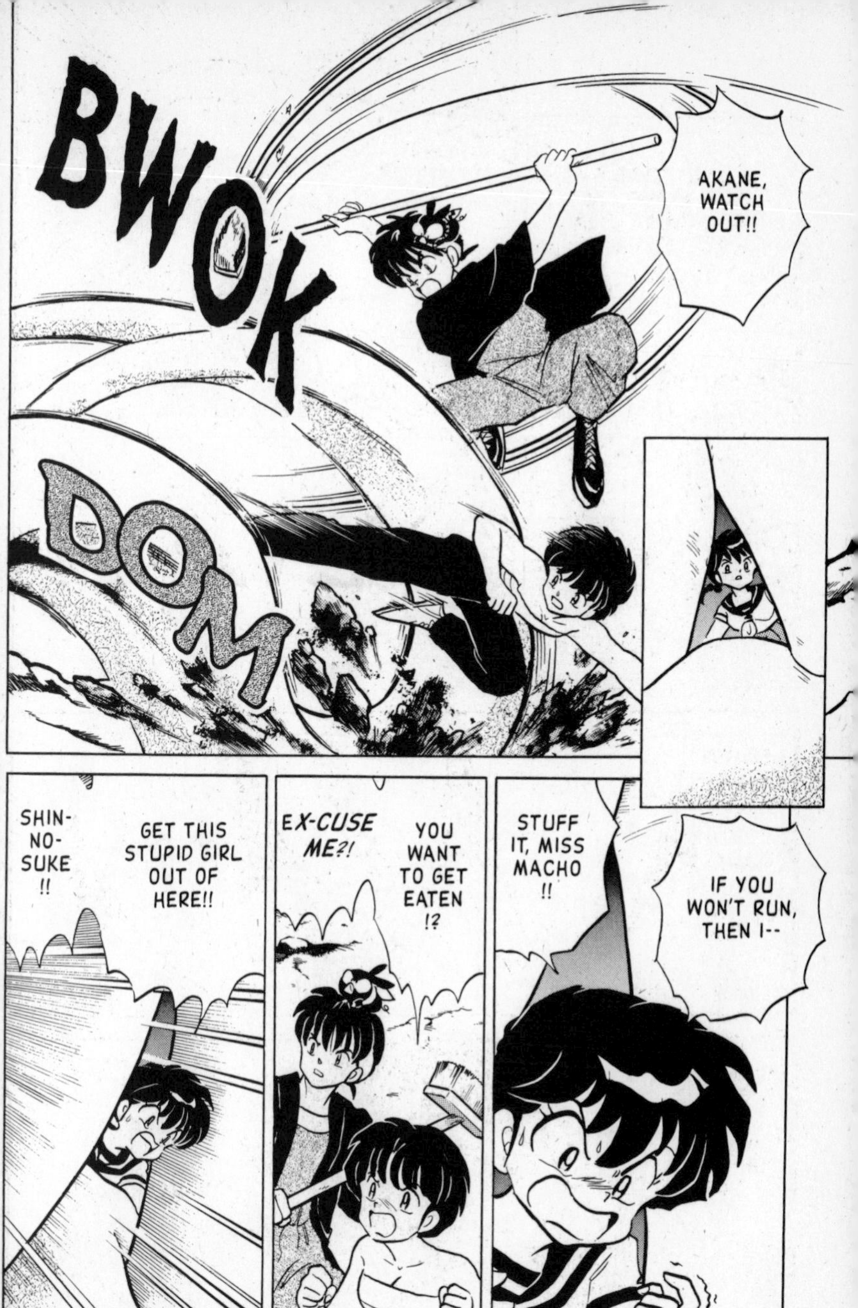
BWOK
AKANE, WATCH OUT!!
DOM
SHIN-NO-SUKE!!
GET THIS STUPID GIRL OUT OF HERE!!
EX-CUSE ME?!
YOU WANT TO GET EATEN!?
STUFF IT, MISS MACHO!!
IF YOU WON'T RUN, THEN I--

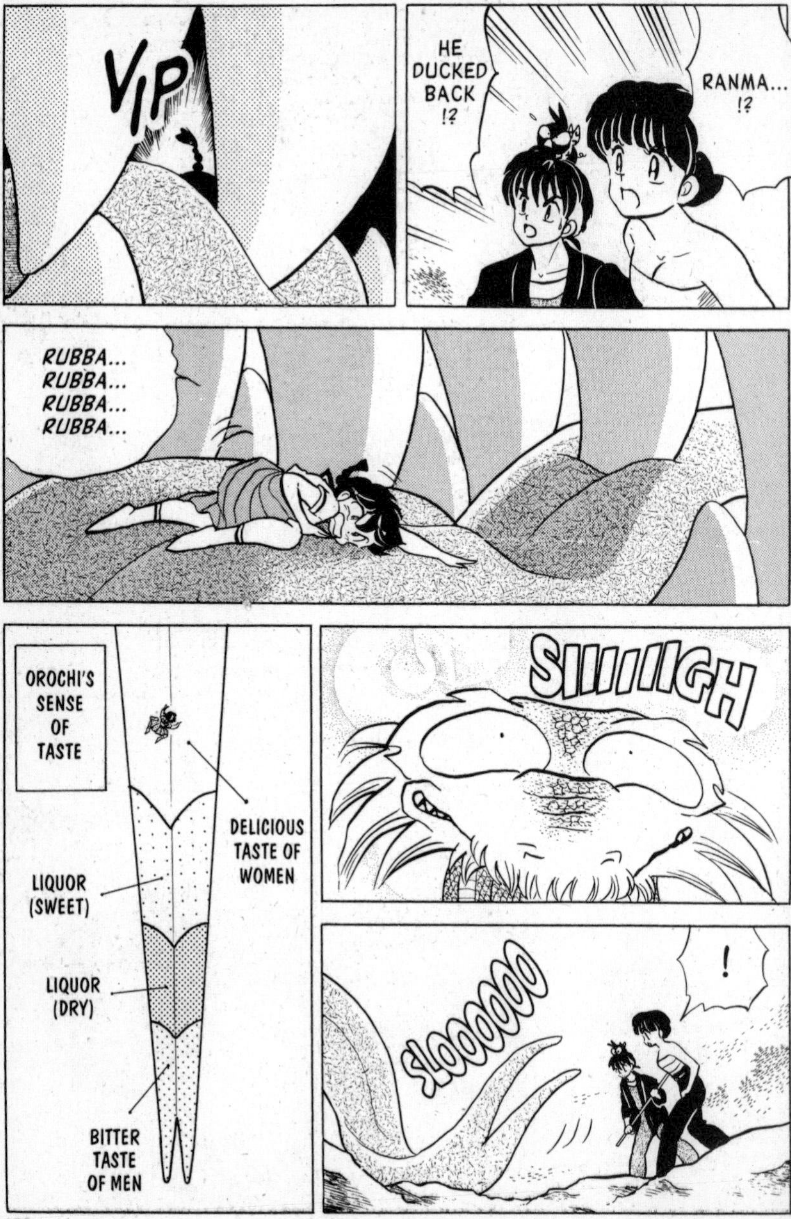
VIP
HE DUCKED BACK !?
RANMA... !?
RUBBA... RUBBA... RUBBA... RUBBA...
OROCHI'S SENSE OF TASTE
DELICIOUS TASTE OF WOMEN
LIQUOR (SWEET)
LIQUOR (DRY)
BITTER TASTE OF MEN
SIIIIIIGH
SLOOOOOO
!

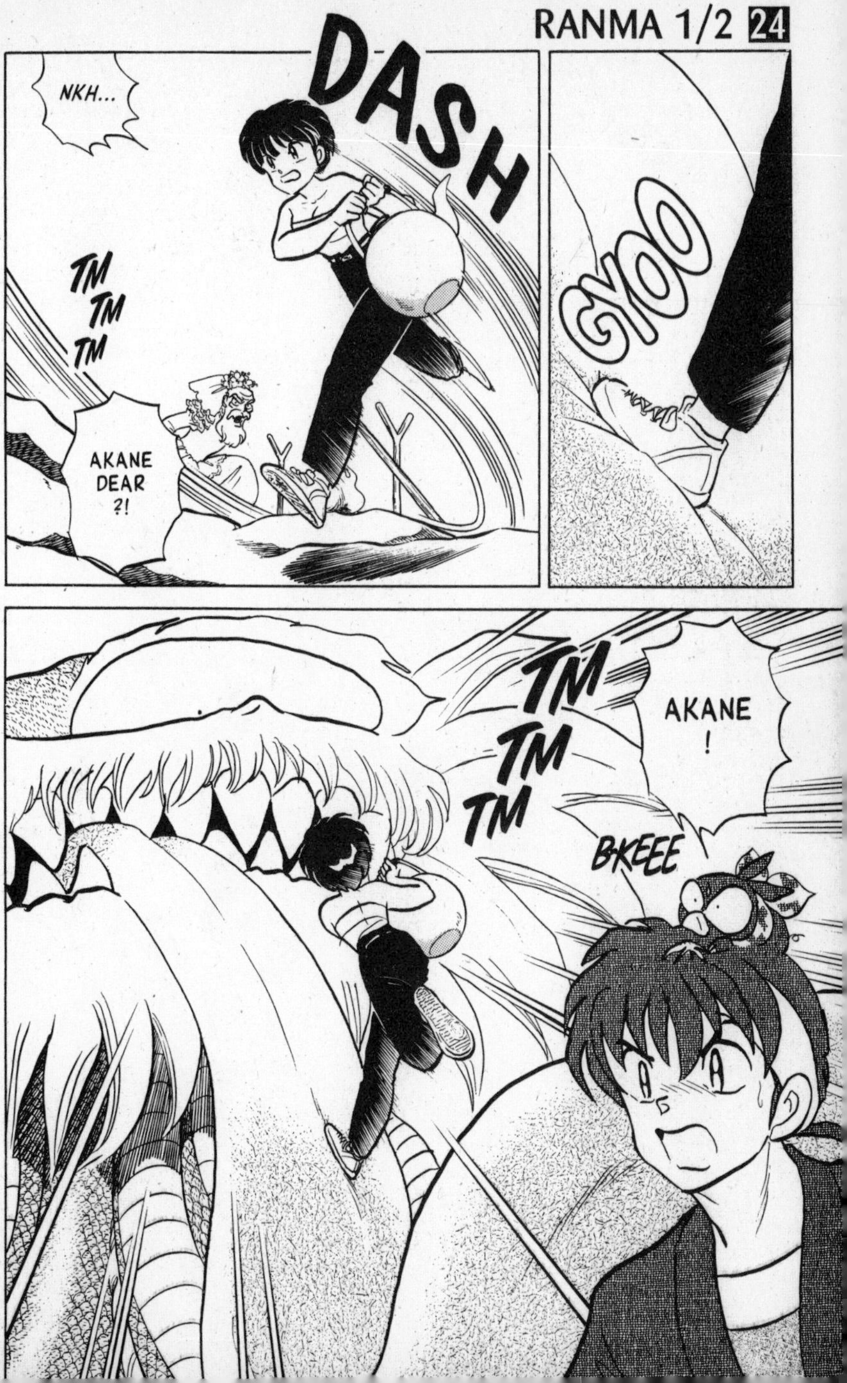
NKH...
DASH
TM
TM
TM
AKANE
DEAR
?!
GYOO
TM
TM
TM
AKANE
!
B-KEEE

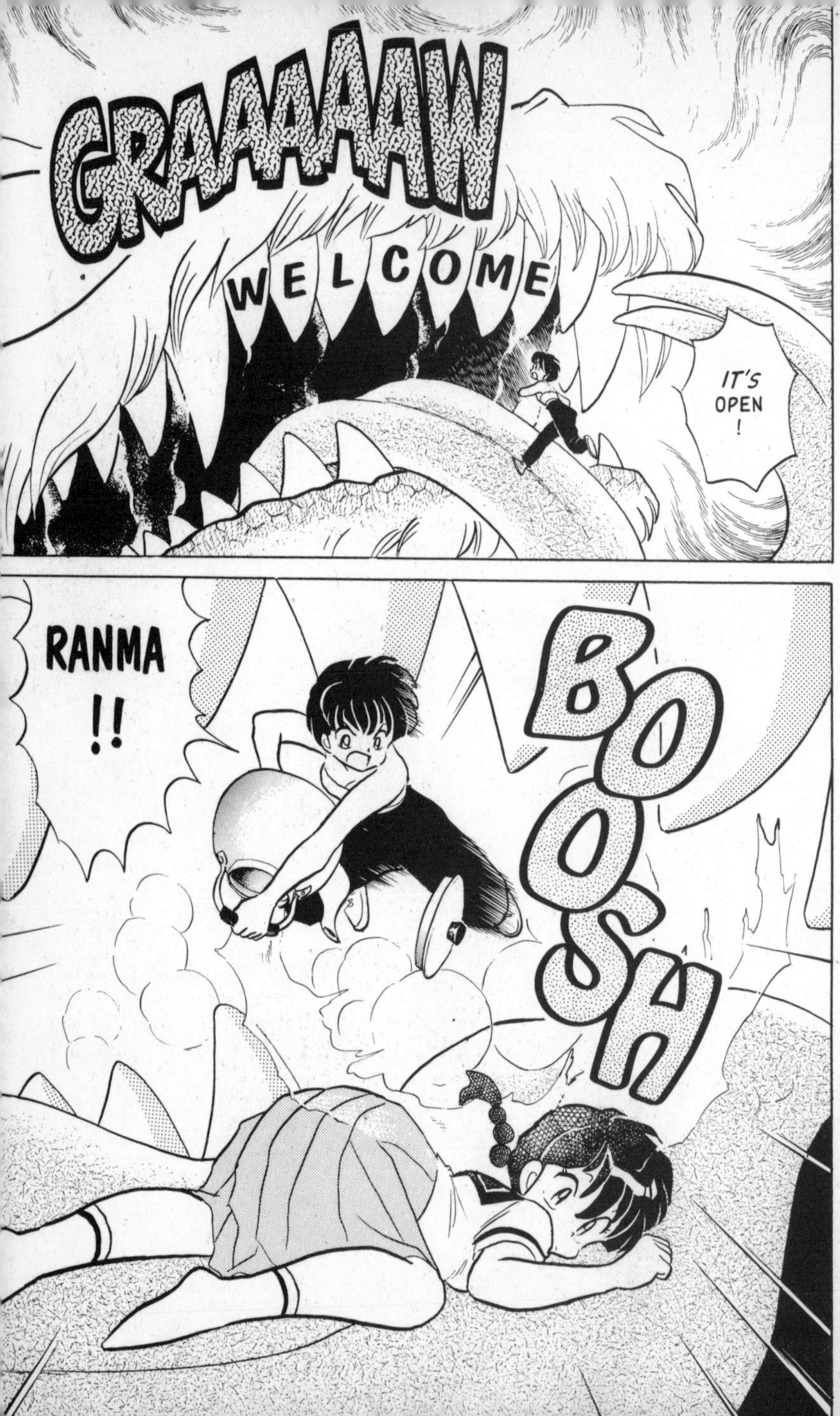
GRAAAAAW
WELCOME
IT'S OPEN!
RANMA!!
BOOSH

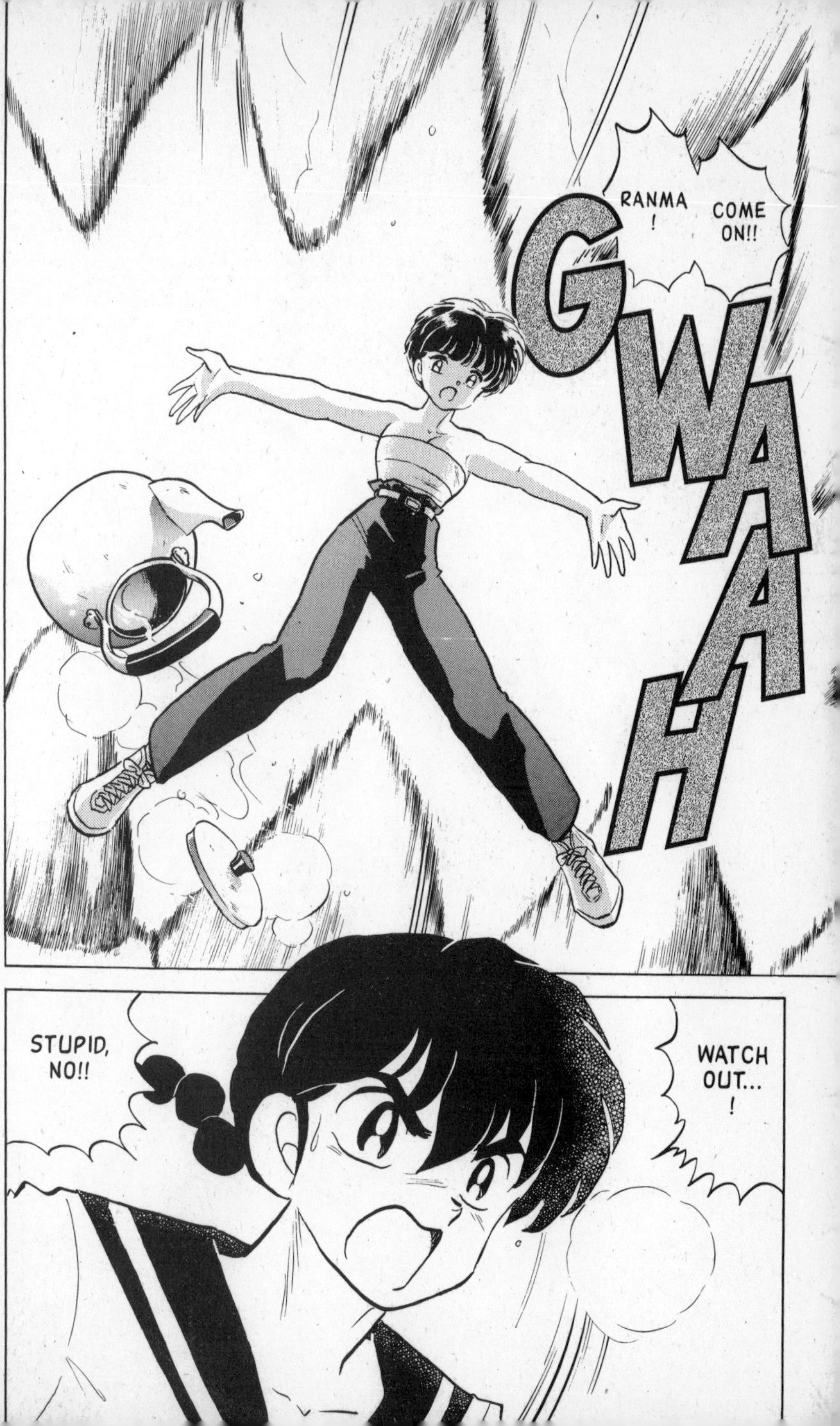
RANMA! COME ON!!
GWAAH
STUPID, NO!!
WATCH OUT...!

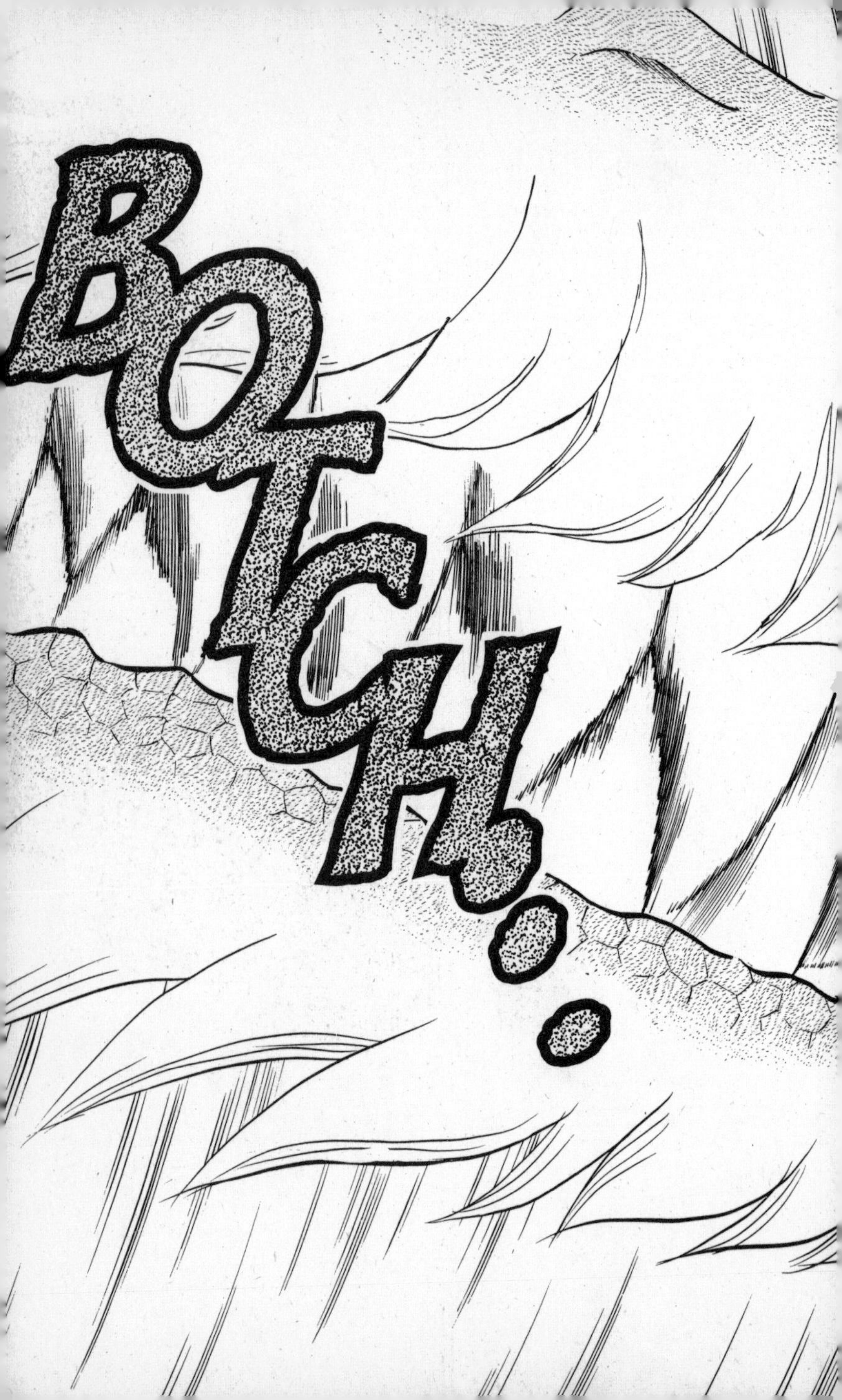
BOTCH!

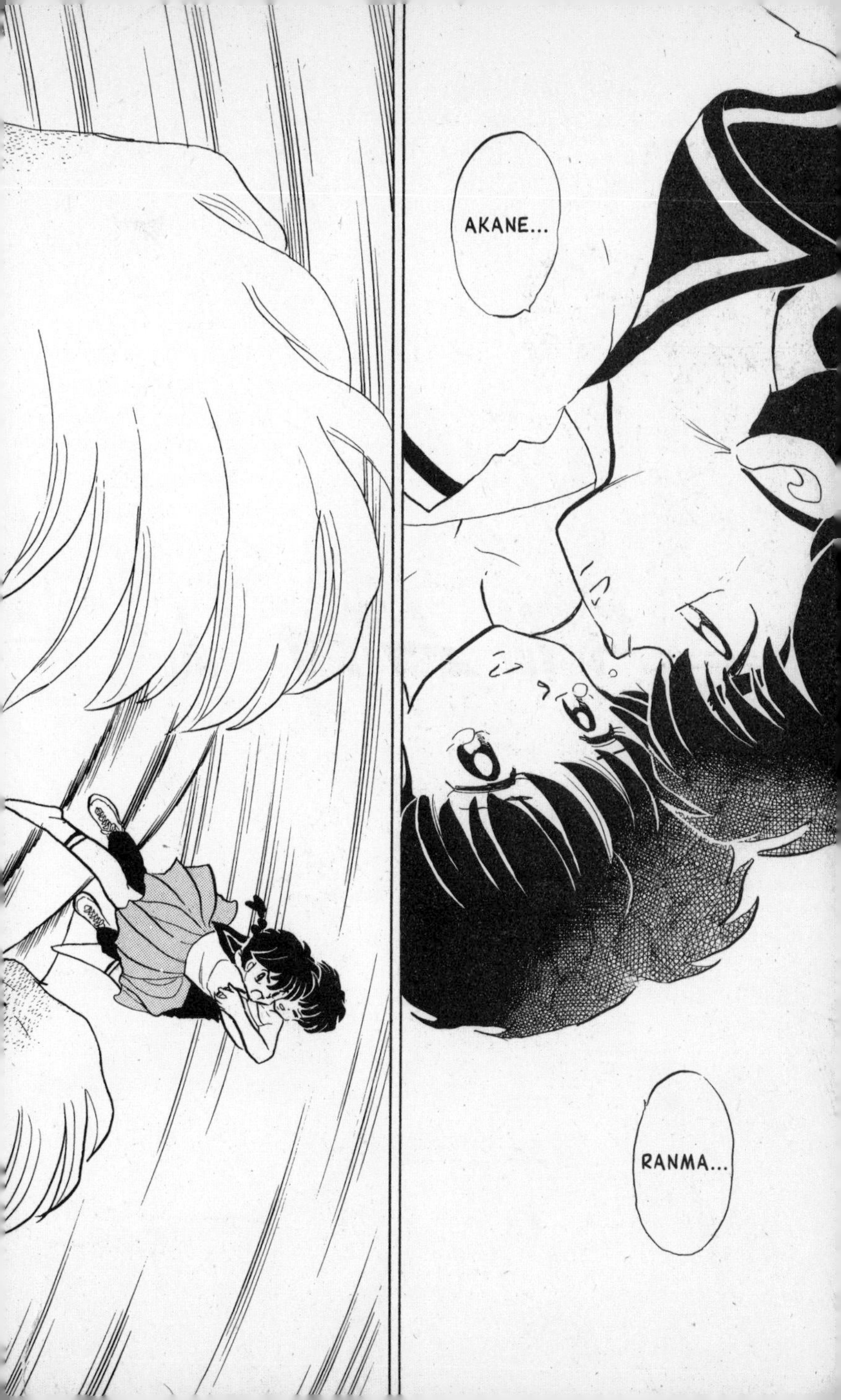
AKANE...
RANMA...

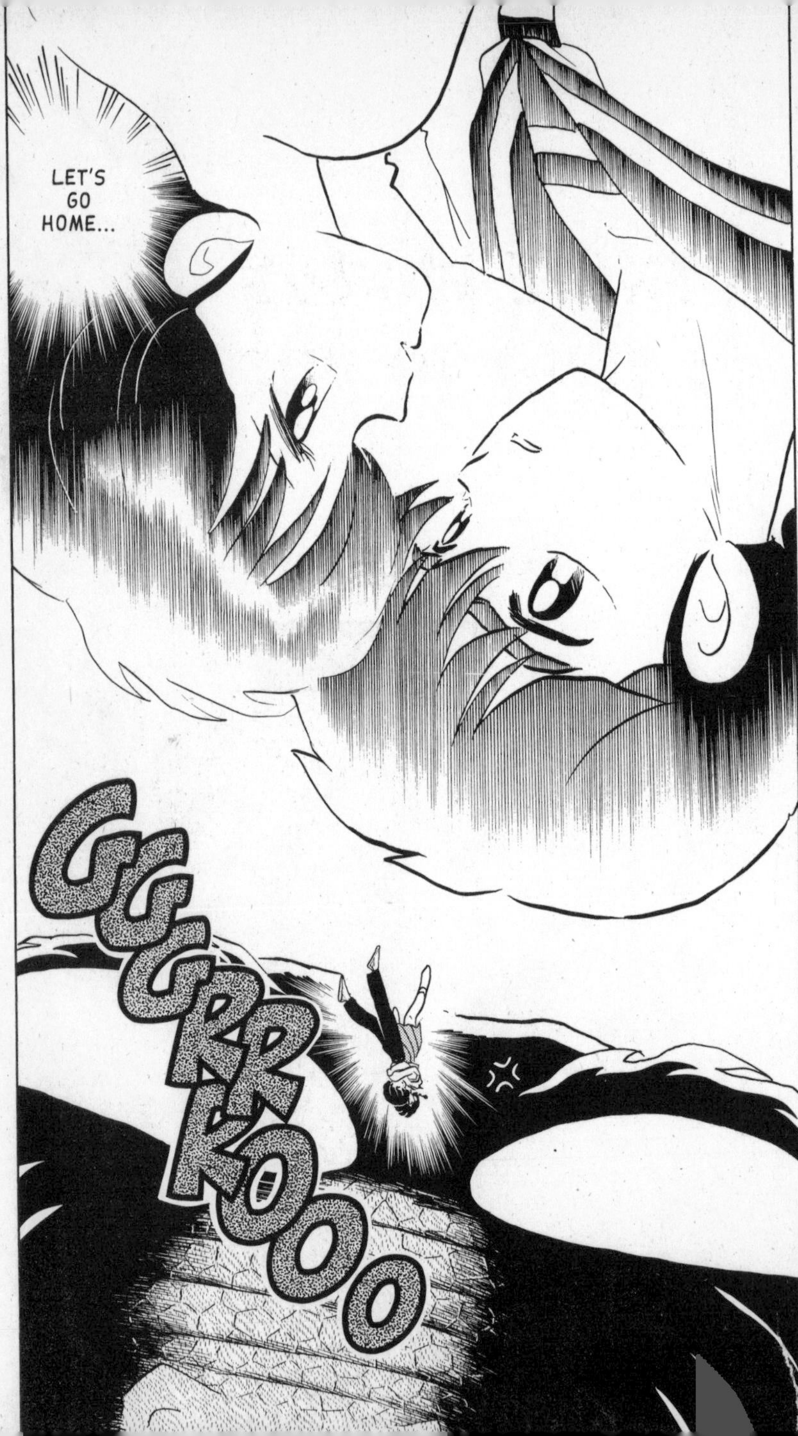
LET'S GO HOME...
GUGRRKOOOO

Part 11

THESE WORDS I SEND TO YOU

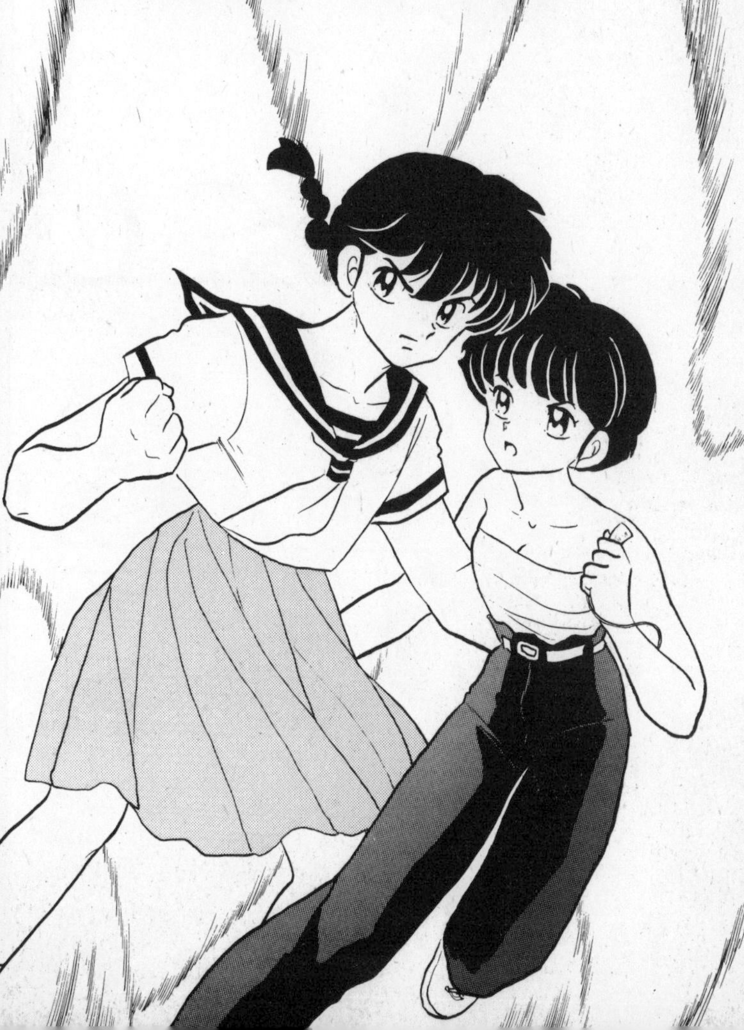

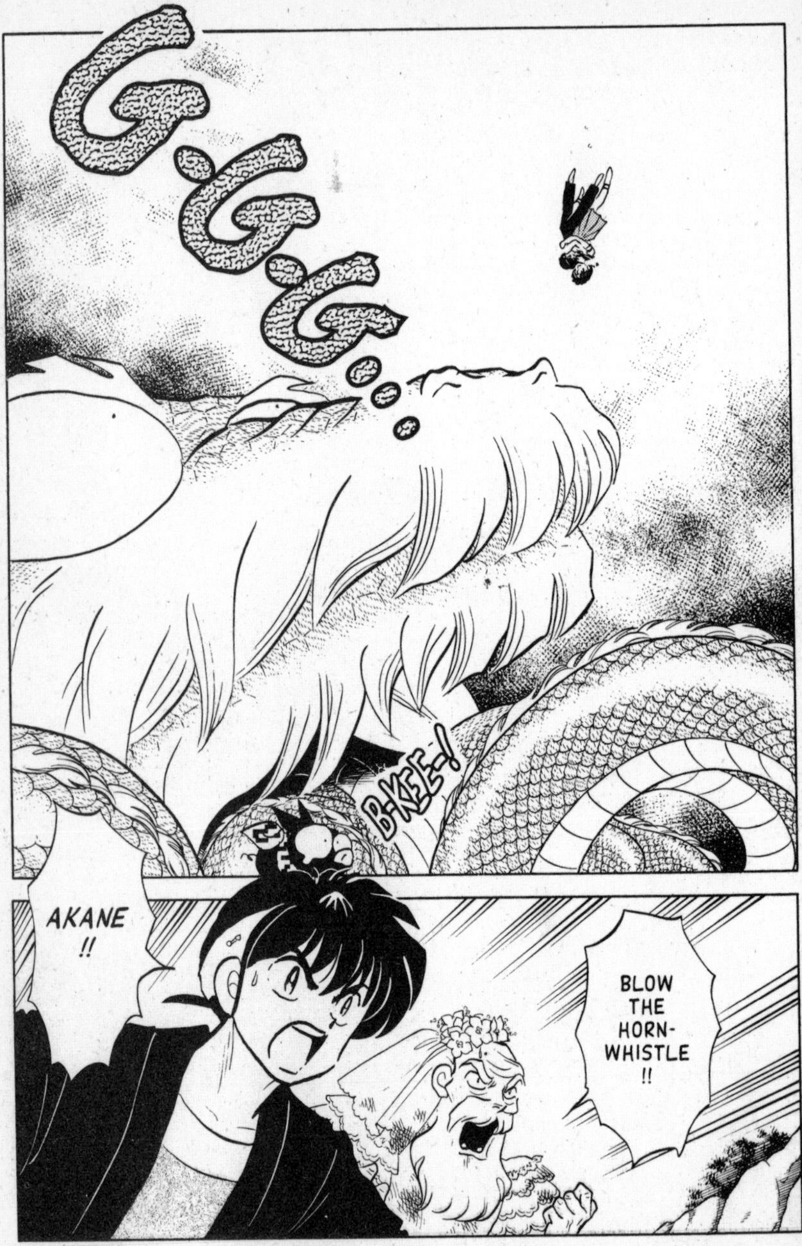
G-G-G-G...
B-KEEE-!
AKANE !!
BLOW THE HORN-WHISTLE !!

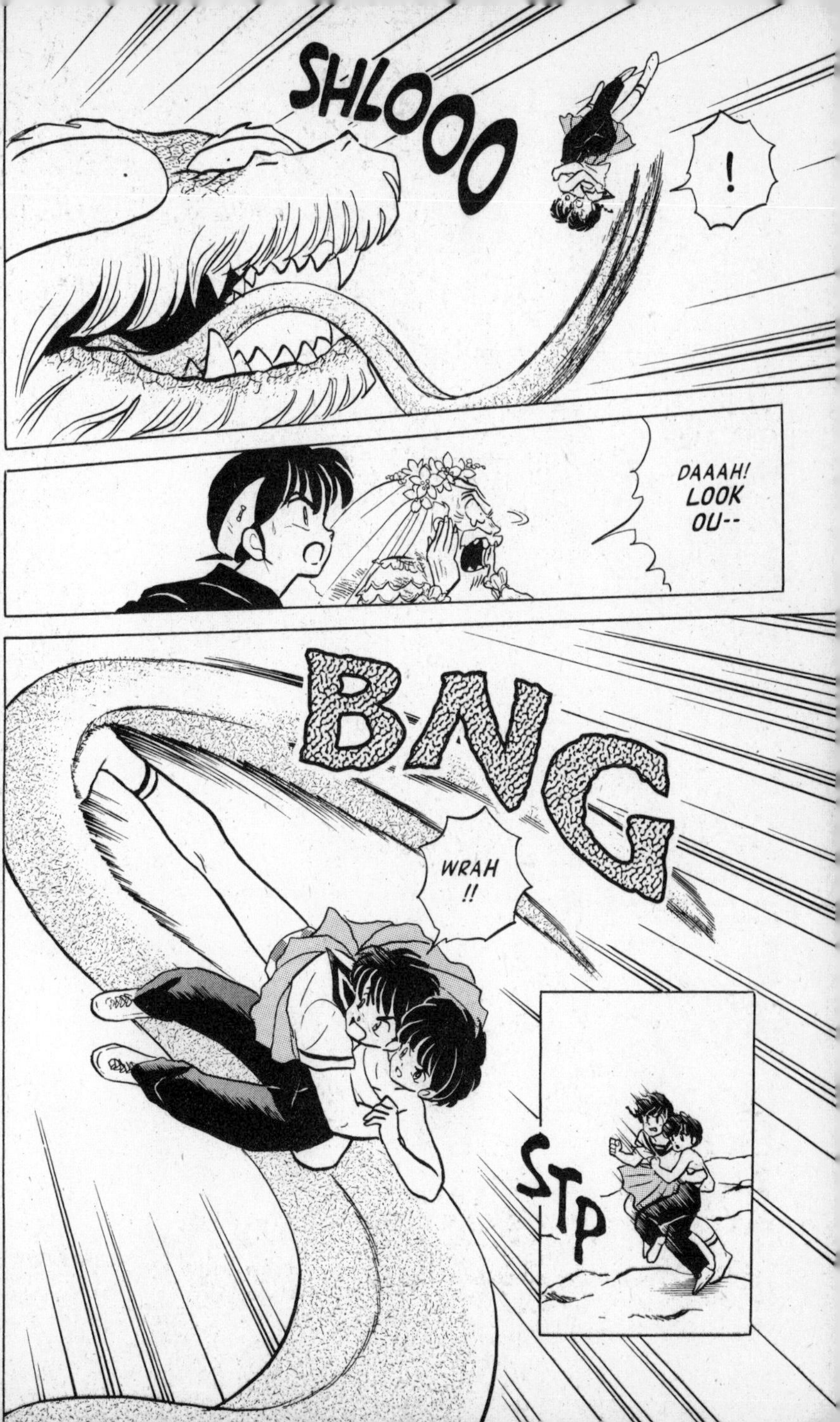
SHLOOO
!
DAAAH! LOOK OU--
BNG
WRAH !!
STP

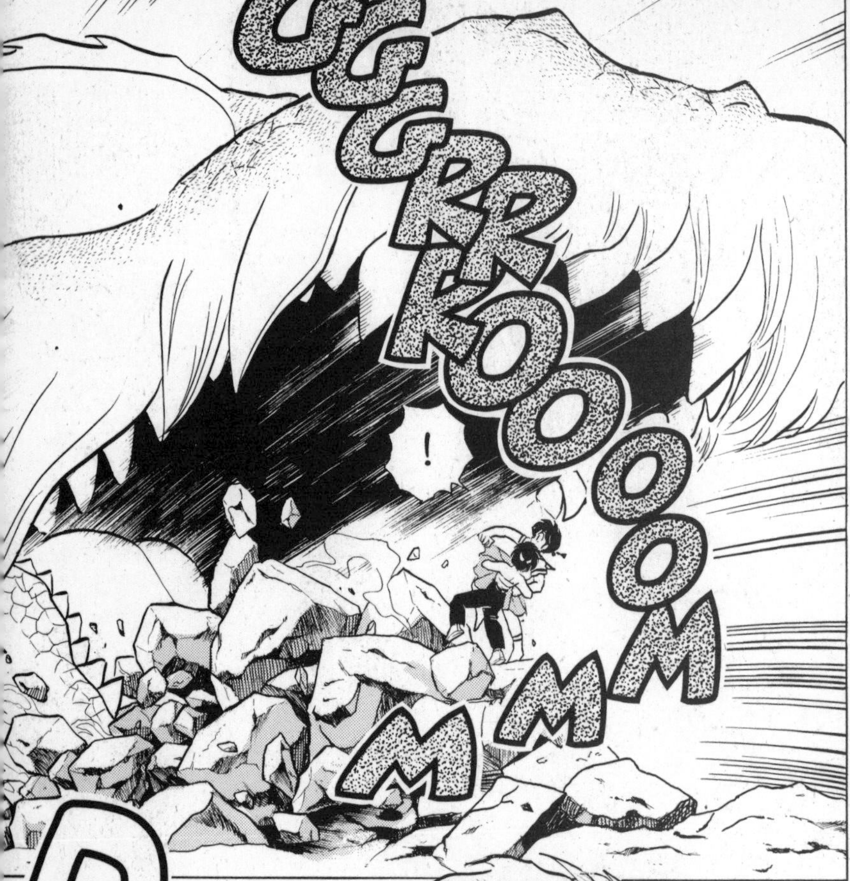
GGGRRROOOOMMM
!
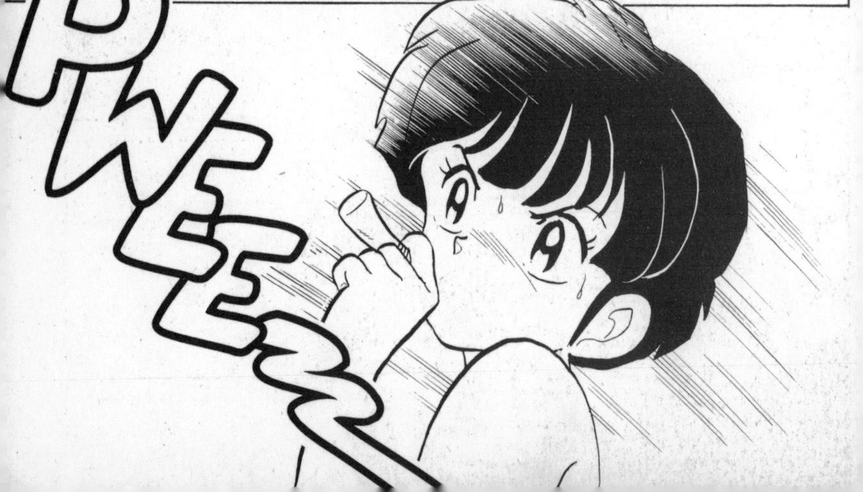
PWEEEE

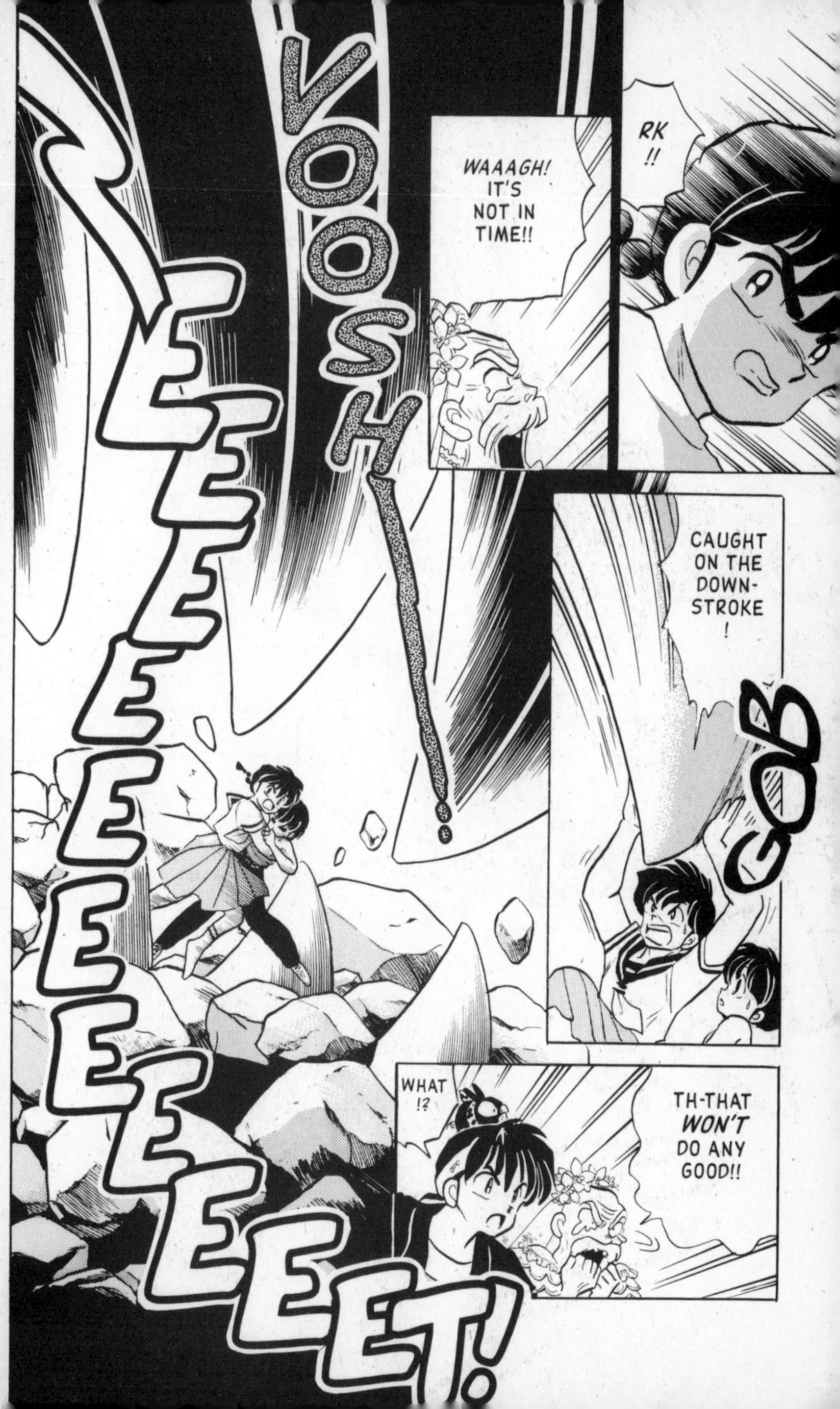
VOOSH
EEEEEEEEEEEEEET!
WAAAGH! IT'S NOT IN TIME!!
RK !!
CAUGHT ON THE DOWN-STROKE !
GOB
WHAT !?
TH-THAT WON'T DO ANY GOOD!!

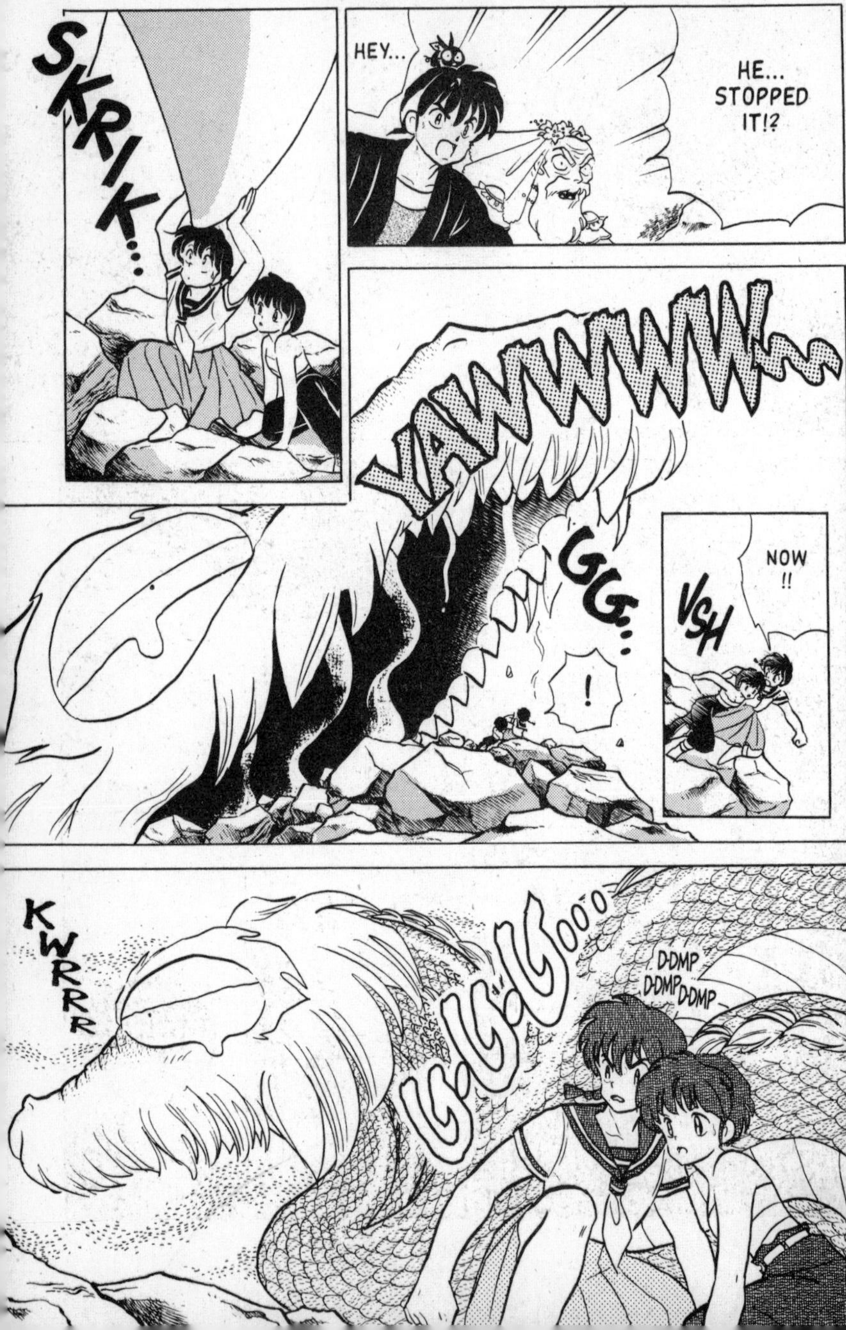
SKRIK...
HEY...
HE... STOPPED IT!?
YAWWWWW...
GG...
!
VSH
NOW !!
KWRRR
G-G-G-Gooo
D-DMP D-DMP D-DMP

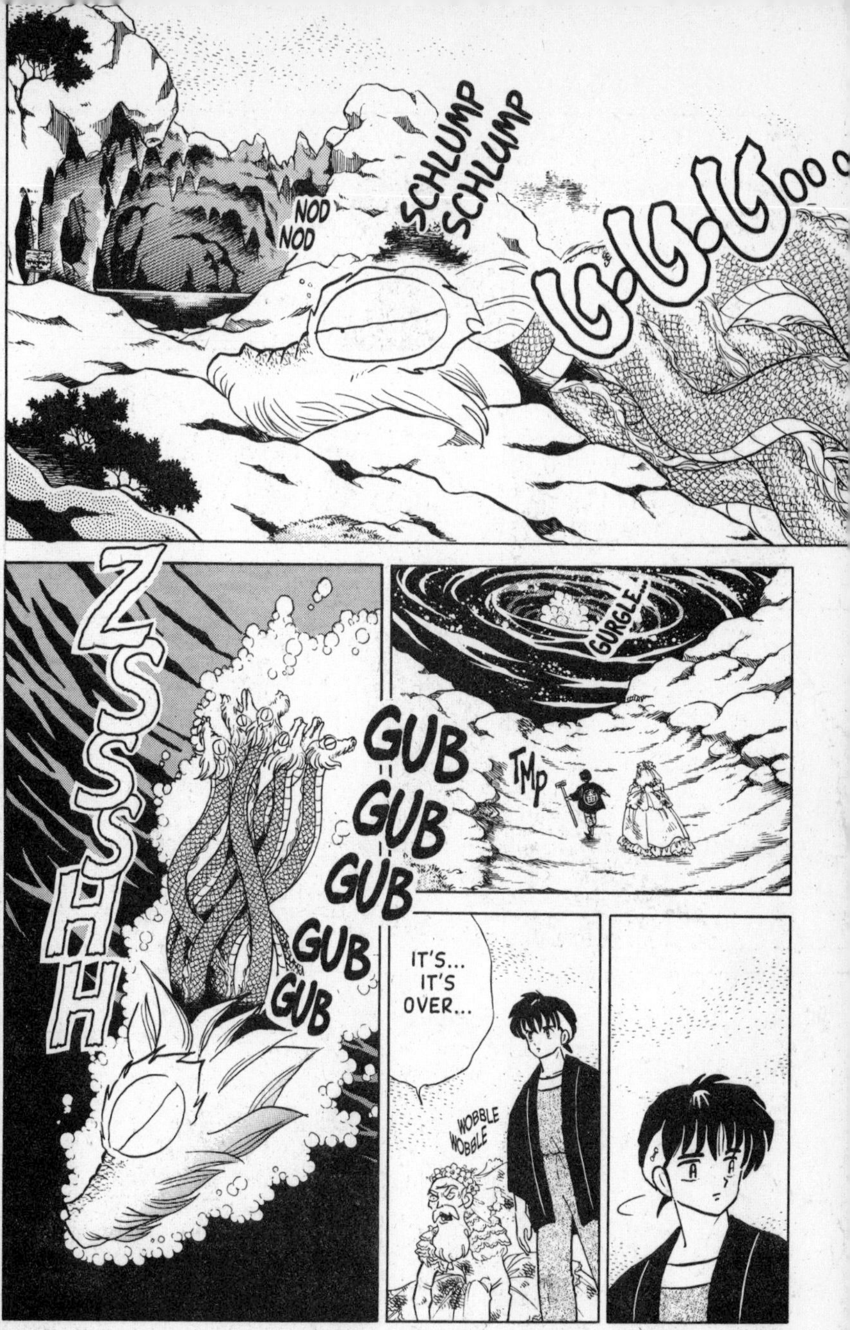
NOD NOD
SCHLUMP SCHLUMP
G-G-G-Gooo...
ZSSSHHH
GUB GUB GUB GUB GUB
GURGLE...
TMP
IT'S... IT'S OVER...
WOBBLE WOBBLE

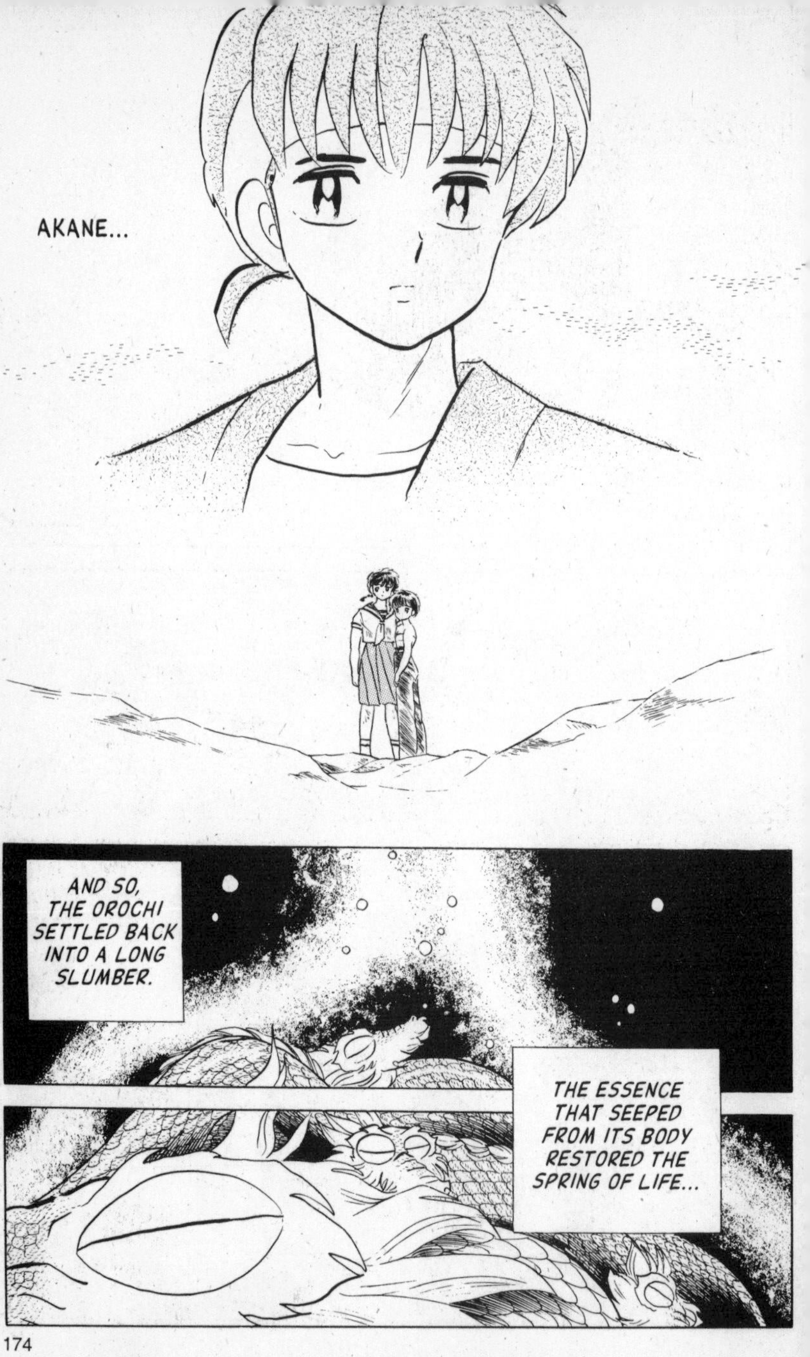
AKANE...
AND SO, THE OROCHI SETTLED BACK INTO A LONG SLUMBER.
THE ESSENCE THAT SEEPED FROM ITS BODY RESTORED THE SPRING OF LIFE...

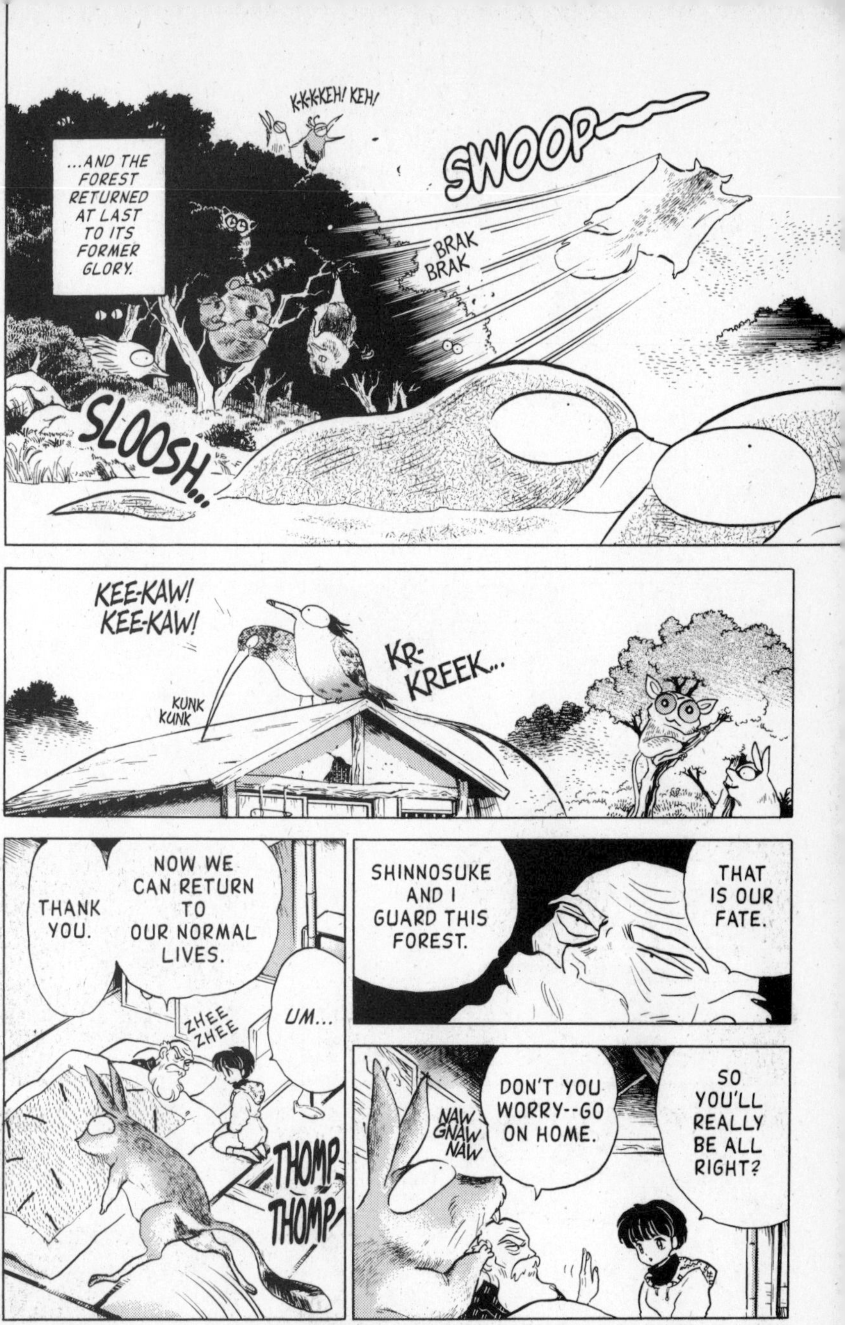
...AND THE FOREST RETURNED AT LAST TO ITS FORMER GLORY.
K-K-K-KEH! KEH!
SWOOP
BRAK BRAK
SLOOSH...
KEE-KAW! KEE-KAW!
KUNK KUNK
KR-KREEK...
THANK YOU.
NOW WE CAN RETURN TO OUR NORMAL LIVES.
ZHEE ZHEE
UM...
THOMP THOMP
SHINNOSUKE AND I GUARD THIS FOREST.
THAT IS OUR FATE.
NAW GNAW NAW
DON'T YOU WORRY--GO ON HOME.
SO YOU'LL REALLY BE ALL RIGHT?

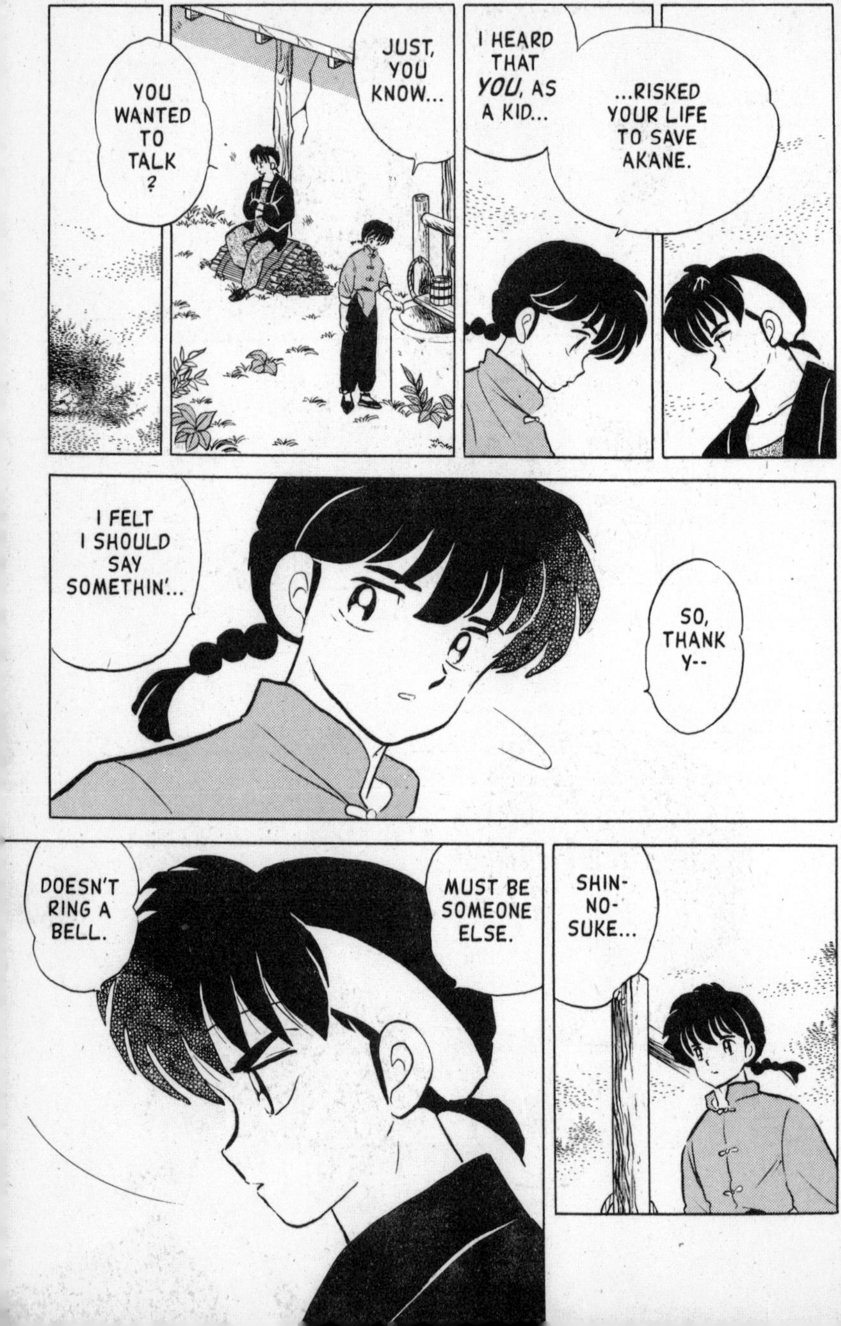
YOU WANTED TO TALK ?
JUST, YOU KNOW...
I HEARD THAT YOU, AS A KID...
...RISKED YOUR LIFE TO SAVE AKANE.
I FELT I SHOULD SAY SOMETHIN'...
SO, THANK Y--
DOESN'T RING A BELL.
MUST BE SOMEONE ELSE.
SHIN-NO-SUKE...

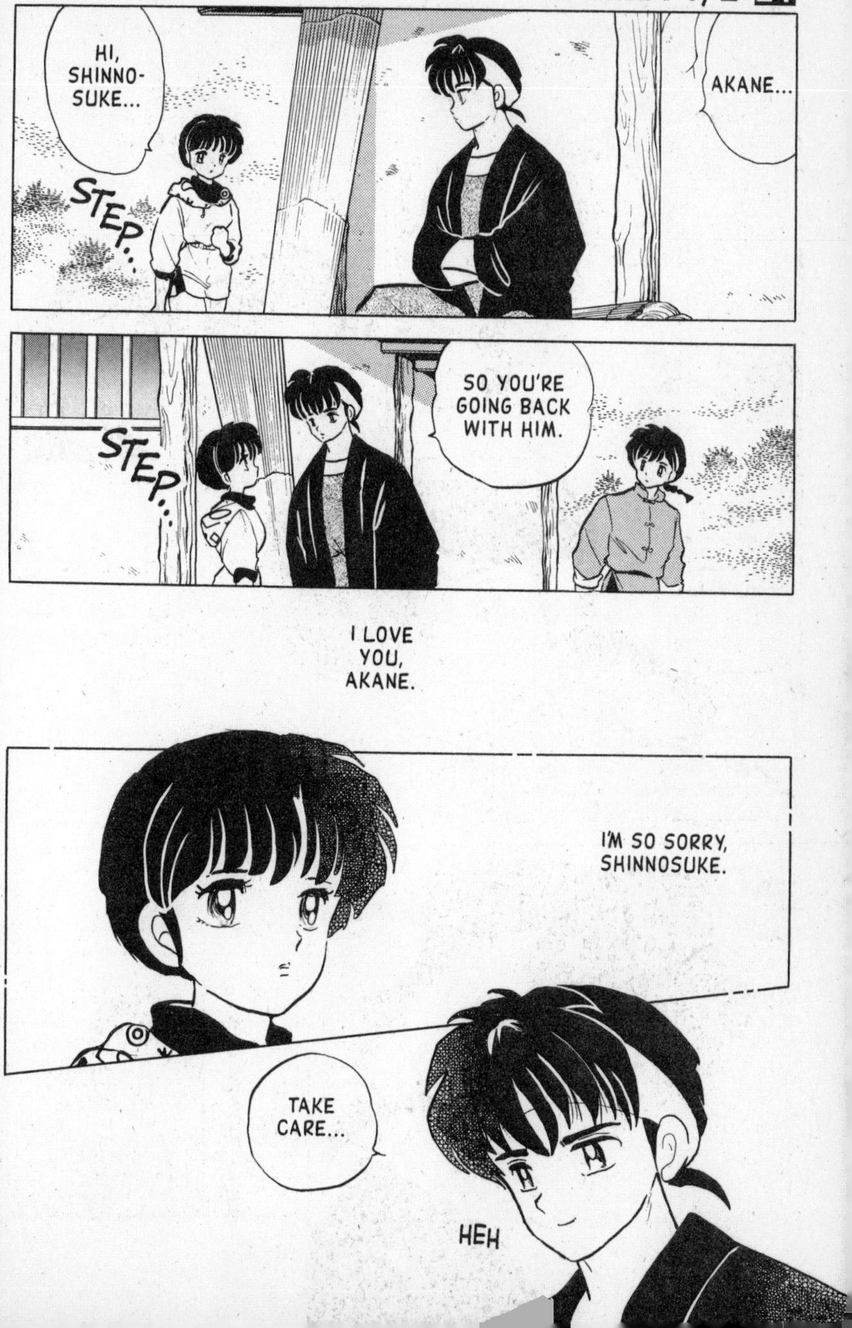
HI, SHINNO-SUKE...
STEP...
AKANE...
STEP...
SO YOU'RE GOING BACK WITH HIM.
I LOVE YOU, AKANE.
I'M SO SORRY, SHINNOSUKE.
TAKE CARE...
HEH

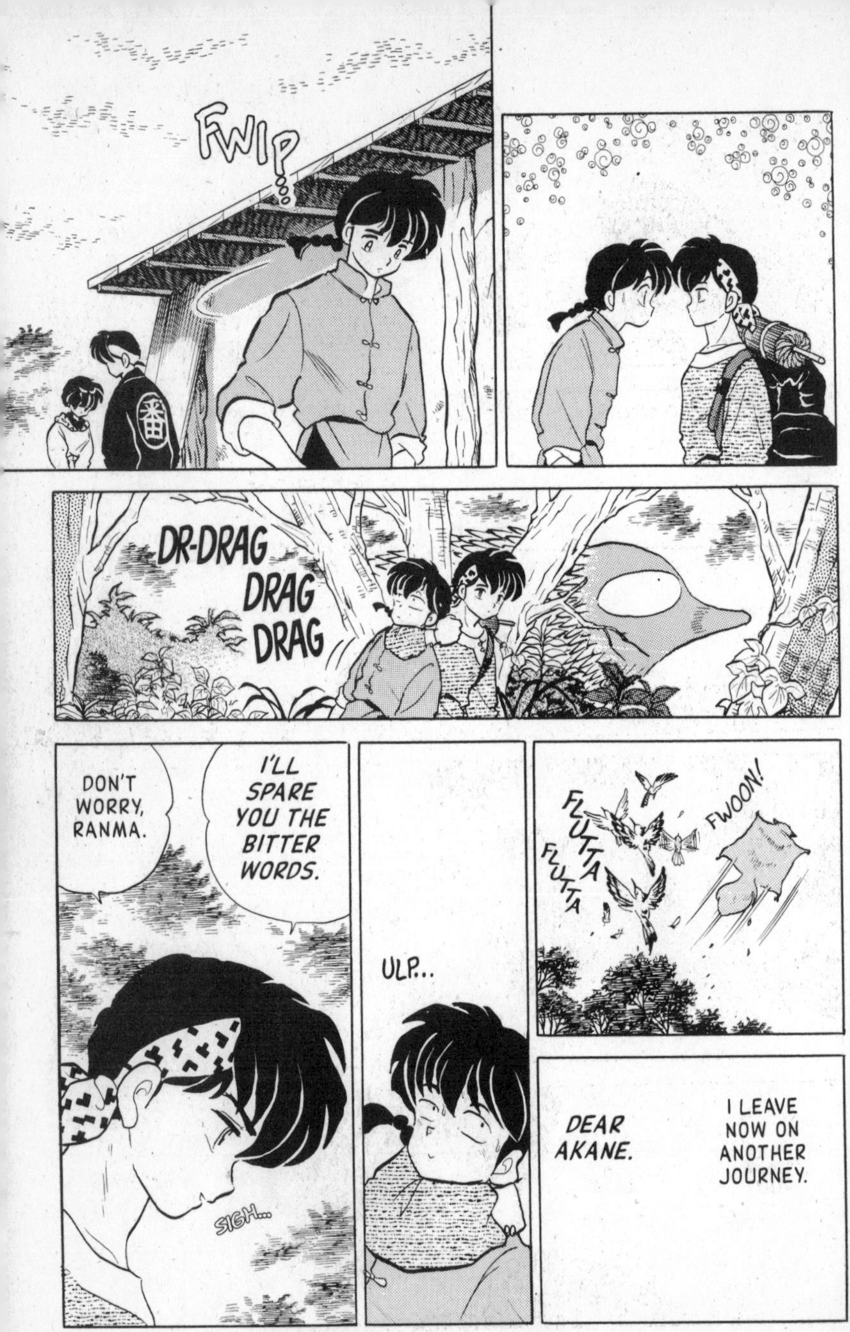
FWIP
DR-DRAG
DRAG
DRAG
DON'T WORRY, RANMA.
I'LL SPARE YOU THE BITTER WORDS.
SIGH...
ULP...
FLUTTA
FLUTTA
FWOON!
DEAR AKANE.
I LEAVE NOW ON ANOTHER JOURNEY.

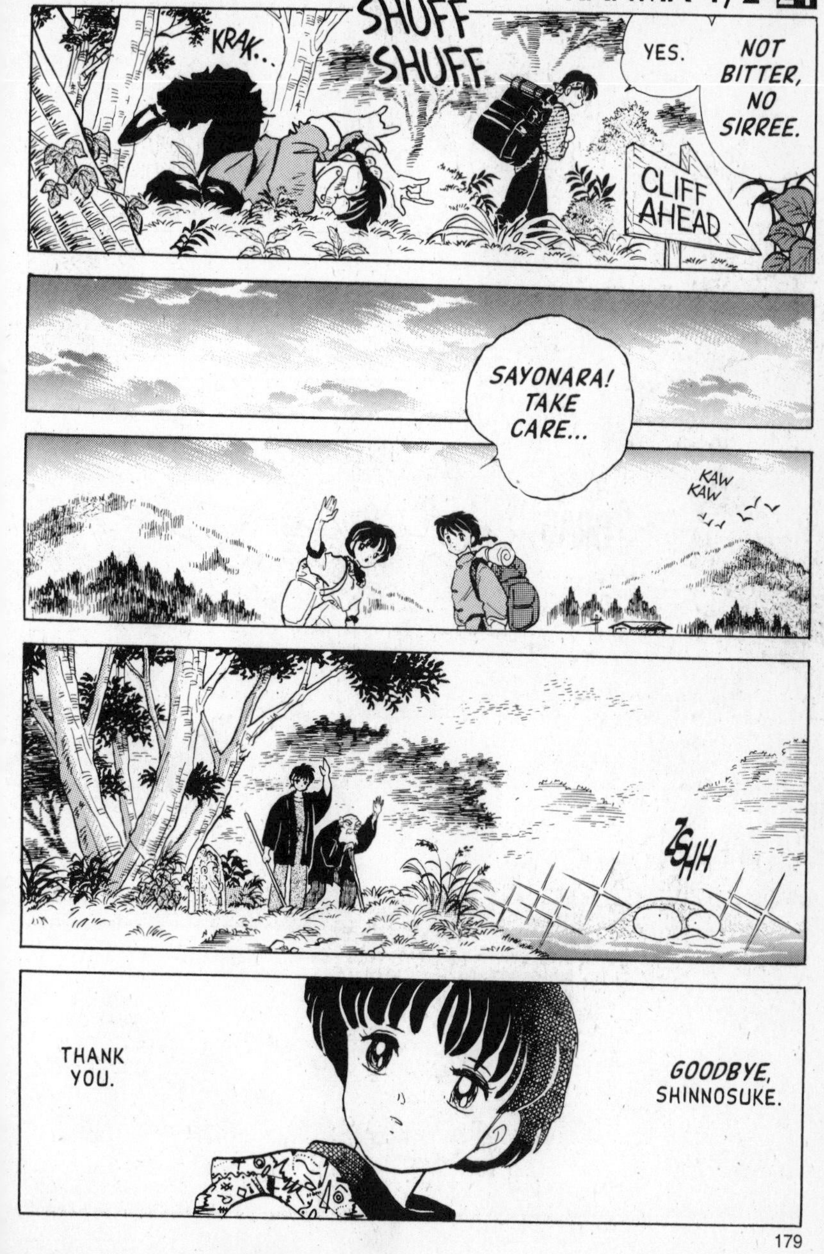
KRAK...
SHUFF SHUFF
YES.
NOT BITTER, NO SIRREE.
CLIFF AHEAD
SAYONARA! TAKE CARE...
KAW KAW
ZSHH
THANK YOU.
GOODBYE, SHINNOSUKE.

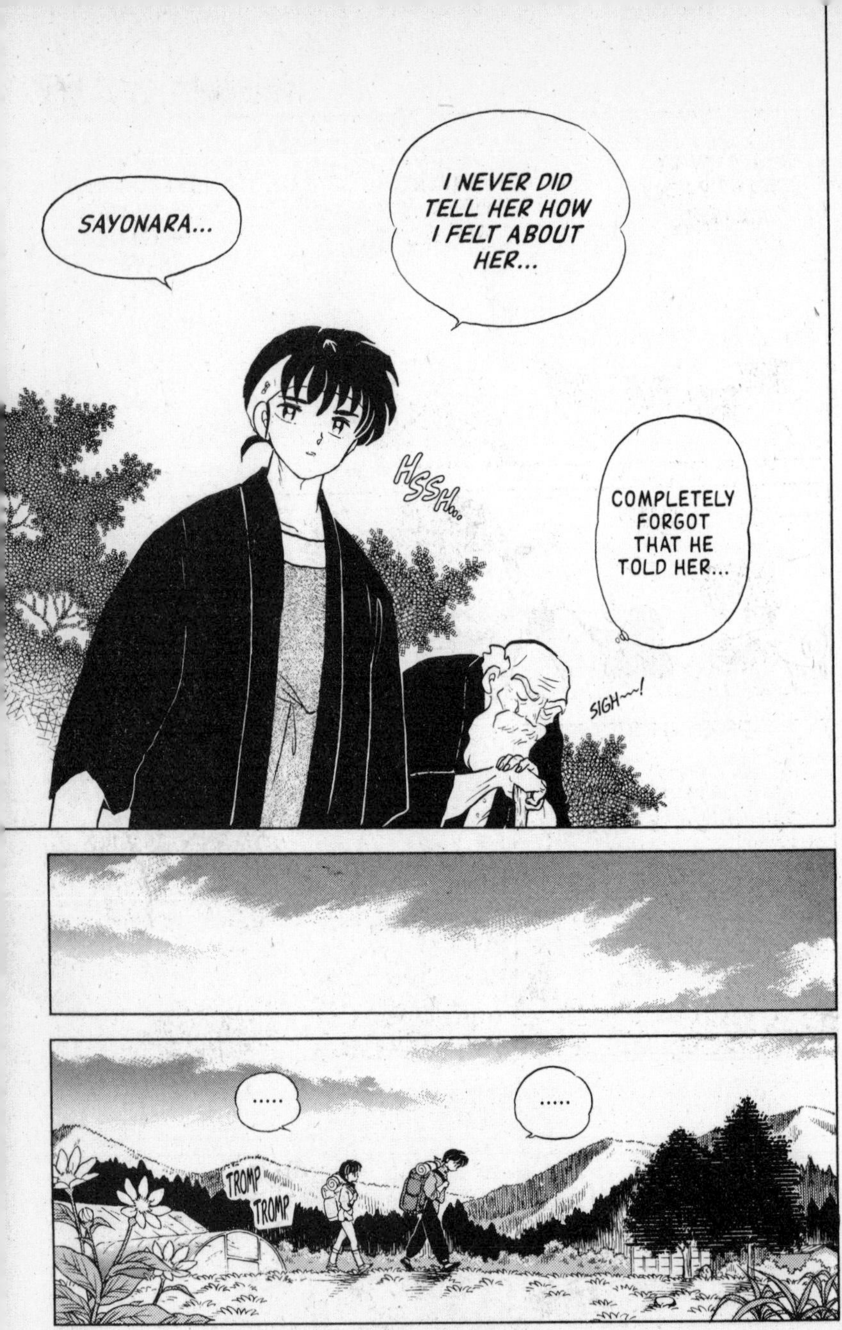
SAYONARA...
I NEVER DID TELL HER HOW I FELT ABOUT HER...
HSSH...
COMPLETELY FORGOT THAT HE TOLD HER...
SIGH~~!
.....
TROMP TROMP
.....

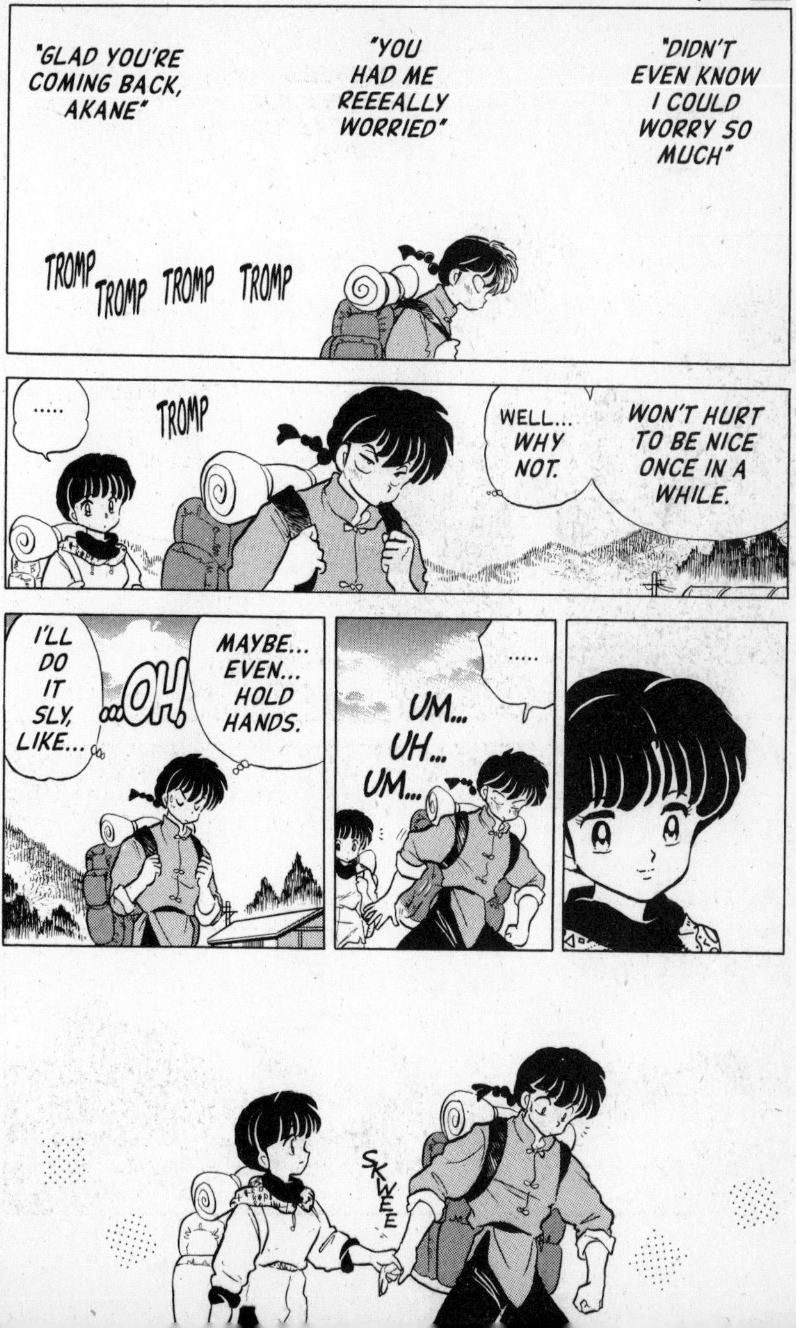
"GLAD YOU'RE COMING BACK, AKANE"
"YOU HAD ME REEEALLY WORRIED"
"DIDN'T EVEN KNOW I COULD WORRY SO MUCH"
TROMP TROMP TROMP TROMP
.....
TROMP
WELL... WHY NOT.
WON'T HURT TO BE NICE ONCE IN A WHILE.
I'LL DO IT SLY, LIKE...
OH!
MAYBE... EVEN... HOLD HANDS.
.....
UM... UH... UM...
SKWEE

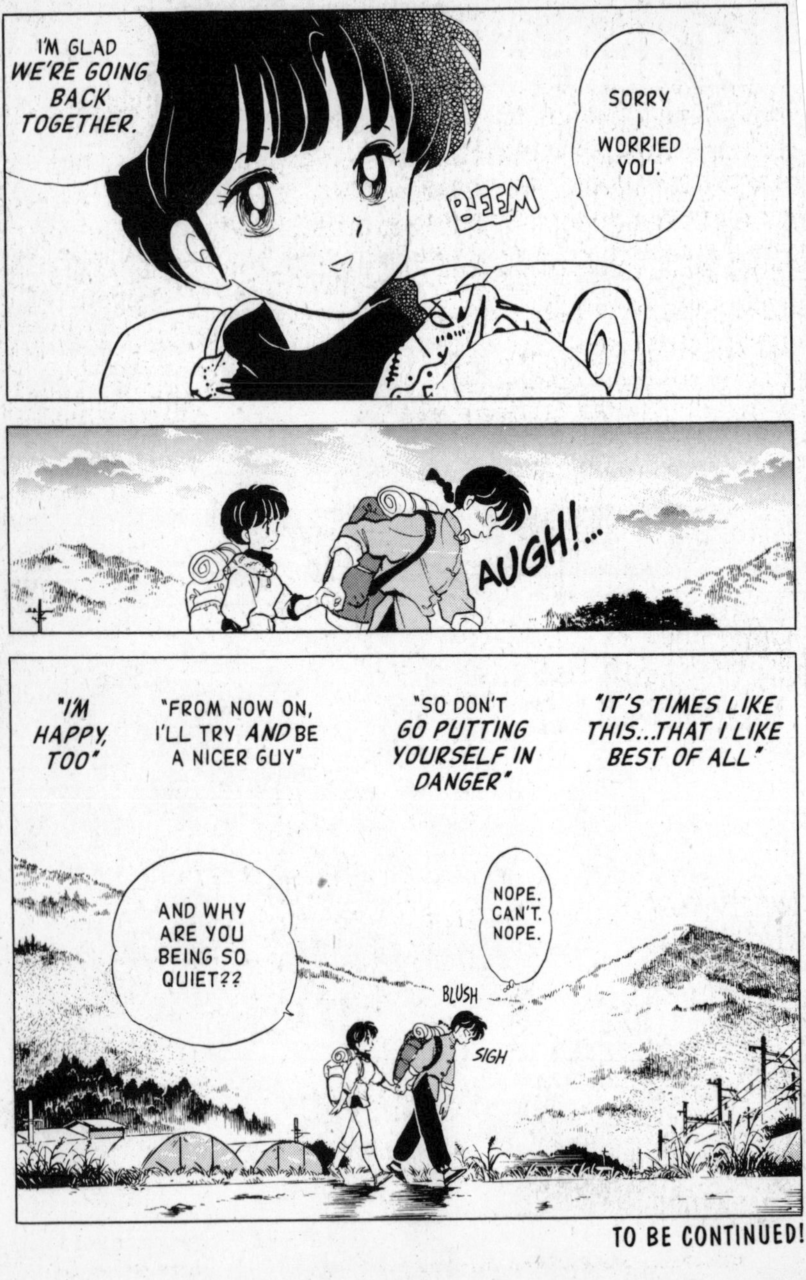
I'M GLAD WE'RE GOING BACK TOGETHER.
BEEM
SORRY I WORRIED YOU.
AUGH!...
"I'M HAPPY, TOO"
"FROM NOW ON, I'LL TRY AND BE A NICER GUY"
"SO DON'T GO PUTTING YOURSELF IN DANGER"
"IT'S TIMES LIKE THIS...THAT I LIKE BEST OF ALL"
AND WHY ARE YOU BEING SO QUIET??
NOPE. CAN'T. NOPE.
BLUSH
SIGH

TO BE CONTINUED!